A Political Companion to Flannery O'Connor

A POLITICAL COMPANION TO
Flannery O'Connor

EDITED BY Henry T. Edmondson III

UNIVERSITY PRESS OF KENTUCKY

Copyright © 2017 by The University Press of Kentucky

Scholarly publisher for the Commonwealth,
serving Bellarmine University, Berea College, Centre College of Kentucky,
Eastern Kentucky University, The Filson Historical Society, Georgetown College,
Kentucky Historical Society, Kentucky State University, Morehead State
University, Murray State University, Northern Kentucky University, Transylvania
University, University of Kentucky, University of Louisville, and Western
Kentucky University.
All rights reserved.

Editorial and Sales Offices: The University Press of Kentucky
663 South Limestone Street, Lexington, Kentucky 40508-4008
www.kentuckypress.com

Cataloging-in-Publication data is available from the Library of Congress.

ISBN 978-0-8131-6940-8 (hardcover : alk. paper)
ISBN 978-0-8131-6942-2 (epub)
ISBN 978-0-8131-6941-5 (pdf)

This book is printed on acid-free paper meeting the requirements of the American
National Standard for Permanence in Paper for Printed Library Materials.

Manufactured in the United States of America.

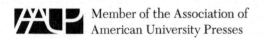 Member of the Association of
American University Presses

Contents

Part I. O'Connor's Politics

Part II. Kindred Spirits

Series Foreword

Those who undertake a study of American political thought must attend to the great theorists, philosophers, and essayists. Such a study is incomplete, however, if it neglects American literature, one of the greatest repositories of the nation's political thought and teachings.

America's literature is distinctive because it is, above all, intended for a democratic citizenry. In contrast to eras when an author would aim to inform or influence a select aristocratic audience, in democratic times, public influence and education must resonate with a more expansive, less leisured, and diverse audience to be effective. The great works of America's literary tradition are the natural locus of democratic political teaching. Invoking the interest and attention of citizens through the pleasures afforded by the literary form, many of America's great thinkers sought to forge a democratic public philosophy with subtle and often challenging teachings that unfolded in narrative, plot, and character development. Perhaps more than any other nation's literary tradition, American literature is ineluctably political—shaped by democracy as much as it has in turn shaped democracy.

The Political Companions to Great American Authors series highlights the teachings of the great authors in America's literary and belletristic tradition. An astute political interpretation of America's literary tradition requires careful, patient, and attentive readers who approach the text with a view to understanding its underlying messages about citizenship and democracy. Essayists in this series approach the classic texts not with a "hermeneutics of suspicion" but with the curiosity of fellow citizens who believe that the great authors have something of value to teach their readers. The series brings together essays from varied approaches and viewpoints for the common purpose of elucidating the political teachings of the nation's greatest authors for those seeking a better understanding of American democracy.

Patrick J. Deneen
Series Editor

Introduction

A Political Companion to Flannery O'Connor offers essays to help the reader appreciate Flannery O'Connor's brilliance as a short story writer, novelist, essayist, and correspondent; and, her importance as a political philosopher, even if political philosophy was for O'Connor an irregular and inadvertent activity. Nonetheless, her contribution to political philosophy should not be surprising: she regularly reviewed books on philosophy and theology for periodicals in the Diocese of Savannah and the Diocese of Atlanta, and she was impressively well read. Her large personal library, housed at Georgia College in Milledgeville, Georgia, includes works by Plato, Aristotle, Aquinas, Nietzsche, and Eric Voegelin, among others. Her stories, moreover, are concerned with questions of human nature, prudence, social change, equality, modernity, and justice. Her essays, posthumously collected under the heading of *Mystery and Manners*,[1] address the problem of untethered theory; the interplay between fiction and politics; and, as the title implies, the nature of social and individual manners. Her collected and edited correspondence, *The Habit of Being: Letters of Flannery O'Connor*,[2] is witty and astute as she deals with many of the same themes found in her fiction and prose. In those letters she often provides trenchant if succinct analyses of authors, philosophers, theologians, politics, the nature of fiction—as well as invaluable insight into her own work. As O'Connor herself once impishly complained: "It is a pity I can't receive my own letters. If they produce as much wholehearted approval at their destination as they do at their source, they should indeed be able to keep my memory alive and healthy."[3]

Aristotle, Voegelin, and the Political

The definition of "political" and "politics" employed in this volume is expansive and rests upon the Aristotelian notion that politics is the overarching discipline, the inquiry concerned with all areas of study having relevance to a virtuous life and with those matters that contribute to "human flourish-ing" (*eudaemonia*)—a "good life"—as most would define it.[4] As Aristotle understood them, those subdisciplines are necessarily far-ranging and ad-dress, for example, individual virtue, friendship, family life, the nature of justice, public discourse, and the place of material goods. These concerns also encompass the manner in which we spend our leisure time and how that activity shapes character, the education of children, the education of leaders, and aesthetics. Informed by St. Thomas Aquinas and the Christian tradition, O'Connor also emphasizes the essential and incontestable dignity of the ordinary man and woman, a threshold never quite reached by the ancients.

That O'Connor's thought might address Aristotelian concerns should not be surprising, given her keen interest in Aquinas. One reviewer, in re-marking upon her essay "The Nature and Aim of Fiction," describes it as "a statement of universal literary theory almost equaling Aristotle's *Poetics*."[5] O'Connor certainly understood the significance of Aristotelian thought: after her residency at the Yaddo artists' retreat in Saratoga Springs, New York, she began to live with the Sally and Robert Fitzgerald family, Rob-ert Fitzgerald being the renowned classicist and translator. O'Connor re-ported: "I am living in the country with some people named Fitzgerald. . . . He teaches Aristotle and St. Thomas at Sarah Lawrence College and has a lot of books which I am getting to read."[6] She also reflected: "I suppose I read Aristotle in college but not to know I was doing it; the same with Plato. I don't have the kind of mind that can carry such beyond the actual read-ing, i.e., total non-retention has kept my education from being a burden to me."[7] Despite O'Connor's whimsical assertion that she read Aquinas "every night"—not to be taken literally—there is no real evidence that she read Thomas's primary writings much, if at all; rather she absorbed them from secondary sources, especially the writings of Jacques Maritain. There is in O'Connor's personal library a one-volume compilation of Thomas's major treatises, but it has been read very lightly at best. Similarly, a one-volume compilation of several of Aristotle's major works is also found in her library, but neither does it appear to have been handled, save for a brief inscription, "M. F. O'Connor, 1943."[8]

Because O'Connor's college philosophy textbook dealt with modern philosophy, not ancient or medieval philosophy, her primary access to Aristo-tle seems to have been through Eric Voegelin, specifically *Plato and Aristo-*

tle, volume 3 of his four-volume series *Order and History.* She has inscribed on the first page, "Flannery O'Connor 1959," but in this case the text is frequently annotated in her minimalist manner.[9] At one point in her marginalia she provides her own brief but intimate commentary on the evolution from the ancients to Aquinas. Voegelin records Aristotle's elegiac passage on behalf of Plato when Aristotle observes that the latter's greatness was such that "it is not lawful for bad men even to praise" him. Aristotle further records, in verse, that Plato taught "by his own life and by the methods of his words / How a man becomes good and happy at the same time." The elegy concludes with Aristotle's assertion, "Now no one can ever attain to these things again." O'Connor, however, has written to the side, "comp. St. Thomas."[10]

With these influences in mind, we might ask what may be O'Connor's enduring value for those interested in politics, philosophy, theology, literature, and culture. Perhaps the most conspicuous political dimension of O'Connor's work is her self-conscious concern with, and response to, the doctrine of nihilism as she saw it emerge and gain vigor in the twentieth century. Although O'Connor conceded Nietzsche's brilliance, especially appreciating his critique of modernity, his ideas nonetheless alarmed her, and she believed the German philosopher's doctrine an empty promise, dangerous to personal morals and hazardous to a sound and productive social philosophy. Her anti-Nietzschean effort is most evident in her first novel, *Wise Blood,* and her short story "Good Country People."[11]

O'Connor understood that Nietzsche's uneasy genius lay not so much in his ability to create a new philosophy but rather in recognizing and diagnosing an emerging social condition, in foreseeing its influence in a future beyond his own lifetime, and in popularizing it. When he pronounced God's "death" in the middle of the nineteenth century, he was prophetically describing a world in which the Judeo-Christian tradition was no longer dominant or persuasive in matters of morals and policy. Famously noting that nihilism is the very "air we breathe," O'Connor held Nietzsche in reluctant respect: the two would agree that an experience of "nothingness" is the logical consequence of a world that has for centuries rejected God or at least acted as if God were irrelevant to modern life. O'Connor argues on several occasions, as do so many others, that when God is ignored, even the exercise of reason turns unreliable.

Accordingly, the deterioration of rhetoric is an indication of the intensity of the battle that has come upon us. O'Connor ends her diocesan bulle-

tin review of Voegelin's *Plato and Aristotle* by comparing the nature of the
rhetorical fight between Socrates and the Sophists to contemporary conflicts: "Plato's enemies were the Sophists and Socrates' arguments against
them are still today the classical arguments against that sophistic philosophy of existence which characterizes positivism and the age of enlightenment." For that reason, she notes that according to Voegelin, "the murder
of Socrates parallels the political murders of our time."[12] This tension is in-
ventively played out in O'Connor's fiction when her crudest characters, including criminal personalities like the "Misfit" in "A Good Man Is Hard to
Find," or the bizarre elder Tarwater, are the ones who speak most plainly,
in contrast to more "sophisticated" personalities like the grandmother and
Rayber, who are the modern-day obfuscators with their self-serving and
self-deluding sophistry.

This modern struggle is also reflected, among other ways, in the use—
or misuse—of our leisure time. Such use, in turn, depends on an education that suits individuals for meaningful enjoyment of leisure. O'Connor
has highlighted Voegelin's summary of Aristotle's distinctions, found in his
Politics, between the activities of "play," "work," and the most important
use of personal time, "leisure," which consists of activity directed toward
moral, intellectual, and spiritual improvement. Work, according to Aristotle, is primarily directed at providing opportunities for leisure; and, play
(or "recreation") provides a respite from work. Voegelin writes, "Education
must, therefore, equip a man with knowledge and train him in intellectual
pursuits" so that he might be equipped for the "supreme fulfillment" of the
"*bios theoretikos,*" or the life of contemplation.[13]

O'Connor's interest in this passage offers insight into two aspects of
her life: First, she is consistently interested in the importance of education, often expressed in her wry and deprecatory observations on her
own formal education; and, her criticism of education more broadly. In
respect to the innovations introduced in her high school by the progressive education movement, O'Connor remarked, "Anything having to do
with this 'learning for life' stuff turns my stomach permanently." She further complained: "They would as soon have given us arsenic in the drinking fountains as let us study Greek. I know no history whatsoever." She
notes, "At that school we were always 'planning.'"[14] With tongue in cheek,
she advised Robert Lowell regarding the education of his daughter: "You
ought to raise her in the South and then she wouldn't have to go to school.

I am really looking forward to the next generation being uneducated."[15] It makes little difference whether education is secular or parochial since, as she said in one lecture, "the average Catholic reader" is likely "a Militant Moron."[16]

The second connection between Voegelin's discussion of leisure and O'Connor is more poignant. By the time O'Connor read and reviewed Voegelin's text, she had been diagnosed with lupus erythematosus, the disease that eventually took her life at the age of thirty-nine, just as it had taken her father's life in his forty-first year. When she was reviewing this edition of Voegelin, the disease was beginning to take its toll. Indeed, six years before she reviewed Voegelin's *Plato and Aristotle,* and four years before it was even published, she wrote to Robert Lowell: "I am making out fine in spite of any conflicting stories. . . . I have enough energy to write with and as that is all I have any business doing anyhow, I can with one eye squinted take it all as a blessing. What you have to measure out, you come to observe more closely, or so I tell myself."[17] Such a confession suggests the beginning of the contemplative life, especially as it is occasioned by the impossibility of the active life.

O'Connor's paramount achievement is to reveal artistically the phenomenon of divine and natural grace, which, for her, is the manifestation of mercy in the life of an individual. Herein is the key to O'Connor's political philosophy, at least insofar as we aspire to a better life—politically, socially, morally, and spiritually: Men and women are rescued from their pride and ignorance—"terrible radical human pride"—by dramatic if not violent interventions of grace in their lives, a grace that brings, above all else, self-knowledge.[18]

It is with respect to grace that we find what may be the most remarkable highlighted passage in O'Connor's copy of Voegelin's *Plato and Aristotle.* The German political philosopher notes that for all his concern over the life of virtue, Aristotle hit a kind of philosophical ceiling beyond which he could not imagine moral improvement prompted by anything like grace, nor could he envision genuine "friendship" between human beings and the gods given the vast inequality in their conditions. It was only in the Christian era that the opportunity for transcendent assistance in moral growth was conceived, and this was ultimately best explained in St. Thomas's systematic moral philosophy and theology.

O'Connor highlights Voegelin's explanation that "there remained in

Aristotle the fundamental hesitation which distinguished the Hellenic from the Christian idea of man, that is, the hesitation to recognize the formation of the human soul through grace; there was missing the experience of faith, the *fides caritate formata* in the Thomistic sense." Voegelin elaborates that for the ancients, "Transcendence does not form the soul in such a manner that it will find fulfillment in transfiguration through Grace in death."[19] Such a passage, in which Voegelin explains the limits of Aristotelianism and the opportunities of Thomism, demonstrates, almost single-handedly, why Voegelin enjoyed such deep resonance with O'Connor. Her stirring innovation on this concept was to demonstrate that such transfiguration may take place, not only through death but through a kind of violence that may or may not be mortal, violence that creates turmoil in the soul.

O'Connor was keenly attracted, moreover, to Voegelin's philosophy of history because the latter declined to recognize an artificial separation between the secular and the divine; accordingly, for Voegelin history consists of a "leap in being toward the transcendent source of order," which is reflected in the title of her second collection of short stories, *Everything That Rises Must Converge*.[20] Indeed, in her review of Voegelin, she quotes from his work that philosophy itself is man's attempt to recover from his fallen state: "For Plato, 'The philosopher is man in the anxiety of his fall from being; and philosophy is the ascent toward salvation for Everyman.'"[21] O'Connor believes, then, like Voegelin, that the political order is not self-contained; rather, it is part of a larger transcendent order.

Men and women need grace, which requires that they accept the limitations of their fallible nature. This means, moreover, that they are in need of redemption; and, in a startling way, O'Connor explains that this desideratum is the basis of all good fiction, however it may be rendered.[22] It need not be addressed theologically; to the contrary, it is often explored far more effectively in an artistic fashion that leaves theology in the background. Thus the silver thread that runs through so many of O'Connor's works is the acquisition of self-knowledge through necessarily violent epiphanies that trigger the operation of grace in the individual soul.

This need for grace and redemption speaks in turn to at least two themes critical to politics: one, it provides a contemporary perspective on the Aristotelian-Thomistic insistence that individual virtue precede social change. That is, O'Connor corrects those social reformers who would skip the less glamorous task of improving individual character before launching headlong into collective reform. Second, O'Connor's principles speak to the twentieth-century collectivist political heresies that have brought such disaster upon the world. The fundamental problems of the world must be diagnosed, in the first instance, on a person-by-person basis. That personal reformation must be voluntary; moreover, even if it is precipitated by grace, it cannot be imposed by external agents, no matter which extreme of the political spectrum they occupy. This may not be the entire solution, but it is the beginning of meaningful political growth. In her copy of Voegelin's text, O'Connor has highlighted a passage that captures as well as anything might her own thoughts. Voegelin writes that "a political society, in so far as its course in history is intelligible, has for its substance the growth and decline of an order of the soul."[23] This position points once again to Aristotle, for whom the foremost task of politics is the cultivation of virtue; indeed, a study of political philosophy begins with a study of moral philosophy. For that reason, it is only at the end of his *Ethics* that he recommends a study of politics, and the conclusion of the *Politics* is concerned with education, culture, and virtue, suggesting a return to a study of moral philosophy.[24]

O'Connor understood that she potentially served as a kind of literary prophet, a self-defined role that she undertook with earnestness, though she avoided the self-referential solemnity that may characterize those who feel a responsibility to speak to the world at large. O'Connor once shared with a friend her delight that she had made a "lucky find" that, according to St. Thomas Aquinas, "prophetic vision is dependent on the imagination of the prophet," by which she suggests that the modern-day prophet need not earn the role by her intellectual brilliance, her moral excellence, or her spiritual aptitude. She sincerely believed that she had things to say that carried prophetic truths and that she possessed the imagination to do so aesthetically. She never seemed to take this role too seriously: in her correspondence to her friend Maryat Lee, she often signed her letters with comic variations of the name of "Tarwater," the prophet in her second novel, *The Violent Bear It Away.* In her typically wry, self-effacing manner, she commented on her inspiration, admitting: "I wish I had Voices anyway, or anyway distinct voices. I have something that might be a continuing muttering snarl like cats courting under the house, but no clear Voice in years."[25]

Such self-deprecation left O'Connor free, at times, to speak unequivocally about her work: "I write because I write well," she told a correspondent. On another instance she admitted, "No one appreciates my work the way that I do."[26]

Others have confirmed O'Connor's view of her role. In an interview shortly before her death, Sally Fitzgerald reflected upon O'Connor's "unique place in twentieth-century American literature," observing, "You know, it's like having Jeremiah suddenly appear."[27] In another place, Fitzgerald elaborates, explaining, "Flannery O'Connor defined the prophet as one whose function is not to foresee the future but to see into the depths of finite reality, of men and manners, to the spirit that enlivens them, and to bear witness to that insight, whether in utterance or in the life he leads."[28] Confirming Fitzgerald's observation, O'Connor scholar Marion Montgomery explained, "O'Connor is a 'prophetic poet,' one who sees the world in its wholeness, natural and supernatural, at once."[29] Ralph Wood argues that, though she at times seemed to hold herself aloof from political concerns, Flannery O'Connor was a writer deeply engaged with the largest matters of political and social order: "Flannery O'Connor's work cannot be conscripted for either conservative or liberal causes because it is imbued with an Augustinian political vision of properly ordered loves." Wood thus explores O'Connor's conception of prophetic vision as "the realism of distances": "If we see with our eyes, she shows, using them as mere optical instruments, we possess sight of things near at hand—namely, immediate and secondary goods. If we see through our eyes, by contrast, with lenses formed by true convictions about God and man and the world, we possess vision of distant things as if they were close up—namely, permanent and final goods."[30]

In terms of her own politics regarding the topical issues of her day, O'Connor might fall into that coveted category today called "independents." Though her family was habitually Republican, she was not uncritically so. It is best to say that, politically, she was Catholic, meaning that she viewed social and political conundrums in light of eternal principles as well as temporal. This does not mean she always approved of the day-to-day politics of the Catholic Church; to the contrary, during a discussion of the Spanish Civil War, she remarked: "God never promised [the Church] political infallibility or wisdom and sometimes she doesn't appear to have even elementary good sense. She seems always to be either on the wrong side politically or simply a couple of hundred years behind the world in her political thinking." More appreciatively, she continued by explaining, in reference to the Spanish Church's uneasy alliance with the Franco regime,

"She tries to get along with any form of government that does not set itself up as a religion."[31]

O'Connor was also a southerner, and that gave her a particular lens through which she assessed the debates and tensions swirling about her, though it would be a mistake to call her provincial. Nor did she militate for the perpetual preservation of an uncompromising southern way of life—she knew the South was badly in need of reform. For example, the more she observed the practice and culture of segregation, the more disgusted she became. She notes that when Guy Wells, the president of Georgia State College for Women (later Georgia College), began to integrate the staff of the college, racial militants burned a cross on his front yard: "The story goes that everything was as separate and equal as possible, even down to two Coca-Cola machines, white and colored; but that night a cross was burned on Dr. Wells' side lawn. . . . The people who burned the cross couldn't have gone past the fourth grade but, for the time, they were mighty interested in education."[32]

She believed, however, that change must come to the South in such a way that its vital infrastructure would not be destroyed until a better social structure could evolve, lest the region devolve into chaos: "Bad manners are better than no manners at all," she observed.[33] O'Connor at times resisted identification as a "southern writer." She felt her fiction offered a certain universality that she did not want obscured by regional categorization; at the same time she was quick to praise her fellow writers, recognizing, for example, the power of William Faulkner's work. By contrast, she held Carson McCullers in low regard and reported that the translations of Erskine Caldwell's work are "usually terrible so that the French think [he] is a great writer."[34]

An undertaking such as *A Political Companion to Flannery O'Connor* runs the risk of regarding the fiction writer's work instrumentally rather than aesthetically. O'Connor once complained about another author: "[Her book] is just propaganda and its being propaganda for the side of the angels only makes it worse. The novel is an art form and when you use it for anything other than art, you pervert it. I didn't make this up. I got it from St. Thomas (via Maritain) who allows that art is wholly concerned with the good of that which is made; it has no utilitarian end." O'Connor, however, did not deny that a work—including her own—might carry political import as she added, "If you do manage to use it successfully for social, religious, or other purposes, it is because you make it art first."[35] This is to say that a novel or a short story is not written with a didactic motive or in a moralistic manner; if so, it is a poor work of fiction, though it might be a useful political tract. But if the reader draws certain moral, philosophical, political, or theological implications from a work of art, so be it.

Fiction may at times convey philosophical ideas in a way that philosophy cannot due to the limitations of philosophical discourse. In his introduction to the *Nicomachean Ethics,* Aristotle warns the reader, "We must not expect more precision than the subject matter admits of, for precision is not to be sought for alike in all discussions." To expect otherwise is not the mark of "an educated man"; rather, it is "foolish."[36] That concession implicitly, if inadvertently, invites other disciplines to aid in achieving the aim of philosophical discourse. Enter literature, for it leads the reader into such inquiries from an oblique angle and from a unique perspective, perhaps even provoking those geographically located cerebral functions not stimulated by even Aristotle's best lectures in the Lyceum.

The Essays

The essays in *A Political Companion to Flannery O'Connor* are concerned with the political context in which O'Connor lived and worked; her incidental yet incisive responses to the critical events and controversies of her day; and the philosophers, theologians, and authors who shaped and illuminated her work. The essays also address the ways in which O'Connor's work confronted the challenges of modernity; and finally, the extent to which these concerns fit into the larger, transcendent order in which political and moral activity takes place.

This undertaking examines O'Connor's work in such a way that should be valuable to O'Connor aficionados and scholars as a background source of her influences and associations. Several of these associations have been barely studied, some not at all; yet, the significance of O'Connor's work in light of, for example, her relationship with the Agrarians, Friedrich von Hügel, Eric Voegelin, and Fr. James McCown is difficult to overstate. Examining O'Connor's work in the context of her spiritual and intellectual "fellow travelers" also grounds these essays so that none should be arcane explorations of her work or try to force O'Connor's thought into theoretical Procrustean beds. These essays also generously integrate such discussions into O'Connor's fiction, prose, and correspondence, providing rich insight into her two novels and many of her short stories. In some cases, it is O'Connor's fiction itself that drives the essay; exploration of her intellectual and spiritual kinships is a by-product of that exegesis.

Some of the writers, philosophers, and authors discussed in this volume are but one step removed from O'Connor; that is, O'Connor herself acknowledges their influence, or they acknowledge hers, or both. Lacking in this collection are essays that are merely interpretive; more important to this project is an exploration of O'Connor's influences, the principles submerged in her fiction; and the implications O'Connor's work might hold for contemporary intellectual life and culture. Other of these essays deal with O'Connor's self-conscious—or inadvertent—responses to various challenges of the modern age, such as the impulse toward nihilism, the loss of human dignity, the denigration of religion, an ignorance of sin and grace, and the danger of misguided benevolence. Some of the essays demonstrate that O'Connor is not simply reacting to modernity but confidently issuing challenges of her own, a quality of her thought, speech, and writing that knowledgeable readers will recognize.

A Political Companion to Flannery O'Connor begins with an exploration of O'Connor's relationship with, and the degree of her affinity to, that all-important group of southern literary figures, the Agrarians. In "Flannery O'Connor and the Agrarians: Authentic Religion and Southern Identity," John D. Sykes Jr. notes that although Flannery O'Connor did not read the Agrarians' manifesto *I'll Take My Stand* until the final year of her life, she had a long, complex relationship with their central ideas. This relationship included an acceptance of much of their literary theory, an echoing of their critique of modernity, an endorsement of their evaluation of southern strengths, and, finally and crucially, a rejection of their understanding of the social function of Christianity. This essay, moreover, pays particular attention to O'Connor's relationship to Allen Tate and his wife, Caroline Gordon. Tate was the instigator of the Agrarian project; Gordon was, at times, O'Connor's professional mentor.

In his essay, "'These Jesuits Work Fast': O'Connor's Elusive Politics," Benjamin B. Alexander draws upon correspondence between O'Connor and Fr. James McCown—much of which is unpublished—to demonstrate how their friendship evoked serious thought and exchanges in three areas of "politics": literary politics, the politics of the civil rights era, and the politics of anticommunism. Fr. McCown offered meaningful encouragement and spiritual guidance to O'Connor; and O'Connor, for her part, gave McCown regular advice on reading material in particular and intellectual growth in general.

In "Desegregation and the Silent Character in O'Connor's 'Everything That Rises Must Converge,'" Michael L. Schroeder argues that the title short story of O'Connor's second collection suggests the story itself reflects the complex challenges of the civil rights movement. Each of the characters in the story represents a flawed approach to a convoluted problem. In this particular essay, Schroeder offers a unique interpretation of the silent but dignified black man on the bus, suggesting that far from being a mere prop in the story, he provides a more sophisticated and nuanced attitude toward civil rights. The essay "The Pivotal Year, 1963: Flannery O'Connor and the Civil Rights Movement" by Margaret Earley Whitt provides a canvass of the civil rights movement as O'Connor would have experienced it in Georgia. Whitt takes up the criticism that O'Connor should have done more by wielding her influence on behalf of integrationists, considering the "sin of omission" as explained by St. Thomas Aquinas. Bridging from the theoretical to the experiential, Whitt offers reflections from her own experience in the early 1960s and, by so doing, attempts to render a balanced consideration of O'Connor's posture.

In "Flannery O'Connor, Friedrich von Hügel, and 'This Modernist Business,'" George Piggford, C.S.C., demonstrates that several components of the religious and philosophical ideas of Baron Friedrich von Hügel (1852–1925) were of particular value to O'Connor. Von Hügel is, however, a controversial figure in Catholic history given his association with Alfred Loisy, George Tyrrell, and others whose "modernist" ideas were condemned in "Pascendi Dominici Gregis" (1907) by Pope Pius X. It was through von Hügel that O'Connor came to understand the lineaments of the modernist controversy in the Catholic Church, and in relation to his heterodoxy she was able to refine her orthodoxy. Many of von Hügel's ideas nevertheless appear in O'Connor's later short stories, most notably "The Enduring Chill" and "The Comforts of Home."

Sarah Gordon's essay, "Flannery O'Connor, the Left-Wing Mystic, and the German Jew: A Reconsideration," is concerned with O'Connor's interest in Edith Stein and Simone Weil, who, as O'Connor remarked, are the "two twentieth-century women" who, as O'Connor noted, interested her the most. Gordon explores the life and thought of these two fascinating women as well as additional references to them in O'Connor's correspondence. She also considers points at which O'Connor's fiction might be understood in terms of her interest in Stein and Weil. In addition, Gordon wonders, given the Jewish heritage of both Edith Stein and Simone Weil, why "Jewishness" is never dealt with directly in O'Connor's fiction, especially in her story "The Displaced Person," which seems to have offered a natural opportunity.

For Aristotle, friendship is so critical to an ethical life and to a life of human flourishing that he devotes no fewer than two chapters to the subject in his magisterial work on ethics, the *Nicomachean Ethics*.[37] Accordingly, Ralph C. Wood invokes Aristotle in his essay on the friendship between Flannery O'Connor and Betty Hester, "Sacramental Suffering: The Friendship of Flannery O'Connor and Elizabeth Hester," which demonstrates that, among other mutual interests, the two were bound together in suffering, though the extent to which that misery was experienced sacramentally differed. The irony is that although O'Connor certainly influenced Hester, Hester's influence on O'Connor, though indirect, may have been the greater because it elicited some of O'Connor's most important discussions about literature, philosophy, politics, spirituality—and friendship— and without these letters it is possible that our understanding of the depths of O'Connor's soul and intellect might have never been evident, at least not as they are known now.

The next essay, "Flannery O'Connor as Baroque Artist: Theological and Literary Strategies," by Mark Bosco, S.J., is an analogy: Although there exists no known concrete connection between O'Connor's work and the Italian baroque painter Caravaggio, Bosco argues that there is a striking parallel between their endeavors. A consideration of seventeenth-century Catholic Counter-Reformation artistic strategies illuminates O'Connor's experience as a Catholic artist in the Protestant South, concerned as she was with the challenges of modernity. In this framework, O'Connor's southern realism, her love of the grotesque, and her often violent epiphanies have much in common with the baroque world of Caravaggio, Bernini, and Rubens.

Farrell O'Gorman's essay, "O'Connor and the Rhetoric of Eugenics: Misfits, the 'Unfit,' and Us," reveals that in the American South of

O'Connor's day, the philosophy and practice of eugenics enjoyed widespread support, and it was conducted as close to O'Connor as Milledgeville's Central State Hospital, which was no more than fifteen minutes from Andalusia. O'Gorman further explains that other authors of the day—principally Erskine Caldwell—integrated a barely veiled sympathy for eugenics in their fiction; O'Gorman then demonstrates that O'Connor's treatment of the poor, even the apparently genetically inferior, is radically different from these disturbing trends that surrounded her.

In "'School for Sanctity': O'Connor, Illich, and the Politics of Benevolence," Gary M. Ciuba deals with a central theme in O'Connor's works: the way in which ideology and humanitarianism become entangled. He explains that from 1961 to 1963 O'Connor corresponded with Roslyn Barnes about her friend's work with the Papal Auxiliary Volunteers of Latin America, a missionary group formed in the aftermath of John XXIII's call for North Americans to engage in evangelization south of the U.S. border. The priest that provided Barnes with her training for such volunteer work was Msgr. Ivan Illich; and, although Illich would later become famous for his radical reevaluation of education and health care, the genesis of his anti-institutionalism lay in his work as a priest at the Center of Intercultural Documentation at Cuernavaca. As Barnes wrote to O'Connor about Illich, O'Connor's reaction to the priest and his ministry was mediated through her recent novel *The Violent Bear It Away*. Just as O'Connor could use her own work to understand Illich, Ciuba argues, Illich's work can likewise be used to elucidate O'Connor's. Illich's critique of the misguided charity of missionaries in Latin America provides a means for considering the politics of benevolence in O'Connor's fiction about a postcolonial South.

The next essay, "'He Thinks He's Jesus Christ!': Flannery O'Connor, Russell Kirk, and the Problem of Misguided Humanitarianism," demonstrates the importance of O'Connor's relationship with conservative man of letters, the late Russell Kirk. She met Kirk only once, but that encounter is described in some detail by both, and for both it was evidently significant. Kirk wrote in his memoirs, "The impression that she made upon me by her presence was as strong as that created by her stories." This essay explains that several of their shared concerns point to a common preoccupation over unmoored humanitarianism that runs a risk of generating more harm than good. In "Flannery O'Connor and Political Community in 'The Displaced Person,'" John Roos opens a dimension of O'Connor's short story "The Displaced Person" in a way few have imagined. As Roos demonstrates, woven into this elegant story is a tension between a Lockean political philosophy on the one hand, with its emphasis on individualism and property rights; and, on the other hand, a Thomistic worldview that prizes belonging and meaningful discourse.

In "Future Flannery, or, How a Hillbilly Thomist Can Help Us Navigate the Politics of Personhood in the Twenty-First Century," Christina Bieber Lake combines her expertise in O'Connor studies with her interest in bioethics and explores issues surrounding the question of personhood in the realm of bioethics. This essay illustrates the way in which O'Connor's fiction provides ways of thinking about the sanctity of the human person that are deeply needed as new technological possibilities arise; namely, she offers a vision of dignity without sentimentality, a model of how the Incarnation can lead us to reconsider the value of each human person, and a unique contribution to the concerns raised by disability studies.

The next essay addresses not only *what* O'Connor said but *how* she said it. In "In Defense of Being: Flannery O'Connor and the Politics of Art," John F. Desmond notes that in a letter to her friend Elizabeth Hester, O'Connor writes: "You have to be able to dominate the existence you characterize. This is why I write about people who are more or less primitive." In this statement, O'Connor indirectly acknowledged that unlike other authors like Walker Percy, Graham Greene, François Mauriac, or Albert Camus, O'Connor does not present an interior view of the modern self-conscious mind in its struggle between doubt and belief, and in its ambiguous search for spiritual meaning. Accordingly, this essay examines the relative success of O'Connor's dramatization of belief. Central to the matter is a discussion of her aesthetic; the narrative authority in her work; her understanding of the representative audience for whom she was writing; and the strategies she adopted to reach them.

This book ends with the essay "Flannery O'Connor, Eric Voegelin, and the Question That Lies between Them" by the late Marion Montgomery, who was a contemporary and friend of O'Connor. In this essay, Montgomery explores the important relationship between Voegelin's and O'Connor's thought, and the sense of mystery that is so conspicuous in their philosophical predilections. O'Connor was obviously taken with Voegelin's philosophical/theological/historicist thought, reviewing as she did several of his works for the Atlanta diocesan newsletter. Montgomery suggests that both writers recognize what lies beyond rational explanation—namely that which involves man's participation in transcendence.

Notes

1. Flannery O'Connor, *Mystery and Manners: Occasional Prose* (New York: Farrar, Straus and Giroux, 1957).

2. Flannery O'Connor, *The Habit of Being: The Letters of Flannery O'Connor*, ed. Sally Fitzgerald (New York: Farrar, Straus and Giroux, 1979).

3. January 22, 1944, Emory Collection. Used with permission.

4. *Nicomachean Ethics*, trans. David Ross (Oxford: Oxford University Press, 1984), 1094a19–1094b10.

5. Charles J. Huelsbeck, "Of Fiction, Integrity, and Peacocks," in *Flannery O'Connor: The Contemporary Reviews*, ed. R. Neil Scott and Irwin H. Streight (Cambridge: Cambridge University Press, 2009), 399.

6. Betty Boyd Love, "Recollections of Flannery O'Connor," *Flannery O'Connor Bulletin* 14 (1985): 64–71.

7. August 9, 1955, Milledgeville, Ga., Emory Collection. Used with permission.

8. *Aristotle: On Man in the Universe: Metaphysics—Parts of Animals—Ethics—Politics—Poetics*, ed. Louise Ropes (New York: Walter J. Black, 1943).

9. John Herman Randall Jr., *The Making of the Modern Mind: A Survey of the Intellectual Background of the Present Age* (Boston: Houghton Mifflin, 1926); Eric Voegelin, *Plato and Aristotle*, vol. 3 of *Order and History* (Baton Rouge: Louisiana State University Press, 1957).

10. Voegelin, *Plato and Aristotle*, 285.

11. Flannery O'Connor, *Collected Works* (New York: Library of America, 1988), 1–132, 263–84.

12. Flannery O'Connor, *The Presence of Grace and Other Book Reviews* (Athens: University of Georgia Press, 1983), 71.

13. Aristotle, *Ethics*, I:5, X:7; Voegelin, *Plato and Aristotle*, 355.

14. O'Connor, *Habit of Being*, 249.

15. Ibid., 311.

16. Ibid., 179.

17. Ibid., xvi.

18. Ibid., 307.

19. Voegelin, *Plato and Aristotle*, 164. Note: "Fides caritate formata" means, literally, "faith formed by charity."

20. O'Connor's title is taken from the works of the French Idealist philosopher Pierre Teilhard de Chardin, specifically, from this quote from his essay "Omega

Point": "Remain true to yourself, but move ever upward toward greater consciousness and greater love! At the summit you will find yourselves united with all those who, from every direction, have made the same ascent. For everything that rises must converge" (*The Future of Man*, 1950).

21. O'Connor, *Presence of Grace*, 71, 70.

22. O'Connor, *Mystery and Manners*, 48.

23. Voegelin, *Plato and Aristotle*, 129.

24. Aristotle, *Nicomachean Ethics*, trans. Ross, 1179a35–1181b23; Aristotle, *The Politics*, trans. Carnes Lord (Chicago: University of Chicago Press, 1984), bk. VIII, chaps. 1–7, 1337a110–1324b135.

25. O'Connor, *Habit of Being*, 204.

26. Ibid., 127, 256.

27. Rosemary Magee and Emily Wright, "The Good Guide: A Final Conversation with Sally Fitzgerald," *Flannery O'Connor Review* 3 (2005): 36.

28. Sally Fitzgerald, "Rooms with a View," *Flannery O'Connor Bulletin* 10 (1981): 22.

29. Ronald Rash, review of Marion Montgomery, *Why Flannery O'Connor Stayed Home* (La Salle: Sherwood Sugden, 1981), 97–99.

30. Ralph Wood, "Flannery O'Connor as Political Prophet," unpublished essay.

31. O'Connor *Habit of Being*, 347.

32. Ibid., 195.

33. O'Connor, *Mystery and Manners: Occasional Prose*, Kindle ed. (Farrar, Straus and Giroux), Kindle locs. 270–271).

34. O'Connor, *The Habit of Being*, 129.

35. Ibid., 157.

36. Aristotle *Ethics*, p. xxix, 1094a, 19ff.

37. Ibid., bks. IX and X.

I

O'Connor's Politics

1

Flannery O'Connor and the Agrarians

Authentic Religion and Southern Identity

John D. Sykes Jr.

Nothing was more instrumental in shaping Flannery O'Connor's politics than her placement in the two polities with which she was constantly identified, the Roman Catholic Church and the American South. Even in the midst of resisting stereotypes associated with Catholics and southerners, she defined herself in relation to them, as she does most explicitly in the essay "The Catholic Novelist in the South."[1] Given her investment in the topic of southern identity, it is surprising that she did not read *I'll Take My Stand: The South and the Agrarian Tradition* until 1964, the year of her death.[2] When she did read it, she wrote her friend Betty Hester that the book marked "the only time real minds have got together to talk about the South."[3] O'Connor's high opinion of the authors of these essays, which were published in 1930, was grounded in personal experience. Four of the twelve contributors would serve at various times as her teachers, editors, referees, and friends. Indeed, it is not too much to say that John Crowe Ransom, Allen Tate, Robert Penn Warren, and Andrew Lytle were the faces of the southern literary establishment for O'Connor when she came of age as a writer—especially if Tate's wife, Caroline Gordon, is added to the list. As may be seen from Sally Fitzgerald's chronology, Ransom, Warren, Tate, and Lytle all interacted with O'Connor at the Iowa Writers' Workshop during O'Connor's two years as a student there.[4] As editor of the *Kenyon Review,* Ransom published a number of O'Connor's stories, beginning in 1953. Lytle later had a similar editorial relationship with O'Connor as editor of the *Sewanee Review*. And after O'Connor left graduate school, Caroline Gordon became her unofficial writing coach. O'Connor would continue to send stories-in-progress to Gordon for the remainder of her career.

Thus, although O'Connor was unfamiliar with the Agrarians' 1930 manifesto, she was very well acquainted with former Agrarians. Although O'Connor took no interest in the policies and programs that the group advanced in the 1930s, she shared their concern to describe and defend a certain type of society. She was decidedly influenced by their characterization of the South. Finally, however, O'Connor's love of the South was outweighed by her devotion to the other polity that claimed her, the Church. O'Connor's explicitly theological notions of human community and history ultimately offer an alternative to the Agrarian vision. Indeed, in her own way, she solved one of the major problems that confounded them.

The Agrarians and the Dilemma of Self-Consciousness

Any treatment of the Agrarian movement must acknowledge two facts at the outset: aside from a few key attitudes and broad principles, the contributors' views diverged nearly as often as they coincided; furthermore, the practical aims of the group were never achieved. By 1940, the movement was, in effect, dead. The Agrarian men O'Connor met in the postwar era had long since abandoned the cause. Nonetheless, the philosophical agenda at the heart of the original enterprise had lasting influence in shaping definitions of the South.

The impetus for what became the Agrarian movement was generated by Ransom, Tate, and their friend Donald Davidson, perhaps the most passionate southern patriot of the group. Having met at Vanderbilt University, where Ransom was a young English professor, and where first Davidson, then Tate, enrolled as students, the three became close associates in the group of poets called the Fugitives. By the mid-1920s, Davidson was an instructor at his alma mater, and although Tate had left for New York and France, the three corresponded regularly.[5] At least two factors drove the three to action. The first was their reaction to the Scopes Trial of 1925 and the attendant criticism directed at the South as a benighted, backward region deserving of H. L. Mencken's scathing appellation of 1917, "Sahara of the Bozart." The second was dissatisfaction with what they considered a "New South" defense of the region put forward by progressives such as those found at the University of North Carolina at Chapel Hill, notably Howard Mumford Jones in English and Howard Odum in sociology.[6] From the point of view of the future Agrarians, the New South strategy of seeking to discredit attacks on the South by insisting that the region was on its way to becoming like the rest of the country was completely misguided. Ransom and Tate in particular took the opposite tack. They maintained that the South was praiseworthy precisely because it had not succumbed to the acids of modernity. It remained a traditional society not yet alienated and fragmented by what they began to call "industrialism."[7] Although the two volumes that eventually emerged from the Agrarian response took up additional issues and included other agendas, the effort to champion the virtues of the South as a cure for the deepest modern social ills remained central.

In making their case for the South, the Agrarians revived an older tradition of conservative political thought in the region, as Eugene Genovese argues in *The Southern Tradition*.[8] However, they combined this line of thought with the critique of modernity Tate found in T. S. Eliot and Ransom found confirmed in Unamuno and Santayana. These contemporary sources for the Agrarian stance were more influential than one might suppose. Tate in particular was driven to a "southern" position only after having fallen under Eliot's influence. During his Fugitive years at Vanderbilt (roughly 1918–1924), Tate scorned southern cultural life as provincial. He detested sentimentality and championed the modernist turn in literature, which had already swept Europe.[9] His animosity toward the southern intellectual establishment of the time was exacerbated by a personal contretemps with Edward Mims, the chairman of the Vanderbilt English Department. With his New South leanings and Victorian tastes, Mims represented the sort of moderation and mediocrity that the brilliant and impetuous Tate could not tolerate. Tate insulted Mims severely enough to sting the older man into refusing to recommend Tate for graduate school, effectively shutting him out of an academic career, at least in the short run.[10] Tate's unhappiness with things southern was not limited to campus politics. Before heading for New York, he complained to friends of the oppressive dullness of southern rural life. As would be true for many southern writers, Tate went "north toward home," in Willie Morris's phrase. He later told an interviewer, "I think if I'd stayed in the South I might have become anti-Southern, but I became a Southerner again by going East."[11] Living outside the south reinforced his "southernness," and the influence of Eliot made him more deeply critical of modernity. In effect, Tate decided to wrest the idea of the South from people such as Mims and rehabilitate it into an ideal that could resist the slide of Western societies into the Wasteland.[12]

Ransom's motives follow a similar trajectory. Unlike Tate, he remained in Nashville during the period that produced *I'll Take My Stand*, but he had already had a lengthy sojourn away from the South, having studied at Oxford as a Rhodes Scholar. Feeling that he was neither adequately appreciated nor sufficiently compensated at Vanderbilt, he left the South for Kenyon College in 1937. But, like Tate, his experience and his reading led him to look to the South for his social ideal.

The crucial run-up to Ransom's participation in the *I'll Take My Stand* project was his book *God without Thunder*.[13] In it, Ransom puts forth a view of religion that anticipates Tate's contribution to the manifesto volume and points us to the key connection between the Agrarians and O'Connor. Ransom's personal history disposed him to see religion as a key component of southern identity. His father and uncles were Methodist ministers in the Nashville Conference, and throughout Ransom's childhood the family moved to a new charge every four years in keeping with the Methodist circuit-riding tradition. Given the argument of the book, it seems a bit odd that Ransom would dedicate the volume to his father, but no doubt he meant to acknowledge that he owed his firsthand acquaintance with religion to his family.

In *God without Thunder*, Ransom argues that one of the great losses in modern, scientific culture is the ability to feel awe. Living in a world he believes he can understand and control, modern man has nothing to fear and nothing to worship. With everything cut to his own measure, man finds that nature has been stripped of mystery, and life has been rendered petty. Insofar as belief in God continues, the God worshipped by moderns is a tamed God, a God without thunder. Ransom urges instead a return to belief in a God of power—unpredictable and terrible, but worthy of worship. Belief in such a God fills a psychological need in human nature; indeed, holding such a conviction is necessary to do justice to the totality of human

experience. Ransom does not flinch from calling the required religious attitude fundamentalism. With the Scopes Trial in the recent past as he writes,
his embrace of the term is an audacious stroke. However, Ransom does not
have in mind a naïve belief that sees no distinction between myth and fact.
His "fundamentalist" is one who understands the mythic nature of his religious affirmation and is able to affirm it nonetheless. He is a sophisticate
bearing little resemblance to the fanatics with which O'Connor scandalized
her secularized readers. Ransom's "fundamentalist," when he speaks religiously, speaks "as if." Ransom defends what may appear to be duplicity on
the part of such a worshiper in this way: "I hardly believe that he would be
either nobler or more intelligent if he elected to cross his fingers whenever
he repeated his creed. It would be asking too much to require him to take
the pains to say to himself each time, 'remember, this is myth, not fact; this
is *als ob,* my hypothesis; don't be taken in.' If he did that he would seem
only pusillanimous."[14] Indeed, in a secularized, scientific culture, Ransom
suggests such religious belief is an act of courage.

Unfortunately, Ransom's argument also threatens to turn belief into
fiction. It is no coincidence that his recommendation to embrace religious
myth as if it were literally true bears a strong resemblance to Coleridge's
"willing suspension of disbelief." Ransom's approach to religion is essentially poetic, and herein lies the chief weakness of his position—one that
O'Connor will assiduously avoid. The reader of poetry knows she must
eventually close the book and adopt the more skeptical attitude of the real
world; even great poetry yields only a secondary reality. Since religion is
supposed to concern ultimate reality, however, treating it as fiction is self-
defeating. When at the end of *God without Thunder* Ransom rallies his
readers, whatever their religion, to *"insist on a virile and concrete God, and
accept no principle as a substitute,"* he is doing so on the basis of a principle
concerning God, namely that "God" has many valid concrete (mythological) expressions.[15] But in that case, how could one take any "virile and concrete God" as more than an expression of a general principle of divinity?
Ransom's advice is incoherent. Belief becomes a self-conscious assertion
that qualifies what only seems to be a wholehearted affirmation. No wonder
Ransom eventually gave up the practice of religion and turned his intellectual energies to literature.

Ransom's unacknowledged dilemma shows itself in a different form in
Tate's essay for *I'll Take My Stand.* When Ransom undertook the writing of

an introductory essay for the volume, the topic of religion fell to Tate. "Remarks on the Southern Religion" is the most ambitious and sophisticated essay in the volume, but the lines of its argument are often obscure, reflecting the difficulty Tate had in writing it. In fact, the essay is in part an attack on the South, or at least a deep criticism of its past. According to Tate, deeply flawed motives marred the very first English settlements. Jamestown was launched as a commercial enterprise. A spirit of competitive, capitalistic individualism was thus present from the beginning, fostered by the Protestant ethos the settlers brought with them. Jeffersonian notions of democracy exacerbated the individualism rooted in Protestantism, compounding the problem. And so although the South managed to develop into a stable society governed by tradition, social hierarchy, a code of manners, systems of kinship, and love of the land, it harbored a fatal flaw capable of bringing it down to the level of its Yankee neighbors. Tate's analysis suggests that the South was undone not by the direct northern "aggression" of the Civil War and Reconstruction but rather by impulses that it had always harbored.

Harking back to the model of medieval Europe, Tate submits that the principal ingredient the South lacked to sustain its social order was the Roman Catholic Church. The South was an anomaly, "a feudal society without a feudal religion."[16] Unlike Protestantism, the Catholic Church presupposes and reinforces social unity, hierarchy, and a sacramental attitude toward nature. A South unified by Catholicism, Tate implies, might have withstood the cultural crisis provoked by the war. However, he stops short of calling for Catholic conversion of the South. Indeed, at this point, Tate himself had not entered the Catholic Church.

On balance, Tate's attitude toward Protestant southern religion is positive. With Ransom, he believes that such religiousness as the South has had, despite its ideological inferiority to Catholicism, has contributed to social cohesion and served as a check on hubris. More specifically, it has preserved a sense of the unavoidability of evil, and perhaps most importantly, it has eschewed the abstract for the concrete, insisting that one pay attention to the actual world in all its unsystematic particularity. "Abstraction is the death of religion," says Tate.[17] However, as Tate acknowledges, his own analysis is itself an abstraction, and thus he faces a dilemma: the argument that must be made to defend religion against modernity requires a detached, analytical stance that kills religion. The problem of self-consciousness rears its head once again.

The dilemma of self-consciousness apparent in Ransom's earlier essay is present in Tate's analysis in at least two ways. As a conservative thinker in the sense Genovese has described, Tate defends the South as a traditional society. Conversely, he attacks modernity for its submission to bureaucratic rational calculation and social engineering. Modern structures of business and government depend upon systems of abstraction that ignore and undermine natural ties of kinship and tradition. Alienation and fragmentation are the inevitable result. Yet Tate's own analysis is a kind of abstraction bent upon provoking change. In the case of religion, Tate finds himself recommending Roman Catholicism, but for entirely instrumental reasons. Anyone who converted as a result of Tate's argument in "Remarks on the Southern Religion" would do so on the basis of an abstract calculation aimed at deriving a benefit—exactly the process used by a business to maximize profits.

In *Three Catholic Writers of the Modern South*, Robert Brinkmeyer details how such dilemmas fuel Tate's poetry. A heightened awareness of himself as an isolated consciousness observing a history from which he stands apart creates the tension in Tate's best-known poem from his Agrarian period. The speaker of "Ode to the Confederate Dead," the first version of which was completed in 1927, mourns not the passing of brave soldiers but his own inability to connect with them.[18] He is alienated from the past and can only retrieve a sense of it through an act of will. As Brinkmeyer observes, the poet is "torn between his desire to affirm the past and his realization of the impossibility to do so."[19] Where religion is concerned, Tate's anguished ambivalence can be measured in the years it took him to take the decisive final step into the Roman Catholic Church, a move he did not make until 1950. Although he recognized the need for the Church well before the end of the Agrarian period, he could not seem completely to surrender his critical faculty and embrace belief. Of course, in this as in all deeply personal decisions, more than one factor came into play, but apparently Tate suffered from the kind of hyperconsciousness and consequent inability to act that Dostoevsky dramatized so effectively in *Notes from Underground*. A second poem from 1927, "Causerie," describes this ambivalence in relation to the Resurrection. In the third stanza the speaker explicitly mentions Ransom and Warren as men "who foundered on / This point of doctrine." At the end of the stanza, the poet asserts: "They lacked doctrine; / They waited. I, who watched out the first crisis / With them, wait: / For the incredible image."[20] The poet seems suspended in unhappy and unwanted doubt, hoping for a miraculous, "incredible" image that will consume his will and sweep him beyond belief into absolute certainty, thus freeing him from the angst of a too-vivid self-awareness.

The figure of the doubt-stricken, paralyzed consciousness appears throughout the literature of the southern renascence, most famously in Faulkner's Quentin Compson. Indeed, it goes part and parcel with the artistic response to history Louis Simpson calls "the aesthetic of memory."[21] Simpson maintains that the fruitful period in southern writing that began in the 1920s was spawned by a cultural crisis. The disjunction between the South's dream of itself as the noble if defeated fulfillment of the American founders' vision, and the reality of the ongoing and indifferent stream of history, became too great to be ignored. Thus Simpson notes that "southern writers discovered the modern resistance to the disappearance of the community of kinship, custom, and tradition; they found, furthermore, that this resistance is complexly, tantalizingly present in southern memory."[22] This discovery coincided with southern writers' embrace of modernists who had worked this ground in other national contexts: Flaubert, Turgenev, Proust, Mann, Joyce, Yeats, and Eliot, to name those cited by Simpson. Simpson terms the modernist turn an "aesthetic of memory" because the loss of community and kinship to which it responds is occasioned by the painful recognition that history has no telos beyond itself. History in this sense is "history as an ineluctable process or series of processes, which may be regarded either as teleological or blank purposelessness."[23] Whether in its Hegelian or Nietzschean form, history in the modern understanding is entirely self-contained. In the absence of larger, commonly shared narratives or other patterns of meaning, it falls to the individual consciousness to supply the lack. For the modernist artist, "memory became, not a spiritual heritage, but a 'life's work.'"[24]

The burden placed upon the artist carrying out this work is tremendously heavy, however. The individual artist takes on the function previously performed by an entire tradition. And at the same time, the artist creates the problem of self-consciousness for herself, placing herself at a remove from the very tradition she is in effect re-creating. Tate and Ransom were correct in seeing that this difficulty is at root a religious one. The question of southern identity is religious because without some telos beyond itself, history is unable to provide any community or individual with a stable identity. The artist's dilemma is inevitable, in other words, without some transcendent reference point. As John Desmond has taken pains to show in *Risen Sons: Flannery O'Connor's Vision of History,* this conviction about history is at the core of O'Connor's aesthetic.[25]

O'Connor and Authentic Religion

"A Late Encounter with the Enemy" offers a vivid contrast between O'Connor and the Agrarians. The thematic trajectory of the story goes from a false ideal of the southern past to a moment of eschatological revelation. O'Connor's conviction that only a transcendent perspective is capable of cutting through illusion and providing a reliable narrative of identity could hardly be made plainer than it is in the case of Gen. Flintrock Sash. The "General" is actually an ancient foot soldier so far removed from battle he cannot remember it. He has become a living monument, promoted, re-named, and costumed in a uniform given to him by a movie public-relations staff. The highlight of his life, blotting out all recollection of his earlier years, is his memory of attending a movie premiere—clearly the Atlanta premiere of *Gone with the Wind.* For all his remaining days he lives on the capital of his celebrity, consenting to be trotted out on ceremonial occasions when a connection to the glorious Lost Cause is needed. His final appearance is at the college graduation of his granddaughter, during which, unbeknownst to the audience, he dies on stage, of an apparent stroke. The climax of the story takes place inside the old man's head. He experiences a kind of personal apocalypse in which he sees his past as it truly was, including the faces of the mother, wife, and son he has not thought of in thirty years. These im-ages, as well as those of the distant battles, catch up with him in his vision and overwhelm him, leaving him desperately to wonder as he dies, "what comes after the past."[26]

The implication is that the "General" had a guilty past for which he had never done the work of repentance, rendering ironic his own role as venerated relic of the Lost Cause. In another sense, however, the General is an apt symbol for a South that has failed to come to terms with its his-tory. O'Connor's satire points to a larger target than the comic-tragic self-deceptions of a crotchety old man. The public ceremony bracketing Sash's inner apocalypse is one that trades on a self-congratulatory version of the past as false as the general's own. O'Connor calls attention to this confusion through the one sentence of the graduation speech that penetrates Sash's consciousness verbatim: "If we forget our past . . . we won't remember our future and it will be as well for we won't have one."[27] The speaker has comically garbled Santayana's famous line, "those who cannot remember the past are condemned to repeat it."[28] Unwittingly, the commencement orator has, with this skewed quotation, pointed to a deep cultural flaw. As long as the South refuses to acknowledge the truth about its past, it has no chance to redeem its errors. It is instead doomed to live out a fantasy version of the past projected as a blueprint for the future. As Sarah Gordon says in her discussion of the story, Sash is "the ridiculous embodiment of the southern veneration of history," a veneration that acts as an escape from history.[29] The official public version of the South, as represented by the city boosters at the film premiere and the dignitaries at Sally Poker Sash's graduation, is captive to the stultifying attitude toward history that Richard King, following Nietzsche, calls monumentalism.[30] According to this view, the accomplishments of the earlier heroic age are unsurpassable, and thus the most that can be done in the present is to ritualistically repeat them. Through Sash's experience, O'Connor suggests both that the South's image of its past is a false one and that the real southern past contains much to be repented of. Like Tate and Faulkner, O'Connor gives us a southern consciousness that is alienated from the past even as it is dominated by it.

In addition to this similarity to Tate, "A Late Encounter with the Enemy" points to O'Connor's more significant departure from the Agrarian approach to the southern need to come to terms with history. The crucial difference has to do with the manner of the old man's final reckoning, when Sash's mind becomes the receptacle for a divine revelation—one he has for most of his adult life stoutly resisted. The pivotal turn in the story comes when "the General felt as if there were a little hole beginning to widen in the top of his head."[31] His vision, when it comes, is poured in from the outside. Sounds and then images make a hole in the top of his skull in order to force their way into his consciousness. The metaphor is primarily one of invasion; this attack issues from the soldier's late encounter with the enemy. Rather than welling up from the repressed depths of memory, Sash's vision crashes in on him as a message from above. He finds himself engulfed by a procession he does not wish to join. He is summoned to face divine judgment, his sins and omissions presenting themselves unbidden. In this sense, the hole in Gen. Flintrock Sash's head becomes the portal of access to the transcendent narrative by which Sash may know the truth about himself:

"the old words began to stir in his head as if they were trying to wrench themselves out of place and come to life."[32] Finally, he cannot dodge the words bringing to life the real past, and they strike him like a volley of bullets: "he felt his body riddled in a hundred places with sharp stabs of pain and he fell down, returning a curse with every hit."[33] He sees not only the old battlefields in their true murderous colors but also the faces of loved ones he has conveniently erased from his selective memory. Thus, before his death, the old man has his judgment day—a divinely initiated reckoning poured in through the aperture bored into his skull.

Flannery O'Connor believed her mission as a writer was to open such portals. As she famously announced, "When you can assume your audience holds the same beliefs you do, you can relax a little and use normal ways of talking to it; when you have to assume that it does not, then you have to make your vision apparent by shock—to the hard of hearing you shout, and for the almost blind you draw large and startling figures."[34] The narrative of transcendence she hoped would enter the minds of her startled readers was the biblical saga of the God of Israel made manifest in Jesus Christ. O'Connor's stories typically strike an eschatological note, as Desmond's *Risen Sons* amply demonstrates. Frequently, characters come to their revelations or moments of grace at the end of her stories, as they face death. Conceptually, however, O'Connor's vision of "the last things" comes at the beginning. Her gaze is fastened upon that one great height in the distance that dominates the pedestrian landscape.

In relation to the Agrarians, O'Connor's prophetic orientation leads to a radical reversal of priorities. They frame authentic religion in terms of cultural need; she judges culture, including southern identity, from within a living religious tradition. Ralph Wood states the matter succinctly: "Flannery O'Connor understood, as Allen Tate and the Agrarians did not, that there can be no identification of Christian faith and Western civilization."[35] Ransom and Tate defined a cultural need and looked for an appropriate religion to fill it. O'Connor, on the other hand, always considered society from a standpoint within the Church. This simple difference is crucial to O'Connor's success in avoiding the problem of self-consciousness: she accepted the transcendent narrative that the Agrarians, along with other figures of the southern renascence, found problematic. Since her view of religion is not instrumentalist, she is not plagued by the tentativeness of Ransom's "as if," and since she feels no need to re-create a tradition through an act of "memory," she avoids the kind of guilty alienation registered by Tate. Thus she was not inclined either to idealize the South or to tailor the history of the Church to fit the requirements of a secular rescue narrative.

The difference shows up plainly in the title of the essay in which she gives the topic her fullest treatment, "The Catholic Novelist in the Protestant South." O'Connor invariably construed the South from her starting point within the Church, which she considered the single most crucial element in her own identity. For her, the Church provided a stable center by which to measure the South, and indeed the world. As a result, O'Connor is more critical of the South and less likely to idealize it. O'Connor can also be scathing in her treatment of religion in the South—both the conventional Protestant churches attended by pillars of the community and fiery sects at the social fringes. Yet at the same time, she finds a commendable zeal and hunger in the latter groups. Ultimately, for her they represent a kind of proto-Catholicism—a response to God's grace that if followed to its end will lead to the faith more fully and accurately revealed in the Roman Catholic Church. With Ransom she affirms a God with thunder, and like Tate she believes Catholicism to represent the fulfillment of the South's deepest cultural need, but her reason for making these claims is different from theirs. For O'Connor, a proper understanding of the South throws into relief the truths proclaimed by the Church. "South" becomes not an ideal to be defended or pursued but, in Augustinian terms, a particular instance of the City of Man that can by contrast point to the City of God. Thus O'Connor's ideal is the Church, or perhaps one should say the Church Triumphant. Since O'Connor is neither inviting her reader nor urging herself to adopt the mind-set of the South she describes, she avoids the dilemma of self-consciousness that befalls the Agrarians.

O'Connor's attitude to the South is ironic without being elegiac. For her, the myth seems to have lost its power. The subject of the southern past seldom arises, and when it does it is as a cliché. As previously noted, in "A Late Encounter with the Enemy" the southern past is subordinated to a religious vision of personal apocalypse; the divine narrative rushes in to subsume the pieces of the now broken myth of the past. Indeed, the pattern whereby a sudden irruption of the divine shatters the pretensions and complacency of self-deceived characters is common to all of O'Connor's fiction, and the view of religion it carries with it is crucially different from that set forth by Ransom and Tate in the 1930s.

The difference might be put in this way. For Ransom, disenchanted modern man needs a God with thunder, and so moderns should, for their own good, will themselves to believe in such a God. For O'Connor, the real God is the last thing moderns want, and thus God must act violently to break down their unbelief. In contrast to Tate, O'Connor sees in southern Protestants not the capital-accumulating individualists of Max Weber, but God-drunk fanatics hungry for sacrament and ritual without knowing it. Where Tate sees proto-Yankees, O'Connor finds proto-Catholics. Two character types found in O'Connor's work illustrate how she differs from the Agrarians in these matters. Ransom's audience corresponds to the enlightened secularist O'Connor parodied in characters such as Sheppard in "The Lame Shall Enter First." Typical of O'Connor's southern proto-Catholics is her first memorable protagonist, Hazel Motes of *Wise Blood.*

Sheppard might be said to represent Ransom's intended audience thirty years later. He is a modern man who refuses to live by illusions. A professional social worker, he attempts to live within the terms of a scientific secularism in which he has placed his entire trust for improving the human condition. In the face of personal tragedy—the death of his wife—he turns his energies to helping others, volunteering as a counselor at the local reformatory. One boy in particular stands out to him as a prodigal who deserves to be saved—a highly intelligent orphan with a club foot. Sheppard hopes to achieve Rufus Johnson's spiritual rescue through enlightenment. Once the boy agrees to live in Sheppard's house, Sheppard exposes him to the thrill of scientific discovery, buying first a telescope and then a microscope. But the teenager refuses to be redeemed. His chief means of intellectual resistance is the Protestant Biblicism he has absorbed from his grandfather. He uses his aggressive religious certitude not only to turn aside Sheppard's efforts to reform him but also to win over Sheppard's own ten-year-old son, Norton, who desperately wishes to see his mother again and who is easily persuaded that she is in heaven. In the end, Sheppard both fails to save Johnson and loses his own son, whom he has neglected.

In terms of Ransom's argument in *God without Thunder,* the rhetorical positions of believer and unbeliever are reversed in "The Lame Shall Enter First." Ransom takes the role of apologist attempting to convince cultured despisers of religion that they are, in fact, behind the curve of intellectual progress, which favors a return to a religious view. In O'Connor's story the secular humanist speaks with the voice of reason, trying without success to dent willful religious ignorance. Yet the implied conclusion of the argument is the same in each case. Sheppard's failure leaves the field to religion. Johnson's devilish triumph and Norton's pitiful death signal that Sheppard's narrow secularism has left out a large portion of reality. Sheppard is blind to both good and evil because he has ruled out God on principle. He has understood neither Johnson's demonic defiance nor Norton's needy innocence.

In comparing Ransom's work to O'Connor's, one must bear in mind the difference in genres: Ransom's book is discursive discourse bent upon rational persuasion, whereas "The Lame Shall Enter First" is art that invites contemplation. Still, O'Connor had a clear, if secondary, didactic purpose in all her fiction, which broadly speaking was to render the otherwise invisible working of God's grace in the world. Like Ransom, she wishes to point to the need for a God with thunder. However, her attitude toward the skeptical, secularized reader is crucially different from Ransom's. He reasons; she confronts. Ransom builds a case through philosophical and historical analysis to convince the intelligent reader that the lessons of science have been misread, and man does need God after all. The human mind requires God as a working hypothesis, he avers. But for O'Connor, God is a reality that may be recognized but cannot be theorized. To put it another way, in O'Connor's work, a God who is the product of human need cannot truly be God. In her role as believing artist, O'Connor plays the part of witness rather than that of apologist. She points but does not explain, or perhaps more accurately, she does not attempt to justify what she points to. In Ransom's terms, she refuses to insert the *als ob* into Christian belief, thinking to the contrary that a tentative faith put forward as an *as if* is actually unbelief in disguise. When O'Connor's characters have revelations, they are stung into them, often through tragedy, which pierces the subterfuges of their reasoning minds.

Flannery O'Connor is a decidedly unapologetic author. The shocks she administers to her educated nonbelievers are designed in part to circumvent the problem of self-consciousness that Ransom and Tate unwittingly created for themselves. "As if" belief, undertaken for instrumental reasons, always threatens to fall apart. To be "useful," religious belief must be sincere, but it can never be completely sincere so long as it is tentatively held. Part of O'Connor's genius lies in connecting moments of faith-eliciting revelation to visceral events rather than cerebral arguments, which is her way of answering the problem of abstraction Tate encountered.

A similar case can be made for O'Connor's treatment of southern Protestants. Allen Tate considered Protestantism to be a great weakness of southern culture, since he believed it sponsored an unhealthy individualism and harbored a dangerous disposition toward market capitalism. A South with a Roman Catholic religion might have been able to sustain the kind of traditional society it developed. But although O'Connor was similarly dismissive of mainline Protestantism, at least in her fiction, she was very much drawn to what John Hayes has called the "folk religion" of the poor, largely shared by blacks and whites, and which often included what Hayes calls a "grassroots sacramentalism."[36] The justification for her fondness takes us both toward and away from Tate's "Remarks on the Southern Religion": O'Connor believed Bible Belt fanatics to be proto-Catholics. The South's chief virtue, so far as O'Connor was concerned, lay in its fidelity to a Bible and a Christ that had to be taken with the utmost seriousness—a cultural context that provided a set of presuppositions and narratives that did not have to be hypothetically entertained or consciously adopted. O'Connor delighted in the excesses of unself-conscious belief that she found all about her, regarding them as signs of spiritual health as well as a source of humor. The South, she famously asserted, was at least Christ-haunted if not Christ-centered. Perhaps less obvious, however, is the fact that in O'Connor's work, Protestant holy rollers are Catholics without knowing it. Thus one might say that the South Tate criticized was more Catholic than he recognized.

Hazel Motes, the protagonist of *Wise Blood,* is typical of O'Connor's proto-Catholic characters. Motes is most remarkable for his hatred of Christ, and his efforts to start a new antichurch. But his hatred is fed by a deeper calling, which he furiously resists. Marked by his itinerant-preacher grandfather as one touched by Jesus, Haze struggles against his election after his hitch in the army exposes him to ridicule and temptation. Having lost his home and all his kin by the time he returns, he takes the offensive against his religious upbringing. However, throughout his story, elements of ritual and belief that have no source in his Protestant past cast shadows across his life. The foolish Enoch Emory, desperate to please his older friend, brings him what he believes to be the New Jesus Haze has proclaimed: a shrunken mummy from the local museum. Enoch makes what can only be described as a small tabernacle to house this unholy Host, a shrine that is violated when the calculating Sabbath Lily Hawkes takes the stolen relic and frightens Haze with a staged Madonna and Child parody. Haze's violent reaction to the sacrilegious New Jesus and the sex-crazed unholy virgin measure the depth of his religious feeling. Apostate though he wishes to be, he is deeply wounded by these blasphemies against distinctly Catholic forms of worship.

Most important of all is the form Haze's penance takes once he knows he is guilty of murder, and once he has lost the treasured symbol of his self-sufficiency, his automobile. He becomes like "one of them monks," according to his landlady.[37] Coffins, with their memento mori associations, haunt Haze throughout the novel, preparing us for his final preoccupation with the world beyond this world, a world that his lime-blinded eyes seem to see in his final days. Equally striking are his efforts to mortify the flesh. He wraps his bare torso in barbed wire and walks on broken glass, apparently to remind himself of his sin and point him toward heaven. His landlady may be confused on many points, but her suspicion that he is "a agent of the pope" is not entirely misguided.[38]

Among O'Connor's characters, Haze's "Catholic" siblings are numerous. Nelson and Mr. Head are transformed before what amounts to an unlikely crucifix in "The Artificial Nigger." Mrs. Greenleaf asks Jesus to stab her in the heart in a sentiment much more compatible with Sacred Heart piety in Catholicism than with anything found in Protestant Evangelical circles. Perhaps most similar to Haze is the protagonist of O'Connor's second novel, *The Violent Bear It Away*. Young Tarwater is another elected prophet who tries to deny his calling until his resistance is brutally broken down. Among his "Catholic" actions is his baptism of the mentally handicapped son of his unbelieving uncle—an action that coincides with his drowning of the boy but that seems also to have assured the boy's salvation. This powerfully sacramental understanding of baptism, typical of Roman Catholic theology, is rare among Protestants in the South. However, it accords completely with O'Connor's description of Tarwater's Sheppard-like guardian, Rayber, who upon overhearing the sermon of a traveling child evangelist, "felt the taste of his own childhood pain laid again on his tongue like a bitter wafer."[39] O'Connor was of course aware of overt attacks on "papists" in the rhetoric of southern Protestants. Yet even when she does depict Bible thumpers in their anti-Catholic colors, she shows that the deeper spiritual hunger behind the fervor is directed toward the forms of faith sustained by the Roman Church. For example, in the last new story she wrote, "Parker's Back," O'Connor gives us a strict Biblicist who condemns religious images as idolatrous. Her iconoclasm leads her in effect to reject the Incarnation, and in the story she rejects her tattoo-loving husband, who has had an icon of Christ inked upon his back. Sarah Ruth's spiritualist extremism is meant to underscore the more authentic God-longing of her spouse, realized in his acquiescence to the summons of Christ by way of a venerated image. Once again the truly Christ-haunted Protestants are drawn to Catholic forms, regardless of the rhetoric of their sects.

O'Connor and Southern Identity

O'Connor is at odds with the Agrarians in her understanding of authentic religion, but in her view of southern identity she is close to them. Although the South as ideal meant little to her and was always secondary to the ideal of the Church, she nonetheless recognized that religion is a cultural phenomenon and that some cultures are more hospitable to the Church than others. She found the South to be the region of the United States most friendly toward Christianity, and for reasons similar to those put forth by the Agrarians. When it came to defining features of the South, O'Connor's list sounds remarkably similar to the one Michael Kreyling identifies as the literary-historical legacy of the Agrarian project. Kreyling cites, from Fred Hobson's *The Southern Writer in the Postmodern World,* this typical list of such a writer's qualities. The southern writer, says Hobson, may be known by "his emphasis on family and community, his essentially concrete vision, his feeling for place, his legacy of failure, poverty, defeat."[40] Similarly, O'Connor discusses southern distinctiveness in the context of literature. In "The Catholic Novelist in the South," speaking of the advantages enjoyed by a southern writer, she opines that "what has given the South her identity are those beliefs and qualities which she has absorbed from the Scriptures and from her own history of defeat and violation; a distrust of the abstract; a sense of human dependence on the grace of God, and a knowledge that evil is not simply a problem to be solved, but a mystery to be endured."[41] O'Connor's catalogue is more theological than Hobson's, but otherwise their lists are quite close, and both lists overlap significantly with Tate's description in his *I'll Take My Stand* essay.

Equally suggestive is Thomas Haddox's commonsense remark that O'Connor's assertion of the compatibility between the South and the Roman Church is both surprising and dubious on the face of it, given the strength of anti-Catholicism in the twentieth-century Protestant South. Surely Haddox is right to find the source of O'Connor's argument "within the context of a concerted effort during the years after the Second World War to redefine southern literature in specifically Catholic terms."[42] The effort he has in mind is, of course, the one led by Allen Tate and his wife, Caroline Gordon, a process that had its genesis for Tate in "Remarks on the Southern Religion." Thus in both her understanding of the hallmarks of southern identity and her disposition to see southern literature in Catholic terms, O'Connor was influenced by the Agrarians and their intellectual heirs. If her devotion to Christian truth saved her from the error of baptizing a culture, she nonetheless fell prey to the Agrarian tendency to use an ahistorical ideal to escape historical realities.

The most serious weakness O'Connor shared with the Agrarians concerns race. This issue, so prominent when O'Connor writes in the 1950s and 1960s, was troublesome for the Agrarians at the end of the 1920s, threatening to derail the *I'll Take My Stand* project. Robert Penn Warren's essay on "the Negro question," which spoke in favor of a Booker T. Washington–style approach to improvement for blacks, so scandalized Donald Davidson with its "progressive" leanings that he told Allen Tate he didn't believe Warren had written it.[43] Aside from the specific issue of racial equality, the Agrarian understanding of southern identity has conceptual difficulties related to race. O'Connor's version of the list of distinctly southern characteristics includes a "history of defeat and violation," echoing an Agrarian theme. However, upon reflection one can see that this reference to the Civil War reflects the history of white southerners, not blacks. It seems obvious now to say that the Agrarians' notion of southern identity is conceived with white southerners in mind. Walker Percy reflected their thinking when he told an interviewer that the reason the South produced good literature was "because we lost the war." Defeat in war, humiliation through Reconstruction, and loss of property and status were experiences not shared by blacks. The "we" Percy had in mind was white, and in approvingly quoting his answer in "The Regional Writer," O'Connor registers her own unrecognized racial orientation.[44]

What this signals is not racism in the conventional sense but rather a considerable blind spot in O'Connor's Agrarian-inspired vision of southern identity. "Southern" identity as defined by the Agrarians is not actually shared by all southerners. This omission is related to Kreyling's valid charge that the Agrarian standard of "southernness" is ahistorical. The point is not that the Agrarians ignore historical events—indeed the Civil War is the crucial point in their narrative—but that the standards themselves become Platonic: they are removed from social reality and not subject to correction. Despite the Agrarians' practical efforts to change public policy in favor of such goals as preserving family farms and promoting self-reliant local economies, their larger aim was the restoration of an order that never existed. Brinkmeyer may well be correct in suggesting, in *The Fourth Ghost*, that in his novel *Lancelot*, Walker Percy is drawing upon an Agrarian-like vision as the inspiration for his mad character's Third Revolution. Finding a disjunction between the America he lives in and the best of the old southern order as he believes it to have been, Lance plans to force society to fit the mold, no matter how wildly unlikely such an unfolding may be.[45]

Although O'Connor has no interest in imposing a stern new social order based on the old verities, her understanding of southern identity is markedly aloof from present historical circumstances. Most tellingly, she is careful to define the South in terms that transcend the turmoil of the civil rights era during which she writes. The problem here is not that she was a segregationist—she was not—but that she theologizes the Agrarian criteria in a way that avoids the topic. In "The Catholic Novelist in the Protestant South," O'Connor in effect makes the point herself: "An identity is not made from what passes, from slavery or from segregation, but from those qualities that endure because they are related to truth."[46] But what kind of truth can there be about southern identity that fails to take account of the role played in it by race? O'Connor, of course, is referring to Christian truth, "those beliefs and qualities which [the South] has absorbed from the Scriptures."[47] However, for many Christians, both black and white, it is those very Scriptural beliefs, qualities, and narratives that require a specific witness in the present, not generalizations about dependence upon God and the inescapability of evil. Although matters of social justice are only settled for good in the Church Triumphant, they may not be ignored by the Church Militant.

A comment in the recently opened letters O'Connor wrote to Betty Hester makes plain how O'Connor's regard for the Agrarians coincided with her reluctance to engage the South's problematic present. Having recommended *I'll Take My Stand* to her friend, she observes of the Agrarians, "You can see why Ralph McGill hates them so."[48] This remark, which Sally Fitzgerald omitted from *The Habit of Being*, indicates that O'Connor respected the Agrarians in part because they avoided what she regarded as

McGill's superficial grandstanding on the moral high ground. Regardless of whether O'Connor's opinion of Ralph McGill is fair or accurate, the comment corroborates her approval of the idea that issues of race should be removed from the question of southern identity.

Despite this troubling lacuna in O'Connor's understanding of southern identity, inherited at least indirectly from the Agrarians, there is much to be said for the Agrarians' criteria as O'Connor applies them. Perhaps the best illustration is to be found in the first item in her list, the South's history of defeat and violation. Understood as an extrapolation from the trauma of losing the Civil War, this criterion is unjustly exclusionary. However, in O'Connor's fiction, it becomes a means to genuine theological insight precisely on the vexed question of race. If O'Connor's notion of southern identity was narrowed by what she appropriated from the Agrarians, her understanding of authentic religion allowed her partially to overcome this weakness. Her Catholic orthodoxy led her to reject racism, and her conviction that the spirit of Christ is at work everywhere in the world led her to see black experience in the South within the terms of salvation history.

O'Connor clearly believed that her story "The Artificial Nigger" made an important statement on the race issue. She refused to let Ransom, by 1954 the editor of the *Kenyon Review,* change the title, precisely because she wanted to draw attention to the racial element he hoped to downplay. The racist statue functions as the crucial, unifying symbol in the story by becoming nothing less than a crucifix. Pointing out this connection is the burden of O'Connor's comment to her friend Ben Griffith: "What I had in mind to suggest with the artificial nigger was the redemptive quality of the Negro's suffering for us all."[49] In the story, Nelson and Mr. Head stare at the statue "as if they were faced with some great mystery, some monument to another's victory that brought them together in their common defeat."[50] Black suffering, represented by the dilapidated Sambo-like figure, is identified with the atoning suffering of Christ, the only "victory" capable of producing the "action of mercy" Mr. Head feels at the story's conclusion. O'Connor has, in effect, extended the "history of defeat and violation" she marks as distinctly southern to the black experience of slavery and Jim Crow. Rather than focus upon white loss and defeat, seeing in it a justification for resentment and violent retaliation, O'Connor finds in southern black experience the ancient Christian paradox of vindication through humiliation. Unlike the white loss of power and property in the war, black suffering is undeserved—innocent, and therefore Christ-like. The unlikely crucifix heals the two whites of their own guilty defeat, at once convicting them of their wrong in turning against each other and making them grateful for their deliverance.

Critics such as Timothy Caron have taken "The Artificial Nigger" to task for operating as yet another dodge of historical responsibility, charging that blacks in the story are perversely seen as having value only insofar as they redeem whites, while the source of their suffering is ignored.[51] In a less tendentious vein, John Duvall has argued that the "artificial nigger" is a means whereby the two poor white characters are able to reclaim their threatened whiteness, and thus their racial superiority.[52] There is a measure of justice in these charges. O'Connor does not bring her black characters to revelatory moments, nor does she call attention to the very real oppression blacks endured. Nelson and Mr. Head are not made conscious of their racism. But these criticisms ignore what O'Connor considered to be a more urgent matter. The most important fact about history is that it harbors the eternal. This is not to say that history is a mere illusion or that the prospect of a heaven after death renders justice in this life a matter of indifference. Rather, it is to say that history is not an autonomous process exhaustively explained through naturalistic analysis. As John Desmond reminds us, "O'Connor's fictional stance was not based exclusively on the dynamic of memory and history as in other southern writers but rather on the dynamic of history and eschatology."[53] Christ's entry into history makes tension between the temporal and the eternal inevitable. Nature is imbued with grace; God is at work in the world. And ultimately, history is moving toward eschatological fulfillment in which the redemption of fallen nature will be complete. If this view of history is true, then O'Connor's emphasis is in the right place—on eschatological fulfillment rather than on what might be termed local justice. The prophet, O'Connor said, is a realist of distances.

Flannery O'Connor thought and wrote about southern identity within the network of ideas supplied by the Agrarians. But her understanding of authentic religion differed so significantly from that of Agrarian architects John Crowe Ransom and Allen Tate that it freed her from many, though not all, of their errors. She was never tempted to hold up the South as an ideal order, and she avoided the circle of self-consciousness to which they fell prey by adopting the stance of testimony rather than that of theory. However, she was subject to bias toward white identity in the Agrarian definition of southern identity, and she was prone to turn her southern marks of distinction into generalizations that ignored present injustice. O'Connor largely overcame this weakness through theological commitments that led her to place black experience within the larger context of salvation history. Ultimately, the politics of Flannery O'Connor is an eschatological politics. Her single-minded focus on how the operations of divine grace manifest themselves in the concrete circumstances of a particular social reality sets her work apart from that of the Agrarians, and indeed from nearly every other significant American writer.

Notes

1. This essay appears in *Flannery O'Connor: Collected Works,* ed. Sally Fitzgerald (New York: Library of America, 1988), 853–64.

2. Twelve Southerners, *I'll Take My Stand: The South and the Agrarian Tradition* (1930; Baton Rouge: Louisiana State University Press, 1977).

3. Flannery O'Connor, *The Habit of Being,* ed. Sally Fitzgerald (New York: Farrar, Straus and Giroux, 1979), 566.

4. O'Connor, *Collected Works,* 1237–56.

5. Paul K. Conkin, *The Southern Agrarians* (Knoxville: University of Tennessee Press, 1988), 32–36.

6. Michael Kreyling, *Inventing Southern Literature* (Jackson: University Press of Mississippi, 1998), 9.

7. Joseph Blotner, *Robert Penn Warren: A Biography* (New York: Random House, 1997), 105.

8. Eugene Genovese, *The Southern Tradition: The Achievements and Limitations of an American Conservatism* (Cambridge: Harvard University Press, 1994).

9. See Malcolm Bradbury and James MacFarlane, "The Name and Nature of Modernism," in *Modernism: 1890–1930,* ed. Bradbury and James MacFarlane (Atlantic Highlands, N.J.: Humanities Press, 1978), 19–56.

10. Conkin, *Agrarians,* 42.

11. Qtd. in Robert Brinkmeyer, *Three Catholic Writers of the Modern South: Allen Tate, Caroline Gordon, Walker Percy* (Jackson: University Press of Mississippi, 1985), 15.

12. See Brinkmeyer, *Three Catholic Writers,* 22–23.

13. John Crowe Ransom, *God without Thunder: An Unorthodox Defense of Orthodoxy* (1930; Hamden, Ct.: Archon, 1965).

14. Ibid., 98.

15. Ibid., 328.

16. Twelve Southerners, *I'll Take My Stand*, 166.

17. Ibid., 156.

18. Allen Tate, *Poems* (New York: Scribner's, 1960).

19. Brinkmeyer, *Three Catholic Writers*, 19.

20. Tate, *Poems*, 79–80.

21. Lewis P. Simpson, *The Brazen Face of History: Studies in the Literary Consciousness in America* (Baton Rouge: Louisiana State University Press, 1980), 233.

22. Ibid., 238.

23. Ibid., 241.

24. Ibid.

25. John Desmond, *Risen Sons: Flannery O'Connor's Vision of History* (Athens: University of Georgia Press, 1987).

26. O'Connor, *Collected Works*, 261.

27. Ibid., 260.

28. George Santayana, *The Life of Reason: Reason in Common Sense* (New York: Scribner's, 1905), 284.

29. Sarah Gordon, *Flannery O'Connor: The Obedient Imagination* (Athens: University of Georgia Press, 2000), 206.

30. Richard King discusses monumentalism in relation to the South in *A Southern Renaissance: The Cultural Awakening of the American South, 1930–1955* (New York: Oxford University Press, 1980), esp. chap, 1. King credits Friedrich Nietzsche with formulating the concept, especially in *The Use and Abuse of History* (Indianapolis: Bobbs-Merrill, 1957).

31. O'Connor, *Collected Works*, 269.

32. Ibid., 260.

33. Ibid., 261.

34. Ibid., 805–6.

35. Ralph C. Wood, *Flannery O'Connor and the Christ-Haunted South* (Grand Rapids, Mich.: Eerdmans, 2004), 71.

36. John Herbert Hayes, "Hard, Hard Religion: Faith and Class in the New South" (Ph.D. diss., University of Georgia, 2007).

37. O'Connor, *Collected Works*, 123.

38. Ibid., 127.

39. Ibid., 412.

40. Qtd. in Kreyling, *Inventing Southern Literature*, 77.

41. O'Connor, *Collected Works*, 861–62.

42. Thomas Haddox, *Fears and Fascinations: Representing Catholicism in the American South* (New York: Fordham University Press, 2005), 114.

43. Conkin, *Agrarian*, 72.

44. O'Connor, *Collected Works*, 847.

45. Robert H. Brinkmeyer Jr., *The Fourth Ghost: White Southern Writers and European Fascism, 1930–1950* (Baton Rouge: Louisiana State University Press, 2009).

46. O'Connor, *Collected Works,* 861.

47. Ibid.

48. Flannery O'Connor to Betty Hester, February 15, 1964, MSS 1064, Manuscript, Archive, and Rare Books Library, Emory University.

49. O'Connor, *Habit of Being,* 78.

50. O'Connor, *Collected Works,* 230.

51. Timothy P. Caron, "'The Bottom Rail Is on the Top': Race and 'Theological Whiteness' in Flannery O'Connor's Short Fiction," in *Inside the Church of Flannery O'Connor,* ed. Joanne Halleran McMullen and Jon Parrish Peede (Macon, Ga.: Mercer University Press, 2007), 163.

52. John N. Duvall, *Race and White Identity in Southern Fiction* (New York: Palgrave Macmillan, 2008), 78.

53. Desmond, *Risen Sons,* 90.

2

"These Jesuits Work Fast"

O'Connor's Elusive Politics

Benjamin B. Alexander

In January 1956, the Reverend James H. McCown, a Jesuit priest serving a small parish in Macon, Georgia, heard that forty miles away in Milledgeville there was a "coming young writer, a Catholic," named Flannery O'Connor who labored at her craft in obscurity at her mother's dairy farm. Afflicted with lupus, yet eschewing self-pity, O'Connor quipped that her suffering taught her more about God's mercy than a trip to Europe.[1] A determined Father McCown enlisted "Mr. Ridley," a member of his congregation described as a "fat big-hearted unacademic whiskey salesman and lover of new Cadillacs," to chauffeur him to the O'Connor dairy farm. When Father McCown stopped to ask for directions on the trip, a neighbor said: "Mary Flannery's a sweet girl and comes to Mass every Sunday. But those stories, she writes! They are terrible. Everybody says so, even the Catholics. Frankly, Father, I am afraid to go near her. She might put me in one of her stories." When Father McCown finally arrived at Andalusia, the modest O'Connor farmhouse, he recalled that from among assorted fowl, including shrieking peacocks, "a damned goose kept coming at me. I stood my ground. He bit me on the leg as though a snapping turtle had me. I bled through my pants." Limping to the front door, he was greeted by O'Connor with an unceremonious "Howdy." Father McCown identified himself and told her: "I read your stories, and I just wanted to meet you. I liked them very much."[2]

For the next eight years, both Flannery O'Connor and her mother, Regina, were delighted when a two-toned Cadillac came up the long driveway to Andalusia, bearing the whiskey salesman and the Jesuit. O'Connor's vital but unexplored friendship with Father McCown, as her unpublished letters reveal, are vital in shedding new light on her elusive political views. The global realignment of nations after World War II, the Cold War with its fears of spreading communism, the prospect of nuclear annihilation, civil rights activism, Southern Agrarian thought, and the dynamic orthodoxy of Catholicism—all had an impact on O'Connor's political ideas, which she often expressed in unpublished letters to Father McCown and others.

O'Connor's dread of political labeling parallels her healthy skepticism about literary categorization. She did not want to be known as *just* a southern or *just* a Catholic writer. In a letter to Louis Rubin from January 24, 1956, O'Connor declined an invitation to speak at a southern literary conference because, as she said, she writes about "two countries" and is ill suited to talk only about the South. In another unpublished letter in 1956, O'Connor wrote a friend about Allen Tate and Caroline Gordon: "The Tates were the only ones that ended up in the Church, although the Church seems a logical end for the principles they began with. . . . That was all part of what is now pompously called the Southern literary renascence." In another letter, O'Connor asks a professor friend who had been lecturing on southern literature, "What is that?" [3]

As O'Connor makes clear in her lectures in *Mystery and Manners*, she did not want to be tarred by a literary brush. She embodied a paradox, remarking once that the only thing that kept her from being a southern writer was Catholicism, and the only thing that kept from being a Catholic writer was being a southerner. [4] This stance also served her well in her determination not to take political positions, especially in regard to civil rights. What can be discerned from her unpublished letters, however, in regard to political topics, may be grouped into three areas: literary politics, civil rights, and anticommunism. O'Connor's views in these areas often evolved indirectly as her friendship with Father McCown developed.

Literary Politics

Unlike Mrs. McIntyre in "The Displaced Person," who tolerated the dutiful calling of Father Flynn, O'Connor looked forward to visits from Father

McCown. Although Mrs. McIntyre in O'Connor's story complains that
religion is unworthy of serious conversation, O'Connor herself actually
discussed theological issues with Father McCown. He became a trusted
friend and often served as her spiritual director. Moreover, in matters of
literary interpretation, Father McCown's Oxford-educated brother, also a
Jesuit, the Reverend Robert McCown, was one of a handful of clergy who
really understood O'Connor's stories. The few letters to Father James Mc-
Cown in *The Habit of Being* are not fully representative of his friendship
with O'Connor (just a handful of her letters to him appear in the Library
of America's *Flannery O'Connor*). The unpublished letters from O'Connor
to Father McCown provide valuable insight into the tensions between
O'Connor and the hierarchy of the Catholic Church on the subject of her
fiction. O'Connor's friendship with Father McCown helped her negotiate
the painful literary politics that still continue a half century after her death.

For example, in 2000 a controversy arose over "The Artificial Nigger,"
listed as required reading at a Catholic high school in the Diocese of La-
fayette (Louisiana). The bishop decreed O'Connor's stories be removed. A
leading Catholic journal noted the political irony of the decision: "The only
Catholic admitted by mainstream secular literary critics to the canon of 20th-
century American authors—now excised by Catholics. A major southern
writer involved in the project of explaining southerners to themselves, now
prohibited in a set of southern schools. A woman known in her own day for
her *anti*-racism now placed on the forbidden list on the grounds of racism."[5]

Father McCown, an energetic motorcyclist-priest, grasped O'Connor's
literary power—one of the few clerics to do so in the 1950s. After the
publication of *Wise Blood* in 1952 and *A Good Man Is Hard to Find* in
1955, Father McCown and his brother stood out as vital clerical emissar-
ies of acceptance and understanding within the ecclesiastical hierarchy. As
O'Connor quipped, Father McCown "was the first priest who said turkey-
dog to me about my writing."[6] He introduced O'Connor's writing to other Jesuits, including Scott "Youree" Watson, of Spring Hill College, Mobile, and
Harold Gardiner, literary editor of the Jesuit journal *America*. O'Connor
wrote her friends Sally and Robert Fitzgerald: "These Jesuits work fast. Ten
days after I had the visit from the one in Macon, I receive a communication from Harold C. Gardiner, S.J., asking me to contribute to *America*."[7]
O'Connor responded, and two years later, on March 30, 1959, O'Connor's
"The Church and the Fiction Writer" appeared in the journal.

The support and recognition of the Jesuits through the efforts of Father McCown were vital to O'Connor's acceptance in Catholic intellectual communities. In the late 1950s, O'Connor's Jesuit admirers were crucial in recognizing the tumultuous orthodoxy of her fiction. O'Connor judged an article by Father McCown's brother Robert McCown—also a Jesuit— on *The Violent Bear It Away,* to be the most illuminating on that difficult work, writing to him: "What you say about the book exactly reflects my intentions when I wrote it. . . . Most of the theories proposed about the book make my hair stand on end."[8] O'Connor, who was impatient with critics and once remarked that she grew tired of reviewers criticizing her fiction, observed, "When I see these stories described as horror stories, I am always amused because the reviewer always has hold of the wrong horror."[9] O'Connor was often provoked by critics who did not recognize her intentions. She traced the crucial title of *The Violent Bear It Away* to "Christ's words" from the Gospel of Matthew that seem to make "no great impression." The novel, she stated, is about the "violence of love giving more than the law demands, of asceticism like John the Baptist's, but in the face of which even John is less than the least in the kingdom." But, as she lamented, "all this is overlooked."[10]

Father Robert McCown provided additional commentary. He was the elusive "good man" who discovered in *The Violent Bear It Away* what other critics did not find: "To those who have properly read her *Wise Blood* and *A Good Man is Hard to Find,* it should come as no surprise that the product is a work of extraordinary literary merit. Unfortunately, however, many and among them would-be admirers, have not got the central message of the novel." Continuing, he observes that there is a "failure to understand Miss O'Connor's use of character-symbols, that is, characters possessing their own living individualities which, however, at the same time function as symbols in a larger and more universal synthesis, in much the same way that the allegorical characters and events of the great mediaeval religious epics, represent certain historical and theological abstractions."[11]

Although Robert McCown, S.J., provided astute analysis, Father James McCown needed instruction and deferred to his brother in literary matters. In his autobiography, *With Crooked Lines,* he notes, "I am a Jesuit" and "you may expect some deep thinking," but "my mental plateaus stop short of the Alpine reaches of abstract thought."[12] Father McCown admits he is not an intellectual; this is one reason why O'Connor liked him. The evolution of their friendship reads like one of her stories. His energy was relentless, and whereas she was increasingly immobile, Father James was peripatetic. He resembled another great Jesuit, the fictional Father Latour of Willa Cather's *Death Comes for the Archbishop.* Recalling Father Latour, as described by Cather, O'Connor writes to Father McCown, "I hope you will be allowed to wear a cowboy hat and spurs, along with the Roman collar."[13] Like Father Latour a century earlier, Father McCown traversed the rugged American Southwest, although on a motorcycle rather than a horse. McCown also went on excursions to Africa, Nicaragua, and Alaska, later regaling the travel-challenged Flannery and her mother with tales of exotic landscapes. He ultimately rode his motorcycle in several countries, while O'Connor wrote him about a driving test she failed in Georgia: "To prove that I aint adjusted to the modern world, I failed the driving test. Now in two weeks I have to go take it again. I barely brought the patrol man back alive so I don't know if he'll relish taking me around the block again."[14]

Thomas Gossett, professor emeritus of Wake Forest University who died in 2005, writes of Father McCown: "He is I believe the best man, the most Christian I have ever known."[15] Gossett and O'Connor were impressed by Father McCown's tireless ministry to poor minorities in Texas in the 1950s and 1960s, and the recurrent retreats he provided for laymen and religious, often at Pass Christian, Mississippi. His friendship with O'Connor provided spiritual renewal, literary edification, and human solace from the demands of the priesthood.

Father McCown lifted his spirits by riding the motorcycle he named "Rosanthe" on summer vacations and mission trips. In one account he wrote that he and Rosanthe "pushed through the plains of north Texas and Southern New Mexico, the mountains of Colorado, the prairies of Southern Wyoming, all of Utah, then home. It was a bizarre achievement that earned a double take even from teenagers, caused a heart-stopping friend to say, 'Father you're too old for that' and a mortician to say 'See you soon.'"[16] Father McCown's letters and visits enlivened daily life at the O'Connor farm. In one letter, O'Connor thanked him for a bottle of wine: "We killed it off in short order and were very much obliged to you. Fr. Tavard negotiated the opening of it and got it all over himself as my mother had shaken it vigorously before bringing it in—she handles liquor as if it were milk of magnesia, or as if it would be better if it were."[17] It is little wonder that fellowship and good times were goals that interested both O'Connor and Father McCown,

since they both pursued unusual vocations in rural Georgia. Father Mc-
Cown recounts that the area was bereft of Catholics and that "Irish, Italian,
and Lebanese Catholics made up 1 percent of the population." He believed
the situation needed "a heightening of the cultural level of the Catholics,
and I was working hard to effect it."[18]

O'Connor educated her friend into the complexity of modern fiction,
while he counseled her about Church doctrine and discipline. In the early
1960s while he and O'Connor were friends, Father McCown was orthodox
theologically and politically a vocal anti-Communist. He was self-effacing
and comical about his literary abilities. He learned from O'Connor and
studied what she recommended. He believed the Jesuits lacked adequate
literary training and ultimately became a discerning reader of modern fiction. Learning about literature from O'Connor, he hoped, would improve
his preaching and catechesis of believers. Venturing beyond the traditional clerical disciplines of theology, philosophy, and apologetics, Father Mc-
Cown became widely read under O'Connor's tutelage. In 1964, he writes
Tom Gossett that he had recently read Joseph Heller's *Catch-22,* James
Baldwin's *In Another Country,* Ralph Ellison's *Invisible Man,* and K. A.
Porter's *Ship of Fools.*

McCown happily accepted O'Connor's criticism of his literary efforts.
She wrote her friends Tom and Louise Gossett (both professors) that "Father McCown breezed in here on his way to give a talk to the St. Joseph
Guild on literary horizons of Catholic Thought or some such grandiose title.
He knows nothing whatsoever about the subject, but was not letting that
deter him."[19] Father McCown observed, however, that "in Macon Catholic
circles, not a profoundly well-educated milieu, I was quite the stuff. And I
could strut around like I did giving my very inept evaluations with no danger of contradiction. So I was only amused by her remark."[20]

O'Connor taught Father McCown about the "integrity of art."[21] When
he approached her "to do some polemical writing to defend Holy Church
against her enemies," O'Connor replied tartly, "That ain't my cup of tea."[22]
She disabused him of the notion that fiction could serve as a "pragmatic
way to rout Protestant error and enthrone Catholic truth in our great country."[23] She decries pietistic Catholic fiction as "propaganda and its being
propaganda for the side of the angels only makes it worse. The novel is an
art form and when you use it for anything other than art you pervert it.
I didn't make this up. I got it from St. Thomas (via Maritain) who allows

that art is wholly concerned with the good of that which is made, it has no utilitarian end."[24]

O'Connor discovered, albeit painfully, that some of the Church hierarchy preferred pious didacticism to the spiritual tumult of her fiction. Seminary education in theology and philosophy did not equip many with the skill to understand O'Connor's often searing stories with their profound ecumenical appeal. The Misfit proclaims in southern vernacular that free will is at the core of Thomistic moral choice, and the hermaphrodite accepts the divine mystery of deformity. Such scenes are not the usual fare of religious orders, seminary classrooms, and diocesan offices. O'Connor once noted that gifted Catholic writers too often became anticlerical; she, however, was devout and revered priests. Admittedly, though, she often found pietistic hagiography annoying. She tolerated books like Bonaventure's *Life of St. Francis of Assisi* but preferred works of religious realism. In 1956, she wrote Father McCown that she had "just read a funny book by a priest named Father Robo on St. Theresa of Lisieux. It's called *Two Portraits of St. Theresa.* He has managed (by some not entirely crooked means) to get hold of a photograph of her that the Carmelites have not touched up which shows her to be a round-faced, determined, rather comical looking girl. He does away with all the roses, little flowers, and other icing. The book has greatly increased my devotion to her."[25]

In dealing with apologetic, didactic writing, O'Connor pursued a difficult path. She admired the craft of "bad Catholics" like Hemingway and Joyce. Unlike them, she remained undeviating in faith and wrote beautiful catechetical letters to Betty Hester, Robert Lowell, Ted Spivey, and others, who were struggling with theological issues. Caroline Gordon, her tutor, taught her the novelist is not a preacher, apologist, or propagandist. In 1951, Gordon wrote to Walker Percy: "I am a Catholic, I suspect, because I was first a fiction writer. If I hadn't worked at writing fiction for so many years, I doubt if I'd have made it into the Church."[26] For Gordon, faith served craft, even if the craftsman was a Catholic rebel like Joyce or a poor Churchman like Hemingway. Piety did not trump good craft.

Gordon's understanding resonated with O'Connor, who, like Thomas Merton, preferred Joyce's (supposedly) apostate writing to works of apologetic uplift. While excoriating Irish Catholicism, Joyce actually affirms it. Through his detailed knowledge of the faith, he confirmed O'Connor's faith and sowed the seeds of conversion in Thomas Merton. The latter "was struck by the respect Joyce retained for the Catholic tradition and the care he took in presenting it believably in fiction—so believably that it could convince the readers in its own right . . . there was something eminently satisfying in the thought that these Catholics knew what they believed, and knew what to teach, and all taught the same thing, and taught it with coordination and purpose and great effect."[27]

Caroline Gordon also admired Joyce and encouraged O'Connor to emulate his skills. Living in Rome and copyediting the stories in *A Good Man Is Hard to Find,* Gordon wrote O'Connor that the first paragraph of "The Artificial Nigger" was not "elevated enough" and encouraged O'Connor to study the Joyce story "Araby," noting with approval "the high and mighty tone he takes throughout that story of something that has happened to every one of us in our time—to be promised a treat as a child and then disappointed."[28]

In heeding Gordon's instructions to study modernist masters, however, O'Connor found herself at odds with the literary expectations of her beloved Church. A faithful parishioner of Sacred Heart parish in Milledgeville, O'Connor dutifully reviewed pietistic works for the local diocesan newspaper. She passed the books on to Father McCown, observing in a letter: "This is a collection of stories taken from the Catholic press; they are therefore guaranteed to corrupt nothing but your taste. I enclose my review."[29] In another letter she defended Graham Greene's *The Quiet American,* criticized as unwholesome in a Catholic newspaper. And in a related letter, she told Father McCown about a Jesuit who wanted to know what he "could read to preserve" his innocence. O'Connor told him to peruse the phone book.[30] O'Connor also wrote to Father McCown of even more fundamental problems: "I have just recently come back from an annual pilgrimage to the Macon Writer's Club breakfast where I was introduced as the author of 'The Valiant Bear It Away.' You go to all them pains to name a book something and then."[31]

O'Connor tolerated her share of inept readers. Perceptive appreciation was limited to a few: the McCown brothers and a few other Jesuits, Robert and Sally Fitzgerald, the Southern Agrarians (Caroline Gordon, Allen Tate, John Crowe Ransom, and Andrew Lytle), and the reclusive Betty Hester. Her Mother, trying to understand modern fiction, once asked O'Connor, "'Who is this Kafka? People ask me.' A German Jew, I says, I think. He wrote a book about a man that turned into a roach. 'Well I can't tell people *that,'* she says. 'Who is this Evalin Wow?'"[32] O'Connor made more progress teaching Father McCown, who assiduously read works she recommended. By her death in 1964, he had completed an unusual apprenticeship with O'Connor and (encouraged by her) with Walker Percy. O'Connor wrote Father McCown in December 1963: "I'm glad you could get shut of Atlanta over the holidays and that you got a visit to Walker Percy. Hep yourself if you want to lend him my book."[33] Like O'Connor, Percy enjoyed McCown's travel narratives and later advised him about his autobiography, *With Crooked Lines.*

Although McCown read works O'Connor suggested, he also advised her about conflicts between obedience to the teachings of the Catholic Church and the practice of her craft. He observed: "As a Catholic writer Flannery O'Connor was abreast of the most advanced theological concerns in the Church, in the early days of the great Second Vatican Council. . . . Yet she was inclined to strictness with herself in anything concerned with morality and having to do with Church discipline."[34] For example, she wrote Father McCown in December 1957 that an ecumenical reading group that met at her home was undertaking the study of André Gide, whose writings were on the Catholic Church's *Index Librorum Prohibitorum.* One of the last vestiges of the Inquisition, the *Index* sometimes amounted to censorship (Dante's *De Monarchia* was on the list until 1922). Writers in the Joycean tradition simply ignored the *Index* or used its strictures, like Stephen Daedalus, to trumpet the Church's repression of artistic creativity. But O'Connor did not defy the Church and sought instead a dispensation from Father McCown about reading prohibited authors:

> Not long ago the local Episcopal minister came out and wanted me to get up a group with him of people who were interested in talking about theology in modern literature. This suited me all right so about six or seven of them are coming out here every Monday night—a couple of Presbyterians, the rest Episcopalians of one stripe or another (scratch an Episcopalian and you're liable to find most anything) and me as the only representative of the Holy Roman Catholic & Apostolic Church. The strain is telling on me. Anyway this minister is equipped with a list of what he would like us to read and upon the list is naturally, Gide, also listed on the Index. I despise Gide but if they read him I want to be able to put in my two cents worth. I don't think there is any use

to ask the local reverend father for permission. . . . You said once you would see if you had the faculties to give me permission to read such as this. Do you and will you? All these Protestants will be shocked if I say I can't get permission to read Gide.[35]

Father McCown wrote an esteemed moral theologian with whom he studied in seminary:

The gal in question has read more fathers of the church, and more St. Thomas than His Excellency ever saw. Now, does any moralist or recent ruling allow me, her spiritual father, to allow her to read Gide? Can I allow the Catholic students of the local state College to read assigned books that happen to be on the Index, or do I have to have *toties quoties* recourse to the bishop? I might say in passing that I agonize over the whole Index anyway. I am sure it is the obstacle keeping countless intellectuals a million miles away from the Church. They laugh at us because of it.[36]

Father McCown's questioning of the *Index* looks forward to issues addressed by the Second Vatican Council, convened from 1962 to 1965. McCown's friend, however, advised him, "You have no faculties to give permission to read forbidden books," but noted: "The law ceases to bind when the keeping of it would result in harm to the Cath. Faith. If what the lady says in her last sentence is true, then it looks as if she could apply this principle to the reading of Gide."[37]

The Politics of Civil Rights

In addition to Father McCown's counsel about the *Index*, he shared with O'Connor the Jesuit dedication to social justice and civil rights activism. However, O'Connor and McCown differed in response to the great domestic political issue of the twentieth century. O'Connor's growing immobility deterred participation in marches and protests, whereas McCown was an activist.[38] Sally Fitzgerald notes that O'Connor "recognized the need for and approved of Martin Luther King's crusade."[39] Fitzgerald observes, moreover, that when O'Connor witnessed a white bus driver verbally abusing African Americans, she became "an integrationist."[40] O'Connor, however, was torn between the social conservatism of her mother and the profound changes introduced by the civil rights movement. The unpublished correspondence reveals she admired individuals on different sides of the racial divide: her mother and other friends were unwilling to challenge segregation, whereas Father McCown, Tom Gossett, Walker Percy, and others were dedicated to ending it.

Regina O'Connor was the matriarch of an active dairy farm where drinking among the black workers could threaten domestic violence. O'Connor wrote a professor friend at Georgetown University, Ward Allison Dorrance: "My Mother is getting ready to sell out the dairy and going in on beef cows. We are now being done in by the local moonshine . . . and she HAS HAD ENOUGH." In another letter she observes: "Our staff has already started celebrating the season with unstamped whiskey. I don't know whether they are still celebrating Thanksgiving or started celebrating Christmas, but the effect is the same."[41] Once a quarrel caused the brandishing of a shotgun. O'Connor admired her mother's cheerful intervention to prevent a shooting, described in a letter to Dorrance: "Now lets [sic] not have any more of this unpleasantness. Bring that shotgun over here and leave it."[42] O'Connor notes such potential violence would have reduced her to "idiocy."[43] In another letter to the Fitzgeralds, O'Connor writes that her mother "delivered several sermons on the theme thou shalt not kill during the Christmas time."[44]

O'Connor also listened carefully to discussions about race at the Monday-night reading-group meeting at her home and informed Father McCown about the deliberations. McCown early on in his ministry criticized segregation. A native of Mobile, Alabama, Father McCown witnessed racial paternalism that would lead him to excoriate its practice in his 1990 autobiography, *With Crooked Lines:*

> We southerners showered our black domestics with shallow affection then exploited them shamelessly. We claimed really to know blacks, but lived with our own self-serving image of them. We paid them starvation wages, then feigned disappointment when they turned out to be ungrateful or shiftless or thieving. . . . We kept them from getting a good education, then complained of their ignorance. We forced them to live in slums, and then condemned them for their violence. We read happiness and contentment in their comedy and obsequiousness and

then were outraged if they expressed their human dignity. For our own use we stereotyped them and their language and habits.[45]

O'Connor was not as outspoken but clearly was aware of Father Mc-Cown's views. She let her stories reveal her oblique view of integration. The desegregation of public transit in Montgomery, Alabama, undertaken by the civil rights heroine Rosa Parks in December 1955 provided the setting of "Everything That Rises Must Converge." The plot concerns black and white characters in conflict on a bus. O'Connor wrote Father McCown, "I'd like to write a whole bunch of stories like that, but once you've said it, you've said it and that about expresses what I have to say on That Issue."[46] She wrote another friend, Roslyn Barnes, in June 1961: "Can you tell me if the statement 'everything that rises must converge' is a true proposition in physics? I can easily see its moral, historical, and evolutionary significance, but I want to know if it is also a correct physical statement."[47] A few months later, she wrote Father McCown, "It looks like we are going to be integrated by the atom, don't it?"[48] O'Connor was thinking apocalyptically about integration reflected in the painful eschatological ending of "Everything That Rises Must Converge," where death bridges racial and generational conflict.

Other letters to Father McCown from O'Connor reveal that she learned fiction writing from some of the Southern Agrarians; however, she was careful not to marshal her writing in behalf of the movement's coded advocacy of segregation. In one letter, she is provoked that a small Georgia college started a lecture series with an invitation to Donald Davidson, one of the original "Twelve Southerners" of *I'll Take My Stand: The South and the Agrarian Tradition* published in 1931. O'Connor wrote: "I hope D. Davidson didn't cure them of having Southern lecturers. At least they started at the extreme. How far to the right can you get?"[49]

Davidson's adroit defense of southern regionalism entailed a shrewd advocacy of segregation. *The Attack on Leviathan*, first published in 1938, features Davidson's brilliant title that puts southern regionalism in the context of the political philosophy of the Enlightenment, an emphasis lacking in the more celebrated *I'll Take My Stand.*[50] In *The Attack on Leviathan* Davidson appears to take a more philosophic approach by criticizing Hobbesian centralization of political power in the "leviathan," a bloated, bureaucratic government presided over by a supermanager figure, the "Sovereign." Davidson defends Jeffersonian decentralization by insisting that an individual state retains the right to "preserve its bi-racial social system." This regional prerogative includes "the furtive evasion to raw violence to which it is now driven when sniped at with weapons of Federal legality."[51] (Davidson does not specify exactly what he means by "raw violence.")

O'Connor kept her distance from Davidson's nuanced defense of segregation, but she was equally wary of civil rights activists from afar who challenged the social patterns of what Davidson calls "regional cultures."[52] O'Connor was not impressed by the notoriety of Father McCown's friend John Howard Griffin. A Catholic convert, Griffin had stained his skin, traveled through the segregated South in 1959, and then later recorded his adventures in, *Black Like Me,* a national best seller in 1961. When McCown wrote O'Connor that Griffin might call on her, she replied: "If John Howard Griffin gets to Georgia again, we would be delighted to see him; but not in blackface. I don't blame in the least any of the people who cringed when Griffin sat down beside them. He must have been a pretty horrible looking object."[53] To O'Connor, Griffin's efforts were postured and flamboyant. By contrast Father McCown admired Griffin's dangerous trek in disguise as a highly visible witness to racial injustice and believed it would encourage other Catholics to engage in activism. M. L. King appreciated Griffin's efforts when the two civil rights activists became friends during King's Alabama protests. In 1964, Griffin received the Pacem in Terris award from the Davenport (Iowa) Interracial Council for his labors to advance social justice.

Although O'Connor kept her distance from Griffin, she did admire Thomas Gossett, whose opposition to segregation would threaten his academic career. Father McCown had introduced O'Connor to the resourceful professor in the 1950s. As their friendship evolved, Gossett became a pioneer in African American history and literature years before such disciplines became fixtures in the academy. In 1958, while Gossett was teaching at Wesleyan College in Macon, Georgia, he publicly supported integration, a position that led the college president to suspend him from the faculty. O'Connor wrote him on November 30, 1958: "You had been treated in a low down fashion. I hope you tear up that briar patch before you leave."[54]

Gossett's seminal 1963 study *Race: The History of an Idea in America* has become a canonical work in African American history. Writing at a time of entrenched segregation, Gossett undertook a thorough analysis of its origins in works such as Thomas Jefferson's *Notes on the State of Vir-*

ginia. Father McCown wrote Tom Gossett in April 1964: "Congratulations a thousand times over, Tom! I am so proud of you and your work and being a friend of yours. . . . The writeup in "Time" which I feverishly found after half of Macon told me about [it], was wonderful. . . . Flannery was so visibly pleased over it that it did me good."[55]

In the foreword to the second edition of *Race: The History of an Idea,* the editors note that "serious readers today and in the foreseeable future will have access to one of the most important books published in the United States in the last fifty years on the subject of race as an idea in the development of American culture."[56] Beginning with anthropological theories of African inferiority prevalent in the eighteenth century, Gossett systematically examines racism in subsequent phases of American history and concludes with a chapter on the civil rights movement. Because of the depth and scope of Gossett's research, O'Connor was steadfast in her support. She wrote him in March 1964: "Thanks for the hog-slopping card. It was real inspiring to me. . . . I was real pleased to see that *Time* took so heavy to your book. Better to have people for you than agin you even though they don't have much sense."[57]

International Politics

Although O'Connor did not actively challenge segregation, she was quietly loyal to friends, like Professor Gossett and Father McCown, who did. She was more vocal as an anti-Communist. O'Connor consistently supported, as did Father McCown, the stern admonitions of President Kennedy in his 1960 inaugural address.[58] The president's aggressive, pro-American foreign policy was personified for Father McCown in John Howard Griffin. Because of the controversy caused in the United States by his book *Black Like Me,* Griffin had retreated to Mexico. Once there, however, he soon found himself in conflict with Mexican Communists. Although McCown and Griffin were social activists, they were critical of Marxist revolutionaries. In McCown's unpublished travel narrative about Mexico, written in 1962, he praises Griffin's defiance of "Marxist thugs."[59] Both O'Connor and her mother read his account and were entertained by McCown's descriptions. O'Connor wrote: "We loved your travelogue. Regina said to tell you it was her kind of literature—places and folks. She also likes to read about wild animals."[60] In another letter she tells McCown: "I don't think you could possibly be too old to go to Mexico if you ain't too old to knock about the states. They just like your face and want to keep it in sight."[61]

In the Mexico narrative, McCown is troubled that the University of Puebla, sponsored originally by the Jesuits, had been "appropriated by the government" and is "controlled, staffed, and run by the Communists. There were no Catholics on the teaching staff—in Mexico!" At the city of Morelia, he recounts, "Communism reached a peak of arrogance" when a mob broke "into a Catholic college and burned in a great bonfire in the street all the furniture, the office equipment, books etc." Father McCown praises Griffin, "a truly great writer" who in the "splendid daily paper in Mexico City, *Excelsior*," used "incontrovertible evidence" to show that "the so called 'students' were simply professional agitators hired and financed by Moscow. This angered the Communists so much that they had a mob gathered and advancing on Griffin's house to burn it and kill him and his family when they were able to escape and return to this country."[62]

While Father McCown praised Griffin's defiance of Marxists in Mexico, O'Connor provided a pithy summation of its theological meaning. Her views are similar to those of Archbishop Fulton J. Sheen in his dramatic television lectures that electrified audiences in the mid-1950s. Witnessing the global expansion of Communist regimes during the Cold War, O'Connor, like Archbishop Sheen, diagnoses the ideology as a theological heresy. O'Connor proclaims, "Communism is a religion of the state and the Church opposes it as a heresy."[63] A reluctant Cold Warrior, O'Connor, once provoked, weighed in with resolute theological conviction. In 1956, after Soviet tanks rolled into Budapest to crush the Hungarian revolution, she wrote her agent: "I wouldn't want my work published in any Russian occupied country as the danger that it might be used as anti-American propaganda is apparent. I understand some of Jack London is now being used that way."[64]

The political turmoil of the 1960s did not shake O'Connor's faith, and she remained an unflinching anti-Communist until her death in 1964. On the other hand, Father McCown's pursuit of social justice would eventually lead him to abandon anticommunism, and to champion liberation theology, popular among the Jesuits in Central America in the 1980s. McCown's drift into theological heterodoxy is evident in October 1974, when, on an extended retreat, he rode his motorcycle to the Jesuit School of Theology at Berkeley. He wrote a communal letter to friends praising campus radical-

ism: "Posters everywhere in gaudy colors and words invited sympathy for
Huey Newton, exoneration of the Rosenbergs. . . . There were announce-
ments for lectures on Socialism, variant sexual lifestyles, transcendental
meditation, yoga, dietary advances, hypnotism, and occultism."[65] McCown
observed that the opening celebration at the Graduate Theological Union
"was held in a beautiful Lutheran chapel, with a mixed denominational
choir, scriptural readings by an Episcopalian woman, a Franciscan monk,
and the main address by a Jesuit faculty member."[66]

O'Connor treated such gatherings satirically. A decade before Mc-
Cown's enchantment with the Berkeley scene, O'Connor wrote him in 1963
about a symposium on religion and art she attended where, she says, "did I
ever get a stomachful of liberal religion." She was left with the "impression
that religion was a good thing (or at least unavoidable) because it was art
and magic. They had a Methodist-Universalist there who talked about how
the symbology of religion was decayed." A third speaker "told them about
how God was a grandfather image and they had better shuck it. I gave them
a nasty dose of orthodoxy in my paper but I think it passed as quaint. It is
later than we think."[67]

Father McCown's later theological and political views, however, would
depart from O'Connor's anchoring in a "nasty dose of orthodoxy" that inspired her anticommunism. She is a tireless, theological apologist in her unpublished letters to Father McCown and in other published correspondence
to friends struggling with their faith such as Betty Hester, Cecil Dawkins,
Robert Lowell, and Ted Spivey. In 1955, she writes Betty Hester that cultural practices should not lead to sudden change in the Church: "If you
are a Catholic you believe what the Church teaches and the climate makes
no difference."[68] She also responds to both Cecil Dawkins and Ted Spivey,
who were critical of the Church for its sinfulness, failures, and flawed personalities, including overworked priests. She writes Dawkins, "Christ never
said that the Church would be operated in a sinless or intelligent way, but
that it would not teach error . . . speaking through the Pope . . . in matters
of faith."[69] To Spivey, O'Connor writes, "You seem to have met nothing but
sorry or dissatisfied Catholics and abrupt priests with no understanding of
what you want to find out." She recommends he "study what the Church
teaches in matters of faith and morals."[70] While Father McCown never
abandoned the faith, his later waywardness would have pained O'Connor.
His evolving favorable views of ecumenism, liberation theology, and the

ordination of women starkly contrast with O'Connor's precise consultation with him before her death about theological orthodoxy and obedience to Church teachings.

In 1964 Father McCown tested his new views out on Walker Percy. That year McCown wrote to Tom Gossett: "Did I ever tell you that a few weeks ago I spent the better part of a day with Walker Percy, author of THE MOVIEGOER? Flannery says he is very good. Certainly he is one of the most charming people I have ever met."[71] Father McCown's friendship with Percy after O'Connor's death is vital in revealing how she and McCown might have had sharp political differences as the political turmoil of the 1960s unfolded. O'Connor endured President Kennedy's assassination but did not live to witness, as did Percy, the senseless murders of both Martin Luther King and Robert Kennedy, or the protracted Vietnam War with all of its vocal opposition. During this tumultuous period, Percy managed to embrace both anticommunism and the civil rights movement. Percy, like O'Connor, maintained allegiance to his southern roots. He had little patience for distant sanctimonious critics of segregation who saw it as a regional failing in places like Percy's native Mississippi; for Percy, Detroit, Newark, and Boston were no paragons of racial accord.[72]

Furthermore, Percy approved of the civil rights movement, but he did not link the quest for social justice to the morality of the Vietnam War. Indeed, Percy was careful to separate himself from antiwar dissenters like Robert Lowell and Dorothy Day. This pattern was not the case with Father McCown and other antiwar religious such as the Trappist monk Thomas Merton, as well as Daniel and Phillip Berrigan. When Thomas Merton sent Percy his article "The Hot Summer of Sixty-Seven," Percy replied that he largely agreed with him, "although I must confess I have reservations about uniting race and Vietnam under the same rubric since I regard one as the clearest kind of moral issue and the other as murderously complex and baffling."[73] Later, in 1969, as fierce fighting continued in Vietnam with many American soldiers killed, Dorothy Day was recommending the study of Vladimir Lenin as well as Ho Chi Minh and Che Guevara because of "their fierce dedication to the common good."[74] Such counsel and the activism it spawned troubled Percy (he probably would have reservations about current canonization efforts in behalf of Day). She refused to pay income taxes, while the Rev. Phillip Berrigan's war protests included pouring duck blood over draft records at a U.S. government office. In the late 1960s, Father

Berrigan and his brother, Daniel, were listed among the "FBI's Ten Most Wanted Fugitives." In 1970, Percy wrote the editors of *Commonweal:* "You and the Berrigans consider the United States' policy in Southeast Asia to be criminal. It is hardly necessary to point out that a great many people, perhaps as decent, as courageous, as equally distressed by the Vietnam War, do not agree with you and the Berrigans. Shall the issue be determined then by the more successful stratagem of violence?"[75]

Later developments in the 1980s such as liberation theology, the movement to ordain women as Catholic priests, and opposition to the Pontificate of John Paul II likewise elicited Percy's disapproval. When the pontiff visited New Orleans in 1987 Percy wrote "If I Had Five Minutes with the Pope." Percy advised him not to suppress the Jesuits of Central America. He noted that liberation theologians "had their hearts in the right place" in wanting to help the "wretched of the earth," but they needed to be disarmed "so they won't go around shooting people."[76] By contrast, Father McCown in a 1988 newsletter about his visit to Nicaragua recounts meeting with members of the Junta of National Reconstruction, led by Daniel Ortega, who had studied revolutionary tactics with Fidel Castro in Cuba. Having also heard liberation theologians preach in Nicaragua, Father McCown writes Tom Gossett that President Reagan should be "impeached" and that he has "been unmasked as not being a man of peace. . . . Bullets for peace is his motto."[77] He also complained to Percy about Pope John Paul II and his successor, known then as Cardinal Ratzinger. Father McCown wrote that the Holy Spirit was "not just in the mind of Pope John Paul via Cardinal Ratzinger. All this from-the-top-down correction of theology will paralyze creative thinking, and we are going to be back in the frozen eras before good Pope John."[78] Walker Percy replied that McCown was adrift, both politically and theologically: "With all your denunciations of U.S.-as-imperialist, Pope-as-monarch, etc. you never once uttered one murmur of complaint against the Sandinistas (e.g. attack on civil liberties, closing down of La Prensa, etc.)."[79]

Had O'Connor lived to see these later developments that elicit Percy's criticism of Father McCown, she probably would have concurred. Father McCown, however, was a bold, remarkable priest: it is a rare person who knocks on the doors of two seminal writers of the twentieth century, Flannery O'Connor and Walker Percy. Father McCown graciously accepted O'Connor's skepticism of his literary talks and Percy's criticism of his political views. McCown admits, "I never claimed to know much about literature . . . and what I do know I think I learned mostly from my conversations and correspondence with the seeress of Andalusia, and things she gave me to read."[80] Finally, Father McCown writes some of the most poignant, comforting words ever written to Tom and Louise Gossett about Flannery O'Connor's untimely death: "Well I know how you feel about our precious Flannery and you know how I feel. God has his own reasons for removing from our needful world such choice souls so soon. But it is an exercise in Faith to accept it. That faith tells me that the souls in Heaven can by their prayer achieve more good among us wayfarers than they ever could by her efforts on earth no matter how skillful they may be. And I believe this. But it's not easy to adjust my human feeling to it."[81] What comforting counsel about "precious Flannery," heretofore known sometimes as flinty, opinionated, and austere!

To Father McCown, Flannery was the loyal friend. O'Connor's letters to him, the Gossetts, and others show that friendship often transcends politics. The global realignment of nations after World War II, the Cold War, the prospect of nuclear annihilation, civil rights activism, Southern Agrarian thought, and the dynamic orthodoxy of Catholicism—all had an impact on O'Connor's political views. For O'Connor, however, political positions and trends did not overrule the loyalties of friendship. Her devotion to her friends—and their devotion to her—was overt and constant. Their politics varied, but joy and good humor quieted the shrill voices of partisanship.

Notes

1. Flannery O'Connor, *The Habit of Being: Letters of Flannery O'Connor*, ed. Sally Fitzgerald (New York: Farrar, Straus and Giroux, 1979), 163.

2. James H. McCown, "Flannery O'Connor," lecture, University of South Alabama, Mobile, April 26, 1985, n.p.

3. Thomas F. and Louise Y. Gossett Papers, Perkins Library, Duke University, Durham, N.C. The unpublished letters cited in this essay have been transcribed from this collection.

4. O'Connor, *Habit of Being*, 105.

5. J. Bottom, "Flannery O'Connor Banned," *Crisis* 18, no. 9 (2000): 48.

6. McCown, "Flannery O'Connor," lecture.

7. O'Connor, *Habit of Being*, 135.

8. O'Connor to Robert McCown, Gossett Papers, Duke University.

9. O'Connor, *Habit of Being*, 90.

10. Ibid., 382.

11. Robert McCown's "The Education of a Prophet: Flannery O'Connor's *The Violent Bear It Away*" was originally published in *Kansas Magazine*. That obscure journal is out of print. A photocopy of McCown's article is in the Gossett Papers at Duke University. All direct quotations are transcribed from this photocopy.

12. James Hart McCown, *With Crooked Lines* (Mobile: Spring Hill College Press, 1990), iii.

13. O'Connor to Father McCown, Gossett Papers, Duke University.

14. Ibid.

15. Gossett's observation is written in his own handwriting beside a picture of Father McCown in the Gossett Papers, Duke University.

16. McCown, "Flannery O'Connor," lecture.

17. O'Connor to Father McCown, Gossett Papers, Duke University.

18. McCown, "Flannery O'Connor," lecture.

19. O'Connor to Tom and Louise Gossett, Gossett Papers, Duke University.

20. McCown, "Flannery O'Connor," lecture.

21. Ibid.

22. Ibid.

23. Ibid.

24. O'Connor to Father McCown, Gossett Papers, Duke University.

25. Ibid.

26. Caroline Gordon to Walker Percy, Walker Percy Papers, Southern Historical Collection, Louis Round Wilson Library, University of North Carolina, Chapel Hill.

27. Qtd. in Paul Elie, *The Life You Save* (New York: Farrar, Straus and Giroux, 2003), 90.

28. Caroline Gordon to O'Connor, Sally Fitzgerald Papers, Robert Woodruff Library, Emory University, Atlanta, Ga.

29. O'Connor to Father McCown, Gossett Papers, Duke University.

30. Ibid.

31. Ibid.

32. O'Connor, *Habit of Being*, 33.

33. O'Connor to Father McCown, Gossett Papers, Duke University.

34. McCown, "Flannery O'Connor," lecture.

35. O'Connor to Father McCown, Gossett Papers, Duke University.

36. Ibid.

37. Ibid.

38. The decade of their friendship from 1956 to O'Connor's death in 1964 saw the social fabric of the United States ripped asunder by violence associated

with the civil rights movement. For example, in December 1955, NAACP member Rosa Parks refused to give up her seat to a white passenger in Montgomery, Alabama, leading to a bus boycott and the eventual desegregation of public transit. In September 1957, nine black students were blocked from integrating Central High School in Little Rock, Arkansas, on the orders of Governor Orval Faubus. President Eisenhower sent federal troops and the National Guard to intervene on behalf of the students, who became known as the "Little Rock Nine." In the fall of 1962, James Meredith became the first black student to enroll at the University of Mississippi. Violence and riots surrounding the incident caused President Kennedy to send in five thousand federal troops. In 1963 Martin Luther King was arrested and jailed during antisegregation protests in Birmingham, Alabama; he wrote his seminal "Letter from the Birmingham Jail," arguing that individuals have the moral duty to disobey unjust laws. In June 1963, just hours after President John F. Kennedy's speech on national television in support of civil rights, an assassin gunned down Medgar Evers in the driveway of his Mississippi home. Later that year, two hundred thousand people joined the March on Washington and listened to Martin Luther King deliver his famous "I Have a Dream" speech. In September 1963, four young girls attending Sunday school were killed when a bomb exploded at the Sixteenth Street Baptist Church, a popular location for civil rights meetings in Birmingham, Alabama. In November 1963, Lee Harvey Oswald assassinated President Kennedy in Dallas. In June 1964, the Ku Klux Klan brutally murdered Michael Schwerner, Andrew Goodman, and James Chaney in Philadelphia, Mississippi,

39. Sally Fitzgerald, introduction to *Habit of Being*, xviii.

40. Ibid.

41. O'Connor to Ward Allison Dorrance, Ward Allison Dorrance Papers, Southern Historical Collection, Louis Round Wilson Library, University of North Carolina, Chapel Hill.

42. Ibid.

43. Ibid.

44. O'Connor to Regina O'Connor, Sally Fitzgerald Papers, Woodruff Library, Emory University, Atlanta, Ga.

45. J. McCown, *With Crooked Lines*, 16.

46. O'Connor to Father McCown, Gossett Papers, Duke University.

47. O'Connor to Roslyn Barnes, Gossett Papers, Duke University.

48. O'Connor to Father McCown, Gossett Papers, Duke University.

49. O'Connor to Thomas Gossett, Gossett Papers, Duke University.

50. Davidson, with other colleagues, had advocated that *I'll Take My Stand* be entitled *Tracts Against Communism* in order to make a wider appeal and to place the volume in the larger context of political philosophy. One of the weaknesses of the collection is its provincial title to which Davidson wisely objected.

51. Donald Davidson, *The Attack on Leviathan* (New York: Peter Smith, 1962), 128.

52. Ibid.

53. O'Connor to Father McCown, Gossett Papers, Duke University.

54. O'Connor to Thomas Gossett, Gossett Papers, Duke University.

55. Father McCown to Thomas Gossett, Gossett Papers, Duke University.

56. Thomas F. Gossett, *Race: The History of an Idea in America*, ed. Shelley Fisher Fishkin and Arnold Rampersad, 2nd ed. (New York: Oxford University Press, 1997), vi.

57. O'Connor to Thomas Gossett, Gossett Papers, Duke University.

58. Kennedy, in the 1960 inaugural, proclaimed: "Let every nation know, whether it wishes us well or ill, that we shall pay any price, bear any burden, meet any hardship, support any friend, oppose any foe, in order to assure the survival and the success of liberty."

59. Father McCown's narrative about his pilgrimage to Mexico is contained in the Gossett Papers at Duke University. Direct quotations are transcribed from this source.

60. O'Connor to Father McCown, Gossett Papers, Duke University.

61. Ibid.

62. McCown, Mexican narrative, Gossett Papers, Duke University.

63. O'Connor, *Habit of Being*, 347.

64. O'Connor to Elizabeth McKee, Gossett Papers, Duke University.

65. Father James McCown, public newsletter, Gossett Papers, Duke University.

66. Ibid.

67. O'Connor to Father McCown, Gossett Papers, Duke University.

68. Flannery O'Connor, *Collected Works* (New York: Library of America, 1988), 956.

69. Ibid., 1084.

70. Ibid., 1102.

71. Father McCown to Thomas Gossett, Gossett Papers, Duke University.

72. This is a consistent theme in Percy's remarkable unpublished essay, "South: Quo Vadis," Walker Percy Papers, Southern Historical Collection, University of North Carolina at Chapel Hill.

73. Walker Percy to Thomas Merton, Walker Percy Papers, Southern Historical Collection, University of North Carolina at Chapel Hill.

74. *All the Way to Heaven: The Selected Letters of Dorothy Day*, ed. Robert Ellsburg (New York: Image, 2010), 458. Day never really understood the Jeffersonian roots of the American social order. Her persistent indignation at the social inequalities of industrial capitalism prevented a dispassionate study of the Ameri-

can founding. Unlike the anticommunism of Percy and O'Connor, Day retained a fascination with Marxist revolutionaries.

75. *Commonweal* 4 (September 1970): 481.

76. Walker Percy, *Signposts in a Strange Land*, ed. Patrick Samway, S.J. (New York: Farrar, Straus and Giroux, 2000), 347.

77. Father McCown to Thomas Gossett, Gossett Papers, Duke University.

78. Qtd. in Patrick Samway, S.J., *Walker Percy, A Life* (Chicago: Loyola Press, 1997), 394. This letter and others are quoted without full bibliographic information about the location of the letters or where they are collected. I suspect the letters between Father McCown and Percy may be in the Jesuit archives of the Southern province in New Orleans. In June 2012 my request to read the letters in the archives was denied.

79. Ibid.

80. McCown, "Flannery O'Connor," lecture.

81. Father McCown to Tom and Louise Gossett, Gossett Papers, Duke University.

3

Desegregation and the Silent Character in O'Connor's "Everything That Rises Must Converge"

Michael L. Schroeder

In spite of all that has been said and written about Flannery O'Connor's attitude toward race and the changes taking place in racial relations in the late 1950s and early 1960s, most scholars continue to see her attitudes on the topic to be, as concisely stated by Brad Gooch, "one of complex ambivalence" (332). Yet it is misleading to say, as Margaret Earley Whitt does, that "O'Connor was silent towards the events of the civil rights movement—in her letters, in her interviews, in her public talks, and, except for a topical reference in Julian's mother's bus ride to the downtown Y for a weight-reducing class in 'Everything That Rises Must Converge,' in her fiction as well" (59). I want to argue that although "Everything That Rises Must Converge" does not become polemical, it certainly goes beyond a mere "topical reference" to reflect her deep concerns with the issues of desegregation and civil rights, and it indicates, subtly, her opinion on how to best deal with those issues.

Whitt's use of "topical" could refer to either of two letters about "Everything That Rises Must Converge" in which O'Connor uses the term. In her first reference to the story in her published letters, dated March 26, 1961, she reports that the story had been sold and adds that it "touches on a certain topical issue in these parts" (*HB* 446). Then, in a letter from September 1, 1963, O'Connor complains: "The topical is poison. I got away with it in 'Everything That Rises' but only because I said a plague on everybody's house as far as the race business goes" (*HB* 537). Those houses presumably include those of the paternalistic but racist establishment that wants to perpetuate segregation, represented by Julian's mother; misguided liberals who want to flaunt their integrationist virtues, such as Julian; and African Americans so fed up with segregation that they are ready to lash out violently even at well-intended condescension. O'Connor appears to be showing all sides to be at fault. Of course, O'Connor's characters rarely demonstrate honorable motives. Yet in this case O'Connor depicts the views and attitudes of all three characters negatively because she wants her story to reflect the complexities of desegregation in the South as viewed by a relatively progressive white southerner at the beginning of the 1960s. As Brad Gooch points out, these complexities are reflected in a 1957 letter to Betty Hester about an incident involving Dorothy Day, the Catholic social activist, who had been shot at after visiting an interracial community in Georgia (333). O'Connor writes: "All my thoughts on this subject are ugly and uncharitable—such as: that's a mighty long way to come to get shot at, etc. I admire her very much. . . . I hope that to be of two minds about some things is not to be neutral" (May 1957, *HB* 218). O'Connor depicts the central characters in "Everything That Rises Must Converge" in "ugly and uncharitable" ways, and she might "be of two minds" on the issues, but that does not mean she is "neutral."

When Julian and his mother board the bus shortly after the desegregation of public transportation, no African Americans are on board, much less sitting in the seats in the front that had formerly been restricted to white riders. Demonstrating commonly held segregationist views, Julian's mother enters into a conversation with another white woman on the bench seat across the aisle. Noting that all the riders on the bus are white, she observes, "I see that we have the bus to ourselves," to which the other woman complains that on her last trip, African Americans had been as "thick as fleas—up front and all through" (*CW* 490). Then, when a professionally dressed black man sits at the other end of her bench seat, this woman feels compelled, in her segregationist mind, to move to the back, and thus out of the story.

Julian's mother is a typical O'Connor mother, well-meaning but proud. Unlike the rural mothers of other stories, her pride is rooted in her ancestry, and her primary flaw is the racism that comes from her romanticized view of slavery and segregation. She is of the Old Guard, like O'Connor's own mother, Regina, ready to acknowledge that change will come, but slowly, and that while African Americans will rise, their social improvement should be "on their own side of the fence" (*CW* 488). She believes that she and her son should be proud of and take strength from their aristocratic heritage as descendants of a governor, and she yearns for the antebellum days, in which her ancestors, the Godhighs, lived in a mansion maintained by slaves. From her own childhood, she recalls fondly "the old darky who was my nurse, Caroline" (488). At the time of the story, however, she endures in genteel poverty, worried over the cost of a new hat and riding a public bus to attend a weight-reduction class with those "who are not our kind of people." But, she adds, "I can be gracious to anybody. I know who I am" (487). Her blindly racist and classist assumptions are clearly not those of O'Connor, though her paternalistic and segregationist impulses reflect ingrained habit more than conscious offensiveness.

As Ralph C. Wood puts it, Julian is "another white liberal who turns a rightful demand for racial justice into a wrongful demand for moral congratulations" (116). Highly critical of his mother's beliefs and ways, he likes to retreat into a "mental bubble" from which "he could see out and judge but in it he was safe from any kind of penetration from without" (*CW* 491). Julian insists to himself that he is open-minded in spite of his mother and the many sacrifices she has made to give him opportunities, particularly a college education. He argues against her in support of integration, yet his fantasies reveal him to be hypocritical and shallow. He wishes to "teach [his mother] a lesson" by bringing home—that is, to her apartment in what used to be a good part of the city—the sort of African Americans who fit his ideal image: a professor or lawyer, or a beautiful but "suspiciously Negroid" (494) woman whom he could introduce as his chosen mate. In addition to his own racist assumptions about the type of African American appropriate for his company, he further displays his hypocrisy by dreaming of the now-decayed family mansion: "He never spoke of it without contempt or thought of it without longing" (488).

We know little about the background or motives of the character who precipitates Julian's mother's literal fall, but her attitude is established from the moment she boards the bus with her young son. She is a large and "sullen" African American woman. "Her face," we are told, "was set not only to meet opposition but to seek it out" (*CW* 495). To Julian's amusement, she wears the same hat as his mother, and while Julian reluctantly continues to sit by her—she is apparently not the sort of African American he wants to associate with—her son starts to play games with Julian's mother, much to the dismay of the child's mother. This woman's irritation continues to seethe until both sets of mothers and sons step off the bus at the same stop. As is her custom, Julian's mother patronizingly gets out a penny for the boy. (She wants to give him a nickel but has none.) Upon this insult to the dignity of herself and her son, the boy's mother whacks the older woman across the head with her pocketbook. As a result of this act of excessive violence, Julian's mother has a stroke, but before she dies she thinks back to her youth and asks first for her grandfather, and then her black nanny. Julian runs for help, but "the tide of darkness seemed to sweep him back to her, postponing from moment to moment his entry into a world of guilt and sorrow" (500).

Anthony Di Renzo discusses the thematic tensions in the stories comprising the collection *Everything That Rises Must Converge*, including the complex depiction of social issues in the title story. He sees "the grotesqueness of much of the death-dealing satire" as "an expression of the author's own ambivalent fascination with the great crisis that disrupted the South in the late fifties and early sixties: the rise of the civil right movement" (197). The author's ambivalence leads to her use of an ambivalent narrator, one who "seems simultaneously to approve of and protest her characters' punishing deaths, to mock and to mourn them" (198). Di Renzo cites two explanations for "this deliberate disjunction between [grotesquely comical] form and [tragic] content." First, the religious perspective: "Since O'Connor deliberately places the social tragedy of her white characters—the destruction of their pride, privilege, and heritage—against the cosmic background of Christian comedy—her characters' moral obligation to see that they and their black neighbors are equal in the eyes of God—she dissociates herself partly from their suffering and humiliation, never allows them to take center stage" (199). Di Renzo's second explanation is more historical: that crisis and change are "open-ended" and that these stories "illustrate the simultaneous losses and gains of social conflict," so "what is tragic for [middle-class white characters] may not be tragic for others" (199). To illustrate the narrator's ambivalence, Di Renzo (referring to Julian's mother as Mrs. Chestny, though Chestny was presumably her maiden name) shows that in "Everything That Rises Must Converge" the narrator "clearly sympathizes with

Mrs. Chestny" (199) but "also sympathizes with the enormous black woman who attacks her" (200). Furthermore, "in some ways Julian's position—for all its snideness and shallowness—has been validated in the story: the old world is 'gone,' and old set of manners 'obsolete,' and Mrs. Chestny's graciousness is 'not worth a damn.'" Yet at the same time Julian "longs for the manners and gentility of the old dispensation—just as Julian can pine away for the lost Chestny mansion while attacking his mother's narrowmindedness" (200). Thus, Di Renzo argues, "This compelling blend of contempt and longing that exists in O'Connor's double-minded narrator perfectly expresses the peculiar schizophrenia created by historical change" (200–201).

Although Di Renzo offers a convincing explanation of the narrator's ambivalence, the bases of O'Connor's views are more complex than he suggests, being rooted as they were in the everyday realities that integration posed for someone in her time, place, and social situation. In light of both her statements elsewhere and a quick review of the political situation in states such as Georgia at the time, the story might also be seen as an attempt to illustrate some of the immense complexities of the racial situation in the South, psychological as well as political, affecting blacks as well as whites. As Sarah Gordon has observed of Julian, his mother, and the African American woman, "All three constitute O'Connor's retort to those . . . who offer simple solutions to the matter of human perfection" ("Maryat and Julian" 35). Or, on a more political level, they comprise a retort to arguments for an immediate and forced solution to the racial dilemmas in the South at the start of 1961.

O'Connor was certainly disturbed by what she saw as oversimplification of the situation by northern liberals. In her letter of September 1, 1963, about getting away with this one "topical" story, O'Connor complained of "all the stupid Yankee liberals smacking their lips over typical life in the dear old dirty Southland" (*HB* 537). As a relatively progressive white Georgian of the time, and particularly one who had been forced by health problems to return from New York and Connecticut to the South a decade before, O'Connor was understandably sensitive to a sense of arrogance of those Yankees who insisted they knew what should be done in the South, and when and how. Life with her mother, Regina, and other members of what had been the respectable white southern establishment led her to be fully aware of the potential conflicts, including the dangers of white backlash. She alludes to some of those conflicts when she writes in April 1959 that she would meet James Baldwin in New York but not in Georgia because "it would cause the greatest trouble and disturbance and disunion. . . . I observe the traditions of the society I feed on—it's only fair. Might as well expect a mule to fly as me to see James Baldwin in Georgia" (*HB* 329).

O'Connor made that observation in one of the letters to Maryat Lee in which she played the role of the southern conservative in contention with the liberal views of her correspondent. Ralph Wood refers to her tone as one of "joshing self-ridicule concerning the race question" (98). Maryat Lee herself wrote of this persona, "I could only believe that she shared with me the sense of frustration and betrayal and impotency over the dilemma in the white South" (qtd. in Cash 149–50). Supporting the view of O'Connor as a progressive are interviews in which she expressed optimism toward integration and stressed the importance of manners, on the part of both white and black folk, in making the changes possible (Cash 155). However, a contrasting view is offered by Sarah Gordon, based on O'Connor's letters to Maryat Lee that were omitted from *The Habit of Being:* "The underlying current of racism in these letters is difficult to ignore or rationalize" (*Flannery* 238).

When Margaret Earley Whitt says that O'Connor was silent on the events of the civil rights movement, she focuses largely on the events of 1963 in Mississippi and Alabama. The Montgomery church bombing and the assassination of Medgar Evers clearly demonstrate the unconscionable extremes to which anti-integration hatred could lead. Yet to judge O'Connor by the standards of our time, more than fifty years later, would be much like the criticism from the "stupid Yankee liberals" that she deplored. Furthermore, if we look at events in Georgia at the time she was writing "Everything That Rises Must Converge," in late 1960 and early 1961, it is easier to see why she would take a more nuanced approach to the issue in her one "topical" story. She would have seen in the daily news many examples of turmoil her society faced, turmoil that underlies the conflicts among Julian, his mother, and his mother's African American counterpart. Yet she also embodies in the story an approach to resolving the inequalities with a minimum of upheaval. But to see that resolution, we must focus on a minor character, the one who says nothing.

One glaring example of the social disruptions posed by integration that would have been prominent in the news is the court-ordered attempt to integrate the University of Georgia at the beginning of 1961. When Charlayne Hunter and Hamilton Holmes attempted to attend classes on January

11, riots resulted, with from five hundred to two thousand students throwing rocks and fighting with police. The university responded by suspending Hunter and Holmes, along with some of the rioters, only to have Hunter and Holmes reinstated by another court order. Although the actions of some of the students and university leaders seem despicable today, students of the time defended segregation not only on the basis of racism and tradition but also on the basis of states' rights and the argument that African Americans had their own institutions of higher learning so had no need to disrupt the segregationist traditions of the University of Georgia (Cohen 624).

Ralph C. Wood refers to Walker Percy's *Signposts in a Strange Land* in his explanation of the depths of feelings that integration could bring to southern institutions: "Like O'Connor, Percy knew that racial justice was a far more complicated matter than many integrationists allowed. Southern colleges and schools, Percy observed, served as social as well as educational institutions." In some public spaces, such as grocery stores, "people do not feel they are sharing the same living space," but "the social body and the student body virtually coincided in the South, Percy argues, far more than in the North. This meant that federally mandated school desegregation was no simple matter of public justice and equal rights; it was an act of aggression against a quasi-tribal society" (104). One need not be a segregationist to be sensitive to social rifts caused by such acts of "aggression," just as O'Connor was sensitive to the social repercussions of meeting James Baldwin in Georgia while still expressing a willingness to meet with him in New York.

Another site of conflict that O'Connor would have been aware of, and that would have certainly demonstrated the dangers of white backlash if changes were pushed too fast, involved the role of the Catholic Church. For decades, the Church in Georgia had reached out to both black and white parishioners, but with racially distinct churches and schools. In 1957, the bishop of the diocese in Atlanta, Francis Hyland, suggested to a group of advisors that the Catholic high schools should be integrated rather than exist as separate institutions for white and black students. However, advisors talked him out of the proposal by emphasizing political realities: not only would integration hurt the Church's attempts to win new parishioners, but it could also provoke the state legislature to retaliate by taxing the schools and taking away teachers' credentials. In addition, Catholic leaders had to acknowledge widespread anti-Catholic feelings of the time, which could be exacerbated by integration of the schools. Bishop Hyland relented then, but the national Catholic Church declared in 1958 that segregation was a moral wrong, and in February 1961 Hyland joined the bishops from Savannah and Charleston in a public announcement that the parochial schools would be integrated as quickly as could be safely achieved. Predictably, many Catholics reacted angrily and withdrew from the Church. As a result of such obstacles and attitudes, Catholic schools were not integrated until after the public schools were (Moore). Such events illustrate the practical obstacles that narrowly focused integrationists like Julian would have failed to take into account but of which O'Connor would have been cognizant.

Just as she was aware of the range of views toward integration among whites, O'Connor would likely have also been aware of disunity within the civil rights movement itself, with one of the most dramatic events occurring about the time she mentioned in a letter that the story was accepted for publication. Boycotts of stores in Atlanta over segregated lunch counters closed seventy downtown stores from late 1960 until February 1961. The boycott was ended by a settlement between the merchants and the black establishment that was widely perceived as a sellout by the more radical participants in the movement. At a March 7 meeting in an Atlanta church, with a handful of white Chamber of Commerce representatives present, the "elders" tried to defend the agreement before a crowd of about two thousand, most of whom were hostile. Martin Luther King Sr. took the pulpit to try to defend the agreement, but he was met by loud boos. About that time, his son arrived, worked his way through the crowd to the pulpit, and accused the crowd of surrendering to the "cancer of disunity." Martin Luther King Jr. defused the situation by praising the black elders and placing the responsibility for upholding the agreement on the white businessmen (Branch 395–97).

O'Connor expresses her views on different approaches to integration in a letter to Maryat Lee dated May 21, 1964. She complains about "the philosophizing prophesying pontificating kind [of 'Negro'], the James Baldwin kind. Very ignorant but never silent." Later she adds, "If Baldwin were white nobody could stand him a minute." In contrast, she writes of Martin Luther King Jr., "I don't think he is the ages [sic] great saint but he's at least doing what he can do & has to do" (CW 1208). She appears to be favoring King's approach as more practical because it reflects his position as a southerner familiar with the social situation as she saw it, in contrast to those arguing for immediate change in spite of the many social forces involved. Yet she saw the change itself as inevitable.

O'Connor believed the resolution of decades of inequality would require not only discretion and understanding of the complex social forces involved but also a recognition of the importance of socially prescribed manners in the process. In one interview with C. Ross Mullins, originally published in *Jubilee* in June 1963 and appended to *Mystery and Manners,* she explains that for the races to live together in the South, they must have "a code of manners based on mutual charity" because "formality preserves that individual privacy which everyone needs and, in these times, is always in danger of losing" (*MM* 233). She adds: "The South has survived in the past because its manners, however lopsided or inadequate they may have been, provided enough social discipline to hold us together and give us an identity. Now those old manners are obsolete, but the new manners will have to be based on what was best in the old ones—in their real basis of charity and necessity" (*MM* 234). When Julian tells his mother that her "manners are obsolete," he is right to a point, but in their place he offers nothing but rudeness to his own mother and misguided and hypocritical liberalism, totally lacking in genuine charity.

O'Connor reveals her meager optimism through the only adult character on the bus who is not depicted negatively. One of Julian's attempts to perturb his mother occurs when a well- dressed African American carrying a briefcase boards the bus, looks around, and chooses to sit on the bench across from Julian and his mother, near the front of the bus. At first Julian sees him only as an example of the "injustice in daily operation," which provides him with "a certain satisfaction" (*CW* 492). When a white woman on the same bench responds by moving to another seat, receiving an "approving look" from Julian's mother in response, Julian takes her place beside the black man in a typically mismotivated display of racial egalitarianism, his "tension" having been "suddenly lift[ed] as if he had openly declared war" on his mother (492). To further irritate her and drive up her already dangerously high blood pressure, Julian wants to strike up a conversation with the man "about art or politics or any subject that would be above the comprehension of those around them, but the man remained entrenched behind" his newspaper (493). Julian tries to open a conversation by asking the man for a light, despite the "no smoking" sign and the fact that Julian has no cigarettes. The man provides a book of matches without looking at Julian, and when Julian returns them with a "sorry," the man gives him "an annoyed look" (493). Julian's attempt to teach his mother a lesson fails because the other man "refused to come out from behind the paper" (493).

Despite the fact that few critics give this man more than a passing reference, certainly O'Connor intends him to serve as more than a prop or foil for Julian. His suit and newspaper connote a professional and social status far different from that of the African American farmworkers or city dwellers of her other stories. He displays dignity in his effort to maintain his privacy. He refuses to take offense at or even acknowledge racist reactions to his presence. And most of all, he expects the right to sit where he wants and to be left alone. These attitudes might be seen as an indicator of O'Connor's vision for progress in the crisis that was continuing to grow around her. In a letter dated October 11, 1963, O'Connor reported on a group of "local Negroes" who "petitioned the city council to do the usual things," one of which was "to integrate the library. It turns out the library has been integrated for a year and they didn't know it. Nine Negroes had cards. That's the way things have to be done here—completely without publicity. Then there is no trouble" (*HB* 542). The man on the bus could have been like one of those African Americans who quietly went about claiming some of their rights, with O'Connor's approval. For O'Connor, change was coming, whether people like her mother, or Julian's, wanted to accept it or not. But it would not be helped along by the likes of Julian, with his misguided motives and provocative actions, or his mother's African American counterpart, with her anger and resentfulness. O'Connor saw the answer to lie in pursuing change quietly and persistently, and most of all with manners.

Note

This essay was originally published as "Desegregation and the Silent Character in O'Connor's 'Everything That Rises Must Converge,'" *Flannery O'Connor Review* 10 (2012): 75–81. Reprinted with the permission of the *Flannery O'Connor Review*.

Works Cited

Branch, Taylor. *Parting the Water: America in the King Years, 1954–63*. New York: Simon, 1988.

Cash, Jean. *Flannery O'Connor: A Life*. Knoxville: U of Tennessee P, 2002.

Cohen, Robert. "'Two, Four, Six, Eight, We Don't Want to Integrate': White Student Attitudes toward the University of Georgia's Desegregation." *Georgia Historical Quarterly* 80 (1996): 616–64. *Humanities International Complete*. EBSCO. Web. March 24, 2011.

Di Renzo, Anthony. *American Gargoyles: Flannery O'Connor and the Medieval Grotesque*. Carbondale: Southern Illinois UP, 1993.

Gooch, Brad. *Flannery: A Life of Flannery O'Connor*. New York: Little, 2009.

Gordon, Sarah. *Flannery O'Connor: The Obedient Imagination*. Athens: U of Georgia P, 2000.

———. "Maryat and Julian and the 'Not So Bloodless Revolution.'" *Flannery O'Connor Bulletin* 21 (1992): 25–36.

Moore, Andrew S. "Practicing What We Preach: White Catholics and the Civil Rights Movement in Atlanta." *Georgia Historical Quarterly* 89 (2005): 334–67. *Humanities International Complete*. EBSCO. Web. March 24, 2011.

O'Connor, Flannery. *Flannery O'Connor: Collected Works*. Ed. Sally Fitzgerald. New York: Library of America, 1988. Cited parenthetically as *CW*.

———. *The Habit of Being: Letters*. Ed. Sally Fitzgerald. New York: Farrar, Straus and Giroux, 1979. Cited parenthetically as *HB*.

———. *Mystery and Manners: Occasional Prose*. Ed. Sally Fitzgerald and Robert Fitzgerald. New York: Farrar, Straus and Giroux, 1969. Cited parenthetically as *MM*.

Whitt, Margaret Earley. "1963, A Pivotal Year: Flannery O'Connor and the Civil Rights Movement." *Flannery O'Connor Review* 3 (2005): 59–72. *MLA International Bibliography*. EBSCO. Web. March 24, 2010.

Wood, Ralph C. *Flannery O'Connor and the Christ-Haunted South*. Grand Rapids, Mich.: Eerdmans, 2004.

4

The Pivotal Year, 1963

Flannery O'Connor and the Civil Rights Movement

Margaret Earley Whitt

The modern civil rights movement, dating from the mid-1950s until Martin Luther King's death in 1968, takes its origins in three distinct events: *Brown v. Board of Education of Topeka* (May 1954), the lynching of fourteen-year-old Emmett Till in Money, Mississippi (August 1955), and the Montgomery bus boycott (December 1955–December 1956). The active days of the civil rights movement and the writing career of Flannery O'Connor have considerable overlap. Interestingly, O'Connor unwittingly predicts her days through one of her female characters, the thirty-two-year-old Joy/Hulga Hopewell, about whom "the doctors had told Mrs. Hopewell that with the best of care, Joy might see forty-five" (*CW* 268). If Mrs. Hopewell is responsible in her caretaking, her daughter will have thirteen years, which, of course, happens to be the length of writing time for O'Connor between diagnosis of her lupus in late 1951 and her death in 1964.

When the civil rights movement kicked into active high gear, then, O'Connor had already published her first novel and first collection of short stories. I would like to focus on those years that the movement and O'Connor are both doing their respective tasks—1955–1964—with a goal of understanding why O'Connor, at best, concerned herself only slightly with the events that were clearly changing the face of the South she knew so well, and then, ever so slowly, bent in the direction of what might have been a new O'Connor had she lived.

For the most part, O'Connor was silent toward the events of the civil rights movement—in her letters, in her interviews, in her public talks, and, except for a topical reference in Julian's mother's bus ride to the downtown Y for a weight-reducing class in "Everything That Rises Must Converge," in her fiction as well. Though she had little to say in direct commentary about the civil rights movement, these times, no doubt, contributed to the O'Connor that might have come to be—had her life not been cut short. For in the last full year of her life, civil rights events in the news offered O'Connor specific subject content that she might have used in her fiction, as her own awareness was beginning to change about the segregated world that nurtured her. Before we get to that last full year of her life, it is helpful to look closely at what we can find about her views before 1963.

O'Connor's published correspondence with Maryat Lee is an obvious starting point because of the often-documented comments that the two women exchanged on the issue of race relations as it was unfolding in the South in particular and in the country at large. O'Connor does make references to Ku Klux Klan activity on August 19, 1962 (*HB* 489), to the White Citizens Council on May 21, 1962 (*HB* 475), and jokingly to sit-ins, wade-ins, and kneel-ins on June 26, 1962 (*HB* 482). In earlier letters to Lee, O'Connor comments, on March 29, 1959, that she has "a friend who predicts that the school crisis in Georgia will take the following course: the issue will come to a head, the Governor will close all the schools, the people will realize that this means no more collegiate football and will force him to open them again" (*HB* 325). She makes this comment at a time when the governors of Arkansas and Virginia had both acted to close the public secondary schools in Little Rock and Prince Edwards County, respectively. In Little Rock, the schools were closed the year following the integration of Central High School, when nine black teenagers had to be escorted to class on a daily basis by soldiers from the 101st Airborne and later by federalized Arkansas state troopers. In Prince Edwards County, the schools were closed for five years in order to resist *Brown*. Again, on school integration, in a letter to Lee in January 1961, O'Connor makes a reference to Georgia's plan: "There is a marked change of atmosphere about all this in Georgia. They are fixing to junk the segregation laws and substitute a more local arrangement. Don't think now we will repeat New Orleans" (*HB* 425).

The reference to New Orleans is most likely to the first-grade black student Ruby Bridges, who spent a year in a classroom, alone with her white teacher, Barbara Henry, because the parents of all the white first-graders had removed their children from Ruby's class. Depicted in one of the more famous Norman Rockwell paintings, Ruby is the little girl being escorted into school by four tall federal agents.

In light of her absolute Christian beliefs and the moral lifestyle to which she was committed, O'Connor knew but did not acknowledge in her fiction the efforts of the civil rights movement and its progress toward justice for all. St. Thomas Aquinas explains the sin of omission as being the nonperformance of some action. According to the *New Catholic Encyclopedia*, it is of concern to the moralist only when a person could and should do what he leaves undone (10:688). We have to ask the obvious question: Why did she ignore what had to be so blatantly obvious? Was she unconscious of an obligation to act? Was it simple nonchoice? Or deliberate choice? St. Thomas explains the difference and establishes the weight of seriousness of these two options. Deliberate choice is serious business; a person makes an explicit decision not to do what he should. I do not think O'Connor's silence was this kind of deliberate choice. The lesser sin of omission, however, is nonchoice; a person does not reach a positive decision not to do what he should, but rather the decision to take action or not is somehow interrupted, aborted. To O'Connor, the civil rights movement offered an opportunity, but the message's importance did not connect to her own talent for fiction; she saw the palette from which she drew the colors of her universe not as the current events of social history but as the earlier events of biblical history. In the reality of mid-twentieth-century Milledgeville, she lived her life on one side of a parallel universe—in the white world, not in the black. In not using her talent to respond to what were among the most important current events of her writing life, she was guilty of a sin of omission, but of the venial classification, the lesser sin of nonchoice, not the more serious mortal sin. Catholic or not, for those living in the Deep South during these years, the sin of omission is a helpful way to understand how countless whites made a similar nonchoice and kept their silences.

In Alice Walker's important essay "Beyond the Peacock: The Reconstruction of Flannery O'Connor," Walker grapples with her own struggles with knowing what to do with O'Connor. Five years before the publication of O'Connor's collected letters, Walker traveled back to the geography of her childhood, just a few miles up the road from Andalusia. Walker admired O'Connor's ability to write about the southern white woman without sentimentality, and she understood that if O'Connor's writing was "'about' anything, then it is 'about' prophets and prophecy, 'about' revelation, and 'about' the impact of supernatural grace on human beings who don't have a chance of spiritual growth without it" (53). But, still, she takes O'Connor to task for using the word "nigger" casually in a letter to Robert Fitzgerald, which he reprints in his introduction to what will be the posthumous collection *Everything That Rises Must Converge;* Walker's response: "I do not find it funny" (53). Nor would she have found the repeated use of the word in letters to Maryat Lee, once *The Habit of Being* was published, "funny." She chastises O'Connor's blindness—what she does not see because, as a white woman, she does not have to see it. After quoting O'Connor on how the southerner sees justice in terms of persons, not races, Walker responds: "Of course this observation, though grand, does not apply to the racist treatment of blacks by whites in the South, and O'Connor should have added that she spoke only for herself" (53). But Walker had come on this trip in search of wholeness, and she does appear to reconcile and approve of the O'Connor who published "The Geranium" in 1946 but continued to struggle with the central black character's development through the years until "Judgment Day" was completed. The former Old Dudley is a compliant sort; the man whom Tanner calls "Preacher" has evolved way beyond compliance.

For a writer who did use the day's often quirky news as the inspiration for her fiction—The Misfit of "A Good Man Is Hard to Find," General Sash of "A Late Encounter with the Enemy," for example—it is worth noting those large and startling events that were breaking down the color divide of her home country. Major events—that received scant to no attention from O'Connor—after those mentioned above that began the movement include a wide array: Little Rock's Central High School's 1957 integration; Greensboro's February 1960 launch of the sit-in movement at a Woolworth's coffee counter and the ensuing April formation of the Student Non-Violent Coordinating Committee (SNCC); the May 1961 Freedom Rides; the explosive, deadly September 1962 integration of the University of Mississippi; the police and fire departments' use of dogs and high-pressure hoses on children in 1963 Birmingham; Medgar Evers's June 1963 assassination in his own driveway; the August 1963 march by a quarter-million people on

Washington, followed within weeks by the September bombing of the Sixteenth Street Baptist Church, and the deaths of four little girls, followed
by President Kennedy's November assassination; and finally the events of
the 1964 Freedom Summer in Mississippi and the deaths of James Chaney,
Michael Schwerner, and Andrew Goodman, whose bodies were unearthed
in the August of O'Connor's death. Each of these events was front-page,
often double-bannered headline news in the daily Atlanta newspapers that
O'Connor read.

Of the above events that attracted the close attention of the southern
public and, in most cases, of people from around the world, O'Connor commented on only two of them in her published letters: the death of President
John Kennedy and the March on Washington. In her fiction, she commented on the results of one event, the integration of public transportation, and
that in a story she first published in October 1961 in *New World Writing*,
"Everything That Rises Must Converge," a full five years after the Montgomery boycott had achieved its goal of integrating the city's buses. About
Kennedy's death, which in her published letters she did not refer to as the
assassination that it was, she made two comments. The first was to "A," who,
since her suicide on the day after Christmas in 1998, the world has come
to know as Betty Hester. O'Connor wrote simply on November 23, 1963:
"I am sad about the President. But I like the new one" (*HB* 549). The other
letter went to the Fitzgeralds, who were out of the country on November 23,
1963, when she wrote the letter: "The President's death has cut the country
up pretty bad. All commercial television is stopped until after the funeral
and even the football games called off, which is about the extremest sign of
grief possible" (*HB* 550). In moments of deep public grief, O'Connor's wit
prevents any possibility of a maudlin response. About the March on Washington, O'Connor uses it to poke fun at her sparring partner on racial jibes.
In a September 10, 1963, letter to Maryat Lee, she alludes to what many
considered a life-altering event as a marker: "Here I have been commiser-
ating with my image of you that was so po and energyless it couldn't go to
Washington to march for freedom with all its natural cousins" (*HB* 538).

During these years and after the appearance of *Wise Blood* and the
first collection, *A Good Man Is Hard to Find*, O'Connor lived to see published one more novel and seven short stories of the nine in her posthumous
collection *Everything That Rises Must Converge*, along with one other
story, "The Partridge Festival," which she decided she did not want in the

second collection. The fragment of what might have been her third novel, then in progress, "Why Do the Heathen Rage?" appeared in the July 1963 *Esquire*. No direct response to the civil rights movement itself exists in any of these works. Issues of race, or, at the very least, black characters, appear in the following five: Buford Munson and his daughter in *The Violent Bear It Away;* Carver and his mother, and mention of Caroline in "Everything That Rises Must Converge"; unnamed African Americans in "Greenleaf" who are serviced by Scofield May, the "nigger-insurance man"; Randall and Morgan in "The Enduring Chill"; the delivery boy and the blacks that offer flattery and work the land on the Turpins' place and later appear in Ruby Turpin's revelation in "Revelation." In "Judgment Day," which did not appear in her lifetime, Coleman and the unnamed black man who is not a preacher round out the references to race. O'Connor draws each of these characters with nobility. She had promised after her earlier failed attempt with one of her thesis stories, "Wildcat," that she would never again try to go inside the heads of her black characters. True to her word, each of these characters appears to do the right thing. As readers, we know only what we hear black characters say aloud, never what they think. Often, they are rescuers, and they are clever—outwitting their white counterparts by a deeper understanding of the worlds both whites and blacks inhabit.

O'Connor was a faithful reader of *the Atlanta Constitution* and *the Atlanta Journal,* especially the combined Sunday issues, yet in all her published correspondence, she makes only one reference to using the newspaper possibly for information about the movement's activities. In a letter to Roslyn Barnes on November 28, 1960, she writes: "Enclose you a clipping from the *Atlanta Journal* in case you might want to give it to your teacher . . . [.] Do you think there are still any closed societies in the South? There are two official ones, Black and White, but they are about to be loosed upon one another" (*HB* 420). Their being "loosed," of course, had been going on in an orchestrated manner for more than five years. Note that the term "closed society" would be made famous by southern historian James Silver's *Mississippi: The Closed Society,* which would not be written for four more years. When asked, O'Connor and every person with a modicum of sense living in the South acknowledged their worlds were separated between races. Every town had its black section, and the rest of the town was the property of the white population. Though the Atlanta newspapers appear most often in her published letters with references to Dr. Frank Crane, the Protestant theologian who offered "salvation by the compliment club," and appeared on the same page as the funnies (May 18, 1955, *HB* 81), O'Connor does make one reference to a mention of her story "Everything That Rises Must Converge," on the book page, "that alert sheet of Sunday criticism," with this cryptic note: "I suspect somebody from Atlanta U. did it" (June 16, 1963, *HB* 524). Atlanta is home to six historically black schools that together form the Atlanta University Center: Atlanta University, which merged with Clark College, becoming Clark Atlanta University in 1988, Morehouse College, the Interdenominational Theological Center, Morris Brown College, and Spelman College. What that unnamed critic said was in a May 12, 1963, "roundup" of short reports from contributors to the *Atlanta Journal and Constitution* book page: "Flannery O'Connor's "Everything That Rises Must Converge" is the first-prize story in the O. Henry awards competition this year. Her basic plot line is provocative and witty: An old-guard Southern lady, afraid to ride the buses without her son since integration, parades out for an evening dressed in a new and expensive hat. On the bus she encounters a Negro woman in the same hat. Unfortunately, the denouement of the story (the good Southern lady drops dead) is uncomfortable. It is pushed just too far." ("Offerings" 6-D)

Perhaps O'Connor's assigning these tepid comments to "somebody from Atlanta U." is a response to the critic's choice of summing up the whole of the story by mentioning Julian's mother's fear of riding the buses since integration, a line that comes directly from the first paragraph of the story itself: "She would not ride the buses by herself at night since they had been integrated" (*CW* 485). Is O'Connor suggesting that only a black person, or a white sympathetic to the civil rights movement, would reduce the story to this particular character description? From O'Connor's comments on *Galley Proof*, a 1955 television hour that showcased the works of just-published books, she refuses to sum up the conclusion of the dramatization of "The Life You Save May Be Your Own" for the host, Harvey Breit, stating that a story's worth is not in a reduction but in the whole of the story itself (*Conversations* 8).

The Montgomery bus boycott lasted 381 days, beginning in December 1955. While over fifty thousand black citizens took to walking to work in neighboring Alabama's capital city, O'Connor was adjusting to crutches, developing a new friendship with Betty Hester, taking cortisone in large doses, and worrying about the departure of her editor Catherine Carver from Harcourt, Brace. The sale of *Wise Blood* to France for translation and publication and the summer release of *A Good Man Is Hard to Find* were presenting O'Connor with a new set of challenges, that of becoming famous. She admitted in a letter to Hester on December 16, 1955, that she categorized her newfound fame as a "comic distinction shared with Roy Rogers's horse and Miss Watermelon of 1955" *(HB* 126). In the fall of 1957, when nine black teenagers were integrating Central High School in Little Rock, and the news was full of the thousand troopers bivouacked on the high school yard that had been sent in by President Eisenhower to protect the lives of the nine students, O'Connor was reporting on September 27, 1957, to William Sessions, who was studying in Germany, that "the Bell House is now down and nothing left but two beechtrees on either side of the lot so it is going to be called The Beechtree Parking Lot. Time Marches On" *(HB* 244). During these events, O'Connor did not have a television set, so, at least at home, she never saw the bus boycotters walking, and she never saw the riots or the troopers at Central High; her knowledge of the incidents and what pictures she might have seen came through the newspaper.

From O'Connor's letters, we know that she supported the Democratic candidates during these years—Stevenson over Eisenhower in 1952 (summer 1952, *HB* 42) and Kennedy over Nixon in 1960 (July 23, 1960, *HB* 404). In her published letters, she yokes the mention of a presidential candidate with a statement about his views on race. She chooses the one who is silent on racial integration. Of anything she could have said about the candidates, it is interesting that the only commentary that connects the election of 1952 with the election in 1960 is a statement in both elections about a race matter. In the earlier election, she is amused by a neighbor who "got herself an Eisenhower button the other day and that afternoon he said he would put a qualified Negro in the cabinet if he could find one. She returned the button before the evening sun went down" *(HB* 42). Whereas her mother supported Eisenhower, O'Connor liked Stevenson. Shortly after Kennedy was elected, she heard from a friend "that there was no truth in the rumor that the Kennedys were going to name their baby Martin Luther Kennedy." She went on to say to Maryat Lee on November 19, 1960, that this rumor "had its genesis in New York. It was not heard in the South. Now that we have elected him, we can begin to cuss him" *(HB* 418).

What is well known among historians of the Kennedy-Nixon election in 1960 was the importance of John Kennedy's well-placed, timely telephone call to Coretta Scott King when her husband was in jail in Georgia that election fall for participating in a sit-in demonstration at Rich's Department Store. The Kennedy name attached to a presidential candidate was influential in getting King released from jail. Word soon spread of Kennedy's supportive call to Mrs. King. Blacks then saw Kennedy as the man whom they most felt would support their causes. The black vote helped win the close election for Kennedy. Theodore White, in his *The Making of the President, 1960,* verified that "the Negro vote and the Kennedy-King calls . . . were the critical ingredient in the outcome of the election" (qtd. in Branch 377).[1] The joke about Kennedy's choosing King's first and middle names for his own son suggests that it was no secret to many northern Kennedy supporters that he owed a debt of appreciation for the votes of blacks in his election.

During Kennedy's presidency, O'Connor claims to be the "conservative in the family," which suggests that the status quo was her preference: "I take several Catlic [*sic*] papers which are always rapping about racial justice. Actually *I* am the conservative in this family. Strictly a Kennedy conservative. I like the way that man is running the country" (*HB* 499). O'Connor makes this statement on November 19, 1962, a full seven months before Kennedy will make his first significant speech on civil rights; that won't happen until June 11, 1963. He responds to the April-May atrocities of Birmingham—Bull Connor's hosing of the Negroes in Kelly-Ingram Park, the arrest and incarceration of both King and children on the very night that Medgar Evers is assassinated. Kennedy made those calls to King's wife in the fervor of his own presidential fever, but once elected he was slow indeed to act aggressively on matters of civil rights.

Ralph Wood and Sarah Gordon have wrestled with the troubling and complicated use of racist language in O'Connor's private letters to Maryat Lee.[2] Gordon extends her discussion more fully into the civil rights movement in her *Flannery O'Connor: The Obedient Imagination,* pointing out, in addition to O'Connor's often barbed exchanges with Lee, the lack of O'Connor's acknowledgment of or perhaps even knowledge about such things as the limited integration of the public library in Milledgeville (238); the work of Lillian Smith in her publication *South Today;* and Smith's pro-integration talk with white girls in her camp in the mountains of North Georgia, especially as depicted in her collection of essays *Killers of the Dream* (237); and the work of *the Atlanta Constitution's* Ralph McGill in support of the efforts of the civil rights movement (237). As Julie Armstrong points out in her "Blinded by Whiteness: Revisiting Flannery O'Connor and Race," O'Connor's "fiction fits squarely into the pattern of color obsession/ color blindness that Toni Morrison identifies" in her *Playing in the Dark: Whiteness and the Literary Imagination* (83). Armstrong sums it up well: O'Connor's "white privilege did allow her to ignore race in ways that African Americans could not" (82). And as Alice Walker puts it in "Choosing to Stay at Home: Ten Years after the March on Washington," "In the South, Faulkner, Welty, and O'Connor could stay in their paternal homes and write because although their neighbors might think them weird—and in Faulkner's case, trashy—they were spared the added burden of not being able to use a public toilet and did not have to go through intense emotional struggle over where to purchase a hamburger" (164).

John Howard Griffin, the white man who darkened his pigment in order to pass as a black man in the early days of the civil rights movement, recalls his experiment in the now classic *Black Like Me*. While in Georgia, he spent some time in the Trappist monastery in Conyers and met O'Connor's friend William Sessions, who invited Griffin to accompany him to Milledgeville to meet O'Connor. The invitation came from "a young college instructor of English—a born Southerner of great breadth of understanding" (134). Griffin, however, turns down the opportunity because with his limited time he wanted to spend the hours he had in the monastery. O'Connor recounts the visit that did not happen in a letter to Father James McCown on October 28, 1960: "If John Howard Griffin gets to Georgia again, we would be delighted to see him; but not in blackface. I don't in the least blame any of the people who cringed when Griffin sat down beside them. He must have been a pretty horrible-looking object" (*HB* 414). A few years later, she clarifies this nonvisit with Maryat Lee on May 21, 1964: "That about [John Howard] Griffin was that Billy Sessions . . . was at the Monastery when Griffin in his black face hove in & Billy was on his way down & was going to bring Griffin but I forget what happened, they didn't get here. If I had been one of them white ladies Griffin sat down by on the bus, I would have got up PDQ preferring to sit by a genuine Negro" (*HB* 580).

From Griffin's book, we know that everybody with whom he writes about coming into contact assumes he is a black man, and he is treated as such—in both overtly rude and subtly snide ways. Where or how does O'Connor arrive at the decision that Griffin "must have been a pretty horrible-looking object"? In the comment, she strips him of his humanity and reduces him to a thing. Griffin gives no suggestion in his book that anyone believes he is anything other than a "genuine Negro." O'Connor reports in this same letter to Lee that she had read Griffin's other two books and has determined that he was "an interesting man but [she] wouldn't have liked him" (*HB* 580). About James Baldwin, O'Connor taunts Lee; her usual question is, "Would this person be endurable if white?" (May 21, 1964, *HB* 580). Perhaps O'Connor redeems herself in the question, for she indicates a response to others based on a larger frame of reference than skin pigmentation, and in wanting the "genuine," a strong resistance to fraud. Still, Griffin-as-object remains an enigmatic remark.

In all the commentary that scholars have made about O'Connor's silence on the times around her, interviews—with direct questions on the subject—offer perhaps the best way to see O'Connor exposed, to see her reduce the importance of the movement, and to see that, as well read and thoughtful as she was about theological matters, she was almost embarrassingly naive about these events before 1963. Interviewed by students when she read on the campus of the College of St. Teresa in Minnesota in the fall of 1960—after sit-ins had occurred in every major city in the South, in every town where there existed a historically black college or university, and after the founding of SNCC—O'Connor's response to the question, "Why don't Negroes figure more prominently in your stories?" is a mixture of her stock answer and then one of the most curious comments she ever made on the subject: "I don't feel capable of entering the mind of a Negro. In my stories they're seen from the outside" [the familiar reply]; "The Negro in the South is quite isolated; he has to exist by himself" [the astoundingly odd reply]; "In the South segregation is segregation" (*Conversations* 59).

What does O'Connor mean by the statement that "The Negro . . . is . . . isolated"? If she is talking about the Negro as a race, she must mean that the Negro as a race exists in its own world, isolated from the white world. If this is the case, then her world does not need to embrace this race or their activities. However, this makes little sense, because she well knew that the black world entered the white world every day to help them do their work, whereas the white world rarely stepped into the black world to return the assistance. If she is talking about the Negro as an individual, her comment is still puzzling. She might be suggesting that Negroes do not have relationships with each other, which is actually close to the position of Richard Wright in his 1945 *Black Boy:* "Whenever I thought of the essential bleakness of black life in America, I knew that Negroes had never been allowed to catch the full spirit of Western civilization, that they lived somehow in it but not of it" (43). However, Wright writes from the inside. His comments are indicative of his views, which certainly include a picture of life squeezed by an oppressive white culture that has left no room for the black person's development. For O'Connor to say the Negro is isolated is more offensive than innocent; it is presumptuous and insulting. The presumably young student interviewers did not push further in this line of questioning. The Negro was dropped.

Unknown to her at the time, 1963 would be the last full year of Flannery O'Connor's life. She lived it out with trips to Smith College in Massachusetts, Hollins College in Virginia, Notre Dame of Maryland in Baltimore, Troy State in Alabama, the University of Georgia, and Georgetown University in Washington, D.C. (see Sally Fitzgerald's "Chronology," *CW* 1255). The rest of the time she was home in Milledgeville, a bird sanctuary.

Elsewhere in the South, 1963 was *the* watershed year for the civil rights movement: in Birmingham in late April and early May, more than 2,500 students from six to sixteen years of age left their schools to participate in peaceful demonstrations that got them arrested. Many of those demonstrations were staged from the Sixteenth Street Baptist Church; the children were met with high-pressure fire hoses unleashed on them by the Birmingham Fire Department under orders from Bull Connor, commissioner of public safety. Connor is the same one who turned the peaceful demonstrators into fodder for their cause by calling out the German shepherd police dogs, while he patrolled the streets from the secure seat of his white armored tank. Martin Luther King Jr., went to jail in Birmingham and wrote his letter in response to white clergymen who asked him to wait. His response, known today as "Letter from Birmingham Jail," ranks in the top ten of the American essay canon; it is difficult to find a composition reader that does not include his brilliant answer. In mid-June President Kennedy made his first serious intentional civil rights talk on television—in response to the events of Birmingham. Just after midnight, in the early hours of June 12, Medgar Evers was assassinated as he walked toward his front door. In late August, a quarter-million people—more or less—showed up in our nation's capital at the foot of the Lincoln Memorial on the one-hundredth anniversary of the signing of the Emancipation Proclamation. African American citizens and those who supported them came to protest the bounced check, the one sent back, as King tells us, marked insufficient funds. Three weeks later four young black girls died in a church bombing back in Birmingham, the same church that was so much a part of the activity during the spring demonstrations. Finally, two months later, President Kennedy himself was assassinated in Dallas. It was more than a remarkable year; it was an extraordinary year.

From O'Connor's front porch at Andalusia to the Sixteenth Street/ Sixth Avenue crossroads hub of Birmingham activity is about 250 miles, about five hours of 1963 driving time. In the last few years of my own life, I have become increasingly interested in how the parallel segregated worlds of mid-twentieth-century southern life managed to entrap our minds and hearts so effectively, isolating us one from another while at the same time we shared a common soil and if not a neighborhood, a near proximity. I wonder, too, about how big moments in history happen, and we live beside them yet do not respond to them, or do not record our response to them. A case in point: my mother kept a diary for at least the last fifty years of her life—never skipping a day of recording the activities of her domestic schedule. On December 7, 1941, she carefully wrote: "Moved Jacqueline to the front room and took her picture." Jackie is my older sister, who would have been three months old at the time. I looked quickly at the entry for December 8 and found that on this Monday, like on all Mondays of her recorded life, my mother washed our clothes. She never mentioned Pearl Harbor. Remembering this moment in my mother's record of life when I was moving my 2001 desk diary to its proper shelf, I turned to September 11 to see what I had written. I see that it was the first day of our fall term, and I had noted the classes I taught that day. I added sometime in early 2002 what America-changing event had transpired on 9/11 in 2001. I clearly did not want my daughter one day, if she ever looked, to think I was not aware of a world outside my office!

And so I return to Flannery O'Connor and the events of Birmingham. Where was this writer who has occupied so much of the last quarter century of my own life positioning herself—or not—in relation to the dramatic events that put the South in the country's headlines in ever more dramatic ways? Though O'Connor had been silent up to this point in the movement, would I discover here something that would help me to see the possibility of a changing O'Connor? By looking closely at O'Connor's life and the events in Birmingham during six months of 1963, I hope to suggest that these activities, and their haunting images, which she ignored for the most part in the currency of their happening, might well have been a source for later thought. *The Habit of Being* includes fifty-seven letters to friends from April through December 1963. One additional letter appears in the Library of America edition of O'Connor's works. Readers of these letters are familiar with O'Connor's epistolary style: she sinks easily and often into the dialect of the local dweller, she writes of books she is reading—those she has heard about and those she wouldn't mind reading. She writes of local happenings, news of who is coming to her home, and places she is planning to visit. She mocks delightfully, and, when asked, she does not mince her words. In all the letters, the only mention of Birmingham during this time appears in a letter to Charlotte Gafford on April 21, 1963; she responds to news of Madison Jones's having been invited to an arts festival, which she believed is "better endured in a state of coma," by adding these lines: "A lady called me up from Birmingham and asked me to something, maybe it was to the same thing. She seemed profoundly puzzled that I could find it in my heart not to come" (*HB* 514). The letter does not indicate why O'Connor has turned down the invitation. Perhaps the timing and the local events of this Alabama city do not necessitate any further comment, but almost a year earlier O'Connor had written Gafford in June 1962 about the Birmingham Festival of the Arts, which took place in February: "Wild horses could not get me into the air in February—that is a dumb time to have a festival. Local festivals are the worst of all. . . . I have no use for panels or any collection of writers" (*HB* 481). Taken together, these passages remind the reader of O'Connor's dislike of festivals, which could be more important to her than her wanting to keep a respectful distance on Bull Connor's antics.

Correspondence with New Yorker Janet McKane is frequent in these latter months of 1963—fourteen letters of the fifty-eight total. North-South opinions often come into play, and O'Connor's swoop of history reminds us that her eye is focused more on a distant past than on history in the making: "I think you have a sense of place up there, but since it is not connected with a historical defeat, I don't think it touches as deep an emotion . . . [.] It's not simply a matter of present-place, but a matter of the place's continuity and the shared experience of the people who live there" (June 5, 1963, *HB* 523). In another letter to McKane on October 11, 1963, O'Connor mentions the activities of the "local Negroes"—their desire to integrate the library when the library had already been integrated. O'Connor, who from the grammar of the letter suggests that she herself might not have known about the library integration, asserts: "That's the way things have to be done here—completely without publicity. Then there is no trouble" (*HB* 542).

When Ashley Brown sent her a story of Eudora Welty's in the summer of 1963, her comments, Welty's own publishing record, and the events of the summer suggest that the unnamed story must be "Where Is the Voice Coming From?" Told from the point of view of the killer of a thinly disguised Medgar Evers character, the story appeared in *the New Yorker* within three weeks of Evers's death. O'Connor is taken with the story: "Nobody else could have got away with it or made it work but her I think. I want to read it again" (August 13, 1963, *HB* 533). But a few weeks later, O'Connor appears to have a change of heart. In a letter to Betty Hester on September 1, 1963, she agrees with Hester's position: "It's the kind of story that the more you think about it the less satisfactory it gets. What I hate most is its being in the *New Yorker* and all the stupid Yankee liberals smacking their lips over typical life in the dear old dirty Southland. The topical is poison" (*HB* 537). O'Connor's response is not to the death of Medgar Evers but to Welty's story about the death of Medgar Evers—not to the event itself but to the literary response to the event.

Welty wrote this story fast; barely three weeks elapsed between the cold-blooded murder of Evers and the story's appearance in *the New Yorker*. What Welty delivers in the story is one way to understand the mind of a racist, one who would kill quickly without any worry that there would be consequences to pay. The story became part of the mix of information about Evers himself and his killer, Byron De La Beckwith. O'Connor's response is less to the story, perhaps, than to the timing of the story, the perception that people such as the unnamed killer in the story may be seen as "typical" in the "dear old dirty Southland." In the same month, O'Connor said in an interview: "Sometimes you need time between you and the story before you can really see it whole. . . . Distance is always a help" (*Conversations* 107). In Welty's story, there is little distance between the event and the literary response.

O'Connor often makes references to her reading of the Atlanta newspapers. In 1963, *the Atlanta Constitution* was the morning paper, and *the Atlanta Journal* was the evening paper. The papers combined to publish as the *Atlanta Journal and Constitution* on Sundays. From May 2 through May 10, 1963, page one of both papers carried news and pictures of events

transpiring in Birmingham. Headlines in the *Journal* were more conservative—"Birmingham Alert for 200 Marchers" (May 3); "Birmingham Jails
100 More Negroes" (May 5); "Peace Looming in Birmingham" (May 8);
"Hope Surges Anew in Birmingham Talks" (May 10). *Journal* pictures include a police dog lunging at a demonstrator, while a police officer holds on
to both dog and man simultaneously (May 4); the firemen turning the water
on racial demonstrators in Kelly Ingram Park, across the street from the Sixteenth Street Baptist Church (May 5); and the huge white "riot wagon" that
"stands by as Birmingham braces for more Negro demonstrations" (May 8).
In *the Atlanta Constitution,* headlines, usually in larger font and often three
lines in length, are bolder in their portrayals: "700 Are Jailed in Negro Protest at Birmingham" (May 3); "Dogs and Hoses Used to Stall Negro Trek
at Birmingham" (May 4); "Birmingham Jails 1,000 More Negroes" (May
7); "Midtown Birmingham Erupts in Melees, Bringing in Patrol" (May 8);
and finally "Birmingham Accord in Sight, King Says, but Mayor Denies Any
Role" (May 10). Atlanta's newspapers, television nightly news, and pictures
of the horrific Bull Connor tactics circled not only the South but also the
whole globe. There were few places on the planet anyone could go and not
know about Birmingham.

In a 2001 anthology called *America's Best on the Civil Rights Movement: Voices in Our Blood,* editor Jon Meacham chose to include a page
that he cites as being from O'Connor's *Mystery and Manners.* Actually the
words come from an interview in June 1963, after the explosive spring in
Birmingham. O'Connor considers the "uneducated Southern Negro" to be
"a man of very elaborate manners and great formality." She recognizes a
new day, one where "those old manners are obsolete," and what will replace
them, she hopes, "will have to be based on what was best in the old ones—
in their real basis of charity and necessity." Whereas the rest of the country
may believe the "race problem is settled when the Negro has his rights," for
the "Southerner, whether he's white or colored, that's only the beginning."
She sees the South as having to work it out the hard way, day to day, and
she believes that "in many parts of the South these new manners are evolving in a very satisfactory way, but good manners seldom make the papers"
(Meacham 267; *Conversations* 104).

At Andalusia, in the spring of 1963, O'Connor spent some time in the
aid of her mother's "colored friend Annie." In late April, Regina received
word from her friend that she would need a piece on "Woman's Day" to

deliver on Mother's Day at Flag Chapel AME. In a letter to Betty Hester, O'Connor indicates that this is not the first time she has written for Annie on command. Context is lacking for her intriguing comment to Hester on April 27, 1963: "An invite to the White House I could decline, but not this, unsuited as the subject is to my taste" (*HB* 515). Is the comment in reference to her inability to decline her mother's request or the delight she finds in the task itself—thinking about her own words on "Woman's Day" being delivered in an all-black rural church on a holiday that honors mothers, the same holiday, a year earlier, for which she had purchased a donkey named Ernest for her mother?

In published interviews that O'Connor gave in the spring and summer of 1963, it is not surprising that O'Connor was often asked questions about integration. O'Connor's responses appear to be deep introspections on a subject that others, particularly northerners, see as current and relevant, yet for O'Connor issues of integration in the headlines of the news are part of an older story, one she sees based in a code of manners that provide protection and privacy, enough understanding so that the races, which have lived together in one way, may forge yet another kind of understanding. Those ways, she implies, are not stable yet. When Ross Mullins interviewed her for the June 1963 *Jubilee,* a now-defunct periodical for the Catholic Church, he wanted to know if these evolving manners made good novels. Her answer was that manners make good novels only when they become stable (*Conversations* 104); O'Connor realized she was living in a time of transition.

In August, she consented to an interview with *Atlanta Magazine,* but when it was published, she confides in a letter to Hester on September 1, 1963, that she was disturbed how they had changed words around in such a way that she thought she sounded as though she did not make much sense. About newspaper people she made this determination: "I think they are the slobber-heartedest lily-mindedest piously conniving crowd in the modern world" (*HB* 537). Others, it seems, wanted to foist upon her a race agenda, and, quite simply, she did not choose to pick it up. From that interview with *Atlanta Magazine,* she does make good sense in this summation: "The Negro will in the matter of a few years have his constitutional rights and we will all then see that the business of getting along with each other is much the same as it has always been, even though new manners are called for. The fiction writer is interested in individuals, not races; he knows that good and evil are not apportioned along racial lines and when he deals with topical matters, if he is any good, he sees the long run through the short run" (*Conversations* 109).

When Sixteenth Street Baptist exploded on Sunday morning, September 15, the *Constitution* carried a number of pictures in its Monday morning paper, among them one that had to have spoken loudly to O'Connor: it is the very face of something that would have appealed to her vision of the world. It is a picture that brings instantly to mind O'Connor's explanation of what she was doing in her fiction to get her vision across to the contemporary reader: for the blind you draw large and startling figures, and for the deaf you shout. In the foreground of the picture, police officers stand at the scene of the blast with guns held at the ready, one officer's gun crossing another's to form a large X, and in the V-shape of the top part of the X is the stained glass window with Jesus knocking on the door, faceless now, after the bomb. It would seem that O'Connor would have responded to a faceless Jesus, and in time, as we know was not granted to her, perhaps she might have.

In time, those stories and images of the spring and summer of 1963 Birmingham might have become to her stories of individuals, issues of good and evil, and not the poison of the topical. In a May 4, 1963, letter to Sister Mariella Gable, O'Connor was also looking into the quiet, asking for prayers: "I've been writing eighteen years and I've reached the point where I can't do again what I know I can do well, and the larger things that I need to do now, I doubt my capacity for doing" (*HB* 518). Those "larger things" were right outside the door and a few miles down the road. The times were giving her images that were the large and startling variety: children being blown to pieces on Sunday morning in their own church, children going to jail, children being rolled on the ground with the force of water that could rip bark off trees.

Had she lived, O'Connor might have seen anew what her segregated world obscured. She did not live long enough to write the essay that she might have, the one that Eudora Welty did write—"Must the Novelist Crusade?" In 1965, Welty answers the questions that were obviously coming her way: "'All right, Eudora Welty, what are you going to do about it? Sit down there with your mouth shut?' asked a stranger over long distance in one of the midnight calls that I suppose have waked most writers in the South from time to time. It is part of the same question: Are fiction writers on call to be crusaders? For us in the South who are fiction writers, is writing a novel *something we can do about it?"* (804). Welty had acted, though, in her quick response to the killing of Medgar Evers. She lived less than four miles from Evers, a driving distance of eight minutes; his home was only a few road turns away from her own. But Mississippi did not quiet down after Evers died; in fact, it became a focal point of civil rights activity. In this essay, Welty, in part, is responding to the incident that was resolved the month O'Connor died: "To deplore a thing as hideous as the murder of the three civil rights workers demands the quiet in which to absorb it" (809). As Welty writes: "Great fiction shows us not how to conduct our behavior but how to feel. Eventually, it may show us how to face our feelings and face our actions and to have new inklings about what they mean" (808). In time, O'Connor's "larger things" may well have given us more great fiction that teaches us how to feel—had she only lived to see a new stability in a changing South. She never got the time to absorb that faceless Jesus in a church over in Birmingham.

Notes

Originally published as "1963, a Pivotal Year: Flannery O'Connor and the Civil Rights Movement," *Flannery O'Connor Review* 3 (2005): 59–72. Reprinted with the permission of the *Flannery O'Connor Review.*

1. See Taylor Branch's Pulitzer Prize–winning *Parting the Waters,* especially the whole of chapter 9 (351–78), for a detailed account of King's arrest and Kennedy's calls. Officials in the Nixon campaign strongly encouraged Nixon to make a call, but he declined.

2. See Ralph C. Wood, where he states, "Neither politically nor theologically was Flannery O'Connor a racist" (92). See also Sarah Gordon, "Maryat and Julian."

Works Cited

Armstrong, Julie. "Blinded by Whiteness: Revisiting Flannery O'Connor and Race." *Flannery O'Connor Review* 1 (2001–2): 77–86.

Branch, Taylor. *Parting the Waters: America in the King Years, 1954–1963.* New York: Simon, 1988.

Gordon, Sarah. *Flannery O'Connor: The Obedient Imagination.* Athens: U of Georgia P, 2000.

———. "Maryat and Julian and the 'not so bloodless revolution.'" *Flannery O'Connor Bulletin* 21 (1992): 25–36.

Griffin, John Howard. *Black Like Me.* New York: Signet, 1996.

Meacham, Jon, ed. *America's Best on the Civil Rights Movement: Voices in Our Blood.* New York: Random, 2001.

New Catholic Encyclopedia. 15 vols. New York: McGraw-Hill, 1967.

O'Connor, Flannery. *Conversations with Flannery O'Connor.* Edited by Rosemary M. Magee. Jackson: UP of Mississippi, 1987.

———. "Flannery O'Connor: An Interview." By C. Ross Mullins. *Jubilee* 11 (June 1963): 32–35. Rpt. in *Conversations* 103–07.

———. *Flannery O'Connor: Collected Works.* Edited by Sally Fitzgerald. New York: Library of America, 1988.

———. "Galley Proof: *A Good Man Is Hard to Find.*" Interview by Harvey Breit on *Galley Proof,* WRCA-TV, New York, May 1955. Rpt. in *Conversations* 5–10.

———. *The Habit of Being: Letters of Flannery O'Connor.* Edited by Sally Fitzgerald. New York: Farrar, Straus and Giroux, 1979.

———. "An Interview with Flannery O'Connor." *Censer* [College of St. Teresa, Winona, Minn.] (Fall 1960): 28–30. Rpt. in *Conversations* 58–60.

———. "Southern Writers Are Stuck with the South." *Atlanta Magazine* 3 (August 1963): 26, 60, 63. Rpt. in *Conversations* 108–10.

"Offerings Span Various Periods." *Atlanta Constitution and Journal* May 12, 1963: 6-D.

Silver, James W. *Mississippi: The Closed Society.* New York: Harcourt, 1964.

Walker, Alice. "Choosing to Stay at Home: Ten Years after the March on Washington." *In Search of Our Mothers' Gardens: Womanist Prose.* New York: Harcourt, 1983. 158–70.

———. "Beyond the Peacock: The Reconstruction of Flannery O'Connor." *In Search of Our Mothers' Gardens: Womanist Prose.* New York: Harcourt, 1983. 42–59.

Welty, Eudora. "Must the Novelist Crusade?" *Stories, Essays, and Memoir.* New York: Library of America, 1998. 803–14.

———. "Where Is the Voice Coming From?" *New Yorker* July 6, 1963: 24–25.

Wood, Ralph C. "Where Is the Voice Coming From?: Flannery O'Connor on Race." *Flannery O'Connor Bulletin* 22 (1993–94): 90–118.

Wright, Richard. *Black Boy.* 1945. New York: HarperPerennial, 1991.

II

Kindred Spirits

5

Flannery O'Connor, Friedrich von Hügel, and "This Modernist Business"

George Piggford, C.S.C.

In a letter dated July 22, 1956, Flannery O'Connor commented to her new friend and recent Catholic convert William Sessions that "I am getting all this Modernist business more or less straight for the first time."[1] The phrase "this Modernist business" refers to the most significant theological controversy in the Roman Catholic Church in the early twentieth century, what historians commonly term the "modernist crisis."[2] Ideas associated with modernism informed O'Connor's thought and writing, especially through the influence of a central figure of the modernists, Baron Friedrich von Hügel.[3] Michael de la Bedoyère's biography of von Hügel, a book likely sent to O'Connor in June 1956, provided her with her first introduction to this movement.[4] Bedoyère's study provides extensive background on the modernist crisis, investigates in detail the historical events associated with it, and considers the aftermath of the crisis for those involved.[5] O'Connor also read and reviewed for the Atlanta diocesan paper, the *Bulletin,* works by Baron von Hügel himself that express the baron's spiritual and religious views.[6]

Through her encounter with such texts, modernism as a crisis in Catholic theology and ecclesial politics became clear to O'Connor. What Pope

Pius X condemned in 1907 as "the poisonous sum-total of all heresy" provided O'Connor with a reaffirmation of the orthodoxy of her own Catholicism.[7] At the same time, her writing evinces openness to some key insights in von Hügel's works, especially those composed after the crisis had abated. O'Connor valued the Baron's Thomistic reading of nature and grace, his exploration of history in relation to God's involvement in creation, his attention to human freedom, and his emphasis on the costliness of the Christian life. Such insights would resonate with O'Connor's own theological thinking in the period leading up to the *aggiornamento,* or "bringing up-to-date," of the Catholic Church at the Second Vatican Council, held in Rome during the last years of her life.

O'Connor and Theological Modernism

Modernism as a set of historical events and controversial ideas remains a contested field of study, and not everyone agrees that what Pius X defined as "modernism" forms a coherent philosophical and theological position.[8] For writers such as Nicholas Lash, modernism was actually a series of related movements focusing especially on Catholic ecclesiology, Christology, and the historical-critical method in Scripture studies: "There were . . . as many 'Modernisms' as there were 'Modernists.'"[9] What originally connected the members of this group were friendships and acquaintanceships with the key figure of von Hügel, the son of an Austrian aristocrat who divided his time in the late nineteenth and early twentieth centuries between England and the Continent, notably Rome. What ultimately unified the modernists was condemnation by Vatican authorities.[10]

The first real surge of what would become a flood of censure and disapproval occurred in 1902, when Cardinal François-Marie Richard of Paris condemned Alfred Loisy's controversial *L'Évangile et l'église* (published in English as *The Gospel and the Church*).[11] The Cardinal placed this ecclesiological volume on the *Index librorum prohibitorum,* or Index of Forbidden Books, on the grounds that it questioned dogmas of the Catholic Church, including the authority of scripture and tradition, the divinity of Christ, and the conscious institution by the historical Jesus of the episcopacy and papacy.[12] Later that year, Rome affirmed this condemnation and added four other works by Loisy to the Index.[13] The crisis then began in earnest in the spring of 1907, when the prefect of the Sacred Congregation of the Index denounced the Milanese review *Il Rinnovamento* (The renewal) as "notably opposed to Catholic spirit and teaching."[14] Named in that text were a number of those who would later be labeled modernists: "[Antonio] Fogazzaro, [George] Tyrrell, [Friedrich] von Hügel, [Romolo] Murri."[15] That summer the Congregation of the Holy Office issued *Lamentabili sane exitu,* which proscribed sixty-five propositions associated with these figures and others. In the fall of the same year Pius X himself, in *Pascendi dominici gregis,* officially labeled as "modernist" the writing and positions of a disparate and international group of unnamed writers and condemned their work as a consistent field of heretical teachings—indeed, as the text of *Pascendi* contends, "the synthesis of all heresies."[16]

According to Pius X in this encyclical, "agnosticism" is the philosophical foundation of modernism, a term associated with the complex epistemological systems of René Descartes and Immanuel Kant.[17] The primary theological claim of the modernists, according to *Pascendi,* is that "God is immanent in man."[18] If one begins philosophically not with God, as in the Scholastic tradition founded by Thomas Aquinas, but with man, then an array of theological errors results. This array is difficult to characterize simply, but Alfred Loisy, in his *Memoires* of 1931, helpfully tries, and even points out the theological perceptiveness of the encyclical. Loisy asserts that Pius X "constructed a sort of encyclopedic doctrine" out of a number of theological threads. These include "[Maurice] Blondel's and [Lucien] Laberthonnière's philosophy of *immanence,*" which perceives the action of the human will as the mediating force between the natural world and the supernatural. Loisy also mentions "Tyrrell's mystical theology," which was thought by Pius to be infected by "Protestant individualism and illuminism" over and against tradition and Catholic doctrine. Finally, Loisy mentions his own books, "wherein there was above all critical history and an evolutionary conception of the Hebrew religion and Christianity, of Catholic dogma, cult and constitution."[19] These emphases on human subjectivity over God's reality, the solitary individual over the Catholic Church conceived as the Body of Christ, and the evolutionary rather than eternal nature of the Church and its dogmas posed a considerable threat to what was in the early twentieth century the Catholic theological consensus reaffirmed in *Pascendi* and other Vatican pronouncements. These official documents employed the tradition of Scholasticism as their theological foundation, forcefully emphasized the magisterial (or official teaching) authority of the Roman Catholic

Church over individual believers, and understood dogma to be unchanging and inerrant.[20]

The "encyclopedic doctrine" of the modernists carefully outlined in *Pascendi* led in 1910 to Pius's "Oath against Modernism" (included in the papal encyclical *Sacrorum antistitum*). All Catholic clergy and professors of philosophy until 1967 were required to assent to its five theological points: (1) "that God, the origin and end of all things, can be known with certainty by the natural light of reason from the created world"; (2) that "miracles and prophecies [are] the surest signs of the divine origin of the Christian religion"; (3) that "the Church . . . was personally instituted by the real and historical Christ"; (4) that "the doctrine of faith was handed down to us from the apostles through the orthodox Fathers in exactly the same meaning and always in the same purport"; and (5) that "faith is not a blind sentiment of religion welling up from the depths of the subconscious . . . but . . . a genuine assent of the intellect to truth received by hearing from an external source."[21] These attestations were intended to combat the theological errors of (1) Kantian agnosticism, (2) an empiricist disbelief in miracles, (3) the notion that the Church is of human rather than divine institution, (4) the idea of the evolution of dogma associated with Loisy, and (5) liberal Protestantism's emphasis on sentiment or "feeling" as the foundation of faith. Those who took the oath also acquiesced to the entire content of *Pascendi*.

It is essential to emphasize that the theological positions in O'Connor's writings are broadly antimodernist. Among other things that *Pascendi* and the "Oath" provided in the early twentieth century was a reaffirmation of the Thomistic and Scholastic foundation for all Roman Catholic theology. Although she received no formal training as a Thomist, O'Connor in a letter to Elizabeth Hester affirmed (perhaps with some exaggeration) that she read passages from the *Summa theologiae* each night before sleeping.[22] In the same letter is O'Connor's declaration that "I cannot help loving St. Thomas," and the implication here is that this love extended both to the theology of the Angelic Doctor and to his personality. She avows, "I feel I can personally guarantee that St. Thomas loved God." This love is evident to O'Connor from stories about his life, and for her it animates and illuminates his theological writing.[23]

In addition, Jacques Maritain's neo-Thomistic *Art and Scholasticism* was perhaps the single most powerful influence on O'Connor's aesthetics, including her sense of herself as a writer. Rowan Williams in *Grace and*

Necessity and Susan Srigley in *Flannery O'Connor's Sacramental Art* have thoroughly explored the importance of Maritain's "revival of the thought of St. Thomas Aquinas" for O'Connor. From Maritain, O'Connor borrowed her definition of art as "the virtue of the practical intellect" as well as the basic insight that "art is not simply the product of the human imagination; it is also the product of reason." The interplay of reason and imagination in an artist "possessed by love" is foundational to Maritain's aesthetics.[24] As Srigley has pointed out, O'Connor often portrayed intellectual characters negatively in her fiction, including Hulga in the 1955 story "Good Country People," and, to use Srigley's example, Rayber in *The Violent Bear It Away*.[25] Such portrayals do not indicate O'Connor's anti-intellectualism but rather foreground her Thomistic aesthetics.

Hulga, for example, in "Good Country People" emphasizes the rational at the expense of other human faculties and believes that reason is independent from the realm of the supernatural. Hulga refuses to employ the term "love" because, as she says to Manley Pointer, "I'm one of those people who see *through* to nothing."[26] Beneath or behind the physical there is, simply, nothing at all. An implication here is that love is ultimately meaningless and imagination futile. By contrast, O'Connor learned from Maritain that imagination and reason interrelate, and that their complementary action opens the self to the working of "supernature" within nature. This is why, for O'Connor, the author "uses his reason to discover an answering reason in everything he sees." For such an artist, "to be reasonable is to find in the object . . . the spirit which makes it itself."[27] Reason, inspired by love and working together with imagination, provides a crucial connection between the physical world—the object—and the interpenetrating world of the spirit that enlivens and gives meaning to creation.

O'Connor equated her orthodox belief in Catholic dogma with the ability to see the world clearly. In "Catholic Novelists and Their Readers," she asks, "Just how can the novelist be true to time and eternity both, to what he sees and what he believes, to the relative and the absolute?"[28] Her answer focuses on dogma as "an instrument for penetrating reality." She continues, "Christian dogma is about the only thing left in the world that surely guards and respects mystery." "The fiction writer is an observer," she claims, but a writer "cannot be an adequate observer unless he is free from uncertainty about what he sees." For the Catholic writer, it is precisely dogma that provides this liberty because such a one "feels no call to take on the duties of

God or to create a new universe."[29] This position might be counterintuitive for some, but it is at the core of O'Connor's theory of the novelist as a prophetic "realist of distances," a realism rooted in Thomistic metaphysics and the Scholastic aesthetics of Jacques Maritain.[30]

For O'Connor, the Catholic writer "feels no need to apologize for the ways of God to man or to avoid looking at the ways of man to God." Such an artist will resist succumbing to a temptation to "tidy up reality"—a phrase that O'Connor borrowed from Friedrich von Hügel—because "open and free observation is founded on our ultimate faith that the universe is meaningful, as the Church teaches." O'Connor's realism is thus the opposite of what Pius labeled modernist "agnosticism." For O'Connor, as for Pius X, dogma neither intrudes on the world nor limits mystery. Its function is precisely the reverse: to describe the world as it is, as God created it, and to preserve, at all costs, mystery.[31]

Further, and in relation to the second point of Pius's "Oath," O'Connor seemed to be open to the possibility of the miraculous, especially given her trip to Lourdes in 1958. Although she declared to Hester that "I am one of those people who could die for his religion easier than take a bath for it," O'Connor nevertheless did make the journey to that holy site "as a pilgrim," and after some resistance and, admittedly, "with bad grace" entered the pool in turn with the other *malades*.[32] By the end of 1958, O'Connor reported to Hester that "the trip to Lourdes has effected some improvement on my bones. Before we went they told me I would never be off the crutches," but in December she was able to walk without them at home, and her "bones were beginning to recalcify."[33] This positive development had been unexpected. O'Connor's mother, her "Cousin Katie" Semmes (who had insisted on the trip), and other Catholic family and friends encouraged her to consider this change in relation to the multitudinous miracles associated with the Marian apparitions at Lourdes, with the ostensibly healing waters of the shrine and the revered space of its grotto. O'Connor was at least open to, and strongly suspected that she had experienced, the power of the miraculous.

As for the third and fourth points in the "Oath"—the institution of the Church by Christ and the invariability of "the doctrine of the faith"— O'Connor voiced no doubts on those matters and always expressed adherence to the dogmatic teachings of the Catholic Church. "Catholics believe that Christ left the Church with a teaching authority and that this teaching authority is protected by the Holy Ghost," she wrote to Alfred Corn. And to William Sessions: "The Catholic believes any voice he may hear comes from the Devil unless it is in accordance with the teachings of the Church."[34] These statements should not be used, however, to imply that O'Connor was an unthinking Catholic. Indeed, she wrote to Hester in 1955: "Dogma can in no way limit a limitless God. . . . For me dogma is only a gateway to contemplation and is an instrument of freedom and not of restriction. It preserves mystery for the human mind."[35] This claim comports with those that she made when articulating her Maritain-influenced aesthetic, which situates the artist as a "realist of distances" grounded firmly in the articles of the Catholic faith. O'Connor could be critical of Catholic hierarchs and the unreflectively pious, but she accepted and believed in all dogmatic teachings of the Roman Catholic Church.

The fifth element of the "Oath," with its warning against "blind sentiment" as a basis for faith, resonates well with O'Connor's admonition to Sessions in 1956 not to overemphasize the importance of feeling, especially at the expense of imagination and the rational faculty as Thomas Aquinas understood it: "Having been a Protestant, you may have the feeling that you must feel you believe; perhaps feeling belief is not always an illusion but I imagine it is most of the time."[36] O'Connor here is open to the role of feeling in faith, especially Sessions's sensation of "pain" rather than "joy" at receiving his first Communion, but there is in this passage a questioning of the spiritual importance of any unthinking sentiment. O'Connor was consistent on this point, especially in a testy November 1961 letter to Hester, who was baptized a Catholic in 1956 and left the Church in October 1961: "I don't really think it's too important what your feelings are."[37] Feeling separated from imagination and reason can lead easily and quickly to error, including both theological error and, as in the case of Hester's departure from the Catholic Communion, what O'Connor must have viewed as intemperate action.

In her initial response to Hester's departure from the Catholic communion, O'Connor provides in passing a decidedly Scholastic definition of faith, which is "a gift, but the will has a great deal to do with it. The loss of it is basically a failure of appetite, assisted by a sterile intellect."[38] Just as she warned Hester about excessive emotion, so here her claim is that the intellect, divorced from other qualities of the human mind, can become "sterile" in the sense both of being cleansed from any admixture of the other elements of the self, and of being unable to procreate or reproduce. The "appetite"—another Thomistic category—cannot rely solely on the rational faculty, understood as separate and independent from other elements of the self. O'Connor learned from Maritain that reason needs to be open to the imagination, and to love. Nevertheless, O'Connor's formulation here echoes Aquinas's rather cold characterization of faith in the *Summa:* "Faith, being a habit, should be defined by its proper act in relation to its proper object. Now the act of faith is to believe . . . which is an act of the intellect determinate to one object of the will's command. Hence an act of faith is related both to the object of the will, i.e. to the good and the end, and to the object of the intellect, i.e. to the true."[39] Retaining faith involves will and intellect for both O'Connor and Aquinas; for O'Connor losing faith consists of a "failure" of the appetite and an intellect that is "sterile."

Aquinas's definition of faith in the *Summa* certainly comes across as highly intellectual and rational. It is important, however, to recall that for Aquinas "intellect" is never rationality divorced from other elements of the self, including the appetite (which comprises our natural and supernatural inclinations) and the will (which provides our impetus to happiness).[40] In the same letter to Hester in which she puts forward a Thomistic definition of faith, O'Connor also emphasizes Aquinas's point that faith is a habit: "Faith comes and goes. It rises and falls like the tides of an invisible ocean."[41] In light of all this, it is plain that O'Connor was Thomistic in her vocabulary and in her theological thinking about subjects such as faith. She was also profoundly influenced by Jacques Maritain's neo-Thomistic aesthetics, with its emphasis on rationality and imagination grounded in Christian love. Finally, O'Connor offered occasional warnings, as does *Pascendi,* against any feeling or sentiment that is "blind," that shuts its eyes to rationality.

Given her declarations of unbending orthodoxy and her thoroughgoing reliance on Scholastic philosophy and aesthetics, it seems odd that O'Connor numbered von Hügel, who was closely associated with the theological modernists, among "the great modern Catholic scholars" (here she uses "modern" largely in its more generic sense of "recent"). As noted above, it was von Hügel who taught O'Connor that it is the artist's responsibility not to "tidy up reality" but to be open to it as it is, and as it is clarified by Church dogma. Resisting the impulse to warp reality—both physical and spiritual—requires what von Hügel calls a "contentment in dimness," an acceptance of and humility about the limitations of human vision in con-

trast to the divine. This theological anthropology, along with her reading of
Aquinas and Maritain, explicitly informed O'Connor's talk "Catholic Novelists and Their Readers" and her articulation that a Catholic fiction writer is
what she terms a "realist."[42]

Two Modernisms

If O'Connor had no substantial objections to the five central points of Pius's
"Oath against Modernism," how then do we reconcile her enthusiasm for a
Catholic scholar who, at least in the early twentieth century, wrote essays
and letters that questioned basic Catholic teaching, and who was mentioned
by name in the 1907 Vatican condemnation of *Il Rinnovamento*? In "Official Authority and Christian Religion" (1904), von Hügel echoes Loisy's
L'Évangile et l'église by stating baldly that the "Church . . . in all but the
very rudimentary, Synoptic-Gospel form . . . is not the direct and deliberate creation of our Blessed Lord Himself."[43] Here von Hügel crosses into
territory that contradicts the later "Oath against Modernism." O'Connor
perceptively wrote in the margin of her own copy of Baron von Hügel's *Essays and Addresses*, "see Newman / Development / of Christian / Doctrine;
/ Guitton."[44] This note alludes to John Henry Newman's 1845 *An Essay on
the Development of Christian Doctrine*, which O'Connor acquired for her
personal library in 1949, and which provided Loisy with a foundation for
his arguments about the evolution of dogma.[45] Jean Guitton, who is also
mentioned, wrote a study of Newman, and O'Connor later reviewed Guitton's *The Modernity of St. Augustine*.[46]

    The relationship between Newman's notion of the development of doc-
trine and Loisy's theory of the evolution of dogma is complex, but its crux is
the distinction between "doctrine," a teaching of the Church that is official,
and "dogma," a teaching that is both official and definitive, and therefore
infallible.[47] Newman himself assumes that his reader is aware of this pivotal
distinction: what he terms the "dogmatic truth" is unwavering, and "religious error" about such transhistorical truth is in itself "immoral" and "to
be dreaded."[48] Dogma provides the starting point for theological reflection.
Doctrine, in contrast, is built upon dogma and develops as ideas develop.
Throughout history, as the Church and its members continue to ponder
original revealed truth, new articulations emerge in an organic way that encompass these reflections.[49]

Loisy, in contrast, asserts that dogmatic truth itself evolves. Rather than beginning with inerrant and revealed truth, as in Newman, Loisy holds that development begins in a "real" moment of change, which is then reflected on (the "theological moment") and eventually becomes a new teaching (the "dogmatic moment"). Loisy characterizes the latter as "the formal consecration of the development by a decision of the church."[50] This departure from Newman is both subtle and extreme. Dogmatic truth is not at the beginning of the process of development for Loisy. It is the end product. Baron von Hügel, in his turn, was influenced by Loisy; he argues in 1904 against the Catholic dogma that Jesus Christ intentionally founded what would in time come to be called the Roman Catholic Church.[51] Certainly O'Connor was well read enough to know that the baron was entering highly problematic theological territory by questioning this basic ecclesiological point. O'Connor's marginal comment provides a brief genealogy of this complex issue by linking von Hügel's assertion back to Newman's essay.

In light of her resolute stance on Catholic orthodoxy, O'Connor would almost certainly have been unaccepting of modernist heterodoxy. This included Loisy's and von Hügel's repudiation of the "teaching authority," as she put it, that Jesus of Nazareth instituted in the Catholic Church. Nevertheless, she expressed sincere admiration for the work of von Hügel more generally. Given this apparent contradiction, it is important to sort out O'Connor's enthusiasm for the writings of von Hügel, an author intimately connected with the modernist heresy, from her rejection of the main theological points associated with the modernists. To do so, it is helpful to make a distinction, as the baron and O'Connor both do, between two kinds of modernism.

In a 1918 letter to Maude Petre, von Hügel writes about these modernisms: "The one is a permanent, never quite finished, always sooner or later, more or less, rebeginning set of attempts to express the old Faith and its permanent truths and helps—to interpret it according to what appears the best and the most abiding elements in the philosophy and the scholarship and science of the later and latest times." In contrast, the other 'Modernism' is a strictly circumscribed affair, one that is really over and done."[52] The second modernism is the heresy denounced by Pius X about a decade before von Hügel wrote this letter, from which the baron separates himself by emphasizing the passage of time ("over and done") and a differing attitude ("strictly circumscribed"). The first modernism is articulated very much in the spirit of John Henry Newman on the development of doctrine. Baron von Hügel reaffirms in this private correspondence his allegiance to the Church and its dogmatic teachings (the "old Faith and its permanent truths") while being open to the development of doctrine. Truth needs to find new expression as thinking develops and theological reflection continues.

It is significant that the von Hügel writing this 1918 letter is not only older than the von Hügel who wrote "Official Authority and Christian Religion," but he is also a chastened man. He had witnessed his friends' excommunication—and, in the case of Tyrrell, an untimely death—and seen himself mentioned in the denunciation of *Il Rinnovamento*, all in relation to an association with the modernist heresy. After the events of the first decade of the twentieth century, and especially after the death of Tyrrell in 1909, von Hügel was disinclined to question official Church positions. Indeed, the baron's biographer, Bedoyère, blames Loisy and Tyrrell for heterodox positions taken on by von Hügel, whose "nervous intensity and concentration . . . played an important part in his unbalanced and inconsistent pursuit . . . of paths impossible wholly to reconcile with his deep Catholic faith."[53] It is reasonable to posit that the younger von Hügel was naïve about the political implications of these friends' positions, with which he associated himself around the turn of the twentieth century. After 1909, the baron expressed openness to a broader notion of modernism, one that would comport with dogmatic orthodoxy, and one that O'Connor found to be congenial in her passionate engagement with the baron's work, as well as in her interest in the less controversial writing of John Henry Newman.

In her own copy of Bedoyère's biography, O'Connor underlined a passage where the biographer makes the point that von Hügel, in his "Official Authority and Christian Religion," "came perilously near confounding the inevitable one-sidedness of official authority, together with the errors and faults of human officials, with the rights of authority itself in Catholic doctrine and tradition."[54] This underlining suggests that O'Connor comprehended the implications of this passage for the modernist controversy, and that if von Hügel in the 1904 essay did not actually cross a line into heterodoxy, he at least came "perilously close." It is perhaps for this reason that when O'Connor associated herself with the epithet "modern," she did so with utmost care, even in a private letter to Hester: "When I call myself a Catholic with a modern consciousness I don't mean what might be implied in the phrase 'modern Catholic,' which doesn't make sense. If you're a Catholic you believe what the Church teaches and the climate makes no difference. What I mean is that I am conscious in a general way of the world's present historical position."[55] The distinction that she makes in this 1955 missive is similar to that made by von Hügel in 1918, in that O'Connor takes pains to separate the notion of a modern sensibility, or "consciousness," from the "circumscribed affair" that was condemned as heresy. She embraces an orthodox modernism, eschewing the version condemned in *Pascendi* and associated with the modernist crisis.

O'Connor and the Post-Crisis von Hügel

It was not von Hügel the theological modernist who attracted O'Connor, although she was well aware of the theologically questionable elements in his thought after her reading of his early essays and of Bedoyère. Rather, her primary fascination was with the von Hügel who, after the crisis passed, chose to focus on mysticism, spirituality, and Christian philosophy in ways that carefully avoided the heterodoxies forcefully rejected in *Pascendi* and the "Oath against Modernism." Like von Hügel, O'Connor was fascinated by Catholic (and other) mystics, including John of the Cross, Teresa of Avila, Catherine of Siena, and Catherine of Genoa, the subject of von Hügel's *The Mystical Element of Religion* (1908). O'Connor worked through that monumental text in 1959, and it doubtless had a strong influence on her thinking about purgation and St. Catherine.[56]

It is the spiritual and mystical von Hügel whose *Letters to a Niece* O'Connor recommends as a "welcome relief" to "the reader who has been fed (sufficiently) on Irish piety"—that is, the popular, post-Famine piety that was devotional, unthinking, and exuberant.[57] O'Connor contrasts this with von Hügel's "intelligent piety."[58] Within this correspondence we find von Hügel as a loving uncle and a spiritual director, as when he writes to his niece Gwendolyn Greene in 1919: "You see, *I* see, how deep, and dear, how precious, is your faith in God and in Christ. I thank God for them."[59] This is von Hügel at his most affectionate and personal, and most insistent on the value of basic Christian faith. This is a von Hügel who has put aside the theological controversies of the first decade of the twentieth century in order to be a chronicler of mysticism and a spiritual mentor.

In addition to the *Letters to a Niece*, the baron's "immanently [*sic*] readable" *Essays and Addresses on the Philosophy of Religion* provided

O'Connor with her most sustained and unmediated engagement with von Hügel's spiritual and religious thought.[60] O'Connor marked this two-volume text with dozens of underlinings, marginal linings, checks, and comments. The vast majority of the essays and speeches, nineteen of the twenty-one total, were written after the condemnation of modernism in *Pascendi,* and after von Hügel's 1908 pivot, in *The Mystical Element in Religion,* to the (theologically safer) topics of mysticism and spirituality. In von Hügel's religious philosophy, as it is outlined in the *Essays and Addresses,* one finds a range of contentions that resonate with, and helped to shape, O'Connor's writing. Baron von Hügel is neither a simple nor a perfectly consistent thinker; nevertheless, as Arthur Kinney has indicated, O'Connor tended to mark a related set of points in her own copy of the *Essays.*[61]

We might summarize these points as follows: first, the fundamentally Thomistic insight that grace, or supernature, is always encountered in and through nature; second, the tension between the historic and the superhistoric or divine; third, the maxim, related to St. Augustine of Hippo, that authentic liberty is freedom not to sin, and that evil is an active force that seeks to constrain human choice; and last, the inevitable cost of the spiritual life as a response to supernatural grace.[62] For von Hügel, it is often the most apparently "very simple" and "unbrilliant" who are likely to respond in a positive way to the promptings of grace through nature, to believe, to be truly free, and to experience the cost of the spiritual life. Worldly sophistication is not helpful for the universal human vocation to the mystical life, a point the baron makes plain in his letters to his niece.[63]

For von Hügel, the unschooled are most attuned to the dynamism behind the nature/supernature distinction because they are less distracted with ideas, and more in touch with the physical world. He claims that "religion . . . deals primarily, not with ideas, but with realities," and it is God who is the ultimate reality.[64] Nature is what it is because of its imperfect reality, which produces an "ethic of the honorable citizen." In contrast, supernature is perfectly real and represents a higher ethic, "of our Lord's beatitudes, of St. Paul's great eulogy of love, of Augustine and Monica at the window in Ostia."[65] Here, von Hügel references the Jesus of the Sermon on the Mount who praises, among others, "the poor in spirit," "those who mourn," and "those who suffer persecution."[66] He points also to Paul's First Letter to the Corinthians, where the apostle extols the most important virtues, the "greatest" being, of course, "charity," or love.[67] Finally, von Hügel calls attention to the scene from the *Confessions* of Augustine of Hippo in which Augustine and his mother, Monica, are afforded, following a spiritual climb "by degrees," a vision of "that eternal wisdom which abideth over all."[68] In each of these cases, serving God and others moves one to greater freedom at a higher cost; disciples inevitably endure suffering before entering the "kingdom of heaven."[69] For Paul, attitudes associated with being a child must be given up to attain Christian love, and Augustine and Monica's vision of eternal wisdom comes to them in the sorrowful context of Monica's impending death.

Ruby Turpin and her vision in the final scene of "Revelation" (1964) might qualify as an instance of this supernatural ethic.[70] In that story a young woman, Mary Grace, whom Ruby encounters in a doctor's waiting room, shocks the older woman out of her spiritual complacency by throwing a book at her, throttling her, and eventually accusing her of being an "old wart hog" from "hell."[71] This moment of shock and suffering leads Ruby to question her identity before God, and she eventually has an experience similar to Augustine and Monica's in Ostia, in that she is arguably afforded a vision of the divine reality at the core of the physical world. "Absorbing some abysmal life-giving knowledge," a "visionary light" settles in Ruby's eyes, and she sees "a vast horde of souls rumbling towards heaven" with "even their virtues burned away."[72] She peers through nature and is afforded a passing view of what is most real—the spiritual usually hidden within or behind the physical.

This divine entanglement with the world includes "knowledge"; that is, it is rational in the Thomistic sense, and in relation to Aquinas's philosophy of natural law. This is so because "God is as truly the God of Nature as the God of Grace. . . . Religion cannot be the leaven in the flour, the salt of the earth, the light of the world, unless itself is truly leaven, salt, and light; neither can it be these things, unless there exist, unless it acknowledges, respects, and comes into close contact with flour and earth and world."[73] One inevitably thinks here of O'Connor's maxim that if you are speaking "to the hard of hearing you shout."[74] It is in a sense the deafness that produces the shout, or at least the need. The "shout" for Ruby Turpin takes the form of Mary Grace's book as projectile, her strangulating hands, and her cruel words to Ruby about being an "old wart hog." And Mary Grace is by no means the only eccentric personality in O'Connor's literary oeuvre. It is important to note here that O'Connor's idiots, lunatics, antisocial personalities, amputees, nymphomaniacs, and hermaphrodites are her equivalent of "flour and earth and world," and she populates her fiction with them. A comment she made in the margins of von Hügel's essay "The Essentials of Catholicism" provides a rationale. Where von Hügel contends that in the Renaissance "science and scholarship [were] turned chiefly earthward, [providing] a wider patience and welcome for things new and strange," O'Connor comments: "the natural now no longer new & strange."[75] This indicates that the natural world—and its inadequacy without God—needs fresh attention.

For von Hügel, supernature must have revealed itself in nature in specific ways and at specific times; he calls this revelation of God in nature "happenedness." This term represents the idea that the Christian religion needs to have a basis in historical events. O'Connor underlined "happenedness" multiple times in her copy of the *Essays*. Despite her resistance to elements of von Hügel's earlier arguments about Church history, O'Connor's incarnational theology accorded well with von Hügel's point that "a certain nucleus of historical happenedness is absolutely essential for the Christian faith." Such faith is "revelational, evidential, factual—this also within the range of sense-and-spirit, and can never become a system of pure ideas or of entirely extra historical realities."[76] This is why when the Misfit in "A Good Man Is Hard to Find" (1953) says, "Jesus was the only One that ever raised the dead . . . [and] He thrown everything off balance," he is correct both theologically and historically.[77] Further, he makes this statement in unconscious preparation for what John Desmond calls "the mysterious intrusion of grace in nature [that] is centered upon transfiguring action within the concrete image."[78] This transfiguration occurs in what O'Connor terms the "soul" of the grandmother, whom the Misfit will in due time kill. A grace-filled change can occur even at the moment of death, for the very reason that the historical Christ "thrown everything off balance."[79]

Von Hügel understands the historical Jesus as supernature breaking into nature, and he also conceives this as a purely free act, a freedom that underlies Jesus's sinlessness. In a 1917 essay, von Hügel notes: "St. Augustine teaches admirably that 'it is a great liberty to be able not to sin; it is the greatest liberty to be unable to sin'—a doctrine which must be true, or God is not free. Thus we can say that even the possibility of sin arises, not from the freedom of the will as such, but, on the contrary, from the imperfection of the freedom."[80] O'Connor underlined this passage about authentic freedom being the freedom not to sin, and it is not clear that she had engaged with Augustine's position before she read about it in von Hügel.

Certainly, some characters in O'Connor's stories are mired in their lack of freedom, perhaps no one more powerfully than Thomas in "The Comforts of Home" (1960), who, the more he gives in to the diabolical voice that he associates with his father, the less control he has over his own actions. This ends in a scene that suggests demonic possession and his obedience to a voice that tells him to fire the gun that will kill his mother. "'Fire!' the old man yelled." The "old man" here is the imagined voice of Thomas's deceased father. The narrator reports simply: "Thomas fired. The blast was like a sound meant to bring an end to evil in the world."[81] The problem for Thomas is that he has become the agent of evil, personified as "the ghost of Thomas's father."[82] His mother, in contrast, is able to see through Sarah Hamm's nymphomania to a deeper goodness, and this perceptiveness results in acts of positive charity. What Thomas perceives to be his mother's "excess of virtue" is von Hügel's heroic charity in action.[83] Thomas's inability to perceive Sarah's lovableness—both a failure of vision and a rejection of authentic freedom—brings about the story's matricidal tragedy.

A fourth element in von Hügel's religious philosophy, one to which O'Connor often alluded in her letters, is "cost." She underlined this word multiple times in her edition of the *Essays*.[84] For von Hügel, the "the work and call" of the Catholic Church is "the awakening, the training, the bringing into full life and fruitfulness the Supernatural Life."[85] This work of awakening believers (and even nonbelievers) to the reality of the supernatural is, however, by no means easy. That is why for von Hügel "this outlook, if the truer, is, where at all complete, by far the costlier—costlier even as a theory, still more in practical execution."[86] The costliness of the Christian vocation represents for the baron an instance of heroic undertaking that requires actions based on a careful perceptiveness of the natural world, and insight into the supernatural found within and beyond nature. Being a Christian requires therefore "heroic Truthfulness" to what one sees, and as von Hügel first put it in "Christianity and the Supernatural," an avoidance of the temptation to "tidy up reality."[87] One major cost is seeing; the second is freely acting according to such prophetic sight.

Such action involves "suffering as a whole person," as John Desmond phrases it, and is nothing less than an imitation of Christ.[88] In order to live this way, "a creative love is . . . required . . . to render lovable in the future what at present repels love."[89] This is just what the most heroic characters in O'Connor's writing do: they love even the unlovable. Such heroic charity appears to be at work in the grandmother's ability to view the Misfit as "one of my own children" at the very end of "A Good Man Is Hard to Find," despite the fact that her actual family members have just been murdered at his command.[90] Heroic charity is a motivating factor for Asbury's mother in her care for her "poor sick boy" in "The Enduring Chill" (1958), despite the putative "insufferableness," for him, of life with her.[91] And it is present in the love Thomas's mother shows Sarah Hamm in "The Comforts of Home," as we have seen above. All of these charitable actions entail cost, whether it is the life of the person offering "creative love," as in "A Good Man" and "Comforts," or the option of doing anything else but care for the beloved other, as in "The Enduring Chill." The implication at the end of that story is that Asbury will long suffer from the undulant fever that he has foolishly, if accidentally, inflicted on himself, while his mother will continue patiently to take care of him.

Painful encounters through nature with God/supernature—encounters that are experiential, real, and partake of the eternal—provide an important element of Christianity for von Hügel. This is also true for O'Connor. Although the Austrian aristocrat and the hillbilly Thomist in some instances diverged in their relation to the institutional Church and its dogma, their spiritual and religious thought has much in common, especially in the time after von Hügel's theologically modernist phase. O'Connor would likely agree with a comment that the baron once made to his niece about possessing a "contentment in dimness": "Religion is dim—in the religious temper there should be great simplicity."[92] This simple and humble attitude represents for von Hügel the proper approach to supernatural mystery.

It appears that the overly sophisticated Asbury has at least begun to learn this lesson by the conclusion of "The Enduring Chill." While his mother has cared for him, a visiting priest, Father Finn, seeks to school the young man in the basics of the Catholicism found in the *Baltimore Catechism*. Frustrated with Asbury's lack of knowledge, Finn insists that Asbury pray for God to send the "Holy Ghost" to "fill [his] soul" with faith. Asbury replies, "The Holy Ghost is the last thing I'm looking for!"[93] However, when it becomes clear to Asbury that his life will likely be lengthy and painful, his sight is purified, faith comes to him, and he is able to peer into a costly and demanding supernature: "The last film of illusion was torn as if by a whirl-

wind from his eyes. He saw that he would live the rest of his days in purifying terror." As the sun descends behind him, so too does a "fierce bird,"
formed of a stain on his bedroom wall, with ice in its beak.[94] This figure
heralds the beginning of his dark night, the dimness of suffering in which
Asbury might find the simplicity of faith. The hope put forward at the end of
this story is for a hard-won faith and a contentment in dimness upon which
both O'Connor and von Hügel would concur.

As the twentieth century unfolded and moved toward what O'Connor
called the "new synthesis" of the Second Vatican Council, the second kind
of modernism that von Hügel outlined to Maud Petre became institutional-
ized.[95] His reference to the need in the Church for "always sooner or later,
more or less, rebeginning" resonates profoundly with the call of John XXIII
in 1959 for *aggiornamento,* a "bringing up to date." In the intervening half
century between the modernist crisis and Flannery O'Connor's efforts to get
this "business . . . straight," an understandable chilling effect had occurred
especially in European Catholic theological writing. Eventually, however,
in the years leading up to the Second Vatican Council, Catholic writers influenced by insights of the modernists would begin to publish. A prominent
example is Pierre Teilhard de Chardin, who, despite the controversial nature of some of his writing, was perceived by O'Connor (in a 1960 review
of his work) as "a great Christian [whose] vision of Christ was as real as his
love for science."[96] O'Connor also held in high regard the ecclesiological
work of Yves Congar, whose "admirable" book *The Wide World, My Parish*
explores questions about the "salvation of 'the others'"—those outside the
Roman communion.[97] Finally, O'Connor expressed a particular enthusiasm
for Romano Guardini. In *Freedom, Grace, and Destiny,* which O'Connor
reviewed in 1961, Guardini perceptively warns against "a chemically pure
faith," which represents a reactive and "austere" orthodoxy.[98] All of these
writers owed some of their insights to figures such as von Hügel who were
associated with theological modernism and who became intertwined with
Roman Catholic ecclesial politics in the early twentieth century.

O'Connor herself did not hold to the notion of the "political infallibility" of the Church, and indeed the Church does not offer its believers a
promise of political inerrancy.[99] O'Connor insisted on a mature, thoughtful, and critical faith on many occasions, including in a letter to Louise
Abbot: "A faith that just accepts is a child's faith and is alright for children, but eventually you have to grow religiously as every other way, though

some never do. What people don't realize is how much religion costs. They think faith is a big electric blanket, when of course it is the cross."[100] Such a declaration relies heavily on the vocabulary and thought of von Hügel, who taught O'Connor that the most useful spiritual experiences—in which one encounters what von Hügel terms "supernature"—are inevitably costly. Faith is simple in that it consists of a choice, or assent, to believe what Christ and the Church teach; it is difficult in that this assent must be daily renewed in the context of suffering and life's uncertainties. The "Modernist business" that von Hügel's life and writing helped O'Connor to get "straight" would both intrigue O'Connor and help her to hone and refine her own sense of orthodoxy. She was wary of the heterodox implications of some of von Hügel's writing but at the same time open to the spiritual and religious insights that comported with the Catholic theological tradition: the relation between nature and grace, the historical "happenedness" of the life of Jesus of Nazareth, the Augustinian definition of authentic freedom, and the costliness of the spiritual life. These resonated with her own experience and struggles with living a life of faith. In this way O'Connor achieved a remarkable balance: unapologetic orthodoxy combined with openness to spiritual and religious insights from whatever source, including the "modernist" Baron von Hügel.

Notes

1. Flannery O'Connor, *The Habit of Being: Letters of Flannery O'Connor*, ed. Sally Fitzgerald (New York: Farrar, Straus and Giroux 1979), 166.

2. The study that provides the most thorough examination of this period in the history of the Roman Catholic Church is Marvin R. O'Connell, *Critics on Trial: An Introduction to the Catholic Modernist Crisis* (Washington, D.C.: Catholic University of America Press, 1994). See esp. 342, for the equivocal nature of the terms "modernism" and modernists" in the Catholic context.

3. Despite the profound influence of von Hügel on O'Connor, only a few critics have noted this connection. Exceptions include Kathleen Feeley, who calls von Hügel one of O'Connor's "kindred intellectual spirits"; Ralph Wood, who notes the baron's influence on O'Connor as one of the "chief interpreters of Christian mysticism"; and William Sessions, who argues that O'Connor tried spiritually to "reach" Elizabeth Hester by recommending works by von Hügel (see Kathleen Feeley, *Flannery O'Connor: Voice of the Peacock* [New York: Fordham University Press, 1972], 10; Ralph C. Wood, *Flannery O'Connor and the Christ-Haunt-*

ed South [Grand Rapids, Mich.: Eerdmans, 2004], 26; and William A. Sessions, "'Then I Discovered the Germans': O'Connor's Encounter with Guardini and German Thinkers of the Interwar Period," in *Flannery O'Connor's Radical Reality,* ed. Jan Nordby Gretlund and Karl-Heinz Westarp [Columbia: University of South Carolina Press, 2006], 65). I have been able to find just one article-length assessment of von Hügel's relevance for O'Connor, written by her friend the Episcopal priest William M. Kirkland: "Baron von Hügel and Flannery O'Connor," *Flannery O'Connor Bulletin* 18 (1989): 28–42. Kirkland points out the tension between Catholic orthodoxy and von Hügel's Christian humanism, the centrality of the distinction between nature and supernature for O'Connor and von Hügel, and the importance to O'Connor of "cost" in von Hügel (see esp. 37–39). Some problems include contentions that Catholicism involves a renouncing of the world and a denial of the body, that O'Connor's writing is dualistic, and that there is no social justice element in von Hügel. This last is especially questionable given the baron's emphasis on heroic charity, so important, as we will see, to O'Connor (see ibid., 34, 35, 41).

4. It was sent by her friend Elizabeth Hester, another religious searcher then contemplating entrance into the Catholic Church (see O'Connor, *Letters,* 161).

5. Michael de la Bedoyère, *The Life of Baron von Hügel* (New York: Scribner's, 1951).

6. Notably *Letters to a Niece,* ed. Gwendolyn Greene (Chicago: Henry Regnery, 1955); and *Essays and Addresses on the Philosophy of Religion,* 2 vols. (London: J. M. Dent, 1924, 1926); O'Connor's June 23, 1956, review of von Hügel's *Letters of Baron Friedrich von Hügel to a Niece* and her August 31, 1957, review of his *Essays and Addresses on the Philosophy of Religion,* vols. 1 and 2, can be found in *The Presence of Grace and Other Book Reviews,* comp. Leo J. Zuber, ed. Carter W. Martin (Athens: University of Georgia Press, 1983), 21–22, 41–42.

7. Qtd. in Michele Ranchetti, *The Catholic Modernists: A Study of the Religious Reform Movement, 1864–1907,* trans. Isabel Quigley (New York: Oxford University Press, 1969), 216.

8. Pius X, "*Pascendi dominici gregis:* Encyclical of Pope Pius X on the Doctrines of the Modernists," 1907. In *The Holy See,* www.vatican.va/holy_father/pius_x/encyclicals/documents/hf_p-x_enc_19070908_pascendi-dominici-gregis_en.html.

9. Nicholas Lash, "Modernism, Aggiornamento, and the Night Battle," in *Bishops and Writers: Aspects of the Evolution of Modern English Catholicism,* ed. Adrian Hastings (Wheathampstead, U.K.: Anthony Clarke, 1977), 52–53.

10. According to Lawrence F. Barmann, "The Modernist as Mystic," in *CatholicismContendingwithModernity:RomanCatholicModernismandAnti-Modernism in Historical Context,* ed. Darrell Jodock (Cambridge: Cambridge University

Press, 2000), 215, "The papal encyclical *Pascendi dominici gregis* not only created *Modernism;* it also created *Modernists*—as though dozens of individuals of varying ages and experiences and of a multitude of nationalities, with different degrees of religious development and levels of intellectual culture, thought with one mind and pursued one goal."

11. Alfred Loisy, *L'Évangile et l'église* (Paris: Picard, 1902)

12. Lawrence F. Barmann, *Baron Friedrich von Hügel and the Modernist Crisis in England* (Cambridge: Cambridge University Press, 1972), 100.

13. On the details of this Vatican action, see ibid., 109; and Michael de la Bedoyère, *The Life of Baron von Hügel* (New York: Scribner's, 1951), 156, 157.

14. Qtd. in Barmann, *Baron,* 183 (originally published in English in the *Tablet* 109, no. 3496 [1907]: 734).

15. Ibid., 184.

16. Pius X, *Pascendi,* ¶39.

17. Ibid., ¶6; O'Connell, *Critics on Trial,* 343. On Flannery O'Connor's own resistance to Cartesian philosophy during her undergraduate years at Georgia State College for Women, see Brad Gooch, *Flannery: A Life of Flannery O'Connor* (New York: Little, Brown, 2009), 113–14.

18. Pius X, *Pascendi,* ¶19.

19. Qtd. in O'Connell, *Critics on Trial,* 343.

20. These positions were grounded in three significant official pronouncements from the late nineteenth century: (1) the First Vatican Council constitution *Pastor aeternus* (1870), which outlines the doctrines of papal primacy over the entire Church and the infallibility of the pope when speaking *ex cathedra,* as successor of St. Peter; (2) Pope Leo XIII's 1873 encyclical letter *Providentissimus deus,* which stressed that it is the role of the Catholic Church, not an individual reader of Scripture, to interpret sacred texts and to pronounce doctrines embedded in the interpretative traditions of the Church; and (3) the same pope's 1879 *Aeterni partris,* which calls for a return to Scholastic philosophy in seminary training and official Catholic teaching. On the relevance of these for the modernist crisis, see O'Connell, *Critics on Trial,* 27, 34–35, 133–49, respectively.

21. Pius X, "The Oath against Modernism," in *Sacrorum antistitum,* 1910, *Papal Encyclicals Online,* www.papalencyclicals.net/Pius10/p10moath.htm.

22. O'Connor, *Habit of Being,* 93.

23. Ibid., 94.

24. Rowan Williams, *Grace and Necessity: Reflections on Art and Love* (London: Continuum, 2005), 6; Flannery O'Connor, *Mystery and Manners: Occasional Prose,* ed. Sally Fitzgerald and Robert Fitzgerald (New York: Farrar, Straus and Giroux, 1970), 81; Jacques Maritain, *Art and Scholasticism with Other Essays,* trans. J. F. Scanlan (New York: Scribner's Sons, 1930), 55.

25. On Rayber's notion of autonomous rationality, see Susan Srigley, *Flannery O'Connor's Sacramental Art* (Notre Dame, Ind.: University of Notre Dame Press, 2004), 32.

26. Flannery O'Connor, *The Complete Stories*, ed. Robert Giroux (New York: Farrar, Straus and Giroux, 1971), 287.

27. O'Connor, *Mystery and Manners*, 82. O'Connor and Baron von Hügel would agree on the relation between the physical and the mysterious, nature and supernature, as Srigley notes (*Flannery*, 23); see also below.

28. O'Connor, *Mystery and Manners*, 177.

29. Ibid., 178.

30. Ibid., 179.

31. Ibid., 178; Baron Friedrich von Hügel, *Essays and Addresses on the Philosophy of Religion* (1924; London: J. M. Dent, 1926), 1:128.

32. O'Connor, *Habit of Being*, 258, 280.

33. Ibid., 306.

34. Ibid., 489, 410.

35. Ibid., 92.

36. Ibid., 164.

37. Ibid., 454.

38. Ibid., 452.

39. Thomas Aquinas, *Summa Theologica* (II.II, Q. 4, a. 1), trans. Fathers of the English Dominican Province (Raleigh, N.C.: Hayes Barton, 1947), 2164.

40. Ibid., 408–10 (I, Q. 80, a. 1 and 2) and 413 (I, Q. 82, a. 1).

41. O'Connor, *Habit of Being*, 452.

42. O'Connor, *Mystery and Manners*, 176, 177; Baron Friedrich von Hügel, *Letters from Baron Friedrich von Hugel to a Niece*, ed. Gwendolyn Greene (Chicago: Henry Regnery, 1955), 23.

43. Hügel, *Essays*, 2:18.

44. In Arthur F. Kinney, *Flannery O'Connor's Library: Resources of Being* (Athens: University of Georgia Press, 1985), 31, the punctuation between "Doctrine" and "Guitton" is a colon. My inspection of O'Connor's copy of this volume suggests a semicolon. The slashes in this quotation indicate the line breaks in O'Connor's marginal commentary.

45. In *L'Evangile et l'église* and elsewhere.

46. For confirmation of O'Connor's 1949 acquisition of Newman's *An Essay on the Development of Christian Doctrine*, see Kinney, *O'Connor's Library*, 44. For the complete text of O'Connor's 1960 review of Guitton's *The Modernity of St. Augustine*, see Flannery O'Connor, *The Presence of Grace and Other Book Reviews*, ed. Carter W. Martin (Athens: University of Georgia Press, 1983), 90–91.

47. On the distinction between these terms, see, for example, *The HarperCol-*

lins *Encyclopedia of Catholicism*, ed. Richard P. McBrien (San Francisco: Harper, 1995), 424, 425.

48. John Henry Newman, *An Essay on the Development of Christian Doctrine* (London: Longmans, Green, 1920), 357.

49. Two examples of such developments are Catholic teachings on the reality of purgatory and on devotions to the Blessed Virgin Mary (see Newman, *Essay on the Development*, 315, 388).

50. Qtd. in O'Connell, *Critics on Trial*, 180.

51. See Hügel, *Essays*, 2:18.

52. Baron Friedrich von Hügel, *The Letters of Baron Friedrich von Hügel and Maude D. Petre*, ed. James J. Kelly (Leuven: Peeters, 2003), 173.

53. Bedoyère, *Life of Baron von Hügel*, 86–87.

54. Ibid., 164–65. O'Connor's underlining is noted by Kinney, *O'Connor's Library*, 14.

55. O'Connor, *Habit of Being*, 103.

56. Confirmation that O'Connor read von Hügel's *Mystical Element* can be found in two letters: (1) the complete version of a May 16, 1959, letter to Elizabeth Hester included in Flannery O'Connor, *Collected Works*, ed. Sally Fitzgerald (New York: Library of America, 1988), 1097; and (2) a letter to Brainard and Frances Cheney dated June 14, 1959, in which O'Connor remarks: "Volume II of the Baron goes back to you tomorrow. I wouldn't say I had been too enlightened by reading it once, but I can always say I've done it" (Flannery O'Connor, *The Correspondence of Flannery O'Connor and the Brainard Cheneys*, ed. C. Ralph Stephens [Jackson: University Press of Mississippi, 1986], 86).

57. O'Connor, *Presence of Grace*, 22. The classic study of the origins of Irish piety in the nineteenth-century Potato Famine is Emmet Larkin, "The Devotional Revolution in Ireland, 1850–1875," *American Historical Review* 57 (1972): esp. 625, 644.

58. O'Connor, *Presence of Grace*, 21.

59. Hügel, *Letters to Niece*, 84.

60. O'Connor, *Presence of Grace*, 42. O'Connor also knew by 1957 von Hügel's argument in *Some Notes on the Petrine Claims*, and she marked up von Hügel's introduction to Ernst Troeltsch's *Christian Thought* (see O'Connor, *Letters*, 165–66, 236; and, on O'Connor's marking up of von Hügel's introduction to Troeltsch, Kinney, *O'Connor's Library*, 64).

61. See Kinney, *O'Connor's Library*, 29–32.

62. All of these points are informed by the baron's *Mystical Element* and its division of religion into three basic features: the historical and institutional, the intellectual, and the mystical. These are helpfully described across von Hügel's oeuvre in Ellen M. Leonard, *Creative Tension: The Spiritual Legacy of Friedrich*

von Hügel (Scranton, Pa.: University of Scranton Press, 1997), 137–51. Leonard points out that for von Hügel "all three must always be present in a mature religious person" (60); see also Hügel, *The Mystical Element of Religion as Studied in Saint Catherine of Genoa and Her Friends* (London: J. M. Dent, 2008), esp. 1:53–55. I am grateful to Michael Bruner, who highlighted this tripartite formulation in his "'Whom Have I in Heaven but Thee?' Friedrich and Flannery in Conversation," presented on October 7, 2011, at "Revelation and Convergence: Flannery O'Connor among the Philosophers and Theologians," a conference hosted by Loyola University Chicago.

63. Hügel, *Letters to Niece*, 159.

64. Hügel, *Essays*, 1:48.

65. Ibid., 1:96.

66. Bible, *The New Testament of Our Lord and Saviour Jesus Christ*, trans. R. A. Knox. (New York: Sheed and Ward 1948), Matthew 5:3, 5, 10. O'Connor acquired this translation of the New Testament in 1949 (see Kinney, *O'Connor's Library*, 43).

67. 1 Corinthians 13:13.

68. Augustine, *Confessions*, trans. Edward B. Pusey (New York: Modern Library, 1999), 187, 188. O'Connor was familiar with the Pusey translation in its 1952 edition (see Kinney, *O'Connor's Library*, 73).

69. Matthew 5:3.

70. O'Connor, *Complete Stories*, 508.

71. Ibid., 500.

72. Ibid., 508.

73. Hügel, *Essays*, 2:45. Although this quotation is taken from an address, "The Place and Function of the Historical Element in Religion," that von Hügel first gave in 1905 as the modernist crisis was worsening, the comments comport well with the baron's later writing.

74. O'Connor, *Mystery and Manners*, 34.

75. Hügel, *Essays*, 1:146; O'Connor qtd. in Kinney, *O'Connor's Library*, 30.

76. Hügel, *Essays*, 1:268–69.

77. O'Connor, *Complete Stories*, 132.

78. John F. Desmond, *Risen Sons: Flannery O'Connor's Vision of History* (Athens: University of Georgia Press, 1987), 45.

79. O'Connor, *Mystery and Manners*, 113; O'Connor, *Complete Stories*, 132. Relevant here as well is the spiritually transformative death of Mrs. May in "Greenleaf" (see ibid., 333–34).

80. Hügel, *Essays*, 1:221.

81. O'Connor, *Complete Stories*, 403.

82. Ibid., 394.

83. Ibid., 385.

84. O'Connor was also carefully attentive to versions of the word "cost" in von Hügel's *Letters to a Niece*. She underlined these on pages 64, 65, 83, 149, and 240 of that work.

85. Hügel, *Essays*, 1:283.

86. Ibid., 1:283–84. Paul Elie has discerned that "in the lonely place that sickness was," O'Connor looked for spiritual "companions" familiar with suffering, in O'Connor's case from lupus and in the baron's from deafness; for both "cost" is often associated with sickness and disability. On this, see Paul Elie, *The Life You Save May Be Your Own: An American Pilgrimage* (New York: Farrar, Straus and Giroux, 2003), 282; on the baron's deafness, see also Barmann, *Baron*, 123.

87. Hügel, *Essays*, 1:288.

88. John Desmond, "Flannery O'Connor and the Displaced Sacrament," in *Inside the Church of Flannery O'Connor: Sacrament, Sacramental, and the Sacred in Her Fiction*, ed. Joanne Halleran McMullen and Jon Parrish Peede (Macon, Ga.: Mercer University Press, 2007), 70.

89. Hügel, *Essays*, 2:160.

90. O'Connor, *Complete Stories*, 132.

91. Ibid., 377, 370.

92. Hügel, *Letters to Niece*, 23.

93. O'Connor, *Complete Stories*, 376.

94. Ibid., 382.

95. O'Connor, *Habit of Being*, 306.

96. O'Connor, *Presence of Grace*, 86.

97. Ibid., 159.

98. Qtd. ibid., 123.

99. O'Connor, *Habit of Being*, 347.

100. Ibid., 353.

6

Flannery O'Connor, the Left-Wing Mystic, and the German Jew

A Reconsideration

Sarah Gordon

In a letter to Betty Hester ("A") in August 1955, Flannery O'Connor wrote: "I am wondering if you have read Simone Weil. I never have and doubt if I would understand her if I did; but from what I have read about her, I think she must have been a very great person. She and Edith Stein are the two twentieth-century women who interest me most" (*HB* 93). The tone of O'Connor's statement here is typical of the voice we recognize throughout the letters, intellectually self-effacing and candid. At the time of the writing of this letter, it might be surprising that the thirty-year-old O'Connor, living in Milledgeville far from centers of intense intellectual activity, should have interested herself in these two European Jews. Nevertheless, we discover in her letters that O'Connor found both women compelling indeed, from the 1950s to the end of her life. O'Connor's private library at Georgia College contains Weil's *Waiting for God*, Stein's *The Science of the Cross*, and *The Writings of Edith Stein*. Furthermore, we learn from the letters that O'Connor's reading in Weil was not limited to *Waiting for God*. Evidently, O'Connor found in Simone Weil and Edith Stein the extremes of religious response that were most compelling to her; for Flannery O'Connor, belief in God is the central and most compelling matter in human life. Simone

Weil, the brilliant Jewish-born intellectual, was much drawn to Catholicism though never able to accept the Church; Edith Stein, on the other hand, forsook her strong Jewish heritage to become a Catholic, then a Carmelite nun. She was finally gassed to death at Auschwitz.

O'Connor's interest in Weil began as early as 1952, when she acknowledged in a letter to Sally and Robert Fitzgerald that, although she had not read Weil, she had read "a good bit about her" (*HB* 40). From then on, every reference to Weil occurs in a letter to Hester, to whom in 1955 O'Connor wrote, "I have thought of Simone Weil in connection with you almost from the first" (*HB* 93). Obviously Hester's initially intense interest in Catholicism seemed to O'Connor to reflect Weil's passionate lifelong attraction to the Church. In this same letter to Hester, O'Connor continues: "I will never have the experience of the convert, or of the one who fails to be converted [Weil?], or even in all probability of the formidable sinner; but your effort not to be seduced by the Church moves me greatly. God permits it for some reason though it is the devil's great work of hallucination" (*HB* 93). Weil's resistance to the "seduction" of the Church deeply moved the creator of Hazel Motes and Francis Marion Tarwater. In Weil, O'Connor undoubtedly found what Leslie Fiedler called "a life which touches the remote mysteries of the Divine Encounter" (vii), a life which, in spite of itself, finally experienced mystical revelation. As Fiedler notes (and O'Connor agrees), few "would be capable of emulating the terrible purity of her life" (vii), for "no 'friend of God' in all history had moved more unwillingly toward the mystic encounter" (viii).

Born in Paris in 1909, Simone Weil was one of two children of Dr. Bernard and Selma Weil, prominent intellectuals who had years before abandoned their Jewish heritage and become agnostics. After a childhood spent following her father's army transfers in World War I, Weil passed her baccalauréat examinations in 1925; from 1925 to 1928 she studied with the philosopher Alain (Emile August Chartier). Having passed—with a first place—the entrance examinations for the École Normale Supérieure, Weil received her agrégation diploma in 1931 and took her first teaching post. From then until her death in 1943, Weil was active on behalf of the underprivileged and the working class, to the extent that she took leaves of absence from teaching in the 1930s to work alongside the poor—as a factory and farm laborer. She picketed with the unemployed; in France she was known as a "Trotskyite" and sometimes called the "Red Virgin." Her intent was "to deny herself what the most unfortunate were able to enjoy[, having refused] at the age of five . . . to eat sugar as long as the soldiers at the front were not able to get it." (Fiedler xv). In 1936 her strong political convictions led her to join the Loyalists in the Spanish Civil War. However, in only a few weeks she was forced to leave the front because of a serious accidental burn.

Throughout these years and in spite of her Marxist sympathies, Weil was increasingly drawn to Catholicism, or more correctly, to the life and teachings of Christ, in whose passion she saw the reality of the suffering of the poor, the outcast, the disenfranchised. Indeed, her notebooks and letters testify to the compelling power of Christ in her life, though she feared the tendency toward abstraction and the urge for power and the selfishness she found in the Roman Catholic Church. To her beloved Father Perrin, her priest-confidant, Weil argued out the question of baptism: Would she lose her intellectual freedom in entering the Church? Did Catholicism have in it too much of those "great beasts" Israel and Rome? Did Christianity deny the beauty of the world? Did excommunication make of the Church an instrument of exclusion? (Fiedler xxvi)

In the end she remained unbaptized, waiting "for an express command from God" (xxvi). As Robert Coles observes: "She was a radical Christian of the beggar and outcast variety. . . . She distrusted success in any form, fearing an avalanche of eager, gullible 'conversions.' She looked anxiously for God's signals, meaning encouragement along the tough and wretched way of daily adherence to a strong faith. . . . Above all, she feared the smothering hug of accommodation" (125–26).

In 1937 Weil spent two days at Assisi, where, in the twelfth-century Romanesque chapel of Santa Maria degli Angeli where St. Francis had prayed, she experienced the urge to pray, writing, "Something stronger than I compelled me for the first time to go down on my knees" (Petrément 307). Yet Weil's growing absorption in Christ's passion still did not lead her into the Church. "Simone Weil remained on the threshold of the Church," Fiedler notes, "crouching there for the love of all of us who are not inside, all the heretics, the secular dreamers, the prophesiers in strange tongues" (xxvi). Indeed, Weil admitted, "I have sometimes told myself that if only there were a notice on church doors forbidding entry to anyone with an income above a certain figure, and that a low one, I would be converted at once"(Petrément 333). Thus the title of Weil's best-known work, *Waiting for God*, is emblematic of her life. Even after her mystical experience at the Benedictine abbey of Solesmes, where she experienced "the Passion of Christ . . . entering my being once and for all" (Coles xxiii), Weil remained the outsider.

Until the late 1930s Simone Weil had been a pacifist, but, observing Hitler's rise to power and foreseeing the cataclysm to come, she renounced pacifism. After a trip to New York with her parents and two weeks in a refugee camp in Casablanca, she journeyed to London, obsessed with the idea of joining the French Resistance headquartered in that city. In 1943 she began work with the Free French organization; *The Need for Roots*, her last work, was part of her reports for this group. Always in frail health in spite of (or because of) her radical activities that often involved physical struggle, Weil was diagnosed with tuberculosis. After the diagnosis, however, she refused to eat, arguing that she could not think of eating when she thought of the French people starving; moreover, she insisted that her own food be sent to French prisoners of war (Petrément 536). Her death—on August 22, 1943—was ruled a suicide. The statement on the death certificate ended with this sentence: "The deceased did kill and slay herself by refusing to eat whilst the balance of her mind was disturbed." Simone Petrément, Weil's biographer, notes, "This is the formula ordinarily used in such cases, since suicide is prohibited by English law" (537).

Fiedler notes that the questions of "eating or not eating" were paramount throughout Weil's life (xxx) and that for Weil there are two kinds of eating: "the 'eating' of beauty and the beloved here below, which is a grievous error . . . and the miraculous eating in Heaven, where one consumes and is consumed by his God" (xxxi). In Weil's view, Fiedler contends, "here below we must be content to be eternally hungry; indeed, we must welcome hunger, for it is the sole proof we have of the reality of God, who is the only sustenance that can satisfy us, but one which is 'absent' in the created world" (xxxi).[1] Eating and feeding are also important themes in O'Connor's work. We remember especially the insatiable hunger of Francis Marion Tarwater in O'Connor's 1960 novel *The Violent Bear It Away*, a hunger assuaged only by Tarwater's vision, at the novel's conclusion, of the feeding of the multitude on the mountainside:

> Everywhere, he saw dim figures seated on the slope and as he gazed he saw that from a single basket the throng was being fed. His eyes searched the crowd for a long time as if he could not find the one he

was looking for. Then he saw him. The old man [his vehemently faithful great-uncle] was lowering himself to the ground. When he was down and his bulk had settled, he leaned forward, his face turned toward the basket, impatiently following its progress toward him. The boy too leaned forward, aware at last of the object of his hunger, aware that it was the same as the old man's and that nothing on earth would fill him. His hunger was so great that he could have eaten all the loaves and fishes after they were multiplied. (*CW* 477–78)

For Flannery O'Connor, as for Simone Weil, this is the eternal hunger that will never be satisfied on this earth. Young Tarwater, initially seeking to destroy his great-uncle's stringent spiritual teaching by declaring himself not hungry, has betrayed himself earlier when Rayber caught him eyeing secretly and greedily the sweets in a bakery window. Yet Tarwater's hunger cannot be satisfied with the real food of this world; it can be satisfied only by the miracle of God's sustenance, the bread of life. That both Weil and O'Connor deeply understood this heavenly hunger should not be surprising; for both, the "miraculous" eating provided by the sacrifice of Christ is what matters.

Obviously a primary reason for O'Connor's interest in Weil was the drama of Weil's struggle for faith. In September 1955 O'Connor wrote to Hester:

The life of this remarkable woman still intrigues me while much of what she writes, naturally, is ridiculous to me. Her life is almost a perfect blending of the Comic and the Terrible, which two things may be opposite sides of the same coin. In my own experience, everything funny I have written is more terrible than it is funny, or only funny because it is terrible, or only terrible because it is funny. Well[,] Simone Weil's life is the most comical life I have ever read about [*sic*] the most truly tragic and terrible. If I were to live long enough and develop as an artist to the proper extent, I would like to write a comic novel about a woman—and what is more comic and terrible than the angular intellectual proud woman approaching God inch by inch with ground teeth? (*HB* 105–6)

O'Connor's affinity with the "comic" force of Weil's life and her sense that her own fiction reflects that same blend of the "Comic and the Terrible" is clearly analogous to Weil's disgust with and attacks on sentimental piety and safe, superficial belief. Fiedler observes that Weil takes "the step beyond the trivially silly; and the ridiculous pushed far enough, absurdity compounded, becomes something else—the Absurd as a religious category, the madness of the Holy fool beside which the wisdom of the world is revealed as folly" (Fiedler xix). Consider O'Connor's Holy Fools, among them Hazel Motes, Francis Marion Tarwater, O. E. Parker, all of whom suggest the "madness" of the spiritual quest, at least in the eyes of the world. Consider also O'Connor's own "angular intellectual proud woman approaching God inch by inch with ground teeth," Joy/Hulga Hopewell.

By 1955 O'Connor had written "Good Country People," creating the character of Joy/Hulga Hopewell, who bears striking comic resemblance to Simone Weil. Furthermore, recent commentators, building on O'Connor's lead in a letter to Betty Hester, also link the character to O'Connor herself, who had to return home because of illness and in her determination to write was doubtless perceived as ridiculous by her relatives and others. The story serves, in part, as O'Connor's self-indictment: Joy/Hulga is a philosopher whose arid intellectualism seems capable of smiting all those around her— that is, until she encounters Manley Pointer, who steals her wooden leg and her glasses, leaving her in the hayloft to confront her own inadequacy before the reality of evil.

What drew O'Connor to Weil was the courageous intensity of her search for God. For Weil, nothing else mattered. Joy/Hulga, for whom the seduction of the Bible salesman is to be essentially the destruction of what she discerns as his simple faith, wants to believe in his goodness and innocence. Commentators in fact often fail to see the urgency of her desire to be proven wrong in her atheism and scorn for believers. Like many modern nonbelievers, she confuses the intellect with the spirit. Indeed, in her comically pathetic loneliness, she imagines that she will comfort the Bible salesman after he loses his innocence. It is she, of course, who loses her mooring, her "innocent" belief in Nothing. In O'Connor's letter to Hester in 1955 after this story was completed, she links Weil and Hulga, acknowledging that their lives are parallel:

> By saying Simone Weil's life was both comic and terrible, I am not trying to reduce it, but mean to be paying her the highest tribute I can, short of calling her a saint, which I don't believe she was. Possibly I

have a higher opinion of the comic and terrible than you do. To my way
of thinking it includes her great courage and to call her anything less
would be to see her as merely ordinary. She was certainly not ordinary.
. . . But I didn't mean that my heroine would be a hypothetical Miss
Weil. My heroine already is, is Hulga. Miss Weil's existence only parallels what I have in mind, and it strikes me especially hard because I
had it in mind before I knew as much as I do now about Simone Weil.
Hulga in this case would be a projection of myself into this kind of trag-
ic-comic action—presumably only a projection, because if I could not
stop short of it myself, I could not write it. . . . You have to be able to
dominate the existence that you characterize. That is why I write about
people who are more or less primitive. I couldn't dominate a Miss Weil
because she is more intelligent and better than I am but I can project
a Hulga. (*HB* 106)

When in 1956 Hester sent O'Connor the *Notebooks* of Simone Weil (oddly
missing from the O'Connor library housed in the O'Connor Collection at
Georgia College), O'Connor was extremely grateful, noting that "reading
[the notebooks] is a way to try to understand the age." She continues, "There
are books that I can't begin to exhaust, and Simone Weil is a mystery that
should keep us all humble, and I need it more than most." For O'Connor,
Weil was "the example of the religious consciousness without a religion
which maybe sooner or later I will be able to write about" (*HB* 189). In
O'Connor's view, then, Weil has no "religion" without the Church, baptism
into which Weil resisted to the end of her life.

Letters to Hester in 1957, 1962, and 1963 affirm O'Connor's continuing interest in Weil; O'Connor describes her in a 1963 letter as "a trifle monstrous," adding that she is "the kind of monstrosity that interests me" (*HB*
522). Robert Coles points out that the "monstrous" Weil took on "the two
major sources of this century's 'faith,'" science and Catholicism. In Weil's
words, "A Catholic directs his thought secondarily toward the truth, but primarily toward conforming with the Church's doctrine" as a scientist does,
"only in this case there is no established doctrine but a collective opinion
in process of formation." Science, moreover, attempts to assert control, "a
means by which compliance is exacted and disagreement punished" (qtd.
in Coles 148). Both "lend themselves to idolatry" (Coles 148). Weil writes:
"Scientists believe in science in the same way that the majority of Catholics

believe in the Church, namely as Truth crystallized in an infallible collective opinion; they contrive to believe this in spite of the continual changes in theory. In both cases it is through lack of faith in God" (qtd. in Coles 148).

To Weil, "idolatry is in our very nature . . . and when disguised (as scientific pursuit, as politics, as a deep affection for nature, as a religious ritual and practice) is no less what it is, though perhaps more dangerous, potentially, because not even acknowledged" (Coles 149). Joy/Hulga Hopewell is just such an idolater. She has made an idol of intellect.

In one of her most candid letters to Father Perrin, Weil laments that some of the saints of the Church "as a social structure" approved the Crusades and the Inquisition. In powerful, paradoxical words, Weil asserts that this social institution is "the domain of the devil," creating "a false imitation of what is divine, an *ersatz* divinity" (Weil 12). Furthermore, she identifies with ordinary folk who tend to be swept away by the Church as institution, writing that she was "afraid of the Church patriotism existing in Catholic circles":

> In so far as [the Church] is a social structure, it belongs to the Prince of this World. It is because it is an organ for the preservation and transmission of truth that there is an extreme danger for those who, like me, are excessively open to social influences. . . . There is a Catholic circle ready to give an eager welcome to whoever enters it. Well, I do not want to be adopted into a circle, to live among people who say "we" and to be part of an "us," to find I am at home in any human *milieu* whatever it may be. In saying I do not want this, I am expressing myself badly, for I should like it very much; I should find it all delightful. But I feel that it is not permissible for me. I feel that it is necessary and ordained that I should be alone, a stranger and an exile in relation to every human circle without exception. (Weil 12–13)

Although certainly Flannery O'Connor would not have agreed with Weil's indictment of the Church and its authority and did not share her intense social and political identification with the poor and downtrodden, Weil's warnings about the tendency toward abstract thought and the powerful hold of the scientific outlook in the twentieth century most surely found a receptive audience in the Georgia writer. The characters of Rayber (*The Violent Bear It Away*) and Sheppard ("The Lame Shall Enter First"), once

one and the same, demonstrate O'Connor's extreme distrust of the empirical habit of mind. The mysteries of the human person cannot be contained
in a theory, for it is just such theories and human manipulation in the name
of science, the social good, and the welfare of the state that led to the horrors of Hitler's Germany. In O'Connor's "The Displaced Person," in which
the boxcars and concentration camps figure importantly, Mrs. McIntyre
herself exemplifies the horrifying power of abstraction, the ability to reduce
other human beings to their importance in *her* scheme of things. Believing
that the world belongs to the "smart thrifty energetic ones" (*CW* 307), Mrs.
McIntyre eventually colludes in the murder of the displaced person, who,
she discovers, does not—after all—"fit in" (*CW* 316).

Simone Weil, obsessed with the Passion of Christ, would have been
horrified by Mrs. McIntyre. Weil would have wholeheartedly affirmed
O'Connor's unshakeable belief that compassion—even with the best of intentions—removed from "the source of tenderness" could lead only to the
most terrible of outcomes; that is to say, the secular humanist's compassion,
removed from the figure of Christ, is not rooted in Love and will inevitably
have an unpredictable outcome. In the introduction to *A Memoir of Mary
Ann*, O'Connor makes perhaps her most revealing and important statement
about suffering and compassion:

> Ivan Karamazov cannot believe, as long as one child is in torment;
> Camus' hero cannot accept the divinity of Christ, because of the mas-
> sacre of the innocents. In this popular pity, we mark our gain in sensi-
> bility and our loss in vision. If other ages felt less, they saw more, even
> though they saw with the blind, prophetical, unsentimental eye of ac-
> ceptance, which is to say, of faith. In the absence of this faith now, we
> govern by tenderness. It is a tenderness which, long since cut off from
> the person of Christ, is wrapped in theory. When tenderness is de-
> tached from the source of tenderness, its logical outcome is terror. It
> ends in forced-labor camps and in the fumes of the gas chamber. (*CW*
> 830–31)[2]

O'Connor's use of the word "theory" here underscores her distrust of the
abstract and empirical, a skepticism that finds a strong echo in Weil. In
fact, Weil always links compassion to the Passion of Christ, for it is "Christ
[who] taught us that the supernatural love of our neighbor is the exchange

of compassion and gratitude which happens in a flash between two beings" (Weil 90). She adds that "almsgiving when it is not supernatural is like a sort of purchase. It buys the sufferer" (Weil 91). On the contrary, "wherever the afflicted are loved for themselves alone, it is God who is present" (Weil 93).

Mrs. McIntyre sees her workers as cyphers whom she needs to fulfill the needs of the farm; she is never able to see them as human beings. Her view, in a typical O'Connor doubling of character, is strangely and almost comically mirrored in her white employee, Mrs. Shortley. Neither can see the wholeness of others; neither can love nor respect the whole human being. Instead, they see only "Legs where arms should be, foot to face, ear in the palm of hand" (CW 301), that is to say, only parts of the whole. That fact is, of course, emphasized in the scene of Mr. Guizac's murder—which is the appropriate word to describe his death—in which Mrs. McIntyre can see only Mr. Guizac's legs extending from beneath the tractor. Perhaps that partial vision "frees" her to complicity in his murder, for neither she nor Mr. Shortley nor Sulk call out to warn Mr. Guizac of impending danger: "She had felt her eyes and Mr. Shortley's eyes and the Negro's eyes come together in one look that froze them in collusion forever, and she had heard the little noise the Pole made as the tractor wheel broke his backbone" (CW 326). Little noise indeed.

In the background of this O'Connor story is the Holocaust itself, although O'Connor's displaced person is a Polish refugee—not Jewish but, presumably, Catholic. As we are all well aware by now, O'Connor chose not to present contemporary political issues at the center of her fiction, though, as I have previously observed, Mrs. McIntyre's outlook is purely Hitlerian.[3] Presumably, had she the power, Mrs. McIntyre would have all of her workers "thrifty, smart, and energetic"; those who do not meet those criteria are "extra" (CW 316).

Robert Brinkmeyer's The Fourth Ghost, his recent and cogently argued study of white writers of the South and their relationship to European Fascism, oddly enough does not include O'Connor, though it well might have. Drawing a forceful comparison between the American South and its insistence on conformity to what W. J. Cash called "the savage ideal" and the repressive and dangerous mind-set of Fascist Germany, Brinkmeyer reminds us that the South's "essentially feudal social system," especially in the years between 1930 and 1950, was responsible for its "terrible economic privation" (3). Indeed, President Franklin Roosevelt in a 1938 speech in

Gainesville, Georgia, warned, "Things will not come to us in the South if we oppose progress—if we believe in our hearts that the feudal system is the best system" (qtd. in Brinkmeyer 3), and implicitly compared the South's feudal system to Fascism (3–4). The late 1920s and early 1930s in fact saw the increasing conflict between the traditional ideals of the Southern Agrarians and the more obviously progressive and democratic ideals of the nation. Some southern writers resisted association with the Agrarians, disliking to be called regionalists, for regionalism had come to be associated with the fearfully provincial, with backwardness and even anti-intellectualism.

Without the time here to trace Brinkmeyer's persuasive argument, suffice it to say that O'Connor was, to a great extent, caught in the middle. Her mentors, part of the Fugitive/Agrarian movement—Andrew Lytle, John Crowe Ransom, Donald Davidson, Allen Tate, Robert Penn Warren—advocated a return to conservative pastoral ideals and away from the encroachment of the industrial North and its ideas of progress. These men were intellectuals and writers who were often seen (often unfairly, one must note) as regressive, even racist. However, for such writers as William Alexander Percy, who came to the Agrarians' defense, "the Fascist-southern connection was ridiculous and dangerous, and [these writers] felt compelled to defend the traditional South and refute the alleged ties to Fascism," for, they believed, "the traditional South was actually the last line of defense against what seemed like a worldwide trend toward corporate capitalism and its final manifestation, the Fascist state" (Brinkmeyer 23). In any case, the slightest hint of Fascism on either side of the argument was red flag indeed.

Ironically enough, however, clinging to those traditional southern ideals often led many of the Agrarian writers to embrace European culture as the forerunner of the culture of the South and to associate the industrial progress "threatening the South" with "the aggressive expansionism associated with westward exploration and pioneering" moving, in the words of John Crowe Ransom, "with an accelerating speed" (Brinkmeyer 27), that is to say, too fast. As Fugitive poets Allen Tate and Donald Davidson began to formulate ideas for establishing a southern "academy" to counter the progressive ideas of the industrialized North, they sought to *create an intellectual situation interior to the South*" (Tate qtd. in Brinkmeyer 32) so that, in Brinkmeyer's words, "they would control the ideas that defined southern culture" (32). In a strange meeting in 1933 between the Agrarians and Seward Collins, editor of the new conservative journal the *American Re-*

view, neither party was honest with the other: the Agrarians hid their hope of turning the *American Review* into a voice for the Agrarian point of view, and Collins did not reveal his pro-Fascist leanings to the Agrarians, though, as Brinkmeyer concludes, the Agrarians probably "knew more than they later let on" (35).

Several years later, in 1936, the journalist Grace Lumpkin interviewed Seward Collins in the February issue of *Fight Against War and Fascism* with two purposes in mind: "to tease out Collins's Fascist beliefs and to link the Agrarians with those beliefs" (Brinkmeyer 38). As it turned out, in the course of the interview Collins boldly "asserts that he and the Agrarians share the same broad aims, calling for the destruction of factories and the establishment of guilds, together with the institution of an educational system for instructing a select few while keeping the masses ignorant" (Brinkmeyer 38). In the most devastating and scandalous commentary of all, Collins states that he wants "a king and royal court in America," a turning away from "modern conveniences," and the segregation of "Jews and blacks . . . [to] bar them from schooling" (Brinkmeyer 39). Needless to say, Lumpkin sounds the alarm about the Agrarians, condemning them along with Collins: "I do believe after reading a number of books like "God Without Thunder" [Ransom], "I [sic] Take My Stand" [Twelve Southerners], and copies of the *Southern Review and The American Review*, that in those who write for them (some of them very sensitive and fine writers) there is the beginning of a group that is preparing the philosophical and moral shirt-front for Fascism with its top hat from which the rabbits come" (qtd. in Brinkmeyer 39).

It is no wonder that Flannery O'Connor eschewed direct political commentary, no wonder that she, too, fiercely resisted the label "regional" writer. The term must be understood as freighted not simply with its frequent association with "local color" but with a political conservatism that could be seen as only limiting for a writer who sought universality. In her published writing O'Connor seems to have adopted a willful blindness to or ignorance of the political persuasion of many of her mentors. Although O'Connor set her work in recognizable southern settings and was initially called a southern writer (often of the grotesque), O'Connor's aim was to create fiction that transcends the quotidian until "it touches the realm which is the concern of prophets and poets" (CW 818). Such was her stated intent, reiterated repeatedly in the essays and letters.

Before the writer is able to transcend, however, she must be rooted in the particular, in the here and now, a stance O'Connor insisted on in her comments on her own writing. The writer must, first, "descend" into herself and to recognize that a "descent into [herself] will, at the same time, be . . . a descent through the darkness of the familiar into a world where, like the blind man cured in the gospels [she] sees men as if they were trees, but walking" for this is "the beginning of vision" (CW 821). A complex interplay this, between the world's reality and spiritual vision—a feat that, for O'Connor, was essentially successful. Turning the horrible facts of the Holocaust into a parable concerned with the necessity for a compassionate, godly vision of the whole human was part of this tactic, and, in a way, this transformation underscores O'Connor's resistance to the catastrophic "news" of history, her refusal to be political.

And yet. O'Connor lived her college years in the midst of World War II, and that horror could not help informing her work. Indeed, Simone Weil and Edith Stein came to the world's attention in large measure because of actions of each in the foreground of the war.

In the life of Edith Stein we see, oddly enough, the antithesis of the life of Simone Weil. Stein was born in Germany in 1891, the youngest of eleven children in a devout Jewish family. Stein's mother, after the deaths of four of her children and her husband, was forced to rely on her faith in God and her determination to raise the remaining seven children. Edith Stein's prodigious intellect led her to the study of philosophy and, like Simone Weil, to an early teaching career. Stein studied with the phenomenologist Husserl in Göttingen; there she hoped to discover a new spirituality, having lost her Jewish faith sometime earlier.

An apt pupil, Stein became Husserl's assistant at the University of Freiburg in 1917. Central to the philosophy of Husserl was the belief that "philosophy practiced as a rigorous science would lead to the discovery of truth" (Herbstrith 14). Stein counted on this. While working with Husserl, she continued to probe her interest in Christianity, which had been affirmed earlier in Göttingen when she had met two impressive phenomenologists, Max Scheler and Adolf Reinach, who had both converted to Christianity. Later, when Reinach died in World War II, Stein visited Frau Reinach to offer consolation, only to find that little consolation was necessary. Stein wrote: "It was my first encounter with the Cross and the divine power that it bestows on those who carry it. For the first time I was seeing with my very eyes the Church, born from its Redeemer's sufferings, triumphant over the sting of death. That was the moment my unbelief collapsed and Christ shone forth—in the mystery of the Cross" (qtd. in Herbstrith 25).

This experience with Frau Reinach was soon followed by Stein's reading of the *Life* of Teresa of Avila, the pivotal experience in her search for God. In St. Teresa she found what confirmed her own experience: "God is not a God of knowledge, God is love" (Herbstrith 30). From that time forward in the life of Edith Stein, as one friend observed, "The eternal truth shone on the Church, not the university" (Herbstrith 34).

On January 1, 1922, Stein was baptized, taking "Teresa" as her baptismal name. However, even after baptism and confirmation and with the certainty that one day she would consecrate herself to God by entering the Carmelite order, she continued to attend synagogue with her mother, to ease Frau Stein's pain at her conversion. In 1933, when Edith Stein became Teresa Benedicta of the Cross and entered the Carmel at Cologne, Frau Stein reportedly demanded: "Why did you have to get to know him? He was a good man—I'm not saying anything against him. But why did he have to go and make himself God?" (Herbstrith 66). To the end of her life Frau Stein never accepted her daughter's conversion to Catholicism and her religious vocation.

For Edith Stein, however, the decision to join the Carmelites marked the beginning of authentic life. Continuing to write and to engage in philosophical research in this contemplative setting, Stein lived a productive, busy life in the 1930s, though she was not oblivious to the increasing threat of Hitler and anti-Semitism. At the time of her entry into the Carmelite order and just before Easter in 1933, Stein wrote to Pope Pius XI "to request a private audience during which to plead for an encyclical condemning Nazi antisemitism" (Carroll 540). In answer to her letter, she was asked to attend "a purely ceremonial audience with the pope," during which, as she well knew, she would have no opportunity to exchange private words with him. Thus she "declined the invitation, appealing the refusal of her request." In response, she received "a papal blessing through the mail" (Carroll 540–41). When, after Kristallnacht in 1938, she was forced to flee from the convent in Cologne to Echt in Holland, she wrote a friend that she had "often wondered since, whether [my] letter [to the pope] may sometimes have come to mind" (qtd. in Carroll 541).

The remainder of Stein's story is quickly told. In 1938, in a Dutch convent at Echt, Stein offered herself, in one Catholic account, "to the heart of Jesus as a sacrifice of atonement for true peace" (Herbstrith 95). At that time she was working on a study of St. John of the Cross, knowing full well that her time was short. Indeed, her respite was brief, for the Germans soon invaded Holland. On August 2, 1942, all Jewish Catholics, including the members of religious orders, were placed under arrest. A week later, on August 9, Edith Stein, along with her sister Rosa, was gassed to death at Auschwitz.

The life of Edith Stein is today both a conundrum and a controversy. As James Carroll observes in his very important work *Constantine's Sword: The Church and the Jews,* Edith Stein did not adhere to the doctrine of supersessionism, that is to say, the belief once officially held by the Roman Catholic Church that "Judaism has been replaced by Christianity" (538), although Stein is understood to have said in 1939 that "the shadow of the Cross . . . is falling upon my people" for their unbelief. Carroll emphatically states that, finally, Stein "refused to see the Jews as disadvantaged before God" (542), but that she nonetheless continued to be concerned about Jewish "unbelief." Stein's attitude toward her Jewish heritage and toward the Jews appears complicated. In drafting her will some years earlier, she is said "to have offered her life in atonement for Jewish unbelief" (542), a version of her martyrdom that contrasts with the abovementioned Catholic account (see Herbstrith 95ff.). Although the Church had "officially rejected" supersessionism by the time of Stein's canonization in 1998, Jews were "hard put to deflect the suspicion that even now the truth was being defined in exclusively Christian terms (538). Atonement is an expression of the need for and belief in Christian redemption. To be sure, at least one of Stein's relatives rejected this Christian rendering of Stein's life: "*L'Osservatore Romano* honored [Stein] for saying, as the SS took them off, 'Come, we are going for our people.' That 'for' implies not only an expiation, but two thousand years of superiority, which is why the saint's niece, Suzanne Batzdorff, who is Jewish, insists that her aunt's fate was 'to die with her people, not for her people'" (Carroll 542).

However, Stein's death at Auschwitz led her Carmelite sisters to establish a convent there and to place a large cross in a nearby field. In Carroll's judgment, "the cross erected in the adjacent field remains the poignant and outrageous symbol of all that still divides Catholics and Jews" (542). After all, Pope John Paul II "had insisted on honoring [Stein] as a formally declared 'martyr' for the faith" (538), seeking "to place Catholics in the position of having been Nazi victims" and to cause the "Church's expressions of sorrow for the Holocaust [to] have been self-exonerating" (543).

The ensuing controversy has endured until the present time. James Carroll, a former Catholic priest who remains in the Church to this day, is repelled by the actions of the Church and determined to bring them to light. He writes:

> In proclaiming Edith Stein a martyr, the Church emphasized that she was killed as a Catholic, in retaliation for an anti-Nazi protest by Catholic bishops. But to Jewish critics, she died as a Jew, pure and simple. If she was a martyr, weren't all who died with her martyrs as well? And doesn't the very idea of Christian martyrdom, with its opening to the infinite consolations of redemption, do a further violence to Jewish victims for most of whom such consolations would have remained forever unthinkable? In these ways, didn't her canonization amount, as some Jews put it, to a "Christianizing" of the Holocaust—the ultimate supersessionism? Edith Stein, in other words, could be taken by Jews, and was, as the symbol of a theology of resurrection imposed on their dead. The cross at Auschwitz is a sacrilege. (538)

Furthermore, Carroll charges that "the canonization itself was based on a knowing deception at the highest levels of the Catholic Church" and demonstrated the "lengths to which the Church was prepared to go to renegotiate its own history during the Holocaust" (539). To this day the complicated role of the Church and especially that of Pope Pius XII in the Holocaust continues to disturb many Catholics deeply. Carroll has brought this painful story to light as part of what he concludes is the "long history of [the Church's] contempt for Jews" (543).

Flannery O'Connor, of course, likely knew nothing of the controversy and does not comment on the Jewishness of either Stein or Weil. Indeed, in none of O'Connor's work is there a Jewish character or specific reference to the *Jews* suffering the Holocaust. As we have seen, allusions to that historic horror in "The Displaced Person" never mention the word *Jew*, never confront the fact that the vast majority of those annihilated in concentration camps were Jews, not Poles. Some may argue, of course, that O'Connor had absorbed the supersessionist teaching of the Church, presenting the displaced person as a persecuted Catholic, not a Jew. Although certainly not anti-Semitic, the story might be said to sidestep the horrific deaths of 6 million Jews in order to present a Christian—indeed a Catholic—narrative of the Fall.

For better or worse, the Holocaust itself seems to function in this story as "that nightmare over there," and unless the reader stops to understand that it is the Jews who are the object of Hitler's horrifying plan, he or she is likely to miss the story's central metaphor—that, in the microcosm of the macrocosm, Mrs. McIntyre embodies the same racial and cultural superiority that led Hitler to his vision of racial purity—at any cost. On the other hand, one might argue that O'Connor is simply underscoring Mrs. McIntyre's and Mrs. Shortley's provincial ignorance by allowing them to overlook—or even not to know—the real victims of the Holocaust. We remember those other provincials Wendell and Cory in "A Temple of the Holy Ghost" calling the singing of the *Tantum Ergo* "Jew singing," the Latin hymn epitomizing the worst singing they can imagine (CW 202).[4]

It seems clear that what was important to Flannery O'Connor in the lives of both Simone Weil and Edith Stein was not the Holocaust itself but the fervor of their longing for God. Put another way, the Shoah provides the catalyst for their urgent search for Truth. O'Connor appears to use the issue of race in much of her fiction in the same way—as crucial background for her white characters' deep-rooted, monomaniacal urge for God. Hazel Motes, in his defiance of his fundamentalist upbringing, screams, "Jesus is a trick on niggers!" (CW 43). Like Karl Marx, Haze wants to believe that Jesus's message is merely pabulum for the poor and ignorant, who will be encouraged to look to the afterlife for the reparation of their suffering on earth.

Interestingly enough, however, background becomes foreground if one understands O'Connor's criticism of our ignorant and selfish human nature. In understanding the manipulative, uncharitable Mrs. McIntyre and the nihilistic Hazel Motes, each of whom commits murder, we come to understand how that destructive impulse takes root in the human heart. From the evil in the individual to the implications in world history, the microcosm mirrors the macrocosm. Flannery O'Connor is indeed more a political writer than she ever intended to be.

Simone Weil and Edith Stein died within a year of each other. At first glance, what different deaths these seem: Weil, to the end, fiercely waiting for God; Stein, confident in the love of Christ; Weil, the outsider drawn to Christ's passion but unable to yield fully to that gracious gift; Stein, the insider embracing that gift and offering herself as atonement—whether for peace or for the Jews remains unclear. Despite their differences, however, O'Connor was easily able to couple the two in her thinking, for she was always drawn to the extreme tests to which passionate belief or search for belief is put. Although O'Connor read both Weil and Stein (even briefly reviewing two Stein books for the Georgia diocesan Bulletin), it was the lives of each that held her. In another letter to Hester, O'Connor writes, "My interest in both of them [Weil and Stein] comes from what they have done, which overshadows anything they may have written" (*HB* 98). In thinking about the life of the one of the two more obviously compatible with her own belief, Edith Stein, O'Connor wrote, "If she were ever canonized, she will be one saint that I don't think they can sweeten up with holy cards and write a lot of 'pious pap' about" (*HB* 173). O'Connor might be perplexed indeed to consider how the Jewish community has resisted just such "pious pap" in the Church's claiming Stein as one of their own.

In the end, O'Connor's faith and Stein's were equally fierce and unwavering. Each faced mortality with an assurance that the grandmother in "A Good Man Is Hard to Find" could not summon. To readers resembling the grandmother or Ruby Turpin, each of whom needed her moment of grace, O'Connor directed her fiction. Yet O'Connor also kept the nonbelievers and outsiders like Joy/Hulga and Simone Weil near the center of her vision. For all of these, for all of us, she drew her large and startling figures.

Notes

This essay is a rethinking and expansion of "Flannery O'Connor, the Left-Wing Mystic, and the German Jew," *Flannery O'Connor Bulletin* 16 (1987) 43–51.

1. In Weil's life, hunger assumed a necessary political and spiritual importance, from her refusal to eat sugar at age five because the French soldiers had no sugar, to her intense and ongoing hunger for the Eucharist, the feast she denied herself because of her need to remain outside the Church.

2. Walker Percy echoes O'Connor in the words of the "mad" priest, Father Smith, in his novel *The Thanatos Syndrome*.

3. See *Flannery O'Connor: The Obedient Imagination* (Athens: U of Georgia P, 2000), 186–92.

4. This is, I believe, the singular reference to the Jews in all of O'Connor's fiction.

Works Cited

Brinkmeyer, Robert. *The Fourth Ghost: White Southern Writers and European Fascism, 1930–1950*. Baton Rouge: Louisiana State UP, 2009.

Carroll, James. *Constantine's Sword: The Church and the Jews, A History*. Boston: Houghton Mifflin, 2001.

Coles, Robert. *Simone Weil: A Modern Pilgrimage*. Radcliffe Biography Series. Reading, Mass.: Addison-Wesley, 1987.

Fiedler, Leslie. Introduction to Simone Weil, *Waiting for God*. Trans. Emma Craufurd. New York: Harper Perennial, 1973.

Gordon, Sarah. *Flannery O'Connor: The Obedient Imagination*. Athens: U of Georgia P, 2000.

Herbstrith, Waltraud. *Edith Stein: A Biography*. Trans. Bernard Bonowitz, OCSO. Enlarged ed. New York: Harper, 1983.

O'Connor, Flannery. "The Displaced Person" and "A Temple of the Holy Ghost." *Complete Works*. New York: Library of America, 1988. Cited parenthetically as *CW*.

————. *The Habit of Being: Letters of Flannery O'Connor*. Ed. Sally Fitzgerald. New York: Farrar, 1979. Cited parenthetically as *HB*.

————."A Memoir of Mary Ann." *Mystery and Manners: Occasional Prose*. Ed. Sally and Robert Fitzgerald. New York: Farrar, 1969.

Petrément, Simone. *Simone Weil: A Life*. New York: Pantheon, 1976.

Weil, Simone. *Waiting for God*. Trans. Emma Craufurd. New York: Harper Perennial, 1973.

7

Sacramental Suffering

The Friendship of Flannery O'Connor and Elizabeth Hester

Ralph C. Wood

In a letter written to her friends Sally and Robert Fitzgerald only a year before her death, Flannery O'Connor reported on the contribution she had made to an ecumenical symposium on religion and art held at Sweet Briar College in March 1963: "I waded in and gave them a nasty dose of orthodoxy. . . . I told them that when Emerson decided in 1832 that he could no longer celebrate the Lord's supper unless the bread and wine were removed that an important step in the vaporization of religion in America had taken place."[1] O'Connor was temperamentally disinclined to self-assertion on social occasions, saying that her function at her mother's tea parties was to cover the stain on the sofa. Yet O'Connor could not restrain herself when, at a New York dinner party hosted by Robert Lowell and Elizabeth Hardwick in 1949,[2] the ex-Catholic writer Mary McCarthy declared that she found the Eucharist to be a useful symbol for her fiction, though of course she did not believe a word of its hocus-pocus: "Well," declared O'Connor—to what must surely have been the astonishment of the other guests—"if it's a symbol, to hell with it" (*CW* 977). In recounting this celebrated incident six years later, O'Connor made clear that she was not indulging in Catholic triumphalism: "That was all the defense I was capable of but I realize now that this is all I will ever be able to say about [the Eucharist] outside of a story, except that it is the center of existence for me; all the rest of life is expendable" (*CW* 977).

American Christianity has been vaporous, O'Connor discerned, to the extent that it has been unsacramental. It has often lacked Christian substance because it has depended largely on pietism and moralism—on religious feelings and ethical deeds. The result is that salvation is conceived as an almost wholly individual matter apart from life in the sacramental community. And the church itself is usually understood as a voluntary society alongside all the other organizations that meet people's personal and social needs. The triune and incarnate God becomes a virtual hanger-on in such an operation. Perceiving with remarkable acuity what was baleful in antisacramental and antidoctrinal Christianity, O'Connor offered a drastic alternative to it, not only in her fiction but also in her essays and letters. "My stories have been watered and fed by Dogma," she confesses (*CW* 930). As compressed narrative summaries of God's self-identification in Israel and Christ and the Church, the creeds are "vehicles of freedom and not of restriction," O'Connor insisted (*CW* 943). "Christian dogma," she added, "is about the only thing left in the world that surely guards and respects mystery" (*MM* 178). By "mystery" O'Connor does not refer to things that balk the mind and stifle understanding but rather to the ultimate mystery of the Trinity itself. This *mysterion* alone can prompt both ever-greater discovery and ever-greater unknowing. For it entails not chiefly intellectual knowledge so much as sacramental participation in God's own life, which by definition is inexhaustible. For O'Connor, moreover, our saving involvement in the divine life centers on sacramental suffering.

In Elizabeth Hester, Flannery O'Connor found an unlikely companion in such suffering. From the outset of their relationship, Hester had announced herself to be an atheist and had labeled O'Connor a fascist (*CW* 948, 951). This is an unpropitious beginning, to put it mildly, for a friendship so deep and abiding that it would last for eleven years, until O'Connor's death in 1964. It is evident that O'Connor saw something not just humanly but also divinely promising in this unknown woman from Atlanta. Having met with blind consternation in most of her Christian no less than her secular readers, O'Connor rejoiced at discovering an unbeliever who saw that her fiction is God-drenched. "The distance [between us] is 87 miles," O'Connor begins, "but I feel the spiritual distance is shorter." "I would like to know," she concludes, "who this is who understands my stories" (*CW* 942, 943).

Elizabeth Hester could understand Flannery O'Connor's stories not only because she was an intellectually keen and theologically astute correspondent but also because she shared a history of suffering not unlike O'Connor's own. Thus did they become far more than epistolary friends; they became sacramental companions in the Body of Christ. The recently opened letters from O'Connor to Hester reveal the remarkable story of their friendship. Taken as a whole, O'Connor's correspondence may come to rank among the most important collections in Anglophone literature, standing alongside Keats's letters for their enduring value. O'Connor's missives to Hester constitute the heart of the Georgia writer's massive postal exchanges. For it was there that O'Connor articulated her central theological ideas and there that she confessed the sacramental character of her faith. After first recounting the formation of the Hester-O'Connor friendship, this essay aims thus to explore three crucial theological issues that bear on the matter of sacramental suffering as it was took shape in these two remarkable women: its initial result in conversion, its later reversal in apostasy, and its final location in the human body itself.[3]

The blessed tie binding the lives of Elizabeth Hester and Flannery O'Connor was lashed with argument from beginning to end. They truly *engaged* each other in hospitable but vigorous disputation, thus justifying William Blake's celebrated saying, "Opposition is true friendship."[4] It is important to note that, in her very first letter to Hester, O'Connor mentions suffering. It's as if she sensed that Hester's fascist accusation may have stemmed from her own suffering at the hands of the Church:

> I think that the Church is the only thing that is going to make the terrible world we are coming to endurable; the only thing that makes the Church endurable is that it is somehow the body of Christ and that on this we are fed. It seems to be a fact that you have to suffer as much from the Church as for it but if you believe in the divinity of Christ, you have to cherish the world at the same time that you struggle to endure it. (*CW* 942)

In her direct epistolary witness to Elizabeth Hester no less than her indirect literary witness made in fiction, Flannery O'Connor is never an uncritical

Catholic. On the contrary, she stresses her own limits and failings as a Christian: "I am not a mystic and I do not lead a holy life" (*CW* 944). As a natal Catholic rather than a convert, moreover, O'Connor admits that "I am only slowly coming to experience things that I have all along [intellectually] accepted. . . . . Conviction without experience makes for harshness" (*CW* 949). "Smugness is the Great Catholic Sin," she adds later. "I find it in myself and don't dislike it any less" (*CW* 983).

Flannery also assures Betty (as she would soon be calling "Miss Hester") that her own Catholicism is the kind that respects Nietzsche's critique of Christianity. Far from being the final enemy to be overcome, the great atheist was right to link the death of God with the death of humanity. "The moral sense has been bred out of certain sections of the population," O'Connor writes, "like the wings have been bred off certain chickens to produce more white meat on them." The eclipse of God in modern life, eliding all transcendent moral and spiritual reference, leads O'Connor to offer her own tart Nietzschean alteration of Jesus's hard saying that he lived among a brood of vipers: "This is a generation of wingless chickens, which I suppose is what Nietzsche meant when he said God was dead" (*CW* 942).

It was evident to Flannery O'Connor that Elizabeth Hester was no pinioned chicken but a potential friend. Friendship is most often defined as shared devotion to particular goods, even to the point of laying down one's life for one's friends. This sentiment is known to pagans no less than Christians. "For without friends," Aristotle declares in the opening lines of book VIII, the celebrated section on friendship in the *Nicomachean Ethics*, "no one would choose to live, though he had all other goods."[5] Yet there is another word in addition to *philia* that describes the Hester-O'Connor friendship. It is the Latin *fiducia:* abiding trust. For Flannery O'Connor to have introduced herself to Elizabeth Hester as a self-critical Catholic who at least partially agreed with the most renowned modern atheist was for her to confess that she could *trust* Hester in mutual truthfulness. "Truth" is in fact a word that originally connoted trust, fidelity, and steadfastness—as in the wedding vow from Cranmer's Book of Common Prayer: "I plight thee my troth." Hester discerned a similar trustworthiness in O'Connor, if only because those whom one has labeled "fascist" do not often reply with a summons to friendship.[6]

In the *Rhetoric*, Aristotle also specifies the activity entailed by the highest kind of *philia*. The noblest friendship, says Aristotle, wants for one's friend "what you believe to be good things, not for your own sake but for his, and [thus makes one] inclined, so far as you can, to bring these [good] things about."[7] It becomes clear, early in their correspondence, that Flannery regards Betty as such a friend, as one whom she desires to give the highest possible Gift insofar as she can offer it:

> This is a peculiar thing—I have the one-fold one-Shepherd instinct as strong as any, to see somebody I know out of the Church is a grief to me, it's to want him in with great urgency. At the same time, the Church can't be put forward by anybody but God and is apt to do great damage by trying; consequently Catholics may seem very remiss, almost lethargic, about coming forward with the Faith. (Maybe you ain't observed this reticence in me.) I try to be subtle and succeed about as well as the gents in Washington Square. (*HB* 134)[8]

This remarkable confession—that O'Connor wants not only Hester but also her other friends to become Catholics—will strike many readers as strange, even offensive. In our late pluralistic age, almost everyone remains politely silent about such matters, as if one's Christianity were strictly a private affair having no public ramifications, certainly not something that one would encroach upon one's friendships. O'Connor anticipates the coming of privatized Christianity in the figure of Mrs. May in "Greenleaf." Upon discovering the white-trash woman named Mrs. Greenleaf prostrate over her mound of newspaper clippings, calling out for Jesus to heal the world's many miseries, Mrs. May winces: "She thought the word, Jesus, should be kept inside the church building like other words inside the bedroom. She was a good Christian woman with a large respect for religion, though she did not, of course, believe any of it was true" (*CW* 506). Flannery O'Connor was convinced that the Gospel is indeed true, but not in an intellectual sense alone. She regarded Christianity as an irreducibly public and sacramental faith, a communal way of life into which everyone may and must be invited.[9]

Yet the Church's invitation to become friends of God can never bypass the massive counterevidence against faith in God. Even Nietzsche's nihilism remains a temptation, O'Connor confesses. That the cosmos seems both accidental and pointless, having only the moral order that the ruthless and the powerful impose on the weak and the cowardly, was a notion that O'Connor could not dismiss out of hand. The daily bulletins from Hell delivered by the newspapers are sufficient evidence to make one fear, as Hulga Hopewell declares in "Good Country People" and as Hazel Motes preaches in *Wise Blood*, that "There's nothing but Nothing."[10] "In or out of the Church," O'Connor confesses to Hester, nihilism "is the gas you breathe. If I hadn't had the Church to fight it with or to tell me the necessity of fighting it, I would be the stinkingest logical positivist you ever saw right now" (*CW* 949).[11]

The chief temptation of nihilism is to employ force in order to accomplish alleged good. There being no transcendent order by which human desires might be reordered to the Good, we must both devise and enforce our own schemes for human betterment. The twentieth century was the Age of Ashes because it was also the Age of Force. O'Connor did not live to the end of this deadliest epoch in human history—roughly 180 million people killed by violent means, most of them slain by their own governments—but she rightly perceived that hers was a culture of death. In one of her most controversial declarations, she linked a sentimental notion of the good with the fatal use of force: "When tenderness is detached from the source of tenderness, its logical outcome is terror. It ends in forced labor camps and in the fumes of the gas chambers" (*CW* 830–31). This statement helps to account for O'Connor's vigorous response to Hester's claim that, because so many of her characters come to the truth about themselves only in violent confrontations with death, she herself advocates the use of physical force:

> I am wondering why you convict me of believing in the use of force? It must be because you connect the Church with a belief in the use of force; but the Church is a mystical body which cannot, does not, believe in the use of force (in the sense of forcing conscience, denying the rights of conscience, etc.). I know all her hair-raising history, of course, but principle must be separated from policy. Policy and politics generally go contrary to principle. I in principle do not believe in the use of force, but I might well find myself using it, in which case I would have to convict myself of sin. . . .
>
> The only force I believe in is prayer, and it is a force I apply with more doggedness than attention. (*CW* 951, 953)

Although remaining open to "just war" sanctions of the use of outward force, O'Connor makes clear that there can be no ecclesial acts of moral or spiritual compulsion. For her, the Gospel is the ultimate Invitation, and thus a matter always of attraction and persuasion, never of coercion. On the contrary, Flannery urges Betty to enter the Church only if her conversion means an enlargement, not a diminishment, of her freedom: "This is what you are doing and you are right, but do not make your feeling of the voluptuous seductive powers of the Church into a hard shell to protect yourself from her. I suppose it [coming into the Church] is like marriage, that when you get into it, you find that it is the beginning, not the end of the struggle to make love work" (August 6, 1955).[12]

Having exhibited such startling candor and humility in making Christian witness to her friend, O'Connor can hardly be accused of inducing Hester's reception into the Church as if the Body of Christ would resolve all her troubles, whether personal or intellectual. The two of them struggled to set their friendship on a basis that would vigilantly avoid all easy affirmations: on a trust that, though it takes human form, has its origin and sustenance in the God who has entrusted his Son to the world.

O'Connor's letters reveal that she regarded herself as Hester's private spiritual advocate long before she became her public baptismal sponsor. Yet as her unofficial tutor, Flannery did not seek to distinguish among the various theological strands of contemporary Catholicism but rather to get at the gravamen and essence of the Faith that O'Connor herself had both received and embraced. It all centers, I believe, on the nature of conversion and the struggle that it entails. Knowing well that faith is always a divine gift, O'Connor scrupulously avoids any ownership of Hester's entrance into the Church. On the contrary, she expresses astonishment at the news: "To my credit it can be said anyway that I never considered you unbaptized. . . . All voluntary baptisms are a miracle to me and stop my mouth as much as if I had just seen Lazarus walk out of the tomb. I suppose it's because I know that it had to be given me before the age of reason, or I wouldn't have used any reason to find it" (CW 982).

How, then, do such conversions of the recalcitrant human heart and mind occur? Not, O'Connor makes clear, by the promise of reward, as if believing the Gospel meant a redress of previous damages and thus the guarantee of ready benefits. Rather than selfish gain, authentic conversion ordinarily entails painful deprivation and suffering: "Some kind of loss is usually necessary to turn the mind toward faith" (HB 159). The longer one

peruses these letters to Betty Hester, both before and after she called herself a Christian, the more it becomes evident that Christian faith has one
requisite above all others—namely, it is the gift of total self-surrender, an
unstinting willingness to participate in the suffering of Christ for the redemption of the world. It's a privilege that baptismal grace lays on cradle
Christians no less than new believers. Nor is it an act performed once and
for all but rather by way of continual, daily reconversion. It lies at the heart
of Paul's summons to "fill up those things that are *wanting* of the sufferings
of Christ, in my flesh, for his body, which is the church" (Col. 1:24, Douay
Rheims, emphasis added).

In O'Connor's case, such sacramental suffering entailed not only the
acceptance of an early death[13] but also a return to the confining circumstances of rural Georgia life under the care of her mother. She had to surrender all hope of working things out "on the surface"; that is, in the social
dimension of life. That she would never have a husband or a family or a life
that she could call her own became the inexorable fact that she came to accept, though painfully:

> You are wrong that it was long ago I gave up thinking anything could
> be worked out on the surface. I have found it out, like everybody else,
> the hard way and only in the last years as a result of two things, sick-
> ness and success. One of them alone wouldn't have done it for me but
> the combination was guaranteed. I have never been anywhere but sick.
> In a sense sickness is a place, more instructive than a long trip to Eu-
> rope, and it's always a place where there is no company, where nobody
> can follow. Sickness before death is a very appropriate thing and I think
> those who don't have it miss one of God's mercies. Success is almost as
> isolating and nothing points out vanity as well. But the surface here-
> abouts has always been very flat. I come from a family where the only
> emotion respectable to show is irritation. In some this tendency pro-
> duces hives, in others literature, in me both. (*CW* 997–98)

Never does O'Connor downplay the difficulty of such sacramental suffering. In one of her most poignant letters to Betty, Flannery acknowledges
that, as a speaker at meetings of the American Legion,[14] her father found
a challenging life beyond the confines of his daily routine: "He needed the
people I guess and got them. Or rather wanted them and got them. I want-

ed them and didn't. We are all rather blessed in our deprivations if we let ourselves be, I suppose" (*HB* 169). The heart of this moving confession lies in its two drastic qualifiers: "rather" and "suppose." She is *rather* blessed for accepting her losses, she *supposes*. Or as O'Connor said in early and wrenchingly honest admission to Elizabeth and Robert Lowell soon after her return to Milledgeville: "I can with one eye squinted take it all as a blessing. What you have to measure out [in small portions], you come to observe more closely, or so I tell myself" (*CW* 910). Once again, the real reservations—namely, the skeptically narrowed eye and the partially convincing self-reminder. Writing to Hester in just her second letter, O'Connor is most candid of all: "When I ask myself how I know I believe, I have no satisfactory answer at all, no assurance at all, no feeling at all. I can only say . . . Lord I believe, help my unbelief. And all I can say about my love of God, is, Lord help me in my lack of it" (*CW* 944).

The essence of conversion from unbelief to belief, by way of repeated acts of self-surrender, is personal transformation—the permanent alteration of the Christian's life. The New Testament word for repentance and conversion is *metanoia*. It indicates a radical reversal, an utter about-face, a redirection of one's life course, and thus a total change of one's very being. It seems evident from their earliest exchanges that Elizabeth Hester wants to probe this question of *metanoia:* To what extent will she and can she be changed? With supreme spiritual sensitivity, Flannery O'Connor discerns that there is a deep ache at the core of her new friend's life, a suffering that O'Connor shrewdly links to *purity*. Yet purity is not only or chiefly a sexual matter, as if the virginal innocence of a prepubescent child were an example of it. "Purity," Flannery declares to Betty in an early letter, "strikes me as the most mysterious of the virtues and the more I think about it the less I know about it" (*CW* 970).

O'Connor illustrates the character of repentance and conversion to purity of heart by answering Hester's query concerning the nameless hermaphrodite in "A Temple of the Ghost." He is a pathetic creature who survives by exhibiting his sexually mixed features to gawkers at carnivals, thus enabling such voyeurs to confirm that they are not as he is. Yet the hermaphrodite repeatedly affirms his wretched condition by declaring that "God made me thisaway and if you laugh He may strike you in the same way. This is the way He wanted me to be and I ain't disputing His way. I'm showing you because I got to make the best of it" (*CW* 206). Flannery cannily (though implicitly) links the hermaphrodite's endurance of his miserable state to Betty's own summons to faith in Christ: "As near as I get to saying what purity is in this story is saying that it is an acceptance of what God wills for us, an acceptance of our individual circumstances. Now to accept renunciation, when those are your circumstances, is not cowardly" (*CW* 976). Such self-abnegation entails no cringing passivity or invertebrate quietism. On the contrary, suffering obedience constitutes the core of the Christian life: "Resignation to the will of God," O'Connor writes, "does not mean that you stop resisting evil or obstacles. It means that you leave the outcome out of your personal considerations. It is the most concern coupled with the least concern" (*HB* 419).

This arduous and passionate and lifelong transformation is not a bleak and grim business but the supremely joyful life. It entails the proper ordering of our own loves to the love of God, renouncing lesser goods for greater. Unsullied faith is thus akin to true humility: to possess it to be unaware of it. "On the matter of purity we can never judge ourselves," O'Connor affirms to Hester, "much less anybody else. Anyone who thinks he's pure is surely not" (*CW* 978). Neither Flannery nor Betty was particularly pure when it came to gossip, especially about their friends. They relished personal details that were both petty and peculiar. O'Connor is especially given to caustic comments about longtime friends who were often her houseguests. They might both have learned the character of Christian charity from the Benedictine nuns of Stanbrook Abbey in Worcestershire. It was remarked of their abbess, Dame Laurentia McLachlan, that "You could say to her face what you would not dare say behind her back."[15]

Laughter directed against others is much more convincing when it is turned against oneself, as when O'Connor's banters with Betty about her forthcoming audience with the pope: "When in Rome, do as you done in Milledgeville." She comically confesses to Hester that she will not seek a miracle at Lourdes: "I am one of those people who could die for his religion easier than take a bath for it" (*CW* 1956). Eventually, though ever so reluctantly, Flannery was persuaded to enter the miraculous waters along with the other *malades*. Yet O'Connor is no less sardonic afterward. She admits that she prayed more for her novel-in-progress than for her lupus. The real miracle of Lourdes, she wryly notes, is not that unaccountable cures occur there but "that the place don't bring on epidemics" (*HB* 280).

In all of her letters to Elizabeth Hester, Flannery O'Connor repeatedly describes conversion as radical participation in the life and death Christ. As we have seen, Flannery doesn't ask Betty to undertake a struggle that she has not undergone herself. Though the Christian life has brought happiness to O'Connor in the ultimate sense, it has also cost her. It has required her to refuse the path taken by Hulga Hopewell in "Good Country People." The autobiographical quality of this story is not to be located in Flannery's frustrated love life and thus in Manley Pointer as a stand-in for Erik Langkjaer, the Danish book salesman with whom O'Connor had a brief romance.[16] It lies, instead, with the question of O'Connor's essential identity. Unlike the bitter Hulga, Flannery has not allowed her physical incapacity to become the all-defining center of her existence. Everything that she does, whether in art or in everyday life, will indeed be limited and marked by her lupus. But her sickness is not the key to her character.[17] With wrenching difficulty, and with only partial success, O'Connor ordered her life and loves to the life and love of God. She is a Catholic Christian first and last, all of her subsidiary identities being defined by this central fact.

We cannot know, alas, what Elizabeth Hester confessed to Flannery O'Connor about her own identity. Yet it is not idle speculation to suggest that it had to do with what O'Connor calls Hester's "horrible history" (*CW* 994). Betty's grievous past included the father's abandonment of his daughter and wife, the suicide of Hester's mother in the thirteen-year-old girl's presence, and Betty's own abandonment by the lover with whom she had eloped. It also encompassed Hester's enormous frustration as a lonely intellectual confined to mind-numbing work at a retail credit office. Nor is there any doubt that Betty's unhappy life story entailed her dishonorable discharge from the U.S. Air Force because of her lesbianism. Although the word "homosexual" appears only once in O'Connor's side of the correspondence, it seems evident that she links the question of Hester's personal identity with her friend's overriding concern with her sexuality.

O'Connor responds to Hester's evident confession that she is a lesbian by admitting her own failures in charity but also promising nothing but charity toward Betty herself: "I have a tendency . . . to dismiss other people's torments out of hand, but this one, being yours, will have to be partly mine too. It only hurts me because it has hurt you and inasmuch as the temporal effects can still hurt you now." Betty apparently feared that her long-delayed disclosure might mean an end to their friendship, as if O'Connor would let Hester simply "drop out of my existence." Flannery answers such delusion by professing the *philia* that is at once human and divine:

> It would be impossible for me to let you [thus disappear]. You have done me nothing but good and you have given me the present you wanted to, but the fact is, above and beyond this, that I have a spiritual relationship to you; I am your sponsor, self-appointed from the time you first wrote me and appointed by you afterwards, which means that I have a right to stay where I've been put. . . . I can see how very much grace you have really been given [Flannery concludes] and that is all that is necessary for me to know in the matter. What is necessary for you to know is my very real love and admiration for you. (October 31, 1956)[18]

Flannery O'Connor's quiet acceptance of Betty Hester's lesbianism is remarkable in several ways. Surely the most obvious is that Flannery has no prying curiosity, no desire to be given any lubricious details. On the contrary, she treats the question with an admirable objectivity, making clear that their friendship is not in jeopardy. Yet though she refuses self-righteously to condemn Betty, neither does she sentimentally congratulate her for wanting to be what is now call an "out" homosexual. Flannery avoids the language of victimization, even though the conventional gender boundaries had done Betty a considerable injustice. Instead, O'Connor reads her friend's condition in theological terms, commending Hester for acknowledging her sexual propensity and for suffering as a consequence of it—suffering not for her own sake so much as for God's.

Yet O'Connor acutely discerns that self-acknowledged guilt is not the key to Hester's potential conversion and transformation as a Christian. So long as she remains sunk in self-reproach, she cannot be free. Self-accusation can always be answered with self-justification. Flannery thus summons Betty to a more excellent way, a way for her to be neither defined nor confined by her lesbianism. Thus does Flannery direct Betty to the divine means for becoming the person she is meant to be. "What you have to accept now," O'Connor graciously insists, "is the forgiveness [of God] and I daresay that is harder to accept [than shame and remorse] and that you have to do it over and over." O'Connor knows that mercy, not guilt, lies at the core of the Gospel. Counterintuitive though it seems, Flannery sees that God's grace will be exceedingly difficult for Betty to embrace. Bondage seems paradoxically preferable to liberty, since the greatest of all Gifts entails the greatest of all responsibilities. Forgiveness flings wide the cell door, leaving the prisoner to walk free. No longer on the lam from the law, the convict is now at large to live a transformed life. Love God, said St. Augustine, and do what you will.

In this all-important yet unpublished letter, O'Connor succinctly summarizes the nature of salvation itself. "The meaning of the Redemption," she tells Hester, "is that we do not have to be our history and nothing is plainer to me than that you are not your history." In a subsequent letter, Flannery slightly modifies this claim by encouraging Betty to remember that "you are more than your history. I don't believe that the fundamental nature changes, but that it's put to a different use when a conversion occurs and of course it requires vigilance to put it to the proper use" (*HB* 184). That a bodily or spiritual condition is inherited rather than chosen does not make it necessarily good. Some people, for example, have inherited an abiding proclivity for anger. Yet such wrathful impatience with the world, rather than condemning us to a life of destructive fury, can be channeled by the grace of God into zeal for the good. Accordingly, O'Connor does not urge Hester to cease being a lesbian, nor does she promise easy freedom from her miserable past. Betty will remain, to no small extent, the person whom her genetics and her "horrible history" have made her. Her entry into the Church will mean that her wretched life-story will not be silenced and ignored so much as confronted and redeemed. So will her sexual orientation not be reversed but redirected toward redemptive ends, perhaps through *homophilia,* the friendship that Flannery and Betty themselves practiced.

Until William Sessions's biography is published, we will not know the extent to which Elizabeth Hester became "more than her history." What we can know, however, is that Flannery O'Connor expressed worry about her friend's faith long before Hester left the Church in 1961. In a letter to the writer John Hawkes, for example, O'Connor voices her distress over Betty's lack of a real outlet for her considerable talent: "It pains me to see this much intelligence with nothing to do with itself" (*CW* 1150). More pertinent, now in retrospect, is Flannery's constant recourse to the topic of conversion—as if to remind her friend that drastic mercy entails drastic judgment: "This notion that grace is healing omits the fact that before it heals, it cuts with the sword Christ said he came to bring" (*HB* 411).[19] Yet again: "I don't know if anybody can be converted without seeing themselves in a kind of blasting annihilating light, a blast that will last a lifetime" (*HB* 427). Most prophetic of all, perhaps, is this caveat against the notion that conversion is a singular, punctiliar occurrence rather than a constant deepening of the moral life: "I don't think of conversion as being once and for all and that's that. I think once the process is begun and continues that you are continually turning inward toward God and away from your own egocentricity and that you have to see this selfish side of yourself in order to turn away from it. I measure God by everything that I am not. I begin with that. Maybe this depends on the person and is different for different people" (*CW* 1144).

The softening qualifier at the end may reveals that, though she wants to avoid accusation, O'Connor nonetheless fears that Hester may be unable to sustain her initial conversion. Even so, Betty's announcement of her departure from the Church proves deeply saddening to Flannery:

> I don't know anything that could grieve us here like this news. . . . I don't think any the less of you outside the Church than in it, but what is painful is the realization that this means a narrowing of life for you and a lessening of the desire for life. Faith is a gift, but the will has a great deal to do with it. . . . But let me tell you this: faith comes and goes. It rises and falls like the tides of an invisible ocean. If it is presumptuous to think that faith will stay with you forever, it is just as presumptuous to think that unbelief will [also stay forever]. Leaving the Church is not the solution. (*CW* 1152–53)

By "a lessening of the desire for life," O'Connor does not mean that Hester will lose her joie de vivre but that she will inhabit a smaller sphere of reality. As Frederick Bauerschmidt acutely comments on this exchange, "In losing that which is beyond our nature, we lose our nature."[20] Hester will still have her human life, but she will have lost her life as a creature dwelling *coram Deo*, before God. Two weeks after the news of Betty's departure from the Body of Christ, therefore, Flannery warns that Hester's increased self-confidence will cause her to occupy a shrunken realm, one limited only to those things that she can comprehend: "Faith is blindness and now you can see. Faith is an over-reaching; now what you reach for is within your grasp" (*CW* 1154). So has Betty also forfeited her ethical focus. "Your views on morality," Flannery tartly declares, "are for never-never land. We don't live in it" (*HB* 526). Perhaps the key to Hester's lapse lies in what O'Connor perceives as her serious misreading of what it means to abandon oneself to God: "What I . . . wonder at is that you were in the Church five years and came out with such a poor understanding of what the Church teaches—that you confuse self-abandonment in the Christian sense with a refusal to be yourself, with self-torture, and suggest that it implies a scorn of God. Accepting oneself does not preclude an attempt to become better. It is, in fact, primary to that effort as the Church has always taught. Self-torture is abnormal, asceticism is not" (*HB* 457–58).

By becoming "better," O'Connor does not imply anything akin to mere self-improvement. Moral advancement means, for O'Connor, embracing the love of God within the constraints of Hester's sorrowful history. Betty's sexual and personal suffering—her history of unhappiness—does not render her baptismal freedom inert. Taking up and bearing the Cross, the instrument of suffering that has been divinely transformed into the means of liberty, is not a perverse self-scourging. Rather does it entail a radical re-ordering of one's inmost desires, redirecting the most urgent inclinations to the worthiest of ends, the love of God. Even so, Flannery the believer seeks to keep patience with Betty the ex-believer.[21]

That Hester had made a theological more than a moral act of apostasy becomes ever more evident in retrospect. Flannery had warned Betty that, as one inclined to the abstract over the concrete, she would be tempted to dwell in the stratosphere of pure ideas, in ungrounded notions, in ethereal realms cut off from ecclesial reality. O'Connor thus declares to her friend that the loss of faith "is basicly [*sic*] a failure of appetite, assisted by sterile intellect" (*CW* 1153). This is a straightforward Thomistic caveat. "Appetite" does not mean physical hunger, of course, but a desire for the good. Nor is "intellect" to be understood as mere calculative thinking but rather the perception and understanding of the good. The right use of intellect thus issues in moral fruition, the fulfillment and realization of our proper end.[22] Having forsaken the sacramental life for the discarnate mind, Hester's thought will become ever less fertile and life-producing, ever more barren. O'Connor laments this worst of all losses in a letter to Cecil Dawkins:

> I'll tell you what's with [Betty], why all the exhilaration. She has left
> the Church. Those are the signs of release. She's high as a kite and all

on pure air. The conversion was achieved by Miss Iris Murdoch, as you could doubtless see by that paper [presumably, an essay by Hester]. [Betty] now sees through everything and loves everything and is a bundle of feelings of empathy for everything. She doesn't any longer believe that Christ is God and so she has found that he is "beautiful! beautiful!" Everything is in the eeeek eeek eureka stage. The effect of all this on me is pretty sick-making but I manage to keep my mouth shut. I even have restrained myself from telling her that if Christ wasn't God he was merely pathetic, not beautiful. And such restraint for me is something! . . . She thinks she's at last discovered how to be herself and has at last accepted herself. She says she's always tried to be somebody else because she hated herself, but now she can be herself. It's as plain as the nose on your face that now she's being Iris Murdoch, but it is only plain to me, not her. What I am afraid of is that the reaction is going to set in in a couple of months, or maybe not that soon, but sometime, and when it does BANG. Everything runs to extremes with her, as you can see. (*HB* 460–61)

It would take thirty-six years rather than sixty days for the lethal shot to be fired, on December 26, 1998. Yet O'Connor's dire prophecy is not the most signal aspect of this searing analysis. Flannery does not fear that Betty has let her lesbianism trump her faith, as if she had now found her essential identity in her sexuality rather than her Christianity. Hester had too much ethical integrity to take refuge in sexual satisfaction. She may have had occasional infatuations, but she would not resort to live-in lovers. Instead, she would continue to share one-bedroom apartments with her elderly aunt, Mrs. Gladstone Pitt, living much as she had all along: chain-smoking, sleeping on the couch, surrounded by mounds of books. O'Connor sees that the problem lies not with Hester's sexuality but with her conviction that she has discovered "how to be herself." For in "being Iris Murdoch," Betty has not accepted but rejected her history, as if she could be "truly herself" apart from it. Like Søren Kierkegaard, she wants God not only to forgive her sins but also to forget them. She wants grace without nature. The scandal of the Gospel is that God does not forget our sinful past but continues to love us in our very sinfulness, thereby enabling us to love both him and ourselves through the acceptance and transformation of our history. Rather than finding herself by losing herself, Hester has changed roles. She now wears the mask of a Murdochian Platonist rather than the persona of a repentant Christian.²³

To put a complex matter oversimply, Iris Murdoch's chief contribution to modern ethics lies in her attempt, by way of a modified Platonism, to find a way to be good without God, to be a mystic devoted to an unformulated idea of the Good. Though ultimately indefinable, the Good is for Murdoch the ultimately sovereign concept. It alone has the power to draw all people to it, even if no one ever achieves perfection. In one of her most lapidary statements, Murdoch declares that "the Good has nothing to do with purpose. . . . The only genuine way to be good is to be good 'for nothing.'" The last word is the operative one, since Murdoch's notion of the Good is virtually void of content, except insofar as it entails an endless aspiration via an endless humility: "The humble man because he sees himself as nothing, can see other things as they are. He sees the pointlessness of virtue and its unique value and the endless extent of its demand."²⁴ As Alasdair MacIntyre observes, such a vacuous notion of the Good not only vitiates Murdoch's philosophy of real moral substance, but it also leaves her late fiction without any genuine sense of closure:

> It is characteristic of Iris Murdoch's later novels that all goodness being referred to the Form of the Good seems to entail that there is no such thing as a good way of life or a good form of human community. Good is an object only of individual aspiration. Social circumstances are not themselves, except accidentally, part of the matter of morality, which is a purely individual enterprise and one that, just because what is good is good "for nothing," leads nowhere. This is why the novels have no genuine endings. They simply stop.²⁵

Like Iris Murdoch, Elizabeth Hester seeks to escape the sacramental scandal, the Christian insistence that the Second Person of the Godhead has enfleshed himself in history—specifically in Jesus Christ and his Church. In finally rejecting the Scandal that makes us *more* than our history, Betty wants to prove that history does not exist. Whereas Plato had posited an immortal and disembodied soul as the human essence, Hester (in an unpublished twelve-page essay dated 1966) argues that human beings participate in a changeless realm, not of the Eternal Forms but of the constant speed of light. We do indeed have souls, but they are physical. What we wrongly call "history" Hester calls the "oscillatory velocity" of our lives.

They are nothing but deception and illusion unless our "oscillations" are related to the changeless velocity of true being—the unchanging One. Hester is a thoroughgoing physicalist:[26]

> To recapitulate: *all matter is constant velocity; all motion is oscillatory velocity.* We perceive ascending degrees of constant velocity as various types and degrees of matter, up to the point of ourselves, beyond which we have no capacity to perceive as we cannot apprehend any velocity excessive to our own. Inconstant, or oscillatory, velocity we perceive as motion, or action. Oscillatory velocity is a perfect obedience to the constant to which it is attendant. Compared to the immensity of the constant velocity to which it is attendant, oscillatory velocity is necessarily just the faintest relatively inconsequential tremor. It is, however, inasfar as it is perfectly captive, *at all times and in all circumstances an absolutely valid reflection of the constant to which it is attendant.* (The immediately obvious meaning of this is that there is no such thing as doing something which is "unlike oneself.")[27]

In what one hopes is a wild exaggeration rather than an actual self-estimate, Hester declares that she is prepared to "out-Aquinas Aquinas." She promises, in fact, to overcome the entire Western intellectual tradition as largely superstitious. She will do it by making "a definition that, for probably for the first time in the history of theology and philosophy, has some meaningful connection with the relatively ephemeral mind and body."

> From the [body] the individual is conceived [so] that in which he dies there is an absolutely constant, totally changeless, and utterly invulnerable "force" (i.e., the velocity) dominating the building of the body and the brain, directing it absolutely faithfully in its likes and dislikes, choosing for it its proper sexual mate, and, in short, changelessly "holding steady" until death abruptly blots it out. Here, then, is the immortal soul: When it is not, it is not; and when it is it is forever in its changelessness. This immortal soul, this that I call velocity, is in every living creature a *total power* which no other identity (or velocity) in the universe can reduce, or increase, or "mold," or touch in any way whatsoever. So much, I declare, is the absolute integrity of every individual existence or personality in the universe.[28]

Despite the opacity of these claims, Hester's aim is sufficiently clear. We cannot be other than we are, except by utterly insignificant "oscillatory" modifications of our essentially changeless physical selves. We can act as if drastic personal freedom were possible, of course, but such illusory liberty produces only war and destruction. As with Murdoch's insistence on accepting the essential nothingness of ourselves, so with Hester's claim that we must recognize the essential immutability of ourselves as the only education into the truth.

Such spiritualized physicalism may seem to be an oxymoronic rejection of Plato, but in fact there are similarities. In a crucial response to Plato's argument that the soul constitutes our immortal essence, Aquinas declares that the soul does not merely inhabit the body as sailors dwell in ships or even as people wear clothes—namely, as something merely incidental to it. On the contrary, Aquinas claims that "being alive is existing as a living thing," as an inseparable unity of body and soul. To deny the necessity of the body for the soul is to deny that we are finite creatures: "So the soul is that by which the human body actually exists. . . . So the human soul is the form of the human body." In a remarkable conclusion that flies in the face of both Murdoch and Hester no less than Plato himself, Aquinas concludes that "soul is not the whole human being, only part of one: *my soul is not me.*"[29] So intrinsic is the body to the soul's perfection, in fact, that its final and complete fullness of being can be found only in the resurrected body.

The supreme irony is that Elizabeth Hester thought that she regarded her body with utmost seriousness when in fact she seems not to have regarded it seriously enough. The chief characteristic of the body is precisely its mutability, its changefulness. Such impermanence has led Platonists to insist on the immortality of the soul despite the perishability of the body. Even many spiritualizing Christians want to say, with Plato, that "my soul is me." Though her body was failing her in a way that proved both spiritually and physically anguishing, Flannery O'Connor never took refuge in false notions of immortality. Instead, she worried about the disembodied quality of her friend's thought. In an early letter to Hester, O'Connor insists, quite remarkably, on the centrality of our corporeal existence:

> For me it is the virgin birth, the Incarnation, the resurrection which are the true laws of the flesh and the physical. Death, decay, destruction are the suspension of these laws. I am always astonished at the em-

phasis the Church puts on the body. It is not the soul she says that will rise but the body, glorified. I have always thought that purity was the most mysterious of the virtues, but it occurs to me that it would never have entered the human consciousness to conceive of purity if we were not to look forward to a resurrection of the body, which will be flesh and spirit united in peace, in the way they were in Christ. The resurrection of Christ seems the high point in the law of nature. (*CW* 953)

The Church's defining doctrines and miracles are the grounds for these thoroughly Thomistic affirmations of the indestructible union of body and soul. The dogmas reveal what all of creation was originally meant to be and what it shall yet become: the indissoluble unity and integration of our bodily and spiritual qualities acting in perfect concord, without mortal and sinful distortions.

It is becoming increasingly evident why Flannery O'Connor gladly embraced the charge that she was a "hillbilly Thomist." It was not only because, as a self-taught theologian residing on a Georgia dairy farm, she read Aquinas twenty minutes before bed every night. Rather it was because St. Thomas, especially by way of Jacques Maritain, taught her how to become a thoroughly sacramental artist. "Art is wholly concerned with the good of that which is made," declares the Angelic Doctor. This "beautifully cold" definition of art enabled O'Connor to devote herself thoroughly to her craft, making it her "habit of being," as she achieved artistic skill and proficiency by long and hard practice. To put oneself into "the service of the thing [one] is making," as Maritain said, is to be freed from two false notions: the subjective notion that fiction is a form of self-expression but also the moralistic idea that fiction must edify its readers. Rather should her fiction contain nothing extraneous and subartistic; instead, it must measure up to its own rules and standards of excellence. Just as divine grace completes and perfects nature, in Aquinas's basic definition, so does art bring human experience into the order and coherence of the aesthetic form suited to it. When asked whether Catholic writers ought to produce "wholesome" work, O'Connor tartly replied: "Exactly so: works that are whole." Meaning and matter, content and form, should constitute a perfect unity.

Yet many readers have had difficulty discerning how St. Thomas's theology shapes O'Connor's religious vision. Her fiction often appears to embody a Jansenist if not an outright Lutheran opposition between nature and grace. Her characters come to recognize their need for salvation only through violence, usually in the moment of death, whether as the grandmother faces the Misfit's gun barrel in "A Good Man Is Hard to Find" or as Mrs. May confronts the charging bull in "Greenleaf." Such drastic clashes seem far removed from the Thomistic conviction that divine grace does not negate and destroy but completes and perfects both the human and the natural realms according to what is already latent in them, even after the Fall. Frederick Bauerschmidt answers, quite convincingly, that we have misread Aquinas in thinking that the nature-grace relation constitutes a seamless unity having no tensions or stresses. On the contrary, says Bauerschmidt, Aquinas discerns grace as perfecting the human only by first prompting "us to reach out beyond the confines of our nature": "For just as form perfects matter by stirring it to act, 'troubling' and 'goading' it into actuality, so too grace perfects nature by disturbing it."[30] O'Connor's characters are not coerced, therefore, so much as they are agitated into a proper response to God. Far from having salvation thrust on them perforce, they finally cooperate with the grace that has been previously prodding them throughout their lives.

In her last completed story, "Parker's Back," O'Connor powerfully displays this Thomistic understanding of the Holy as "disturbing" human nature into saving action. And since there is no salvation apart from the sacraments, she indicates the manner in which the sacramental life entails bodily suffering. O. E. Parker, the story's protagonist, is an early-day enthusiast for tattoos. He has a natural instinct for Mystery that prompts the needled figuration of his skin. A religious rube with nothing akin to Thomistic training, he nonetheless recognizes that the universe is a woven web of analogies, a realm rife with outward and visible signs of inward and invisible grace. Yet Parker seeks Transcendence not by faith through grace but by way of his own will-to-power. He gradually becomes obsessed, therefore, with the potency that his tattoos provide him, especially his erotic power over women. Covering his body with images of predatory violence—a tiger, a panther, a cobra, and hawks on both thighs—Parker comes to think of himself as an all-conquering sexual raptor. Yet none of Parker's tattoos satisfies him. He remains uneasy and discontent, as if there were a Thomistic turbulence at the core of his unquiet soul, an Augustinian restlessness seeking the rest that only God can grant. Hence the peculiarity of his attraction to a rawboned and unappealing woman named Sarah Ruth Cates. She is not a hedonist like him but a puritan who is always "sniffing up sin." Thus does she have nothing but contempt for Parker's tattoos. His attraction to her is thus doubly paradoxical: he wants to prove that no woman, even the ugliest, can finally resist the lure of his tattooed body; yet he also wants to fathom Sarah Ruth's strange penetration of his ache, her secret knowledge of his soul.

Cates is utterly antisacramental and thus anti-ecclesial in her spirituality. She insists on a civil wedding, refusing to marry Parker in a church: such earthly mediations of divine grace are "idolatrous." She denounces the images covering Parker's body, calling them "vanity of vanities," even demeaning the lordly eagle tattooed on Parker's arm as a mere "chicken." So shameful are these similitudes that she requires Parker to wear a long-sleeved shirt. She also despises sex, and only in the dark will she let him undress. Sarah Ruth Cates is thus a gnostic kind of Christian scandalized by all forms of human embodiment, whether in erotic nakedness or in artistic figures: "At the judgement seat of God, Jesus is going to say to you, 'What you been doing all your life besides having pictures drawn all over you?'" (*CW* 663–64). Yet Parker remains determined to suborn Sarah Ruth to his own will, if only by having his back incised with a Christ-identifying tattoo that his Christian wife will surely be unable to resist. At first, Parker pages through images marked by the sentimental piety that O'Connor regarded as religious pornography: "The Good Shepherd, Forbid Them Not, The Smiling Jesus, Jesus the Physician's Friend." Parker hurriedly flips past the one page that contains eyes so arresting that they eventually command him to "GO BACK." Almost against his will, Parker returns to the image of a drastically different sort of Savior: "the haloed head of a flat stern Byzantine Christ with all-demanding eyes" (*CW* 667). Unlike his wife's "ice-pick eyes" of accusation, these are the divine orbs of allurement, even as they pierce Parker to the very marrow. Ever so reluctantly, therefore, he decides to have the all-demanding Pantocrator etched on his back and thus to embrace sacramental suffering.

Sarah Ruth will have none of this husband who, as a literally ensouled body and thus "a new creation" (2 Cor. 5:17), is also her brother in the Faith. When Parker finally forces her to behold the Christ on his back, she confesses the terrible truth: "It ain't anybody I know." This Christ-denying "Christian" continues her barrage of gnostic rejections when Parker at last identifies the Christ image that she cannot recognize: "God don't look like that!" she insists. "He don't *look*. . . . . He's a spirit. No man shall see his face. . . . Idolatry!" Sarah Ruth screams. "Idolatry! Enflaming yourself with idols under every green tree! I can put up with lies and vanity but I don't want no idolator in this house!" As if she were scourging her own Lord, Cates beats Parker with a broom "until she had nearly knocked him sense-less and large welts had formed on the face of the tattooed Christ" (*CW* 674). The story ends as Parker staggers out of his house and into the yard. Sarah Ruth still glares at her husband with her God-blind eyes, while he leans "against the tree, crying like a baby" (*CW* 675). Parker is learning the hard truth that a gnostic and antisacramental Christianity seeks to deny: Christians are called to follow the *via dolorosa* of holy tears, suffering both *for* and *with* his Lord.[31] It is such sacramental Christian identity and its at-tendant suffering that the Bible-citing Sarah Ruth refuses. She cannot come to the Father who is Spirit because she will not embrace the Son who is Flesh (1 John 14:6).

No Christian can ever embody the fullness of Christ's inward and spiri-tual suffering, of course, if only because none of us is the incarnate Second Person of the Trinity. He alone, as the God-Man, could experience what it means to be utterly abandoned by his Father as well as by his human sisters and brothers. Hence the Christian insistence that we bear our own cross, not the Cross of Christ Himself. Thus are we followers of the *Way* of the Cross that leads Home in the ultimate sense. Yet there is one regard in which ev-eryone is capable of embracing Christ's own suffering—namely, through the inevitable affliction and final death of our bodies. "Bodily suffering," writes John Sykes, "is our incarnational connection to the history of salvation."[32]

Flannery O'Connor sought to lead Elizabeth Hester toward such a sav-ing conviction about her own bodily suffering. Thus does she offer acute theological discernment in reply to Hester's complaint that she is "stuck" with people who neither love nor understand her: "I love a lot of people," O'Connor replies, "understand none of them. This is not perfect love but [it is] as much as a finite creature can be capable of. It all comes under the larg-er heading of what individuals have to suffer for the common good," Flan-nery adds; "[it's] a mystery, and part of the suffering of Christ" (*HB* 543).[33] O'Connor also gestured at the mystery of our participation in Christ's suf-fering in her introduction to *A Memoir of Mary Ann*. This remarkable little book recounts the short life and early death of a young girl who had been

horribly consumed by cancer and who had been cared for by a congregation of Dominican nuns at Our Lady of Perpetual Help Home in Atlanta:
"She and the Sisters who had taught her had fashioned from her unfinished
face the material of her death. The creative action of the Christian's life is
to prepare his death in Christ. It is a continuous action in which this world's
goods are utilized to the fullest, both positive gifts and what Père Teilhard
de Chardin calls "passive diminishments" (*CW* 828).

This may be O'Connor's most radical and thus also her most Christian pronouncement. It is her literal affirmation of Wittgenstein's declaration that "The face is the soul of the body." This girl's wretchedly disfigured
visage,[34] O'Connor declares, "is the material of her death" (*CW* 828). Because she learned to make her affliction into a sacramental participation
in Christ's own suffering, the child's soul enabled her body to take its true
form in a graciously embraced death. In the absence of such faith, the suffering inherent in the natural order is no longer the means of redemption.
Nature is, instead, a purposeless realm awaiting human manipulation. The
logical conclusion, therefore, is that Mary Ann's life is a mistake of nature
and should have been aborted, since she made no "contribution to society."[35]

Such a thoroughly embodied and sacramental participation in the suffering of Christ is the suffering that Betty Hester was finally unable to embrace. She abandoned the basic premise on which everything stands—the
conviction, namely, that the cosmos is not an unsponsored and undirected
process but a magnificent gift-universe mysteriously ordered to the love and
truth and beauty of God. She fled from it into the discarnate and antisacramental philosophy of Iris Murdoch. Rather than discerning her soul as the
form of her body, she envisioned even her bodily self-destruction as the inevitable outgrowth of her unalterable spiritual self. In a late poem, recently
discovered but until now unpublished, called "Metaphysical Extremity, or
Knee-dangle on the Edge of the Moral Universe," Hester thus anticipates
her own act of self-slaughter:

> Job & Jesus had in common
> This:
> That knee-bent to the One
> of God
> Without argument, in whole consent
> There yet had to be

Rage and rant
That consent
Was not.
How to love God
Without
Inventing the Devil?
Say only of suicides
That they are
Impatient people.

The last three lines of Hester's poem do not offer antecedent censure of her forthcoming act, as if she were confessing the sinfulness of self-murder. Rather does Hester seem to commend suicides for their refusal to wait, as her essay declares, "until death abruptly blots [them] out." Bravely, well in advance of the end, without suffering unto the last, such self-executioners give themselves to the Oneness that is also the Nothingness toward which everything tends.[36] This reading is confirmed, I believe, by Hester's mysterious postscript to the poem:

Aye, Flannery—There was not a lot further
One could go
Than where you were.[37]

This final riposte to her long-dead friend does not condemn O'Connor either for her lifelong act of self-surrender to the will of God or for the sacramental formation of her bodily life. For Betty, such faithfulness was the noblest thing of which Flannery's unchangeable self was capable. Yet Hester claims to have gone a step further, if only barely, by traveling in unabashed accord with her own fixed velocity toward self-induced death, denying that her body could be formed by her soul. It was an immensely sad even as it was also a deeply Emersonian and antisacramental act. Just as Emerson refused to offer the bread and wine as the sacrament of Christ's suffering, so was Hester finally unable or unwilling to offer her own suffering as the sacramental locus of the divine sacrifice.

In an uncannily prescient letter from 1958, O'Connor wrote to Hester about a man who had killed himself: "His tragedy was I suppose that he didn't know what to do with his suffering" (*HB* 287). It not maudlin to suggest that the same holds true of Betty Hester: she did not know what to do with her suffering. In a similar letter, Flannery dealt with the suicide of the poet Hart Crane. She pointed out that, "though the act [of self-slaughter] may not have been good, good did come out of [it]. . . . The Communion of Saints has something to do with the fact that the burdens we bear because of someone else, we can also bear for someone else" (*HB* 178). This last clause provides a telling summary of the eleven-year relationship of Elizabeth Hester and Flannery O'Connor. Burdened *by* each other's suffering, they were able to bear it *for* one another. Their long Blakean opposition made their friendship unbreakable. In one of her final letters to Hester, Flannery goes out of her way to confess her own fault, while praising Betty for keenly perceiving the worth of their mutual friend Bill Sessions: "Your great grace is finding the good in people. It's a real gift. I never been bothered with it myself" (*HB* 587).

It's important to remember that, while the Church has declared many souls to be definitively saved—they constitute what Scripture calls the "great cloud of witnesses" (Hebrews 12:1–2) and what the Church calls "the communion of saints"—it has never pronounced a single soul to be definitively damned, not even Judas. Whether human bodies have or have not been sacramentally ensouled and thus redeemed is a judgment that only God can ultimately make. Yet proximate judgments remain altogether necessary. O'Connor's remarkable response to Hester's first confession of her lesbianism is a profound instance of such discernment. She remarked that Job's alleged friends are the ones who are damned, but not the suffering and doubting, the impatient and furiously protesting Job himself: "Compared to what you have experienced in the way of radical misery, I have never had anything to bear in my life but minor irritations, but there are times when the sharpest suffering is not to suffer and the worst affliction is not to be afflicted. Job's comforters were worse off than he was though they didn't know it" (October 31, 1956).

If "the sharpest suffering is not to suffer," then the keenest faith is to join our own bodily affliction to the broken body of Christ. Betty Hester was finally unable or unwilling thus to offer her suffering to God. Yet neither was she afflicted in the dreadful and damning way of Job's false comforters—namely, by remaining immune to affliction. Instead, she confessed her affliction to her friend, in eleven years of remarkable correspondence. Hence our immense gratitude to Elizabeth Hester, though not for her self-immolation, but surely for enabling Flannery O'Connor to gain a fuller understanding, indeed to make a fuller embrace, of her own sacramental suffering.

Notes

Originally published as "Sacramental Suffering: The Friendship of Flannery O'Connor and Elizabeth Hester," *Modern Theology* 24, no. 3 (2008): 387–411. Reprinted with the permission of Wiley and Sons, Ltd.

This essay began as a plenary address at an Emory University conference on *"The Prophet's Country": A Celebration of the Life and Work of Flannery O'Connor* in September 2007. I am grateful to Steve Ennis, Director of the Manuscript, Archives & Rare Book Library at Emory, for the original invitation as well as for the splendid hospitality that he and his colleagues at the Robert W. Woodruff Library provided me during my visit.

1. *Flannery O'Connor: Collected Works*, ed. Sally Fitzgerald (New York: Library of America, 1988), 1180. All quotations from O'Connor are from this edition of her work, which is cited as *CW*. O'Connor's *The Habit of Being*, ed. Sally Fitzgerald (New York: Farrar, Straus and Giroux, 1979) is cited as *HB*. *Mystery and Manners*, ed. Sally and Robert Fitzgerald (New York: Farrar, Straus and Giroux, 1970) is cited as *MM*.

2. "Having me there [at the party] was like having a dog present who had been trained to say a few words but overcome with inadequacy had forgotten them" (*CW* 977).

3. Though there is a gathering body of work devoted to the sacramental quality of Flannery O'Connor's fiction, very little of it has scrutinized her letters. The most notable examples are Marion Montgomery, *Hillbilly Thomist*, 2 vols. (Jefferson, N.C.: McFarland, 2006); Susan Srigley, *Flannery O'Connor's Sacramental Art* (Notre Dame, Ind.: University of Notre Dame, 2004); Christina Bieber Lake *The Incarnational Art of Flannery O'Connor* (Macon, Ga.: Mercer University, 2005); and John D. Sykes Jr., *Flannery O'Connor, Walker Percy, and the Aesthetic of Revelation* (Columbia: University of Missouri, 2007).

4. Flannery O'Connor's friendship with Elizabeth Hester was utterly unlike her relation to Maryat Lee. With Lee—who enacts the role of the pluperfect Yankee liberal with reflexive responses to every controversial subject, especially race—O'Connor adopts an equally artificial pose. She and Lee banter and joke and pontificate, calling each other belittling and self-mocking names. O'Connor often impersonates the reactionary southern conservative, offering outrageous

opinions in ways that cannot be taken unironically, as I have sought to demonstrate in "'Where Is the Voice Coming From?' Flannery O'Connor on Race," *Flannery O'Connor Bulletin* 22 (1993–94): 90–118.

5. *Nicomachean Ethics* (1155a), in *The Complete Works of Aristotle*, vol. 2, Revised Oxford Translation, ed. Jonathan Barnes (Princeton N.J.: Princeton University Press, 1984), 1825. Aristotle quotes Heraclitus as, like Blake, making a case for opposition rather than likeness as the basis for friendship: "'It is what opposes that helps' and 'from different tones come the fairest tunes' and 'all things are produced through strife'" (1155b, p. 1826).

6. Soon O'Connor is forced to be blunt: "Find another word than fascist, for me and St. Thomas too. And totalitarian won't do either" (*CW* 948).

7. *Rhetoric*, 1380b36–1381a2; ibid., p. 2200. Yet Aristotle rules out all friendships with those who are "bad": "For the sake of pleasure or utility, then, even bad men may be friends of each other, or good men of bad, or one who is neither good nor bad may be a friend to any sort of person, but for their own sake clearly only good men can be friends; for bad men do not delight in each other unless some advantage can come of their relation" (*Nicomachean Ethics*, 1157a18–21; ibid., p. 1828). Such constraints are unacceptable to Christians, of course, called as we are to love even our enemies (Matt. 5:44; Luke 6: 27), and love can never exclude the possibility of friendship.

8. The final reference is not to Henry James's novel, I suspect, but to the drag queens whom O'Connor had seen frequenting Washington Square during her brief stay in New York in 1949. They are not the butt of the joke, of course, but rather O'Connor herself.

9. Pope Benedict XVI shares this concern for Christian candor and truthfulness: "Only if the Christian faith is true does it concern all men; if it is merely a cultural variant of the religious experience of mankind that is locked up in symbols and can never be deciphered, then it has to remain within its own culture and leave others in theirs. That, however, means that the question about the truth is the essential question of the Christian faith as such, and in that sense it inevitably has to do with philosophy" (Joseph Cardinal Ratzinger, *Truth and Tolerance: Christian Belief and World Religions*, trans. Henry Taylor [San Francisco: Ignatius Press, 2004], 184).

10. Motes's cornpone nihilism derives more from O'Connor's reading of Jean-Paul Sartre than Friedrich Nietzsche. That humanity is its own autonomous project, as Sartre endlessly iterated, is not our dread existential fate but rather Motes's hot new gospel:

No truth behind all truths is what I and [the Church Without Christ] preach! Where you come from is gone, where you thought you were going to never was there, and where you are is no good unless you can get away from it. Where is there a place for you to be? No place."

"Nothing outside you can give you any place," he said. "You needn't to look at the sky because it's not going to open up and show no place behind it. You needn't to search for any hole in the ground to look through into somewhere else. You can't go neither forwards nor backwards into your daddy's time nor your children's if you have them. In yourself right now is all the place you've got." (*CW* 93)

11. Roughly defined, logical positivism holds that the only truth-claims to be credited are those that can be empirically verified by scientific evidence or else logically demonstrated by philosophical proof. Metaphysical, theological, and ethical claims are said to fall short of what is commonly called the "verifiability criterion of meaning." They have only emotive or figurative or expressive significance.

12. Unpublished letters. Copyright 1955, 1956 by Flannery O'Connor. Copyright renewed 1983, 1984 by Regina Cline O'Connor. Permission granted by the Mary Flannery O'Connor Charitable Trust. All rights reserved.

13. O'Connor ruefully admits that she would never live to become a little old lady in tennis shoes.

14. Ed O'Connor served as commander of the American Legion for Georgia, and young Flannery heard him give speeches all over the state.

15. The character of this tough-minded abbess is set forth by D. Felicitas Corrigan, in *The Nun, the Infidel and the Superman: The Remarkable Friendships of Dame Laurentia McLachlan with Sydney Cockerell, Bernard Shaw and others* (Chicago: University of Chicago Press, 1985).

16. For such a wrong-headed reading of the story, see Mark Bosco, S.J., "Erik Langkjaer: The One Flannery 'Used to Go With,'" *Flannery O'Connor Review* 5 (2007): 44–55.

17. Not until they have corresponded for more than a year does O'Connor finally mention that she is seriously ill with lupus erythematosus.

18. Unpublished letters. Copyright 1955, 1956 by Flannery O'Connor. Copyright renewed 1983, 1984 by Regina Cline O'Connor. Permission granted by the Mary Flannery O'Connor Charitable Trust. All rights reserved.

19. The message received by the boy-prophet Francis Marion Tarwater at the end of *The Violent Bear It Away* puts this matter most memorably: "GO WARN THE CHILDREN OF GOD OF THE TERRIBLE SPEED OF MERCY" (*CW* 478).

20. Frederick Christian Bauerschmidt, "Shouting in the Land of the Hard of Hearing: On Being a Hillbilly Thomist," *Modern Theology* 20, no. 1 (January 2004): 176.

21. There is nothing so scorching, for instance, as O'Connor's response to Robert Lowell's announcement that he had left the Church: "That you are not in the Church is a grief to me and always has been and will be and I know no more to say

about it. I severely doubt that you will do any good to anybody 'outside' as you call it, but it is probably true that you will do good for yourself in as much as you will be the only one in a position to" (*CW* 924).

22. "Now it was the inmost lie of the Manichees that they identified purity with sterility. It is singularly contrasted with the language of St. Thomas, which always connects purity with fruitfulness; whether it be natural or supernatural" (G. K. Chesterton, *St. Thomas Aquinas: The Dumb Ox* (1933; Garden City, N.Y.: Doubleday Image, 1956), 109.

23. The two women were in fact to correspond for thirty years, their letters ending only with Murdoch's descent into Alzheimer's in the mid-1990s; she died in 1999. Murdoch had a high regard for Hester as a thinker, often discussing with her the notoriously difficult work of Ludwig Wittgenstein.

24. Iris Murdoch, *The Sovereignty of Good* (1970; London: Routledge, 1989), 103–4.

25. Alasdair MacIntyre, "Good for Nothing," *London Review of Books* 4, no. 10 (June 3–16, 1982): 16.

26. This term is more apt than *materialist,* since Christians regard material reality as inherently good; indeed, as that which the soul shapes into form. The Incarnation made the redemption of pagan materialism (perhaps as figured in Lucretius) virtually inevitable, says Chesterton: "There really was a new reason for regarding the senses, and the sensations of the body, . . . with a reverence at which great Aristotle would have stared, and no man in the ancient world could have begun to understand. . . . It was no longer possible for the soul to despise the senses, which had been the organs of something that was more than man. Plato might despise the flesh; but God had not despised it. The senses had truly become sanctified; as they are blessed one by one at a Catholic baptism. . . . When once Christ had risen, it was inevitable that Aristotle should rise again" (*St. Thomas Aquinas,* 118–19).

27. H. E. Hester, "A Metaphysics," 7; quoted with permission of William Sessions, her literary executor.

28. Ibid., 8–9.

29. Thomas Aquinas, *Selected Philosophical Writings,* ed. Timothy McDermott (New York: Oxford University Press, 1993), 188, 192, emphasis mine.

30. Bauerschmidt, "Shouting in the Land of the Hard of Hearing," 176.

31. I owe this point to my former student John Sykes, *Flannery O'Connor,* 52. Sykes also remarks the story's emphasis on Parker's iconographic *silence* and *vision,* especially in contrast to Sarah Ruth's wordy biblicizing. The whole of O'Connor's work moves, according to Sykes, toward a deeply Catholic stress on the primacy and finality of the visual over the aural: "The purpose of speech is to bring words to an end, leaving only vision and contemplation" (ibid., 54).

32. Ibid., 76.

33. On the preposition "of" hangs the real weight of this final phrase. Our refusal to suffer both *for* and *with* Christ becomes the occasion *of* his own renewed suffering, as he is crucified afresh.

34. She suffered from a neuroblastoma that pushed an eyeball out of its socket.

35. At his worst Rayber, the father of the imbecile child in *The Violent Bear It Away*, succumbs to this conviction: "His normal way of looking on Bishop was as an *x* signifying the general hideousness of fate. He did not believe that he himself was formed in the image and likeness of God but that Bishop was he had no doubt" (*CW* 401).

36. Hence Hester's "Androgynous Prayer" to the bigendered universe and in parody of the Our Father:

Oh universe which is the all of being—Reverence to You—Your rule be
   known—And acceded to in darkness as in light.

Feed us by the truth of our need

Let us not be deluded

That we may transgress or be transgressed upon.

Deliver us from the violence of the false.

Amen.

37. These quotations are used, once again, with the kind permission of William Sessions.

8

Flannery O'Connor as Baroque Artist

Theological and Literary Strategies

Mark Bosco, S.J.

Flannery O'Connor often described herself to friends and colleagues as a "thirteenth-century lady." Brad Gooch, in his biography of the writer, offers many instances of this in O'Connor's own correspondence. The most striking is a secondhand reference in a letter written by the musicologist Edward Maisel to Yaddo director Mrs. Ames, encouraging her to invite O'Connor back for the winter term at the artists' retreat: "I have been on several evening walks with her, and find her immensely serious, with a sharp sense of humor; a very devout Catholic (thirteenth century, she describes herself)."[1]

Given her singularly Catholic literary vision, O'Connor's brand of religious orthodoxy is often discussed in light of the medieval philosopher-theologian Thomas Aquinas, and of twentieth-century interpreters of Aquinas, such as Jacques Maritain and Etienne Gilson. She takes great pleasure in telling Robie Macauley in a 1955 letter that readers of *Wise Blood* think her a "hillbilly nihilist," when in fact the term "hillbilly Thomist" would be more accurate.[2] O'Connor, moreover, admits to Betty Hester that she "cut [her] aesthetic teeth" on Maritain's *Art and Scholasticism* and suggests that Hester read Gilson's *Art and Reality*.[3] Both of these seminal works of Neo-

Scholasticism appropriate the Angelic Doctor's understanding of the nature and function of artistic creation. O'Connor imbibed the mysticism and synthesis of a medieval Catholicism that saw reason and faith not as adversaries but as collaborators in the production of knowledge and the arts.

Yet, as critic John Desmond suggests, O'Connor's self-identification as a hillbilly Thomist masks a more complex intellectual and artistic engagement with modern and progressive writers of the twentieth century—Catholic, Protestant, and Jewish.[4] Alongside Newman, von Hügel, and Maritain she read Freud, Jung, and Buber. She recommended to Hester her own regimen of reading, including the crisis theologians of the Protestant tradition: "They are the greatest of the Protestant theologians writing today and it is to our misfortune that they are much more alert and creative than their Catholic counterparts. We have very few thinkers to equal Barth and Tillich, perhaps none. This is not an age of great Catholic theology. We are living on our capital and it is past time for a new synthesis. What St. Thomas did for the new learning of the 13th century we are in bad need of someone to do for the 20th."[5]

Ted Spivey's claim about O'Connor is arguably the most accurate: "What is deepest in her writing is a tension that exists between her medieval self and her modernist self."[6] Though not a theologian, O'Connor sought in her art to embody the crisis of meaning in the twentieth century, while simultaneously confronting, and perhaps embracing, the contours of a medieval Catholic vision of life. The dramatic settings of her short stories are riveting precisely because they extend outward and upward toward transcendent mystery. Her success in capturing this mystery depended on her ability to shock readers into acknowledging that the human and the divine literally, and sometimes violently, collide.

The tension between O'Connor's synthesis of a medieval Catholic vision and her intellectual awareness of modernist thinkers made her art "counter, original, spare, strange," to borrow a phrase from Hopkins's poem "Pied Beauty."[7] There is indeed something "counter" about O'Connor's art, something akin to the Catholic Baroque aesthetics of the seventeenth-century Counter-Reformation. As an artistic and a religious response to a culture reeling from the effects of the Protestant Reformation, the Catholic Baroque offered a theological vision that was as accessible as it was excessive in its sensory overload. Artists such as Caravaggio, Bernini, and Rubens communicated religious insight in strange, expressive ways, rendering theatrical or revelatory moments in painting and sculpture. These artists looked back toward a medieval synthesis that fostered positive doctrines of Catholic faith and culture, even as they responded to the spiritual-cultural exigencies of a Catholic society living in the wake of hegemonic Western Christendom.

An apt comparison can be drawn, for example, between Michelangelo Merisi da Caravaggio (1571–1610), an exemplar of a religious revival in painting during the early decades of the Church's Counter-Reformation, and Flannery O'Connor, an exemplar of a Catholic literary revival during the Church's confrontation with modernity in the twentieth century. Both artists labored in cultural moments at odds with competing discourses on the validity and expression of religious faith. Caravaggio's works reacted against the Protestant Reformation's distrust of art and, at the same time, resisted any easy congress with the more propagandistic desires of his Catholic patrons. O'Connor's texts reacted, not against a Protestant dispensation but against an "enlightened" intellectual's secularist distrust of faith on the one hand, and the pietistic aesthetics of a triumphant American culture on the other. Both artists' strategies challenged any religiosity that sought merely comfort and consolation from religious practice. In their shared use of the grotesque and their often violent epiphanies, Caravaggio and O'Connor, though centuries apart, nonetheless offer a larger frame of artistic reference in which to explore the contours of a Catholic Baroque aesthetic.

The word "baroque," from the Portuguese word *barroco* (an imperfect pearl) came to be applied to a seventeenth-century artistic and architectural style that emphasized dramatic, often strained effects typified by bold, complex forms and elaborate ornamentation. The *Oxford English Dictionary* defines the adjectival form as "irregularly shaped, whimsical, grotesque, odd." Catholic Baroque was a conscious turn from the intellectual qualities of the previous generation of Mannerist painters (Tintoretto, El Greco) to a visceral style aimed at the senses. With the emergence of new religious orders there arose an evangelical call to capture in art an experience of faith. Over time, Baroque became an international fashion, divested of religious content and purpose; however, the Catholic, or Italian, Baroque, which combined a virtuosic naturalism with kinetic emotionalism, was used in churches as both a response to the Protestant Reformation and a pedagogical tool of faith formation.

The early Baroque was as much a political strategy of the Counter-Reformation Church as it was an artistic one. The prelates and theological advisors at the Council of Trent (1545–1563) understood that art did not exist in some pure form, that it, too, had ideological implications. If the constant theme of John Calvin was that the senses cannot be trusted to lead one to faith, then the Catholic response was to accentuate the opposite, extending deeper the sacramental ramifications of the image as a way to understand art's effects on faith. The ideological strategies of the Catholic Baroque attempted to teach, to delight, and to persuade the viewer that a religious vision impinged upon human life. In its simplest terms, it professed aesthetically the Jesuit argument that all the senses should engage empathetically with the events of religious martyrdom and ecstasy. Evonne Levy argues in her work *Propaganda and the Jesuit Baroque* that the aim of this Counter-Reformation tactic was to use art as a "directed communication" of the Church's message.[8] Levy claims that the propagandistic element of Baroque art was essentially intended to provoke a positive response to the Church's message of salvation. Through a highly developed naturalism that engaged the viewer both physically and emotionally, the Catholic Baroque drew on the theological doctrine of *Imago Dei*—made in God's image—as the foundational insight into mimetic reform, or the process of conversion to God through identification with the image of Christ. Levy notes that when St. Paul says "we reflect as in a mirror the glory of the Lord, thus we are transfigured into his likeness," he envisions salvation as a matter of becoming Christ's image.[9] The reform of the soul through mimesis makes dramatization extremely important, for one must constantly perform—through story, ritual, and art—the ongoing conversion of the soul. Both the realism and the theatricality of the Catholic Baroque made demands on the viewer. The aesthetic is annunciatory, an invitation into a decisive moment in the life of Christ, or of His saints, as a shared experience of one's own life with God.[10] Imagination and artistry became critical tools in the formation of faith.

The energy of the Counter-Reformation inspired great artists of the time, many of whom were sincere, conforming Christians. The cultural historian Kenneth Clarke assessed this revival in the early modern Catholic Church: "Guercino spent much of his mornings in prayer; Bernini frequently went on retreats and practiced the Spiritual Exercises of St. Ignatius; Rubens went to Mass every day before beginning work. This conformity was not based on fear of the Inquisition, but on the perfectly simple belief that the faith which had inspired the great saints of the preceding generation was something by which a man should regulate his life."[11] Though Caravaggio is not on Clarke's list of artists, his work presents a powerful illustration of the early Catholic Baroque. Caravaggio's revolutionary realism, his dramatically intense form of chiaroscuro, and his idiosyncratic—and sometimes transgressive—reworking of traditional iconic piety all suggest a medieval theological vision that was very much in tension with his modern, more secular way of reflecting on the spiritual.

Counter-Reformation theology presumes that the presence of God is quite accessible: the experience of the holy, of mystery, is available to everyone, even the unlearned. The Catholic Baroque advocated a populist conception of theology, one that eschewed abstraction and theory. Faith is not an epistemological concept but a dramatic experience that moves the human being to respond—in joy, in triumph, in pity, or in fear. Caravaggio's *Madonna of the Pilgrims* (1604) is a perfect example. The painting reveals, not a distant and ethereal Madonna, but what Peter Robb calls a "sexy young housewife coming to the front door of what looks like a very ordinary Roman home."[12] Mary is a warm, fleshy, welcoming mother. The poverty-stricken pilgrims look as if they have just arrived, gazing up at the child Jesus who is ready to squirm from Mary's grasp. Heaven's doorway is accessible to all who knock, a mere step away from the pilgrims' earthly path. Both Mary and the pilgrims have dirty feet—a provocation, certainly, in a painting that hangs over an altar during liturgical celebrations in a city that feared the poor's growing presence. The painting places the poor directly before the eyes of the clerical and courtly elites. The theologian Nathan Mitchell suggests that Caravaggio is "rewriting an icon, bringing the human condition—unwashed—smack into the middle of the space for celebrating liturgy."[13] What Helen Langdon calls Caravaggio's "harsh vernacular" creates a shock of humility for the moneyed class of Rome.[14]

Although the Catholic Baroque is accessible, it is also often excessive, as the experience of the holy becomes an overwhelming sensory encounter. Images stun the viewer: their vibrant color and dramatic lighting transmit theatrical energy and movement. Disequilibrium is fostered as clichéd categories of religious signification are destabilized. Caravaggio's *Martyrdom of St. Matthew* (1599), for instance, illustrates a Mass being interrupted by a murder. At its center, Matthew, already wounded and bleeding, catches his attacker's eye at the instant of his own death. As biographer Peter Robb observes, "In that triangle of killer and victim locked together by their hands and their gaze and in the infinitesimal pause of mutual recognition before the murder, is a powerful immobility," in which the murderer stands "seemingly drained of all his strength."[15] Likewise, Caravaggio's *Seven Works of Mercy* (1607), which hangs above a church altar in Naples, reinterprets acts of piety in the street life of the city. Instead of showing idealized virtue, it depicts "mercy as the satisfaction of basic needs." The starving old prisoner "sucked milk from his daughter's breast, as she hitched up the rest of her bodice as best she could" and looked around as if to dare anyone to comment.[16] Caravaggio, in an altarpiece intended to frame and interpret the participation of the faithful in a liturgical celebration, depicts the dark conditions under which humanity works out its salvation in turbulent Neapolitan life.

This notion of access and excess through visual representation responded directly to the Lutheran and Calvinist reformers whose theology focused on the absolute transcendence of God, and the unfathomable distance between the Lord in His heaven and the human being mired in earthly sin. The iconoclasm of the Protestant reformers is well documented. In Protestant principalities, cathedrals removed their statues and paintings. The aesthetics of the Catholic Baroque, however, stood in direct contrast: heaven and earth were falling into one another, and the Roman Catholic Church—its physical and ecclesial structure—was the place where that crash happened. The sweeping sense of verticalization in the ceilings of many Baroque churches suggests human passage toward some divine realm, but there is a countereffect as well, as if the heavens are tumbling down into the world. Andrea Pozzo's ceiling in the Church of St. Ignatius in Rome (1691) illustrates this well. The massive painting portrays the worldwide mission of the Jesuit order, dramatically visualizing Luke 12:49, when Christ said, "I have come to cast fire on the earth, would that it were already kindled!" The diffusion of the name of Jesus, through Jesuit intermediaries, to the four known continents connotes that the Church represents a portal that brings heaven and earth together, peopled with angelic figures grasping clouds, lest they plummet to the ground. This tumbling effect is evident in Caravaggio's *Martyrdom of Matthew* and his *Seven Works of Mercy* as well. In these paintings, heavenly figures are precariously balanced, reflecting not only the proximity of the divine but also the probability that the divine will collapse upon—and perhaps injure—those in the world below. The gap between the human and the hallowed, the natural and the supernatural, the secular and the religious, is momentarily glimpsed as fluid and indeterminate.

Caravaggio's preeminent biographers—Peter Robb and Helen Langdon—argue that the painter, however reckless his life, was thoroughly conversant with current artistic practice and theory. Before his sudden departure from Rome in 1606 (prompted by his having killed a man in a brawl), he spent years assimilating the aesthetics of religious art, although he never gave way to the easy triumphalism that marked the work of later artists patronized by the Church. Though critics are quick to argue that Caravaggio's personal religious experience is unimportant to his work, such criticism falters when one views his compositions. The significance of his Catholic vision, and its influence on his creativity, cannot be denied, even though his work does not fit easily into the conventional pieties of his day. What can be said with certainty is that his genius awakens the imagination to an entirely new way of comprehending the experience of faith in art. Such provocation is due in part to his technique. Caravaggio perfected a heightened chiaroscuro, called "tenebrism," which intersperses dark, murky spaces with areas of spectacular intensity. The violent contrasts of light bring high drama to his subjects. Illumination directs the viewer's attention both to the subject of the painting, and to a source of light outside the painting— a source of revelation. As light strikes a figure's face or body, the force of that figure's psychological interaction is directed toward a glimpse of the divine. The divine is represented as a literal enlightenment of the human frame, thus revealing a highly intimate, incarnational vision of reality.

Caravaggio also reinterpreted the use of the grotesque in painting. The motif had been prevalent since the fourteenth century, when Hieronymus Bosch set his eschatological themes—heaven and hell, the seven deadly sins, the Last Judgment—in a shockingly indeterminate and alien landscape. But whereas Bosch subverted the natural order to produce a surreal world of alienation and depravity, Caravaggio used the grotesque to accentuate the outward expression of his subject's inner anxieties. His biblically inspired paintings transgress static notions of religious meaning; the faces and actions of his characters make the familiar seem unfamiliar; his stories of salvation are drawn from an aesthetic perspective that renders them suddenly strange in a terrifying, or sometimes even a comic, manner. Such distortions demand a fresh perspective toward the work of art and its underlying, essentially theological, inspiration.

The faces of Caravaggio's figures often disclose an interiority fraught with sympathy, danger, or surprise. In his *Judith Beheading Holofernes* (1598), all three faces capture different emotional responses. One senses the horror and surprise of witnessing a violent death in the face of the Assyrian warrior; in Judith's courtly countenance resides fascination, even a reflective concern for what she is doing; and in the hardened visage of Judith's maid, there is an ugly and almost greedy satisfaction with vengeance. This is seen, too, in Caravaggio's *Call of St. Matthew* (1599): the light from outside the edge of the painting falls upon the tax collector's startled, incredulous expression as Christ's hand reaches out to claim him. In the *Martyrdom of St. Matthew,* which hangs opposite the *Call of St. Matthew* in San Luigi dei Francesi in Rome, every face, every limb on the canvas is fixed by the shock of recognition, by the immensity of Matthew's murder. In both of the St. Matthew paintings, the demands and implications of religious faith are felt in the prosaic rituals of ordinary life, as Matthew collects taxes or celebrates the Mass.

Caravaggio draws upon violent or melodramatic biblical tableaus that bow to realism while at the same time allowing for anagogical interpretation. The magnification of light and action through these episodes becomes an epiphany of grace, often shown in a facial expression that reveals the subject of a painting—and the viewer—as unprepared for the consequences of divine intervention. The painter's use of chiaroscuro and the grotesque subverts the natural order, yet the effects of this disharmony paradoxically imply a transcending principle of order underneath the surface. Caravaggio deconstructs the culturally normative paradigms of the religious imagination for the sake of a harsh *metanoia,* a recognition of religious mystery breaking through the Roman manners of his day. The vitality of his art lies precisely in his holding together such grotesque disruption with the affirmation of mystery. The viewer is caught between these extremes.

To claim that Flannery O'Connor's methods are comparable to those of Caravaggio is to suggest that both the religious properties of Counter-Reformation ideology and the techniques by which those principles were rendered into art have an affinity with the cultural ideologies of literary modernism as creatively reworked by O'Connor from within her premodern Catholic sensibility. As Caravaggio created a fresh, accessible aesthetic from new modes of artistic theory and practice, so too does O'Connor fashion an accessible mode of literary realism that reflects both her modernist, formal-

ist credentials and an orthodox Christian faith often at odds with a complacent and compromising American culture.

By the time *Wise Blood* was published in 1952, O'Connor was already
commenting on ways to write about the movement of grace in the lives of
her characters. In a letter to Winifred McCarthy, she notes, "There is a moment in every great story in which the presence of grace can be felt as it
waits to be accepted or rejected, even though the reader may not recognize
this moment."[17] Her most famous pronouncement on this particular kind
of grace is at the heart of her work: "I have found that violence is strangely
capable of returning my characters to reality and preparing them to accept
their moment of grace. . . . This idea, that reality is something to which we
must be returned at considerable cost, is one which is seldom understood
by the casual reader, but is one which is implicit in the Christian view of
the world."[18] O'Connor's artistic strategy is, in part, a response to her assessment of the mores of a post–World War II America where religious discourse was frequently displaced by narratives of economic progress, and by
psychological therapies. Her critique of modern America echoes that of her
contemporary, the Protestant theologian H. Richard Niebuhr, who claimed
that American religious communities had come to understand faith as a
story where "a God without wrath brings man without sin into a kingdom
without judgment through the ministrations of a Christ without a cross."[19]

The incongruity of religious faith in a secularized modern world produces many of the tensions within O'Connor's texts. As a Catholic and a
literary modernist in midcentury America, she self-consciously committed
herself to the task of fashioning a religious vision of art within the confines
of the New Criticism's formalist theories. Her regard for the fundamentals
championed by Allen Tate, Caroline Gordon, and John Crowe Ransom resonated with her Christian impulses. She created jewels of formalist structure, modern-day Christian parables situated in southern life that generate
the internal paradoxes and ironic contrasts so important to New Critical
analysis. Her short stories climax with the disordered thoughts, words, and
actions of characters stripped of their significance, only to reveal to the
reader, if not to the character, an ordered, even hierarchical structure of
religious meaning. A character's internal conflicts suggest some insight partially revealed through grotesque, and often fierce, action. Like Caravaggio's brutal canvases, which draw the viewer in and force a revaluation of
the biblical stories he paints, O'Connor's parabolic story lines violently de-

construct preconceived notions of righteousness and social order, drawing her characters into the real struggles and costs that come with attempts to live a coherent and authentic life.

The logic of O'Connor's purpose is asserted in her essay "The Fiction Writer and His Country":

> The novelist with Christian concerns will find in modern life distortions which are repugnant to him, and his problem will be to make them appear as distortions to an audience which is used to seeing them as natural; and he may be forced to take ever more violent means to get his vision across to this hostile audience. When you can assume that your audience holds the same beliefs you do, you can relax a little and use more normal ways of talking to it; when you have to assume that it does not, then you have to make your vision apparent by shock—to the hard of hearing you shout, and for the blind you draw large and startling figures.[20]

In order to shake the reader out of such false conceptions, O'Connor affects a realistic narrative style that routinely ends in horrendous, freak fatalities or, at the very least, a character's emotional instability. These grotesque distortions shine a light, in a manner much like a painter's use of chiaroscuro, on a moment that penetrates the self-delusions of her characters. The revelatory flash of insight unexpectedly becomes the interpretive center of a story.

As with Caravaggio's naturalism, O'Connor's level of specificity in her narratives gives her an opportunity to manipulate her characters until she has revealed a superfluity of potential meanings. Farrell O'Gorman describes the aesthetic as an "emphasis on the concrete and a faith that the immediate world itself holds a mystery and a meaning that does not have to be imposed by the artist but is already present, if only recognized."[21] It is the function of her grotesque characters to engage the reader in this present mystery. And Paul Giles argues that the grotesque affects a gap between what is surface realism and the mystery within the complex motivations of her characters: "The traditional function of the literary grotesque is to rip things open, to render moribund systems vulnerable to the very forces they are seeking to exclude. . . . [T]his is the advent of 'mystery' alongside 'manners,' the interruption of observable social reality by the latent force of divine truth."[22] O'Connor says as much in her essay "Some Aspects of the

Grotesque in Southern Fiction," affirming that what appears "on the surface will be of interest to [the artist] insofar as it can be gone through to an experience of mystery itself" so that her art is "always pushing its own limitations outward toward the limits of mystery . . . until it touches that realm that is the concern of prophets and poets."[23] Mystery, she claims, must be described, realized, and felt on the literal level of natural events, if it is to have any real power.

Hence, where Caravaggio's works are accessible to the viewer immediately as a religious moment that is nonetheless destabilized by the artist's refusal to sanitize his subjects or their situations, O'Connor's tactic, as Gilbert Muller notes, is to "maneuver her characters through dark and impenetrable mazes which seemingly lead to nowhere, but which unexpectedly reveal an exit into Christianity's backyard."[24] Her stories are not built upon biblical moments but rather conform to the biblical structures of a parable. We gain easy access to her realistic settings and psychological portrayals, only to have the dramatic action magnified to the point where she achieves what she calls the "essential displacement" of the reader.[25] If her art is effective, then, readers experience a transformation of consciousness in which the story—on the surface horrific and nihilistic—becomes imbued with a new perspective, a deeper possibility of meaning. O'Connor's aim is to affect this aesthetic moment, much as Caravaggio did on canvas: he deconstructs iconic forms of religious faith, only to reinscribe them in realistic, natural expressions of human life; she conceals orthodoxies of Catholic faith within the Protestant mores of her southern characters, only to have them tested and evaluated, accepted or rejected, in light created by grotesque ruptures within the plot. Both Caravaggio and O'Connor explore the shock of divine grace as a complement to suffering humanity.

The aesthetic strategies of the Catholic Baroque—an accessible experience of God through the lens of realism, an excessively dramatic action that leads to a superfluity of meaning, and the violent crash of a transcendent moment falling upon characters—provide a fascinating way to understand O'Connor's context within the larger artistic responses to Catholic faith. If, as Levy suggests, the Catholic Baroque of the Counter-Reformation created an emotional response to religious martyrdom and ecstasy, then one can find this quest in all of O'Connor's fiction. She uses her own "harsh vernacular" to critique contemporary Christianity's self-satisfied manners. A brief look at four of her short stories—"A Good Man Is Hard to Find,"

"The River," "A Temple of the Holy Ghost," and "Revelation"—reveals this Baroque strategy.

O'Connor's most famous story has a fairly simple plot line: a deceitful and scheming grandmother presides over a dysfunctional family on their way to Florida on vacation and ends up causing the death of her entire family at the hands of an escaped convict called "the Misfit." We laugh at the reactions of her son Bailey and her grandchildren—June Star and Wesley—as the grandmother complains, scolds, and wears them down in order to get her way. But when the grandmother meets the Misfit, it is, quite literally, the beginning of the end for them. Having entered the story through O'Connor's familiar humor and use of detail, the reader experiences a sharp reversal of role expectation. After the grandmother witnesses each member of her family being escorted into the woods and shot by the convicts, she summons up every bit of religious virtue she possesses in order to save herself. But despite her pleas that the Misfit "turn to Jesus," we discover how narrow and naïve the grandmother's faith actually is when she confronts this diabolical criminal. Her rhetoric of Christian conversion—"turn to Jesus"—does not allow her to understand the religious crisis that haunts the Misfit. At the same time, the banal, complacent religiosity of the grandmother's own call to be a Christian is revealed.

The Misfit replies to the grandmother that Jesus "thrown everything off balance," and that there are only two choices for us: "If He did what He said, then it's nothing for you to do but thow away everything and follow him, and if he didn't, then it's nothing for you to do but enjoy the few minutes you got left the best way you can—by killing somebody or burning down his house or doing some other meanness to him."[26] There is a genuine, if grotesque, logic to the Misfit's words. In discerning the brutal truth of what he says, the grandmother's own religious scaffolding falls apart: she mumbles that the Misfit might be right. And here O'Connor captures a moment of literary chiaroscuro: the Misfit, suddenly aware of his own moral bankruptcy, cries out, "Listen Lady . . . if I had of been there I would of known and I wouldn't be like I am now." The grandmother, feeling real compassion for the Misfit for the first time, murmurs, "Why, you're one of my babies. You're one of my own children!" and touches him on the shoulder. The Misfit's precarious sanity is shattered by this touch, and he shoots her, for as O'Connor comments on her story in a letter to Andrew Lytle, "This moment of grace excites the devil to frenzy."[27] O'Connor stretches the notion of grace to the breaking point: grace smashes into all of the familiar categories—even moral categories—that the grandmother holds. In her own disequilibrium she sees what she did not see before—a person in need. She is left dead but with "her face smiling up at the cloudless sky," affecting an intimacy with the heavens above and with the earth below.

O'Connor's "The River" builds more explicitly on a portal where the natural and the divine merge, this time in the baptismal waters of a river. As Caravaggio's paintings are framed by the churches where they hang, the liturgical discourse of baptism provides a framework for the dramatic ending of this story. O'Connor suggests that the young Harry Ashfield's drowning is a spiritual encounter through baptism, and the reader is startled by any staid associations he or she might have regarding baptism's significance for Christian life. Harry doesn't seem to understand the workings of grace any more than the adults in the story, but he manages to penetrate the surface of the sacramental ritual in his deadly plunge toward the "Kingdom of Christ." In terms of a Baroque aesthetic, O'Connor dramatizes a strange combination of Catholic sacramentalism and fundamentalist practice. A sacrament is a visible "sign" (*sacramentum*) that both bears within itself and at the same time points beyond itself to an invisible "reality" (*res*) that is, in the final analysis, the Creator. It implies a vision of the world as a composite of two interpenetrating planes of reality: seen and unseen, created and uncreated, natural and supernatural. Within the story, then, the river becomes the composite site, both place and moment when these two planes of reality merge. O'Connor pushes the sacramental system to its precarious edge, because the unseen, uncreated, supernatural reality of baptism (the *res*) is not discovered in the performance of a formal ritual, but in Harry's tragic death.

Once again, O'Connor's humorous portrayal of dialectically opposed worlds—the urban wasteland of Harry's family life and the rural, religious home of his babysitter, Mrs. Connin—draws us into the child's predicament. Harry is a mere afterthought in his parents' lives and looks forward to an adventurous day away from them. Mrs. Connin sets him on a new course of discovery, culminating in his baptism at the river by the preacher. Early on, Harry hears mention of the itinerant preacher's name, Bevel Summers, and the boy unthinkingly takes the name as his own. The naming ritual of baptism is evoked here, and also biblical name-changing, which is often accompanied by violence (Saul becomes Paul and is at once blinded on the road to Damascus), and which therefore sets the stage for the story's violent ending.

O'Connor develops a realistic psychology in the newly named Bevel. Though a stranger to spiritual experience, the boy weaves together the information that he has collected over the course of his day. He learns that Jesus Christ was a carpenter. He learns that Jesus made him (and is not the curse word he has heard at home). This same Jesus makes pigs come out of a man. A pig has snorted in his face and chased him into Mrs. Connin's arms. He then learns that a man named Mr. Paradise with a cancerous growth on his ear resembles a pig. At the river he hears that being baptized "is not a joke," and that he now counts when "he didn't even count before." Finally, when he returns to his parents and reports that he has been baptized, they mock and belittle his experience. Bevel awakes next morning to the stale smell of cigarettes and alcohol, and his desire to go back to the river seems inevitable. He decides that this time he will not "fool with preachers any more but Baptize himself and keep on going until he finds the Kingdom of Christ in the river."[28] During his second attempt, Bevel sees what looks like a giant pig bounding after him. On one level, he is reliving the pursuit of the shoat from the day before, but on a more significant level, O'Connor suggests that in fleeing Mr. Paradise, Bevel instinctively is fleeing the devil. And in his effort to swim away from the false Mr. Paradise, the child finds himself pulled toward the paradise he is seeking.

Heaven does not come crashing down upon Bevel; rather, he must go in search of a more promising future beneath the water's surface. A Baroque aesthetic is evident, for the encounter with the river becomes the indeterminate place where the temporal and the eternal meet. As Bevel gets pulled under the current, the reader is left with the image of Mr. Paradise, touched by the mystery before him, staring "with dull eyes as far down the river line as he could see."[29] The ramifications of such a liturgical act—that in baptismal waters one dies and is reborn into the death and resurrection of Christ—is provocatively rendered. The tragedy of the boy's drowning is countered by the reader's overwhelming conviction that his naïve faith has somehow led him to God, just as surely as Mr. Paradise emerges from the river of life "empty handed."

If the grandmother in "A Good Man Is Hard to Find" looks up above to the blue sky in her moment of death, and if young Bevel in "The River" meets his supernatural fate in the undertow of a stream, then in "A Temple

of the Holy Ghost" O'Connor anchors the human-divine encounter in bodies: sexual bodies, martyred bodies, sacramental bodies. O'Connor weaves
all the disparate threads of the story to a moment of revelation in which the
Body of Christ—the consecrated Host of Eucharistic adoration—becomes
the transcendent reality that, paradoxically, holds together the secular body
of a hermaphrodite, and the body of these young girls, as dwelling places
of God.

The unnamed twelve-year-old protagonist, naïve about sexuality and
filled with "ugly" thoughts, must help her mother host her two fourteen-
year-old cousins from Mount St. Scholastica Convent school for the weekend. The older girls—Susan and Joanne—call themselves "Temple One
and Temple Two," mocking their teacher Sr. Perpetua, who told them what
to do in the face of ungentlemanly behavior: "Stop, Sir, I am a temple of the
Holy Ghost."[30] From the beginning, the story is a transgressive comedy on
the themes of theological anthropology—humanity made in the image and
likeness of God—and the sexual awakening of the teenage girls. The reader
laughs at the sharp-witted child as she pokes fun at her older cousins and attempts to put together the many dissociated facts that she has accumulated
during the day. When her cousins stay away at the fair, she is reminded of
the grotesque bodies in the circus tent advertisements. Thinking that the
freaks look like the pained bodies of the martyrs of the early church, the
young girl ruminates on her future career. She moves from wanting to be a
doctor to an engineer to a saint and settles on a romantically comical reverie
of martyrdom as the only option for her proud and ornery disposition. The
story dances around this notion of vocation, of the consequences of being
called a temple of the Holy Ghost.

O'Connor affects something akin to the Baroque strategies of Caravaggio in the wonderful play between Protestant and Catholic discourses.
Catholic girls Susan and Joanne are wooed by the boys from the Church of
God, Wendell and Cory Wilkins. In the midst of their flirtation, the reader
senses *counter*-imaginations at work: the young men sing their evangelical hymns, "I've Got a Friend in Jesus" and "The Old Rugged Cross," in
response to which the young women literally chant the *Tantum Ergo*. The
Protestant hymns of personal righteousness and witness to Jesus are juxtaposed with the Catholic contemplative hymn of Eucharistic adoration. And
when the cousins arrive home from the fair and report to the young girl that
the Hermaphrodite told them not to laugh, because "God may strike you

the same way," the twelve-year-old is left wondering how the freak could be a man and a woman both.[31] Unable to fathom this mystery, the young girl merges, in her dream, the circus tent with a tent from a Protestant revival meeting; so the freak becomes "a temple of the Holy Ghost," preaching a sermon about the holiness of the body and the ruin that comes from desecrating it.

We see this *counter*-imagination at its fullest in the final scene, the Benediction at the convent school. The young girl's "ugly thoughts" halt, and she realizes that she is "in the presence of God," a realization that provokes her to confess her sins mindlessly. But her mechanical thoughts turn to something unimaginable as she sees the priest raise the monstrance with the Host shining ivory-colored like the sun. Immediately, she thinks of the Hermaphrodite at the fair saying: "I don't dispute hit. This is the way He wanted me to be."[32] The Eucharist becomes the mysterious place in which two dissimilar realities are held together. It is wonderfully transgressive and at the same time absolutely orthodox: the strangeness of the Incarnation of Christ's dual nature as divine and human is found in the strangeness of the Hermaphrodite's intersexed abnormality. O'Connor juxtaposes the Hermaphrodite's suffering of indignities with the incarnate Christ's suffering on the cross, as made present in the sacramental bread, the broken body of Christ, in the Eucharist. It is, I think, O'Connor's most daring analogy, revealing in an original and striking way something about the nature of God and of human life that the reader has not seen before. Indeed, the story suggests that God is to be found, enfleshed, in the freak, the stranger, and the alienated of society.

One last story, "Revelation," is a fitting illustration of O'Connor's Baroque aesthetic sensibility as it highlights more than any other her disdain for conventional Christian piety. Where Caravaggio's aesthetic reimagines acts of charity and Christian piety in representations that profoundly undermine the comfortable orthodox considerations of faith, O'Connor's aesthetic makes Christian piety an object of satire. O'Connor structures "Revelation" like a parable in which God's providence violently overturns the proud Ruby Turpin in her conceit—a triumph of the comic grotesque.

Like the grandmother in "A Good Man Is Hard to Find," the self-indulgent Ruby Turpin is made grotesque largely by her own doing. Ruby confuses the righteousness of faith with the hypocrisy and pride she feels as a white, Christian lady, whose sense of moral superiority is wrapped up in her race and economic class. O'Connor builds up Ruby's spiritual deformity in the first part of the story, where the character sits in a doctor's office, assessing the worth of various representatives of the South's class structure. The reader witnesses her duplicity as she comments aloud about her "good disposition," in contrast to her classist and racist inner monologue about those around her. The Wellesley girl, Mary Grace, strikes Ruby in the eye with a book and tries to strangle her. Mary Grace tells Ruby to "go back to hell where you came from, you old wart hog," a violent revelation that Ruby finds hard to understand, even though she cannot deny the force of truth it contains.[33] The key theological turn in the text is thus set as the paradox of a Christian anthropology: how is Ruby Turpin "a hog and me both"? How is she saved, and also from hell? Or, in theological language, how is she redeemed by her identity with Christ, and yet still a sinner?

In the second part of the story, Ruby wrestles with her revelation as she marches out to her pig parlor, "going single-handed, weaponless, into battle."[34] O'Connor's use of a realistic, natural setting allows a chiaroscuro-like moment in the story. A transformative light shines upon this duplicitous Christian woman as she journeys out to meet her apocalypse. From the brightness of the late-afternoon setting to the deepening blue hue of evening, Ruby rages at God as she angrily hoses down her pigs: "The color of everything, field and crimson sky, burned for a moment with a transparent intensity. . . . Mrs. Turpin stood there, her gaze fixed on the highway, all her muscles rigid. . . . Then like a monumental statue coming to life, she bent her head slowly and gazed, as if through the very heart of mystery, down into the pig parlor at the hogs. They had settled all in one corner around the old sow who was grunting softly. A red glow suffused them. They appeared to pant with a secret life."[35] Literary realism and religious vision blend perfectly as Ruby's long view of the highway at the edge of the horizon is juxtaposed with the close view of the pigs panting beneath her.

O'Connor paints with words the final revelation, where the heavens and the earth open up before the reader: "There was only a purple streak in the sky, cutting through a field of crimson and leading, like an extension of the highway, into the descending dusk. . . . A visionary light settled in her eyes. She saw the streak as a vast swinging bridge extending upward from the earth through a field of living fire."[36] In this visionary light the "battalions of freaks and lunatics" go ahead of her and her husband Claude through the purgatorial living fire. Ruby stands immobile in this verticalized, reordered vision, where the last shall be first and the first shall be last. The scene is dramatically rendered as the spiritual corrective to Ruby's journey of faith. O'Connor suggests that this theological vision must not only be seen but also felt, as a harsh conversion, a metanoia that recomposes one's vision in a critical moment of time.

O'Connor not only paints familiar scenes in realistic terms, but she also invites the viewer/reader into a transformed perception of such scenes. This mirrors a Baroque aesthetic because it suggests that reality has not changed; rather, the measure of that reality has been changed by grotesque and violent dramas that reorient one's perspective. Whether in the chiaroscuro paintings of Caravaggio or in the parable-like stories of O'Connor, Catholic Baroque modes of expression force one to recognize and respond to this aesthetic. The ideology of the Baroque requires conversion; an interior act that is not merely psychological but one that requires a dramatic turning of the self toward the otherness of reality. For Caravaggio and for O'Connor, that otherness ultimately means God. Conversion is thus a recomposition— on canvas or on the page—in which we move from accessibly smug, comfortable versions of religious experience to a moment of sensory overload. In this moment, we return to a reformulation of the promise of salvation as something close to us but made distant by our disordered sensibility. Both O'Connor and Caravaggio create an aesthetic strategy that deconstructs our preconceptions of what religion is, and also how we evaluate religious experience. These artists force us, through their work, to take off the blinders of a rationalized and distorted faith, and so to see clearly the image of God in an unworthy, unwanted, ungrateful, and ungodly people. And by doing so, they reawaken us to the risks, to the stakes, of Christian witness. They allow us a moment of participation in the drama of salvation while still in the flesh.

Notes

1. Brad Gooch, *Flannery: A Life of Flannery O'Connor* (New York: Little, Brown, 2009), 156.

2. Flannery O'Connor, *The Habit of Being: Letters*, ed. Sally Fitzgerald (New York: Farrar, Straus and Giroux, 1979), 81.

3. Ibid., 216, 279.

4. John F. Desmond, "By Force of Will: Flannery O'Connor, the Broken Synthesis, and the Problem with Rayber," *Flannery O'Connor Review* 6 (2008): 138.

5. O'Connor, *Habit of Being*, 305–6.

6. Ted R. Spivey, *Flannery O'Connor: The Woman, the Thinker, the Visionary* (Macon, Ga.: Mercer University Press, 1995), 10.

7. www.poetryfoundation.org/poem/173664.

8. Evonne Levy, *Propaganda and the Jesuit Baroque* (Berkeley: University of California Press, 2004), 115.

9. 2 Cor. 3:18; Levy, *Jesuit Baroque*, 116.

10. Levy, *Jesuit Baroque*, 117.

11. Qtd. in Thomas E. Woods, *How the Catholic Church Built Western Civilization* (Washington, D.C.: Regnery, 2005), 127–28.

12. Peter M. Robb, *The Man Who Became Caravaggio* (New York: Henry Holt, 2000), 265.

13. Nathan Mitchell, *Meeting Mystery: Liturgy, Worship and Sacraments* (Maryknoll, N.Y.: Orbis, 2006), 170.

14. Helen Langdon, *Caravaggio: A Life* (New York: Farrar, 1999), 5.

15. Robb, *Caravaggio*, 137.

16. Ibid., 371.

17. O'Connor, *Habit of Being*, 118.

18. Flannery O'Connor, *Mystery and Manners: Occasional Prose*, ed. Sally Fitzgerald and Robert Fitzgerald (New York: Farrar, Straus and Giroux, 1969), 112.

19. Richard H. Niebuhr, *The Kingdom of God in America* (Middletown, Ct.: Wesleyan University Press, 1937), 193.

20. O'Connor, *Mystery and Manners*, 33–34.

21. Farrell O'Gorman, *Peculiar Crossroads: Flannery O'Connor, Walker Percy, and Catholic Vision in Postwar Southern Fiction* (Baton Rouge: Louisiana State University Press, 2004), 108.

22. Paul Giles, *American Catholic Arts and Fictions: Culture, Ideology, Aesthetics* (New York: Cambridge University Press, 1992), 361.

23. O'Connor, *Mystery and Manners*, 41.

24. Gilbert H. Muller, *Nightmares and Visions: Flannery O'Connor and the Catholic Grotesque* (Athens: University of Georgia Press, 1972), 18.

25. O'Connor, *Mystery and Manners*, 45.

26. Flannery O'Connor, *Collected Works*, ed. Sally Fitzgerald (New York: Library of America, 1988), 152.

27. O'Connor, *The Habit of Being*, 373.

28. O'Connor, *Collected Works*, 170.

29. Ibid., 171.

30. O'Connor, *Collected Works*, 199.

31. Ibid., 206.

32. Ibid., 209.
33. Ibid., 646.
34. Ibid., 651.
35. Ibid., 653.
36. Ibid., 654.

III

O'Connor and Modernity

9

O'Connor and the Rhetoric of Eugenics

Misfits, the "Unfit," and Us

Farrell O'Gorman

Medical historians Todd Savitt and James Harvey Young have offered one of the most straightforward answers to the question, "What has, historically, made the South such a distinctive region of the United States?"—or, to put it more negatively, "What has made the South such an American problem?" Their book chronicles the region's long-standing experience of, and particular reputation for, diseases linked to climate, to socioeconomic factors, or to both, from the colonial era through World War II.[1] The most devastating diagnosis of the region's ills ever presented, however, was surely that of H. L. Mencken. In an influential 1917 essay Mencken damns postbellum Dixie in general and Georgia in particular as "but little removed from savagery."[2] Noting that real "scientific investigation" of the region's benighted population has yet to be conducted, he nonetheless does not hesitate to offer his own analysis: "The south has simply been drained of all its best blood. The vast blood-letting of the Civil War half exterminated and fully paralyzed the old aristocracy, and so left the land to the mercies of the poor white trash." Such "trash" was essentially irredeemable, for it "is highly probable that some of the worst blood of Western Europe flows in the veins of the southern poor whites. . . . [Even] the original strains, according to every honest historian, were extremely corrupt."[3]

The notion of inherent inferiority in a certain ethnic or racial stock, implicit in the Mencken passage, became distasteful to most educated readers after the Holocaust. In the early twentieth century, however, such sentiments were far from eccentric. Edward Larson quotes a respected Atlanta pediatrician who, in 1937, in a piece entitled "Human Rubbish," essentially agreed with Mencken when he stated that "the South's 'poor white trash,' so aptly named by the Negro, is no doubt the product of the physical and mental unfit, left in the wake of the War Between the States."[4] The pediatrician strongly recommended that such "rubbish" be forcibly sterilized—a policy made legal in Georgia that same year. The sterilizations were carried out almost exclusively on poor whites in an era when wealthier whites found themselves acutely embarrassed, not by African Americans, from whom they rigorously separated themselves, but by poorer European Americans. Larson's study, *Sex, Race, and Science: Eugenics in the Deep South,* documents the development of this policy and records how recommendations such as those of the pediatrician came to be accepted within the political and medical mainstream.[5]

Such scholarship helps to contextualize crucial aspects of O'Connor's fiction, which in this regard may be usefully contrasted with that of Erskine Caldwell. When O'Connor was growing up in the 1930s, Caldwell and Margaret Mitchell were Georgia's only nationally prominent fiction writers. The image of the state presented by Caldwell in novels such as *Tobacco Road,* however, differs radically from that made famous by Mitchell in *Gone with the Wind.* Caldwell's fiction does not dwell on the glories of an older South but instead on the squalid lives of contemporary poor whites. Caldwell casts those poor whites—who were often literally diseased—as diseased portions of the social organism, largely because they do not "fit" into newly prevailing economies.

O'Connor's mature fiction resembles Caldwell's more than Mitchell's; yet, the resemblance is superficial, for Caldwell and O'Connor ultimately present entirely different visions of poverty, disease, and human identity. Though his degenerate whites were often received by the American public as objects of humor, Caldwell at times adopts Marxist rhetoric in claiming to speak on behalf of the working class. Yet scholars investigating Caldwell's relation to the eugenics movement have shown that his professedly progressive inclinations also led him to portray such seemingly unfit families as the Lesters in *Tobacco Road* as plausible candidates for forced sterilization. By contrast, O'Connor's misfits, flawed though they are, offer no easy aesthetic consolations and prove themselves resistant to simple political or medical remedies. In fact, O'Connor relentlessly insists upon the inevitability of having the poor and the ill always with us and, most provocatively, upon the ways in which they challenge reductive modern notions of poverty and "fitness." Her own belief that poverty, broadly construed, is in some sense a natural and inevitable part of the human experience is perhaps most concisely reflected in one of her most memorable titles: "You Can't Be Any Poorer Than Dead."[6] Elsewhere she maintained that, in the final analysis, "everybody, as far as I am concerned, is The Poor," in the sense that each individual should properly recognize his or her own incompleteness and innate hunger for communion with God.[7]

Alien as her flawed poor whites might seem to some audiences, O'Connor intends that her readers not merely laugh at but instead recognize their strange kinship with such characters, as she herself did. In those characters' stories she, unlike Caldwell, ultimately affirms both the necessity and the dignity of kinship itself. She stresses the roots of human identity within family and the natural process that extends family, even when that process results in unexpected and perhaps undesirable children. Furthermore, she affirms the proper freedom of the individual: not a freedom to declare independence from family, nature, or God but rather a freedom from abstract systems of categorization, such as those favored by eugenics advocates. For O'Connor, such freedom is in fact grounded in relationship with God, and with other people. It is most profoundly reflected in the Adamic gift—which is also a responsibility—given to the individual: to name creation properly, an essentially poetic act that the rhetoric of eugenics fails to accomplish.

Writing Georgia's "Unfit" in the 1930s: The Legacy of *Tobacco Road*

In Caldwell's *Tobacco Road*, sharecropper Jeeter Lester resists the lure of the new Savannah River textile mills that have attracted the most successful of his children, preferring to remain instead on the decrepit farm once owned by his father. Although there is no overt call to sterilize the Lester

family in the novel, Caldwell's flat, naturalistic characterization of Jeeter
and his brood make the rural poor out to be little more than alarmingly
fertile parasites, carriers of a genetic threat in need of extermination. Both
Karen Keely and Sarah Holmes have demonstrated that *Tobacco Road* has
this eugenic subtext, something that would have been readily recognized by
educated readers in 1932, when the novel was published and when eugenics
legislation was first proposed in Georgia.[8]

There are three parts to Keely's argument. First, she describes the
"family study" genre favored by eugenicists, wherein the expert author assumes a purportedly objective stance while organizing data regarding, and
damning testimony from, members of "degenerate" families. Keely then
argues that the third-person narrative voice in *Tobacco Road* follows this
model, in part by presenting "no characters with whom the reader can com-
fortably identify"—except, that is, for occasional city dwellers who laugh at
the Lesters or look upon them with disgust. Second, Keely cites a family
study written by Caldwell's own father, a progressive Presbyterian minister who favored economic solutions to poverty until he attempted to improve the lot of a rural white Georgia family whom he eventually dubbed
"the Bunglers." He moved the poor, illiterate, family—suffering from hookworm—into a small town, where he "arranged a job for the father at the
local mill, enrolled the children in school, orchestrated donations of clothes
and food from the local community, and encouraged the entire family to attend services at his church." The ultimate failure of this experiment led Ira
Caldwell to speculate, in the journal *Eugenics*, that some families were so
irreparably damaged that sterilization would best "lessen the pressure from
the lower levels of society. In the Bungler family it appears that [only] 40
or 50 per cent could be rehabilitated and brought to a higher level." Keely
also documents the extremely close resemblance of Ira Caldwell's Bungler
family to Erskine Caldwell's supposedly fictional Lester family. Finally, she
examines the use of extended metaphors in *Tobacco Road* in relation to
eugenics, concluding that "once we cease to think of the Lesters as human
and think of them as a ruined car or a boll weevil infestation, it becomes
much easier for Caldwell to convince readers that the family has outlived
any usefulness and should be eliminated, or at least kept from reproducing
any further."[9]

Keely and Holmes both claim convincingly that, as Holmes phrases it,
Tobacco Road "converses with other eugenics utterances in the larger cul-

tural landscape."[10] However, such claims could be given even greater force. First of all, one might simply note how frequently the Lesters have sexual intercourse, both in and out of wedlock, and frequently with natural consequences: Jeeter's wife, Ada has borne seventeen children. The eugenics-based interpretation is also bolstered by the scene in which Jeeter, influenced by a simplistic reading of the Gospel injunction to remove offending body parts, briefly considers castrating himself. Pearl's distinctive identity as the most attractive Lester child further supports the eugenics argument because she has been fathered by a man other than Jeeter, as Holmes notes. The text strongly implies that the most successful Lester boy, Tom, has a different father as well.[11]

More broadly, *Tobacco Road* is consistent with the position of many eugenics advocates in its cynicism regarding traditional Christianity, its accompanying critique of long-standing Western notions of charity, and, most profoundly, in its antagonistic view of nature. The novel consistently suggests not only that American society is defective but also that nature and the God who made it are deeply flawed. Human beings, moreover, must actively combat such a God. Jeeter prefers to envision a benevolent, New Testament deity who will one day raise up the rural poor, but his own experience seems to tell a different story. He imagines that God might punish the Lesters if they leave the land and go to the mills—punish them "slow-like, and hounding us every step, until we wish we was a long time dead in the ground." But he fails to see that the family has in fact already been punished in this manner. They have been born, with debilitating mental and physical shortcomings, into a challenging environment that they seem manifestly unfit to cultivate.[12] Perhaps modern farming equipment could help the Lesters—although probably not: they immediately ruin the one piece of machinery that they do purchase, an automobile. Or perhaps medical technology could "fix" them by, for example, correcting daughter Ellie Mae's cleft lip, if only Jeeter would take her to a physician. The novel, however, consistently suggests that the Lesters are not victims of a problematic nature but rather walking embodiments of it, and that charitable attempts to help them can only perpetuate the problem.[13] This reading is encouraged from the very beginning of the novel when Jeeter, contemplating the infestation of his turnip crop, the family's main source of food, by parasitic worms, remarks, "What God made turnip-worms for, I can't make out." Caldwell's rhetoric in *Tobacco Road* inevitably leads the reader to ask:

What did God make the Lesters for? And how can we fix God's mistake? Forced sterilization would have been a compelling answer in 1932, an answer soon endorsed by the Georgia state legislature despite opposition from some Christian groups.[14]

O'Connor and the "Population Problem": Faith, Family, Fertility, Fear

In *Tobacco Road,* Caldwell depicts the backwoods Christianity of families such as the Lesters as merely ineffectual and self-serving. Furthermore, he implicitly endorses a shallow modern Gnosticism that posits the natural world as deeply flawed yet correctible, a problem to be analyzed and mastered. For all these reasons, Caldwell's great adversary in chronicling the lives of poor southern whites is Flannery O'Connor. Her Catholic views on bioethical issues were antithetical to those of eugenics advocates just as her views on literature were antithetical to those represented by the family study genre.

O'Connor did not see herself as directly engaged in advocacy against eugenics programs: she firmly believed that "the topical is poison" to art and never sought to be a literary activist of any sort.[15] She rejected, however, the principles of eugenics and necessarily had some awareness of eugenic practices, since by 1950, the State Hospital in her hometown of Milledgeville was Georgia's primary facility for carrying out enforced sterilizations. The hospital, which had been founded in 1834 to house "idiots, lunatics, and the insane," had, by the mid-twentieth century, become an asylum for as many as twelve thousand human beings whom the state deemed "unfit" for life outside its confines.[16] William Monroe has brought attention to this often overlooked aspect of O'Connor's milieu, arguing that the "aliens and outcasts" who populate her fiction often reflect her "sympathetic awareness" of the asylum's inmates.[17] That population included those singled out as unfit to reproduce. Larson reports that whereas forced sterilizations of such individuals declined in most of the United States after World War II, they actually increased in much of the South, including Georgia. Tellingly, in "a 1959 Pulitzer Prize–winning exposé [of improper practices at the Milledgeville hospital], the *Atlanta Constitution* raised the issue of involuntary sterilization only briefly—reporting that doctors' practice of treating employees and their relatives was consuming operating room time that could be used for sterilizations."[18] Such reporting indicates that the sterilizations themselves were apparently known and accepted by the newspaper's readers. The scandal, as reported by Atlanta journalists, was not that the sterilizations were being conducted but that they were not being conducted efficiently enough.

The Catholic Church, by contrast, rejected eugenics. Pius XI's 1930 encyclical, *Casti connubii*, affirmed that "the family is more sacred than the State" and further argued that human identity could not be fully analyzed using purely naturalistic criteria and therefore should not be controlled by those criteria.[19] There was, moreover, ongoing Catholic resistance to eugenics legislation in Georgia and other southern states in the early to mid-1930s, when O'Connor was attending parochial school in Savannah.[20] The mature O'Connor clearly indicated her own rejection of the eugenic mentality in her 1960 essay "Introduction to *A Memoir of Mary Ann*," wherein she states that the ostensible compassion of the modern West's post-Christian scientism—its desire to create a human race that conforms to some abstractly conceived ideal—can only lead "to the gas chamber."[21] Furthermore, as she remarked in a 1959 letter to Cecil Dawkins: "The Catholic can't think of birth control in relation to expediency but in relation to the nature of man under God. He has to find another solution to the population problem. Not long ago a lady wrote a letter to *Time* and said the reasons the Puerto Ricans were causing so much trouble in New York [that is, 'overrunning' the city] was on account of the Church's stand on birth control. This is a typical 'liberal' view, but the Church is more liberal still."[22] Just a few years before O'Connor wrote this letter, Puerto Rico itself had been the site of extensive clinical trials for the Pill (in a program that has recently been criticized for taking advantage of, and demeaning, uneducated non-Anglo women on the island).[23] Whether O'Connor was aware of such trials is unknown, but her statement conveys her understanding of how programs that advocate artificial birth control can be bound up with the desire to manipulate or eliminate seemingly unfit or troublesome groups of human beings—whether Puerto Rican or poor white. The Church's first concern is with granting all human beings the freedom to exist.

A number of O'Connor's plots turn on anxieties about fertility, at times specifically with regard to intrusive poor whites or other apparently threatening populations; and, at other times, more generally with regard to the proliferation of children who are, for one reason or another, unwanted. These concerns first appear in her 1947 story "The Crop," part of her

M.F.A. thesis at the University of Iowa. The story reflects O'Connor's effort to define her own future as an artist, in this case by painting a satirical portrait of what an artist should not be, and she alludes to Caldwell in
the process. In "The Crop," a lonely middle-class southern woman, Miss
Willerton, aspires to be a fiction writer and decides to follow the *Tobacco
Road* model for achieving fame: she will write about sharecroppers, a subject that "would give her that air of social concern which was so valuable to
have in the circles she was hoping to travel." "I can always capitalize," she
tells herself, "on the hookworm."[24] Her fiction, she imagines, will therefore
have to contain "some quite violent, naturalistic scenes, the sadistic sort of
thing one read in connection with that class."[25] This last reflection emphasizes Miss Willerton's perceived distance from, and condescension toward,
the poor. However, as previously noted, each human being is, in O'Connor's
view, one of "The Poor," and her concern as an author is that her protagonist
should come to realize what it is that she or he lacks.[26] One thing Miss Willerton lacks is physical affection, as is revealed when her attempts to write
fiction degenerate into romantic fantasizing about herself and an imagined
sharecropper. (This sharecropper becomes increasingly attractive to her,
perhaps reflecting the subtly pornographic dimension of Caldwell's fiction.)
Miss Willerton's daydream culminates in the birth of a baby during the
spring harvest season; but, when she is awakened from this dream to run an
errand, she is repulsed by a real world filled with overly affectionate lower-
class couples and "trifling domestic doings," including children who need
their noses wiped, who jump all over their grandmothers, and who seem to
strain at the ends of leashes.[27]

O'Connor herself would find in such scenes the manifestation of a larger cosmic drama, one with eternal consequences for all involved. Miss Willerton, however, senses only the inconvenience and hardship of having to
care for difficult children—a notion that afflicts other O'Connor characters,
female and male alike, in more disturbing ways. Ralph Wood has demonstrated how O'Connor's concern with what Pope John Paul II deemed the
twentieth century's "culture of death" begins in *Wise Blood*, with Sabbath
Lily Hawkes's strange monologue regarding an inconvenient child—perhaps her own—murdered by its parents.[28] "A Stroke of Good Fortune," a
revised fragment from that novel, develops such concerns with more easily
identifiable eugenic undertones. Ruby Hill fears pregnancy not only because
it seems a personal hardship but also because she fears the worst in her own

genetic makeup: "She was the only one in her family" ever to have "had any get," the only one ambitious enough to escape her poor rural upbringing for the life of the city. Accordingly, she dreads the prospect of birthing a child who resembles any one of her seven siblings, including the brother who has recently come to live with her and whom she views as a parasite.[29]

Viewed through a certain feminist lens, "A Stroke of Good Fortune" seems "a story in which . . . pregnancy becomes a kind of Gothic horror, imprisoning its reluctant victim in a biological identity with her mother which is perceived as tantamount to death."[30] This is indeed Ruby's own perception of her situation. O'Connor herself, however, would affirm that the parent-child relation is the "primal" human relationship and therefore has an implicitly "theological quality."[31] If Ruby's desire to reject her pregnancy is also a rejection of her genetic inheritance, and of her parent—the natural source of her being—it becomes a temptation not only to infanticide but also to deicide. This concern, which goes hand in hand with the eugenic concern, is reflected in O'Connor's statement that "A Stroke of Good Fortune" is "Catholic" precisely in its disapproving depiction of Ruby's willful "rejection of life at the source"—though it is also, she believes, "too much of a farce to bear the weight."[32] To be sure, this early story is, like "The Crop," not one of O'Connor's strongest. By the mid-1950s she would become both more masterful as an artist and more extensively and explicitly engaged with eugenic concerns. "The Displaced Person" and "Greenleaf," two major stories from that time, both have protagonists who fear growing populations.

In "The Displaced Person," the controlling and childless farm owner Mrs. McIntyre is convinced that the world is "swelling up" because, she asserts, "people are selfish"—"they have too many children." In an increasingly overpopulated world, she believes, life necessarily becomes a Darwinian struggle in which "only the smart thrifty energetic ones are going to survive." Hence, she claims that in her years spent managing the farm she has been simultaneously hiring migrant workers and "*fighting* the world's overflow," since she views the workers themselves as parasitical.[33] This population overflow has generally consisted of native poor whites but now appears in the form of a family of Polish Catholic refugees fleeing the aftermath of the Holocaust—the most infamous manifestation of eugenics. The Polish father proves to be a good laborer. Nonetheless, when he proposes a marriage between his cousin and an African American farmworker—with the implication of mixed-race offspring—he falls out of favor with Mrs. McIntyre. The foreigner reveals that he and his family are not only "displaced" but also apparently "unfit"—notice the essential similarity of the two terms—for responsible reproduction in the South, circa 1950. Accordingly, Mrs. McIntyre becomes complicit in putting the Pole to death, part of a silent conspiracy in which the mechanistic murder of this refugee who threatens impurity recalls the fate of Jews in his homeland.

This conflation of Catholic and Jewish identities carries theological import: the "Displaced Person" offers, arguably, the most obvious Christ-figure in all of O'Connor's fiction. His identity must also be understood in historical context, however, in relation not only to anxieties regarding overpopulation and racial purity, as voiced by Mrs. McIntyre, but also to the kind of general xenophobia and quasi-Puritanical anti-Catholicism professed in the story by the Shortley family. The first decade of O'Connor's life saw a revitalization of the Ku Klux Klan in reaction to new waves of immigration, and "many [U.S.] Catholics recognized the fact that eugenics—especially calls for sterilization—were supported by Protestant Anglo-Saxons who vilified the Eastern Europeans who became a growing part of the Catholic and Jewish communities." A similar pattern characterized the eugenics movement in Great Britain, where among the disturbingly fecund unfit, Irish Catholic and Jewish immigrants were quickly identified as primary targets.[34] "The Displaced Person" not only directly addresses such historical patterns in Anglo-American culture but also presents Catholicism as properly offering an antidote to the sectarian habits of categorization that underlie them. Immediately after the Pole proposes the mixed-race marriage to Mrs. McIntyre, she perceives his body as multicolored and further notes that "his whole face looked as if it might have been patched together out of several others."[35] To her, he seems a sort of Frankenstein's monster, his body patched together from the stacks of foreign bodies in concentration camps, as described earlier in the narrative.[36] O'Connor, however, has a very different analogue in mind for this patchwork image of the Displaced Person: the multicolored peacock that roams the farm and functions in this story in its traditional symbolic role, as representative of both the risen body of Christ and the Church. In Catholic ecclesiology, the Church is understood as composed of many different bodies that simultaneously exist as one communal body, a body that crosses racial, national, and temporal boundaries.

Yet O'Connor would also insist that the peacock in this story is simply itself: a part of the natural world. Her understanding of the continuity between the natural and the supernatural is essential to her rejection of eugenics. This understanding is made explicit at many points in her nonfiction, as in this 1959 review of a study of Jesuit paleontologist Pierre Teilhard de Chardin, whom she greatly admired: "In his early years Teilhard was oppressed by a caricature of Christianity . . . which sees human perfection as consisting in escape from the world and from nature. Nature in this light is seen as already fulfilled. [But the mature] Teilhard, rediscovering biblical thought, 'asserts that creation is still in full gestation and that the duty of Christianity is to cooperate with it.' . . . Actually Teilhard's work is a scientific rediscovery of St. Paul's thought."[37] Given O'Connor's emphasis on "gestation" here, her reference to Paul is likely Romans 8:22, where Paul describes all of creation as "groaning in labor pains even until now."[38] All of creation, in other words, is progressing with difficulty but also with hope under God, toward some future completion; yet for Paul—and for O'Connor—the form of creation's completion has already been revealed, mysteriously, in the body of the risen Christ. Such a view of creation is radically countercultural in a modern "Anglo-American intellectual milieu" wherein "the dominant view of nature is atomistic and the dominant view of biological life accords with Darwin's most draconian interpretation of the survival of the fittest."[39] These modern views are, as we have seen, entirely consistent with the character of Mrs. McIntyre in "The Displaced Person," and they also complemented twentieth-century arguments for eugenics, insofar as those arguments advocated a sort of active Social Darwinism that separated, and then sought to eliminate, unfit members of society.[40]

An anxious Darwinian view of nature also afflicts Mrs. May, the landowning protagonist of "Greenleaf." Like Mrs. McIntyre, she fears the rising fecundity of what she sees as a threatening population—in this case the poor white Greenleaf family, which she has long employed and deemed "scrub-human."[41] The story's concern with fertility is overt. The characters have telling surnames, and the setting is a farm in springtime where a stray bull threatens to "ruin the breeding schedule."[42] The Greenleaf patriarch consistently plants fields with "the wrong seeds."[43] There is also a surprisingly foreign dimension to the ever-expanding Greenleaf clan, propagated as it is by French Catholic women whom the twins O. T. and E. T. met and married during their service in World War II. The twins' mother, Mrs. Greenleaf, a Pentecostal Christian, is associated with an *eros* that is inher-

ently bound up with fertility and hospitable to new life.⁴⁴ Mrs. May memorably meets this woman—her foil—in the woods, where Mrs. Greenleaf is
engaged in "prayer healing" on behalf of the world, clutching the dirt with
her four limbs as if she "were trying to wrap herself around the earth" while
ecstatically moaning the name "Jesus." On hearing this, "Mrs. May winced.
She thought the word, Jesus, should be kept inside the church building like
other words inside the bedroom. She was a good Christian woman with a
large respect for religion though she did not, of course, believe any of it was
true."⁴⁵ Mrs. May's priggish reaction to Mrs. Greenleaf's "dirty" passion is
O'Connor's roundabout satirical commentary on what she saw as an increasingly liberal and sterile mainline U.S. Protestantism. Such Protestantism
acknowledged little intrinsic connection between nature, God's revelation,
and a desirable human destiny—and therefore did little to resist eugenics,
or even supported it, as in the case of Caldwell's father.⁴⁶

"Greenleaf" was written at the same time as "The Displaced Person"
but is best understood in light of its essential place in O'Connor's final collection, *Everything That Rises Must Converge.* In a pointedly titled article, "'Blood Don't Lie': The Diseased Family in *Everything That Rises
Must Converge*,"⁴⁷ Susanna Gilbert demonstrates just how many of this collection's stories turn directly on attempts to control inherited family traits.
Gilbert reads the stories as primarily reflecting O'Connor's subconscious
struggle with lupus, the disease that had killed her father and would eventually kill her. This approach is disappointingly reductive.⁴⁸ It does, however, correctly emphasize that disease and genetic inheritance were not
merely abstract concerns for O'Connor. Gilbert is right to note a thematic
concern with the diseased family in this collection; yet, when stories such
as "Greenleaf" are read in relation to the rhetoric of eugenics rather than as
veiled autobiography, they in fact reveal just how arbitrary any designation
of the genetically "diseased," the "unfit" (or "scrub-human"), can be. The
Greenleaf family, which Mrs. May deems genetically inferior, is not only
proliferating but also beginning to prosper, while her own allegedly supe-
rior (but spiritually bankrupt) family is in steady decline. Here the apparently unpredictable, or scientifically indeterminable, nature of "blood," and
of human identity, squares with O'Connor's emphasis on a nature that is not
closed off from the supernatural: a nature that continually surprises, as with
unexpected children. In "Greenleaf," then, and in the collection of which
it is a part, O'Connor begins to articulate her most profound response to

the vision of diseased family offered by Caldwell and his ilk. Understanding that response, however, which is at the very heart of her second novel, *The Violent Bear It Away*, demands a more direct consideration of how O'Connor saw the rhetoric of eugenics, as a threat to a proper understanding of human identity.

O'Connor, Individualism, and the Rhetoric of Eugenics

O'Connor's understanding of individual human identity in relation to the concerns of eugenicists, and, accordingly, to government programs and to scientism, must be considered in historical context. In the decade of O'Connor's birth, the 1920s, the U.S. Catholic Church increasingly found that its ongoing "attempts to provide charity for the poor were regarded [by eugenicists] as short-sighted, sentimental acts that were contributing to the degeneration of civilization." In response, some "Catholic narratives of the 1930s" more openly endorsed the "noble" goal of eugenics, that is, improving the material future of humanity, even while suggesting radically different means for achieving it. Those means "did not involve birth control but rather improvements in social justice," including "traditional notions of charity, child welfare, maternal benefits, and higher wages."[49] *Casti connubii* itself might be read as consistent with such narratives. It not only condemned the notion that the state should interfere with procreation but also supported, to a degree, activist government, calling upon state officials to "do their utmost to relieve the needs of the poor" and to ensure that laborers' wages matched their family needs, a call very much at the heart of the major social encyclical *Quadragesimo anno*, issued four months later.[50] Significantly, some of O'Connor's most obviously flawed characters oppose government-funded programs intended to aid the poor and disabled, though always for blatantly selfish reasons. Mrs. Flood in *Wise Blood*, for example, "felt that the money she paid out in taxes returned to all the worthless pockets in the world, and that the government not only sent it to foreign niggers and a-rabs, but wasted it at home on blind fools and every idiot that could sign his name on a card."[51] Mrs. May is similarly bitter that the Greenleaf twins have benefited from the G.I. Bill, studying agriculture at the state university while American "taxpayers . . . support their French wives."[52]

Implicitly, then, government programs that provide aid to those in legitimate need are not, in O'Connor's view, necessarily flawed. But what is very much at issue in her fiction with regard to such programs is the danger that expert authorities operating under their auspices will reductively categorize, or explain away, the value of individual human beings. The threat of such reductive categorization and accompanying dehumanization has always been the crux of the eugenics issue for the Church. Even in the earliest Catholic reactions to the emerging concept of eugenics, some of which were somewhat positive, the Church strongly asserted that the "physical well-being" of humanity "cannot be taken to override moral and spiritual well-being" and insisted that the "irreplaceable value of the individual person" never be forgotten. Always there was a "trend to defend the dignity of the individual" on the part of the Church: the belief that every individual has a God-given "freedom and responsibility explains why no one is to be considered merely an instrument for the survival or purification of the race."[53]

Perhaps it is not surprising that eugenics programs took root in Western culture in the early twentieth century, at a time when words like "liberty" and "freedom" were "considered to represent outmoded and unscientific ways of thinking" and when the expectation was that science would, one day, eliminate our illusion that such things exist.[54] In such an environment, it was relatively easy for Oliver Wendell Holmes Jr., for example, to mandate the sterilization of unwilling human beings such as Carrie Buck, asserting in *Buck v. Bell* (1927) that "three generations of imbeciles is enough."[55] Buck was a poor white woman who, as Holmes's remark makes clear, was seen as both the inevitable result of and the propagating agent for a diseased family. She was forcibly sterilized at the State Colony for Epileptics and Feebleminded in Virginia—the equivalent of Georgia's State Hospital in Milledgeville.

In depicting the essential worth of human beings who resemble those confined in such facilities, O'Connor strongly affirms a form of freedom that is bound up with a proper understanding of individualism: not an ontological individualism that denies one's essential relationship and obligations to a larger community but a less radical individualism that Robert Bellah defines as affirming "the inherent dignity and, indeed, sacredness of the human person."[56] O'Connor's work suggests that this form of individualism was threatened in the twentieth century, not by modern science but rather by modern scientism, which inevitably tends to devalue individual human beings—as eugenic practices made clear. This threat explains why, in so many of O'Connor's stories, rugged and often violent southern individual-

ists—invariably poor whites—strive to resist scientific attempts to categorize and thereby control them.

This pattern, which becomes more pronounced in O'Connor's later
work, is subtly present in the collection *A Good Man Is Hard to Find*. In
the title story, the Misfit rejects any reductive attempt to categorize him
as criminally deviant, whether due to nature (his biological inheritance) or
nurture (his childhood environment), when he affirms the grandmother's
flattering remark that he has "good blood." "Yes mam," he says, his parents
were the "the finest people in the world": "God never made a finer woman
than my mother and my daddy's heart was pure gold."[57] Similarly, he rejects Freudian theory as a basis for explaining his entry into a life of crime:
"It was a head-doctor at the penitentiary said what I had done was kill my
daddy but I known that for a lie."[58] Here the Misfit explicitly rejects expert
opinion and implicitly asserts the mystery of his own freedom to choose
good or evil, a freedom that is not entirely susceptible to rational analysis.
The disabled tramp Mr. Shiftlet follows suit in "The Life You Save May
Be Your Own," asserting that all the "doctors in Atlanta" who dissect "the
human heart" finally "don't know no more about it than you or me."[59]

In *Everything That Rises Must Converge*, tension between scientific expertise and the free-willed individualist figures most directly in "The
Lame Shall Enter First." Here the young delinquent Rufus Johnson is valued by Sheppard for his IQ, yet he clings relentlessly to his physical deformity as the badge of his individuality and freedom, attributes that the older
man then seeks to erase in his quest to correct nature. O'Connor's ongoing
quarrel with such men is emphatically outlined in her essay "Introduction
to *A Memoir of Mary Ann*," in which she forthrightly condemns Nathan-
iel Hawthorne's scientist, Aylmer, a figure whom she sees as the predeces-
sor not only to Sheppard but also to Rayber in *The Violent Bear It Away*.
In Hawthorne's story "The Birth-mark," Aylmer devotes himself to trying
to remove the distinguishing mark he believes mars his wife's existence,
and in the process, he kills her. O'Connor wrote that such scientists "multiplied" in her own day: "busy cutting down human imperfection, they are
making headway also on the raw material of human good."[60] In a roundabout allusion to Weimar Germany's increasing acceptance of eugenics and
euthanasia as a prelude to the Holocaust, she proposes that the supposed
"tenderness" of the Aylmers, Sheppards, and Raybers of the world can lead
directly to "the fumes of the gas chamber."[61] Such characters' desire to re-

make, and ultimately eliminate, human beings who do not resemble their own idealized image of humanity is, O'Connor suggests, inevitably tied to their desire to categorize human beings, thereby devaluing individual identity. What they hope to establish is a form of despotism that Tocqueville feared some Americans might come to welcome, a "gentle, administrative despotism that would relieve people of the burden of thinking about and caring for the future, for their humanity, for their own good."[62]

If Sheppard, Rayber, and unnamed "doctors in Atlanta" function as such potential despots in O'Connor's fiction, then a host of poor rural whites, including Rufus Johnson, Mr. Shiftlet, and even the Misfit, serve as violently self-reliant rebels against technocratic despotism. In some respects, the latter fit into a quintessentially American pattern along the lines of figures such as Revolutionary War hero Francis Marion, a guerrilla who attacked the modernized British army from the Carolina swamps, and who is also, plausibly, the namesake of Francis Marion Tarwater. Tarwater is the protagonist of *The Violent Bear It Away*, a novel that continues to explore the tension between the reductive scientific expert and the free-willed individualist.[63] It also critiques, more directly and at greater length than O'Connor's other fiction, both the goals and the narrative methods of the eugenics movement.

O'Connor's Tarwater clan, a diseased rural family, in some respects resembles Caldwell's Lesters, even down to those successful family members who have escaped. At the beginning of the novel, Rayber, a secular urbanite who is ashamed of his rural and religious roots, is writing a callous study of his elderly uncle, Mason Tarwater, for "the schoolteacher magazine," a social science journal.[64] Rayber's methods are essentially those of Caldwell's father in his "family study" of the Bunglers, but Rayber is seeking to understand, and thereby control, what he fears may be his own inherited tendency toward feeblemindedness and insanity. His anger that he cannot control "blood" is directed toward old Mason, whom he inevitably attempts to categorize not as an individual member of his family, or of the human family, but as a mere type, a "type that's almost extinct."[65] Rayber's open hostility toward the old man, and his desire to drown his own feebleminded son, Bishop, whom he labels a "mistake of nature" and who functions as the old man's double throughout the novel, make it clear that he would indeed like to see Mason's type eliminated from the face of the earth.[66] While Rayber is not a eugenicist per se, his broadly eugenic anxieties regarding his and all humanity's apparently flawed "blood"—the word appears repeatedly in the novel—are ultimately bound up with his desire to euthanize Bishop, whom he consistently labels an idiot. "Idiot" was in common use as a technical term in the late nineteenth and early twentieth centuries, at the Milledgeville hospital and other such facilities.

The use of such language demonstrates the particular relevance of eugenics to this novel, although the threat of scientism to human individuality is also developed here in more general terms. Rayber's most openly embraced project involves not the eradication of old Mason or Bishop but rather the forced reformation of young Francis Marion Tarwater. Rayber sees himself as the emissary of both modern science and modern individualism: "being born again the natural way—through your own efforts. Your intelligence."[67] Yet he acknowledges that Tarwater's independent nature is precisely what hinders his reformation. Rayber views the boy as marked not by "a constructive independence but one that [is] irrational, backwoods, and ignorant."[68] Tarwater steadfastly refuses to conform to his uncle Rayber's expectations or to learn and perform "the duties of a good citizen"; he instinctively heeds the old man's early warning that in school he would become merely "one among many, indistinguishable from the herd."[69] Young Tarwater, though, is no mere truant. He is finally, if disturbingly, heroic in his resistance to Rayber's proclivity for "laying out" individual human beings "in parts and numbers," for turning "every living thing" into "a book or a paper or a chart."[70] Old Mason has, rightly, warned the boy that submitting himself to his uncle's rigid scientism will inevitably destroy his God-given dignity and liberty: "I saved you" from Rayber, he shouts, "to be free, your own self! . . . and not a piece of information inside his head!"[71]

The boy's own insistence that he is free—both free-willed and free of Rayber's categorizing habits—leads Rayber to proclaim him a "goddam backwoods imbecile."[72] This use of "imbecile," another term employed to categorize some of the inmates of the Milledgeville State Hospital, and also used in *Buck v. Bell*, is highly significant.[73] It is ultimately Rayber's own reductive voice that demonstrates how O'Connor resists the eugenic mentality most profoundly. She juxtaposes that voice with her own multifaceted and biblically resonant narrative of the Tarwater family, a narrative that renders the one-dimensional rhetoric of eugenics unsatisfactory to all but the tone-deaf.

Such rhetoric is all that is available to Rayber. Insofar as he can resist old Mason's lingering influence, "every living thing that [passes] through" his "eyes into his head" can only be dissected, "turned by his brain into a book or a paper or a chart."[74] Rayber views Bishop himself only "as an *x* signifying the general hideousness of fate."[75] Hence Rayber's study of his family yields only "dead words. What it bore was a dry and seedless fruit, incapable even of rotting, dead from the beginning."[76] Young Francis Tarwater, by contrast, is drawn in spite of himself to some larger and more vital narrative, as he recognizes that his great-uncle's prophetic "madness" is "hidden in the blood and might strike some day in him":

> He tried when possible to pass over these thoughts, to keep his vision located on an even level, to see no more than what was in front of his face and to let his eyes stop at the surface of that. It was as if he were afraid that if he let his eye rest for an instant longer than was needed to place something—a spade, a hoe, the mule's hind quarters before his plow, the red furrow under him—that the thing would suddenly stand before him, strange and terrifying, demanding that he name it and name it justly and be judged for the name that he gave it.[77]

Young Tarwater is called to name the world and its creatures, most pointedly his human family, much as Adam was; he is made in the image of a speaking God to recognize and name God's image in others.

It is noteworthy, then, that O'Connor's only recorded comments on the fiction of Erskine Caldwell condemn it not on moral but on aesthetic grounds: translations of his work in Europe were so bad, she wrote in 1956, that the French actually thought he was a great writer.[78] Yet for O'Connor the moral and the aesthetic are finally inseparable: "The moral basis of poetry is the accurate naming of the things of God," and the duty of the fiction writer is "to render the highest possible justice to the visible universe," which "is a reflection of the invisible universe."[79] O'Connor's fiction is therefore most profoundly anti-eugenic in its concern with proper naming—including the act of baptism, the naming of Bishop not as unfit idiot but as child of God.

Proper naming is what challenges young Tarwater to become something more than the Francis Marion, or even the Huckleberry Finn, of his day. He is called to be, in R. W. B. Lewis's famous phrase, an American Adam. O'Connor had a strong sense that any such Adam was necessarily a fallen one. As "The Displaced Person" makes clear, she had little sympathy with the Yankee notion that the United States had become, or ever could become, a New Jerusalem, let alone a New Eden. Yet what was once said of Walker Percy is undoubtedly true of O'Connor as well: "The swirling transformations in American history and culture" are such that these twentieth-century Roman Catholic writers endorse "a new-fangled version of the antinomianism of those original Puritans, a reversal of the terms of their rebellion against authoritarianism." Both she and Percy, that is, rebelled against newly regnant authorities in an increasingly "post-Christian technological world."[80] O'Connor's protesting (if not quite Protestant) critique of technocratic despotism is, however, uniquely her own in its concern with the poor southern whites whom eugenicists wished to wipe from the face of the earth even while at times professing compassion for them. In her treatment of such individuals, O'Connor remained faithful to both Catholic teachings regarding eugenics and her conviction that finally all human beings are the Poor, the unfit—yet also called in hope not to dominate but rather to cooperate with an ongoing Creation that is still in gestation.

Notes

1. Todd L. Savitt, and James Harvey Young, *Disease and Distinctiveness in the American South* (Knoxville: University of Tennessee Press, 1988).

2. H. L. Mencken, "The Sahara of the Bozart," in *The Literature of the American South: A Norton Anthology*, ed. William L. Andrews (New York: Norton, 1998), 369–78.

3. Ibid., 372, 373–74. This essay is often credited with inadvertently spurring the Southern Literary Renascence, which began in the 1920s and ended, arguably, with O'Connor and Walker Percy.

4. W. L. Funkhouser, "Human Rubbish," *Journal of the Medical Association of Georgia* 26 (1937): 199.

5. Edward J. Larson, *Sex, Race, and Science: Eugenics in the Deep South* (Baltimore: Johns Hopkins University Press, 1996), 1.

6. O'Connor gave this title to an early version of the first chapter of *The Violent Bear It Away*, which was published separately in 1955 (see Sally Fitzgerald's note in O'Connor, *Collected Works*, 1258).

7. O'Connor, *The Habit of Being*, 103.

8. Caldwell is also given prominence in Susan Currell's study *Popular Eugenics*, which opens with a consideration of his fiction's widespread influence.

9. Karen A. Keely, "Poverty, Sterilization, and Eugenics in Erskine Caldwell's *Tobacco Road*," *Journal of American Studies* 36, no.1 (2002): 27, 34, 39; Ira Caldwell is quoted ibid., 37.

10. Sarah C. Holmes, "Re-examining the Political Left: Erskine Caldwell and the Doctrine of Eugenics" in *Evolution & Eugenics in American Literature and Culture, 1880–1940,* ed. Lois Cuddy and Claire Roche (Lewisburg: Bucknell University Press, 2003), 242. Holmes reports that Erskine Caldwell was himself a registered member of the American Eugenics Society and concludes that "*Tobacco Road* may be one of the most successful eugenics tracts in history, and one that puts into serious question the ideologies and goals of the political left" (257).

11. Erskine Caldwell, *Tobacco Road* (Athens: University of Georgia Press, 1995), 6, 108–9, 159; Holmes, "Re-examining the Political Left," 252.

12. Caldwell, *Tobacco Road,* 23.

13. Holmes traces the novel's case against charity in some detail. The narrative's recurrent insistence on the futility of "traditional" ways of burning fields—that is, purifying ground to ensure its proper fertility—might also be read as corresponding to Caldwell's sense of the futility of traditional notions of charity in eliminating the problem of poverty. "Weeds" such as the Lesters, the text suggests, always grow back.

14. Caldwell, *Tobacco Road,* 9. Georgia governor Eugene Talmadge vetoed eugenics legislation in 1935, but it passed successfully in 1937 (see Larson, *Sex, Race, and Science,* 131–34).

15. Flannery O'Connor, *The Habit of Being: Letters,* ed. Sally Fitzgerald (New York: Farrar, Straus and Giroux, 1979), 537.

16. Peter Cranford, *But for the Grace of God: The Inside Story of the World's Largest Insane Asylum, Milledgeville!* (Augusta, Ga.: Great Pyramid Press, 1981), 3.

17. William F. Monroe, "The 'Mountain on the Landscape' of Flannery O'Connor," *Chronicle of Higher Education* 47, no. 16 (2000): B16.

18. See Gayle White, "Georgia May Join Others in Issuing Apology for Involuntary Sterilizations," *Atlanta Journal Constitution,* February 6, 2007, www.ajc.com/search/content/shared/partners/Special_Edition/stories/2007/02.

19. Pope Pius XI, www.vatican.va/holy_father/pius_xi/encyclicals/documents/hf_p-xi_enc_31121930_casti-connubii_en.html.

20. Larson, *Sex, Race and Science,* 138 passim.

21. Flannery O'Connor, *Collected Works,* ed. Sally Fitzgerald (New York: Library of America, 1988), 831.

22. O'Connor, *Habit of Being,* 365–66.

23. See, for example, Laura Briggs, *Reproducing Empire: Race, Sex, Science, and U.S. Imperialism in Puerto Rico* (Berkeley: University of California Press, 2002).

24. O'Connor, *Collected Works*, 733–34.

25. Ibid., 736.

26. O'Connor, *Habit of Being*, 103.

27. O'Connor, *Collected Works*, 739–40.

28. Ralph Wood, *Flannery O'Connor and the Christ-Haunted South* (Grand Rapids, Mich.: Eerdmans, 2005), 236–42. Sabbath, like Enoch Emery in the same novel, is an unwanted child herself.

29. O'Connor, *Collected Works*, 185.

30. Claire Kahane, "The Maternal Legacy: The Grotesque Tradition in Flannery O'Connor's Female Gothic," in *Female Gothic,* ed. Julian Fleenor (Montreal: Eden, 1983), 245.

31. Wood, *Christ-Haunted South*, 211.

32. O'Connor, *Habit of Being*, 85.

33. O'Connor, *Collected Works*, 307–8, emphasis added.

34. Marouf Arif Hasian, *The Rhetoric of Eugenics in Anglo-American Thought* (Athens: University of Georgia Press, 1996), 101, 90.

35. O'Connor, *Collected Works*, 313.

36. Ibid., 287.

37. O'Connor's review of Claude Tresmontant's 1959 book *Pierre Teilhard de Chardin,* in *The Presence of Grace and Other Book Reviews by Flannery O'Connor* (Athens: University of Georgia Press, 1983), 87.

38. New American Bible, Rev. Ed. (2011).

39. Peter Casarella, "Waiting for a Cosmic Christ in an Uncreated World," *Communio* 28 (2001): 25.

40. As Louis Caruana carefully notes, eugenics is "a kind of 'reverse-engineered' version of Social Darwinism," an attempt at "the self-direction of human evolution." Nonetheless, "the *aim* behind eugenics is very often in line with Social Darwinism" (see "Darwinism, Mind, and Society," in *Darwin and Catholicism,* ed. Louis Caruana [London: T&T Clark, 2009], 146).

41. O'Connor, *Collected Works*, 507.

42. Ibid., 504.

43. Ibid., 506.

44. Much could be said about subtly Marian aspects of this story, the final paragraph of which depicts a chastened Mrs. May at the center of an unexpected pieta image. See Casarella's view of "Marian receptivity" as providing the Christian model for cooperation with—as opposed to domination of—the natural world.

45. O'Connor, *Collected Works*, 506–7.

46. See Wood, *Christ-Haunted South*, chap. 1, esp. 34–35 regarding the Scopes Trial, on O'Connor's general preference for "fundamentalist" Protestants over Laodiceans.

47. Susanna Gilbert, "'Blood Don't Lie': The Diseased Family in *Everything That Rises Must Converge*," *Literature and Medicine* 18, no. 1 (1991): 114–31.

48. Most glaringly, Gilbert fails to address the three great final stories—"Revelation," "Parker's Back," and "Judgment Day"—which end the collection on a note both overtly theological and altogether beyond the reach of autobiographical analysis.

49. Hasian, *Rhetoric of Eugenics*, 94, 110–11.

50. See John T. McGreevy, *Catholicism and American Freedom: A History* (New York: Norton, 2003), 162–63.

51. O'Connor, *Collected Works*, 120.

52. Ibid., 508.

53. Caruana, *Darwinism, Mind and Society*, 146–47.

54. Hasian, *Rhetoric of Eugenics*, 26.

55. Buck v. Bell, 274 U.S. 200 (1927).

56. Robert N. Bellah et. al., *Habits of the Heart: Individualism and Commitment in American Life*, rev. ed. (Berkeley: University of California Press, 1996), 334.

57. O'Connor, *Collected Works*, 147.

58. Ibid., 150.

59. Ibid., 173–74.

60. Ibid., 830.

61. Ibid., 831. For the history of eugenics and euthanasia in Weimar Germany, see Sheila Faith Weiss, "The Race Hygiene Movement in Germany, 1904–1945," in *The Wellborn Science: Eugenics in Germany, France, Brazil, and Russia*, ed. Mark B. Adams (New York: Oxford University Press, 1990), 8–68.

62. Peter Augustine Lawler, *Postmodernism Rightly Understood: The Return to Realism in American Thought* (Lanham, Md.: Rowman and Littlefield, 1999), 3. Bellah, like Lawler, sees such "administrative despotism" as increasingly welcomed in the late twentieth-century United States (see esp. 208–9).

63. On a deeper level, the scientific expert and the free-willed individualist can bear striking resemblances to one another in O'Connor's fiction. This is perhaps most evident in "A View of the Woods," a story that is as relevant to eugenic concerns as any treated here. Mr. Fortune, a despotic figure in the vein of Aylmer, reacts to the violence that he sees in nature and in family by turning to a greater violence himself, finally destroying that which he meant to master in the person of his granddaughter Mary. His professed desire to eliminate suffering, and his hidden desire that Mary become a sort of subservient clone—both resembling him and subject to him—make the story akin to dystopian fictions such as Aldous Huxley's *Brave New World*. It is also one of O'Connor's most astute explorations of radical individualism: via the Fortune family "she views prophetically the attempt

of Americans to live the Lockean dream of rationally calculating individual selves, united only for convenience in the mutual domination and transformation of nature" (see John Roos, "The Political in Flannery O'Connor: A Reading of 'A View of the Woods,'" *Studies in Short Fiction* 29, no. 2 [1992]: 177).

64. O'Connor, *Collected Works*, 331.

65. Ibid., 339.

66. Ibid., 403. The narrative repeatedly links Mason Tarwater and Bishop. To Rayber, "Bishop looked like the old man grown backward to the lowest form of innocence" (400). To young Tarwater, the old man's eyes resemble "two fish straining to get out of a net of red threads" and Bishop's eyes are "fish-colored" (335, 461).

67. Ibid., 451.

68. Ibid., 393.

69. Ibid., 398, 341.

70. Ibid., 341.

71. Ibid., 339.

72. Ibid., 422.

73. Thomas Merton perhaps sensed as much when, in his 1965 paper "The Other Side of Despair: Notes on Christian Existentialism," *Critic* 24 (1965): 12–22, he cast Tarwater's struggle with Rayber in terms of O'Connor's intuitive "Christian existentialism," arguing that the boy presents "the existentialist case against the scientism and sociologism of positivist society," "a brief for the person and the personal," for "spiritual liberty" and therefore "against [the] determinism and curtailment" which inevitably accompany Rayber's habits of generic categorization (14–15).

74. O'Connor, *Collected Works*, 341.

75. Ibid., 401.

76. Ibid., 341.

77. Ibid., 343.

78. O'Connor, *Habit of Being*, 129.

79. O'Connor, *Collected Works*, 981.

80. J. Donald Crowley, "Walker Percy: The Continuity of the Complex Fate," *Critical Essays on Walker Percy*, ed. J. Donald Crowley and Sue Mitchell Crowley (Boston: G. K. Hall, 1989), 263.

10

"School for Sanctity"

O'Connor, Illich, and the Politics of Benevolence

Gary M. Ciuba

> The compulsion to do good is an innate American trait. Only North
> Americans seem to believe that they always should, may, and actually
> can choose somebody with whom to share their blessings. Ultimately this
> attitude leads to bombing people into the acceptance of gifts.
>
> —Ivan Illich (*Celebration*)

From 1961 to 1964, Flannery O'Connor corresponded with Roslyn Barnes about her friend's membership in the Papal Auxiliary Volunteers for Latin America (PAVLA). Formed in 1960 during the pontificate of John XXIII, PAVLA was a kind of Catholic precursor of the Peace Corps, which was formed a year later under the presidency of John F. Kennedy.[1] The program sent lay missionaries to help the Church in Latin America as it confronted socioeconomic injustices, government hostility, a critical shortage of priests, and possible threats from communism.[2] Barnes was one of almost a thousand volunteers, generally young, well educated, and involved in their local churches, who brought their faith and professional skills to the decade-long enterprise.[3] On July 26, 1961, O'Connor wrote to Barnes that she would be "delighted to recommend [her] for PAVLA."[4] After Barnes was accepted as a volunteer, she received her training as a missionary from Msgr. Ivan Illich (spelled "Illych" by O'Connor) of the Center for Intercultural Formation (CIF) in Cuernavaca, Mexico. As O'Connor later wrote to Barnes, "he is supposed to be a powerhouse."[5]

The dynamic Illich was a paradoxical mentor for Barnes and the many other volunteers who studied at CIF because he was a missionary *malgre lui*. The monsignor made it *his* mission to undermine the Catholic Church's politics of benevolence in conducting missionary work. John L. Hammond has studied the "politics of benevolence" in the revival-inspired activism of nineteenth- and early twentieth-century America. Newly filled with Christian zeal, the saved in the North and Midwest organized meetings and used the ballot box to oppose slavery and to advocate temperance.[6] Mine Ener has, likewise, traced the "politics of benevolence" in the competing efforts of Europeans and Egyptians, and of rival groups within Egypt, to care for the poor and thus justify their claims to rule.[7] As these case studies suggest, the "politics of benevolence" names the nexus between the quest to assert ideological power and the desire to serve the public good. At this intersection, the impulse to promote a benevolent agenda may lead to political action; or, political parties may adopt a benevolent agenda as a means of winning and maintaining support. Illich saw missionaries in Latin America proclaiming the gospel while advancing the flag of Western values, so he formed his Center outside Mexico City to separate the benevolent message of Christianity from the narrowly political implications of evangelical work. Cuernavaca is almost 1,400 miles from Milledgeville, but Illich's school and think tank fascinated O'Connor. Illich, in turn, looked toward what O'Connor termed her "true country" when he imagined that, despite geographic differences between North and South America, the innermost zones of the self are territories held in common.[8] He claimed that "a critical examination of the effect that intense social change has on the intimacy of the human heart in Latin America is a fruitful way to insight into the intimacy of the human heart in the United States."[9] To explore how Illich reschooled Barnes and other missionary volunteers is to explore, in an equally "fruitful way," how O'Connor's fictional home missionaries are educated in the self-deceptions behind their apparently good deeds.

When Barnes asked O'Connor to support her application to PAVLA, she could not have been more politic in her choice of referees. The two women became friends while Barnes was a student at Georgia State College for Women, where O'Connor had received her bachelor's degree in

1945; the friendship continued through the early 1960s, while Barnes pursued a master's at the University of Iowa and studied at the Iowa Writers' Workshop, where O'Connor had received her M.F.A. in 1947.[10] Converging interests in religion, science, and literature deepened the academic ties between O'Connor and Barnes. While at Iowa, Barnes began to explore the Catholicism that was so foundational for O'Connor, and she eventually decided to enter the Church despite her family's objections. "Prayer will do more for them than argument," a supportive O'Connor counseled in January 1961.[11] Barnes even considered becoming a nun, although her immediate focus in the Department of Humanities at Iowa was science and writing.[12] Early in 1961, O'Connor sent her friend *The Divine Milieu* by the Jesuit theologian and paleontologist Pierre Teilhard de Chardin. Like Teilhard, Barnes had a streak of mysticism in her that prompted O'Connor to group her with "these people who are always lying in the grass feeling God."[13] Later in 1961, O'Connor wrote to Barnes as "the only scientist I am acquainted with" to ask her if "Everything That Rises Must Converge," the Teilhard-inspired title of the short story that she had recently sold, was actually "a true proposition in physics."[14]

Barnes's interests in religion and the natural world informed her thesis "Gerard Manley Hopkins and Pierre Teilhard de Chardin: A Formulation of Mysticism for a Scientific Age." The work was a testament to friendship, as Barnes dedicated the thesis to O'Connor and sent her a copy in 1962. The thesis argued that both Hopkins and Teilhard saw such Christian mysteries as Creation, the Incarnation, and Redemption as ongoing moments in the progress of the world toward God. Barnes might also have been describing O'Connor's work, as both Jesuits helped to shape the fiction writer's vision of a divine dynamism, deep at work in her characters and in their country.[15] The thesis "impressed" O'Connor, although she cautioned that whereas "the technical jargon of writers on mysticism" was appropriate for such an academic undertaking, "you need something more human for public presentation." O'Connor further proposed that her Latin America–bound friend might work on revisions "if in those jungles, or wherever it is, you have time on your hands."[16]

In preparation for her seemingly exotic assignment, Barnes studied that summer at CIF in Cuernavaca, Illich's pioneering effort to make missionaries more sensitive to life in Latin America. O'Connor was inquisitive about CIF. On June 29, 1962, she asked Barnes how many recruits were attending the training session; she also wondered if her friend had a room-mate, if she would be studying theology, and if she needed any supplies from home. "You must need somebody violent to run an outfit like that," O'Connor speculated, and in a postscript she added, "just let me know what I can do to support the troops."[17] O'Connor's charged language typifies how her correspondence often makes Illich's Center at Cuernavaca seem on the verge of being borne away. She also wrote Barnes that Helen Green, a pro-fessor at Georgia State College for Women who had returned from a visit to Cuernavaca, reported "her relief that you were among nice people. All along she must have been thinking that you had fallen in with cut-throats and assassins."[18] In an earlier letter to Barnes, on August 4, 1962, O'Connor had interpreted such violence along spiritual lines. She expressed her plea-sure in learning about Illich's work, and she claimed not to be worried that half of the students at Cuernavaca reportedly never completed the priest's intensive program: "He won't send you home I don't think. That is a school for sanctity and he must know that he can't create saints in 4 months though he has to try. This is surely what it means to bear away the kingdom of heav-en with violence: the violence is directed inward."[19]

Despite written reassurances, O'Connor was concerned enough about Barnes's candidacy at Illich's boot camp that on August 5, 1962, she asked Fr. James McCown, who himself wanted to be a missionary in Mexico but was deemed ineligible because of his age, to pray for her friend in Cuernava-ca: "Her family are violently opposed to what she is doing but she goes her own way. She says Msgr. [Illych] is straight out of Dostoevsky."[20] O'Connor, who always gravitated more toward Dostoevsky than toward Tolstoy,[21] men-tions a telling fictional provenance for "Msgr." Although Ivan Illich bore the name of the self-absorbed judge in the title of Tolstoy's famous novella, a man who learns compassion only as he faces his own death, the impos-ing monsignor from Cuernavaca, as a man who criticized ecclesiastical in-volvement in state affairs, might rather have come from "The Legend of the Grand Inquisitor," Dostoevsky's attack on church corruption.[22] Later in Au-gust, O'Connor wrote to Barnes that she was "much cheered that you have got over the mid-term and are still there, not that I had any doubt about it."[23] O'Connor's rejoicing over Barnes's fortitude bespeaks her continued concern about the rigors of Illich's program. When Barnes completed her training, O'Connor sent her "a graduation or survival present. Take yourself to dinner or something in honor of the occasion & consider me present in ghostly form."[24] "She survived the Msgr. [Ivan Illych]," O'Connor reported to McCown on November 2, 1962. "He left his imprint strongly on her. Regina [O'Connor's mother] was shocked at some of her tales."[25]

The shocking Illich seems like one of those "large and startling figures" that might have been drawn in O'Connor's own audacious fiction.[26] Although O'Connor wrote to Barnes that she had heard much about Illich from the novelist Caroline Gordon and her friend Eric Langkjaer, she did not mention precisely what she knew about the priest.[27] O'Connor's awareness of Illich is hardly surprising, for the charismatic monsignor—the youngest clergyman in America to have been awarded that honor—had become one of the most celebrated and controversial Catholic priests in the country.[28] Helen Green glanced at the reasons for the furor when she opined that the radical cleric was the "'growing tip'" and "anti-American."[29] As if applying postcolonial theory to missiology, Illich sought to purge priests, religious, and PAVLA recruits of their gringo presumptions so that they might embody the Word in new cultural contexts.[30]

Illich's anti-imperialist approach to ministry abroad was inspired by his earlier work among Puerto Rican immigrants on New York's West Side. If missionaries are those who "have left their own milieu to preach the Gospel in an area not their own from birth," Illich lived out this vocation at Incarnation Parish from 1951 to 1956.[31] Born in Vienna in 1926, he earned a master's degree in theology and philosophy at the Gregorian University in Rome and a Ph.D. in the philosophy of history from the University of Salzburg, as well as pursuing studies in crystallography at the University of Florence.[32] Illich's education, aristocratic background, and fluency in languages might have earned him a career as a Vatican diplomat, but he chose instead to serve in an archdiocese where one-fourth of the population had its origins in Puerto Rico.[33] At Incarnation Parish, Illich embodied his conviction, which would become central to his training of missionaries, that the "mission of the Church is the social continuation of the Incarnation."[34] To make the Word again become flesh, Illich understood that he must not impose his own cultural traditions on the parishioners that he was supposed to be helping. Rather, he must put aside his Old World heritage and immerse himself in Puerto Rican life; hence, the polyglot Illich learned Spanish from conversing on the street corners of Washington Heights. He established camps where Puerto Rican children might find respite from the slums, and he founded a center that provided child care as well as a gathering place for neighborhood women.[35] In 1955, Illich organized a San Juan Day Fiesta at Fordham University, which brought together thirty-five thousand people for the first major celebration of Puerto Rican life and culture in New York.[36] Illich's success resulted in his being appointed vice rector of the University of Puerto Rico, where he established a program that prepared American clergy for ministry to emigrants from the island. After five years, however, Illich left Puerto Rico because of a controversy involving church-state relations. In 1961 he founded, along with two friends, CIF at Chula Vista, an abandoned villa in Cuernavaca. Chosen by the American Church to train its recruits for work in Latin America, CIF hosted thirty-five lay Catholics and twenty-seven priests and nuns as its first cohort. The group was typical of those who would attend the four-month sessions that were offered twice yearly throughout most of the decade.[37] CIF was only in its second year when Barnes spent the summer and early fall of 1962 at Cuernavaca.

O'Connor's description of Illich's Center at Cuernavaca as a "school for sanctity" indicates her understanding that CIF provided missionaries not just with professional training but with spiritual formation. In a 1956 address entitled "Missionary Poverty," Illich articulated the theology behind the demanding program that schooled Barnes. He claimed that the missionary must embody the kenosis, or self-emptying, of the Incarnation described in Philippians 2:5–8. Just as "God had to assume a nature which was not His, without ceasing to be what He was," the missionary "leaves his own to bring the Gospel to those who are not his own, thus becoming one of them while continuing to remain what he is."[38] The missionary must leave behind not just his or her home but also the language and culture that, covertly or openly—sometimes even arrogantly—bear the values and economy of the evangelist's native land to the far ends of the earth. Illich recognized that, as O'Connor jokingly reminded a friend who had left the country, "the American traveler abroad is a salesman of the USA."[39]

Although Illich did not oppose missionary work or international aid in theory, he insisted that both be purified of the kind of imperialist agenda that infiltrated the proselytizing of Spanish and Portuguese priests who came to Latin America in the sixteenth and seventeenth centuries. These missionaries left a legacy of cozy relations between the civil and religious hierarchy—thus exemplifying O'Connor's claim that the Church "tries to get along with any form of government that does not set itself up as religious."[40] Illich's radicalism actually typified the political tendencies of the post–Vatican II Church, when Rome began to promote a pastoral approach to social issues rather than supporting specific parties.[41] But, in "The Seamy Side of Charity" (1967), he charged that latter-day missionaries often "fulfill the traditional role of a colonial power's lackey chaplain."[42] They import "a foreign Christian image, a foreign pastoral approach and a foreign political message." Although their programs are seemingly motivated by an "outburst of charitable frenzy," missionaries actually prop up the local power structure through self-serving cooperation with the state, and they inhibit more pervasive social change that would empower the poor and the laity. They proclaim the virtues of American capitalism and make the Latin American Church more costly to operate by imposing a highly clericalized bureaucracy and by sponsoring new services (parishes, universities, radio stations), many of which benefit only the middle class.[43] Illich had particular reservations about the program that attracted Barnes to Cuernavaca. In "Dear Father Kevane," a 1965 letter to the national director of the Papal Volunteers, he criticized PAVLA because it took jobs away from native Latin Americans, promoted short-term stays rather than longer and more meaningful commitments, and indulged idealistic recruits in their fantasies that such work was actually a way of serving God.[44] Illich explained that he accepted such volunteers for his seventeen-week course in intercultural education so that they might "shed their misguided missionary zeal."[45]

As O'Connor's worried letters to and about Barnes imply, there was nothing obviously benevolent about Illich's efforts to undermine the politics of benevolence at his self-described "center of de-Yankeefication."[46] Students gained experience in the field and registered for courses in missionary work as well as in Latin American history and culture, but their primary focus was on learning Spanish.[47] Would-be missionaries took five hours of language instruction in groups no larger than four students—three hours of drilling in repetitive exercises, an hour in a language lab, and a final hour to practice conversation. Even more difficult to learn than Spanish vocabulary and grammar were the silences of the language. Illich insisted that missionaries must understand the quiet intervals necessary for receptivity, contemplation, and movement toward the ineffable.[48] Although CIF became renowned as a language school, it does not seem to have helped Barnes very much. "She knows as much Spanish she says as a three-year-old," O'Connor wrote after her friend's last visit to Andalusia, "and she is going to teach chemistry in it. Lord help us all."[49] Yet since Illich believed that learning a new language provides "a deep experience of poverty, of weakness, and of dependence on the good will of another," Barnes's limited Spanish might just have prepared her for the self-surrender of missionary work.[50]

The formation that Illich provided missionaries extended far beyond the academic. To teach the Latin American disregard for punctuality, Illich might appear an hour late for a meeting. To foster an appreciation for the Mexican diet, he might serve two weeks of *favos*. To shatter North American ways of thinking, he might deliver stinging aphorisms, utter koan-like pronouncements, scream "I hate Yankees!" at a nun from New Jersey, or launch into acerbic polemics about the dropouts from his program.[51] The effects of Illich's countercultural education might be reflected in Barnes's reservations about teaching English in South America, which she shared with O'Connor toward the end of her stay in Cuernavaca. O'Connor disagreed, "I cain't for the life of me see how learning *anything*, unless it is evil, is going to make them less Ecuadorian," but Barnes's sensitivity to the political implications of language instruction demonstrates the kind of self-questioning that master Illich sought to provoke by his iconoclastic pedagogy.[52] When O'Connor commented that the violence at Cuernavaca was directed "inward," she echoed exactly what Bishop Méndez Arceo of Cuernavaca meant when he observed: "I love the way Illich tortures his missionaries. Sometimes I cry with emotion at seeing aged men, old priests, shed their old selves under his care."[53] It is hardly surprising that O'Connor's mother might have been "shocked" by some of Barnes's stories about Illich. When the PAVLA recruit left Cuernavaca, the monsignor, who had never gotten along with his Irish clerical colleagues in New York, advised her, "Don't try to be an Irish Catholic, but you'd better read some more theology."[54] Barnes was mystified by the admonition until O'Connor later explained with a bow that *she* was an Irish Catholic.

Although Barnes raised the possibility of the novelist's teaching a course in English, O'Connor did not have to journey abroad to pursue missionary work.[55] As a sufferer from lupus and a self-professed "hermit novelist," she often took a wry view toward traveling to foreign shores.[56] However, O'Connor might have found Barnes's vocation so fascinating because the Milledgeville writer was herself a missionary by Illich's standards. Indeed, the monsignor from Cuernavaca recognized that such work was not defined by its foreign geography; one could be, for example, a "home missioner in the South of the United States."[57] O'Connor grounded her "incarnational art" in the same fleshly mystery that defined Illich's views on missiology.[58] Her mission, as novelist and as believer, was exactly what Illich defined as *mission* itself—"the transformation of signs (words, gestures) which traditionally meant worldly reality into representations of revealed meaning."[59] Yet although O'Connor incarnated her faith in her fiction, she insisted that a story should not be turned into propaganda: "if you do manage to use it successfully for social, religious, or other purposes, it is because you make it art first."[60] O'Connor's artistry, like Illich's missionary shock tactics at Cuernavaca, inclined toward the edgy, the extreme, and the outré as she explored state-side versions of the politics of benevolence.

Much as O'Connor knew that the bomb dropped on Hiroshima had reverberations felt along the Oconee River, Illich understood that the harmful effects of American benevolence were not limited to Mexico, Chile, or Brazil. In "Violence: A Mirror for Americans" (1968) he pointed to the "link between minority marginality at home and mass margination overseas." [61] Illich proposed that if America could understand how its goodwill was perceived abroad, it might better understand why its social programs had failed in its own slums. He claimed, for example, that in Harlem just as in Latin America and Viet Nam, American benevolence was motivating the spread of the national gospel of wealth and democracy, and possibly also provoking violence as a way to reject such "foreign gods." [62] Illich brought his critique of self-serving charity home to O'Connor's Dixie when, in "Yankee, Go Home: The American Do-Gooder in Latin America" (1968), he told a group of would-be volunteers that the differences between themselves and the Mexican villagers whom they sought to help was so great that the North Americans "imagine [them]selves exactly the way a white preacher saw himself when he offered his life preaching to the black slaves on a plantation in Alabama."[63]

Illich's stinging analogy between antebellum missionaries in the U.S. South and contemporary volunteers who work south of the U.S. border anticipates the increasingly global perspective that has remapped the geography of southern studies. Reflecting on his bond with Faulkner, García Márquez described the Caribbean as having "a homogeneous cultural composition which extends from northern Brazil to the U.S. South," and he concluded that "not only Faulkner, but the majority of the novelists from the U.S. South, are writers possessed by the demons of the Caribbean."[64] These *diabolos* preside over a shared history of slavery, conquest, class stratification, economic underdevelopment, and a plantation-style society and economy, as well as wrenching industrialization and modernization. Most pointedly, both "Souths" were dependent on and exploited by a "North."[65] In *Look Away!*, Jon Smith and Deborah Cohn complicate such broadened regional affiliations even further by arguing that the U.S. South serves as "the uncanny double of both the First and Third Worlds." It is "a space simultaneously (or alternately) center and margin, victor and defeated, empire and colony, essentialist and hybrid, northern and southern (both in the global sense)."[66] O'Connor herself glimpsed this new U.S. South–South American axis. "I hadn't realized that life in Brazil might resemble life here in the South," she wrote to Elizabeth Bishop, who had a residence in Rio de Janeiro, "but I guess there are many similarities." When Bishop sent O'Connor a copy of *The Diary of Helena Morley*, a memoir (translated by Bishop) about late nineteenth-century life in rural Brazil, O'Connor was reminded of the diary of a woman who left New York and came to Georgia before the Civil War.[67]

In the fiction of O'Connor's postcolonial South, the heirs of Illich's Alabama missionaries, and the counterparts of his Yankee interlopers in Latin America, live on. Typical of their professed benevolence is Manly Pointer, the Bible-selling con man in "Good Country People," who "wanted to become a missionary because he thought that was the way you could do most for people. 'He who losest his life shall find it,' he said simply."[68] As early as the nineteenth century, the establishment of foreign missions to India, China, and the Near East ran parallel to the South's domestic missions to slaves and Native Americans. O'Connor's missionaries, unlike Walker Percy's, typically do not cross oceans.[69] Although such southern contemporaries as Katherine Anne Porter, Reynolds Price, William Styron, and Eudora Welty all set stories abroad, O'Connor did not feel comfortable in wandering there in her imagination any more than in fact. She confessed to Robie Macaulay, some of whose stories take place in Germany and Japan, "I wonder at how you can pick up the feeling of foreign places like that as I cannot put down any idiom but my own. I presume there are some advantages to not being a Southerner."[70] O'Connor did, however, find the foreign right in the familiar territory of her native land.

What Illich critiqued in Latin America had its counterpart in O'Connor's South.[71] Her region knew the politics of benevolence from Smith and Cohn's hybrid perspective—as both "victor and defeated."[72] As the defeated, the South had encountered a host of Yankee benefactors—postbellum carpetbaggers, apostles of industry, and the kind of moral zealots that often irked O'Connor.[73] As the victor, it perpetuated a chivalric tradition of noblesse oblige that made acts of generosity into a cultural ideal. However, its rigid social hierarchy and post–Civil War siege mentality militated against purely selfless regard for the other. The result was that benevolence might blur into self-interest and condescension. O'Connor's fiction exposes such egotism and shows how her lords and ladies of the South get schooled when their misguided largesse meets head-on with modern upheaval. Proffering imperial charity, they find themselves dismissed, decentered, and dethroned as a result—and then they may cross the line between Illich's First World benefactor and his Third World beneficiary.[74]

A seemingly good man is not at all hard to find in O'Connor's fiction—nor is a similarly benevolent woman. In "Everything That Rises Must Converge," Julian's mother, proud of her plantation heritage, offers a shiny penny to an African American boy whom she has recently met on a bus. Likewise obsessed with the South's racial and class divisions, Mrs. Turpin in "Revelation" thinks: "To help anybody out that needed it was her philosophy of life. She never spared herself when she found somebody in need, whether they were white or black, trash or decent."[75] As O'Connor's down-home evangelists try to practice the same Christian gospel carried by Illich's Latin American missionaries, or a humanistic version of it, they stumble over the same arrogance and insensitivity that the priest's Center at Cuernavaca sought to eliminate. Julian's eleemosynary mother is struck by the black child's aggrieved mother and then struck again when her own son lectures his paternalistic parent, "The old manners are obsolete and your graciousness is not worth a damn."[76] The magnanimous lady proves the truth of Illich's maxim that "it is hard to help by refusing to give alms," for like the missionary programs in Latin America, the white benefactress offers only "palliatives to ease the pain of a cancerous structure."[77] And the unstinting Mrs. Turpin witnesses the rebuke of her proud virtue when in her culminating vision she is among the least of the last on the happy-go-lucky parade to heaven. The elision between victor and defeated that Smith and Cohn locate in their New World South becomes, in O'Connor's world, the reduction of the high-minded and helpful to a state of abject helplessness. Yet humiliation may be the prelude to insight. Just as St. Catherine of Siena spent three years in the "cell" of self-knowledge before she "emerged to change the politics of Italy," these soul-shocked altruists may be the beginning of a new South.[78] O'Connor's "school for sanctity" is a kind of inverse version of Paulo Freire's "pedagogy of the oppressed."[79] Whereas the Brazilian educator, who was admired by Illich, sought to develop critical consciousness in the victimized, the fiction writer shows how victimizers may learn startling lessons about the limits of their benevolence.

O'Connor's focus on the missionary, not just at home but in the homes of the South, accords with Illich's own view of the political as originating in the domestic. Although Illich argued for depoliticizing missionary work, he was hardly apolitical. Rather, he campaigned against church-state partisanship and gospel-inspired colonialism because he favored empowering Latin Americans at the local level. He resembles the German philosopher and hermeneutist Hans-Georg Gadamer in regarding wider solidarities as growing out of the sharing and intertwining of individual lives.[80] Returning politics to its radical origin, Illich argues that the ancient Greeks "conceived of friendship as the supreme flowering of the interaction which happens in the *politea,* the good political society."[81] Yet, he believes that technology has so obstructed relationships by devaluing face-to-face conversations and by redefining individuals as objects for engineering that today the political must grow out of *philia,* out of friendship. Illich asserts that the "I" is only realized in the context of the other, especially the eye of the beholder. The pupil "is not a mirror of me. It is you making me the gift of that which Ivan is for you."[82] The self achieves its humanity through the loving donation of the other who stands eye to eye. Such friendship is the foundation of the virtuous community, and this community may then find its expression in political life. Illich himself lived out this evolution from priest to activist, and the primacy of the interpersonal encounter became his foundation for opposing how self-interest can taint missionary work.

O'Connor's fiction repeatedly returns to Illich's threshold of political life, the place where friendship begins as "the possibility of leading somebody through the door."[83] Although her work registers an American anxiety about invasion that, as Jon Lance Bacon has demonstrated, was so typical of Cold War culture, it also explores a startling receptivity.[84] Let a stranger stand before a doorway in O'Connor's fiction, and the story will tell of what happens when the outsider gets welcomed into the house. Her staging of this liminal moment has its precedent in a much older story. Illich observes that, whereas in the ancient world food and lodging were offered to fellow Hellenes but denied to barbarians, Jesus used the parable of the good-hearted Samaritan to expand the limits of sociability beyond the favored group of one's own kind. Inspired by this challenge to xenophobia, O'Connor's fiction carries southern hospitality—that most legendary aspect of its regional manners—to the extreme. Such cordiality forces all of her good country and city people to face what Illich would identify as the entryway into the *politea:* "I have to decide who I will take into my arms, to whom I will lose myself, whom I will treat as that *vis-à-vis,* that face into which I will look and lovingly touch with my fingering gaze, from whom I will accept being who I am as a gift."[85]

When, in 1959, O'Connor rejected the prospect of meeting James Baldwin in Georgia, she placed respect for local manners over the mysterious welcome that Illich envisions.[86] O'Connor's fiction is less conventional than a 1950s Milledgeville door closed on an African American, although it often imagines less racially charged encounters. In *Wise Blood* (1952), her first novel, the crowded streets and rented rooms of Taulkinham are so filled with the lonely-hearted that the possibility of Illich's loving gaze emerges only at the end in Mrs. Flood's growing tenderness toward the self-blinded Hazel Motes. The hollowed eyes of the ex-preacher may yet guide the landlady to a home beyond her boardinghouse. The generous folk in O'Connor's subsequent works readily offer hospitality to the odd and the outcast who appear on their doorsteps. One domestic triangle keeps getting redrawn in O'Connor's fiction: a parent reaches across a less socially-conscious son or daughter, and out toward a wayward young person who seems to need a home. However, such amiability leads to no heartwarming redefinition of family boundaries but rather to a struggle for household mastery that rivals the intramural conflicts explored by Pinter in such closely contemporary plays as *The Caretaker* (1960) and *The Homecoming* (1965). O'Connor's missionaries fail to the extent that they brazenly pursue power under their own roofs and forego genuine benevolence. Clinging to their home rule, they take their possessions to heart or seek to dominate their invasive guests by imposing on them a benignly inadequate ideology to explain away their trespasses. O'Connor's fiction tests the deep-down goodness of her seemingly admirable do-gooders in order to expose the self-protection, self-satisfaction, and self-aggrandizement that militate against the politics of friendship.

In "A Circle in the Fire" (1954), Mrs. Cope tries to follow Illich's pre-scription that charity should begin at the threshold and extend to the table. She is convinced of the benevolence with which she has received three ill-behaved teens from the housing projects in Atlanta who arrive at her farm, all unannounced, in the hope of having a country vacation. Although Mrs. Cope does not allow the trio to reside in her house, they stay on her prop-erty and enjoy her land despite the playfully murderous animosity of her daughter Sally Virginia. "I think I have been very nice to you boys. I've fed you twice," she tells the youths after they have steadily failed to appreciate her calculated efforts as hostess.[87] Mrs. Cope's charity seems motivated by gratitude to God for her good fortune, but her kindness is really a delimit-ing strategy for defending her fiefdom. It enables her to exclude most of the threatening world from her narrow family circle, so that she does not feel any blood-and-bone kinship with those who suffer. Yet after Mrs. Cope be-holds the fire that the youths have started in her woods, she knows in her flesh the fellowship of misery that might produce true charity. Glimpsing the sorrow on her mother's face, Sally Virginia is initiated into a daughter-hood of woe that might likewise mollify her fierce heart.

"The Comforts of Home" (1960) offers a more benign portrait of be-nevolence and a more lurid exposé of household politics. Thomas's moth-er exceeds Sally Virginia's mother in her wild charity, for she allows the lying, thieving Sarah Ham not just onto her property but into her house and family. "I keep thinking it might be you," Thomas's mother tells her son about the nineteen-year-old that she virtually adopts.[88] After the good woman tries to save Sarah from an apparent suicide attempt, the benefac-tress finds that her sympathy for her guest widens to become "mourning for the world."[89] At the end, Thomas's mother goes even further than Mrs. Cope in her discovery of heartfelt agony, for she lives out a maternal love born of knowing such all-encompassing sorrow. When the lady of the house tries to protect Sarah during the randy guest's climactic confrontation with Thomas, the mother is shot by her son. Whereas Sally Virginia remains a hostile onlooker to her mother's measured hospitality, Thomas comes to the foreground in this story as the active opponent of his parent's mistaken liberality. He is so intent on preserving his comfortable domesticity that he reduces Sarah to a "moral moron"[90] so that he might then expel her from his virtuous mind, heart, and hearth. Instead of repelling this home inva-sion, Thomas fires at his scapegoat of a mother and is arrested as if he were

a tawdry killer out of pulp fiction. The unwelcoming host is shockingly dis-
comfited—but O'Connor does not show whether Thomas, like Mrs. Cope,
opens himself to the grief that could make him more hospitable to the next
stranger at his threshold.

In "The Lame Shall Enter First" (1962), Sheppard combines the missionary benevolence of Thomas's mother with Thomas's own predilection
for domination and theorization. At first, he provides entrée to the lame
Rufus Johnson, a thirteen-year-old recently released from a reformatory,
who blatantly admits that his wickedness is a sign of his bondage to Satan.
The open house serves Sheppard's enlightened agenda. The widower hopes
that his hospitality might teach his son Norton, grieving over the death of
his mother, to be less selfish. And Sheppard seeks to validate his sociological interpretation of the juvenile delinquent by showing that if Rufus can
experience enough compassion and enough educational opportunities, he
can be saved—not merely from a life of crime but from his belief in the
devil. Sheppard fails because he regards each of the boys as a project rather
than a person. Rufus exposes the lameness of Sheppard's efforts at social
renovation when, just before being arrested and removed from his patron's
home, the youth denounces his benefactor as a false messiah. The scorned
host and stunned father realizes that he "had stuffed his own emptiness
with good works like a glutton. He had ignored his own child to feed his vision of himself."[91] Even more devastating is Sheppard's discovery that his
neglect has driven Norton to hang himself because Rufus had suggested
dying as a way for the bereft boy to recover his dead mother. Confronted by
the dangling body of his son, Sheppard stands in heartsick community with
Mrs. Cope and Thomas's mother. Their stories offer variations on Illich's
imprecation and brief meditation, "To hell with good intentions. This is a
theological statement,"[92] for they trace the altruism-paved road that leads,
if not to perdition, then at least to an agonizing denouement for parents and
children alike, for guests and hosts. Only if O'Connor's missionaries pursue
their heart-piercing sorrow toward profound compunction, as Richard Giannone illustrates, do they have the possibility of connecting with others
and keeping the violence from completely bearing them away.[93]

O'Connor's fictions about home missionary efforts that go awry seem to converge in *The Violent Bear It Away* (1960), a novel that shows how the politics
of benevolence may move beyond violence to rediscover the table fellowship

that should be the source of *politea*. When O'Connor described the "school for sanctity" in Cuernavaca as a place that realizes "what it means to bear away the kingdom of heaven with violence: the violence is directed inward," she might have been reading Illich's work by way of her second novel.[94] *The Violent Bear It Away* takes its title, which O'Connor considered the book's best feature, from Jesus's pronouncement in Matthew 11:12 about the use of force and the coming of the kingdom of heaven.[95] O'Connor's interpretation of Barnes's training in Mexico suggests, conversely, how her second novel might be read by way of Illich's work. Alluding to O'Connor's titular passage, Illich observes, in "Mission and Midwifery" (1964), how violence was directed outward during the recent counterrevolution in Brazil, where both church and state lobbied against socialism: "The violence needed to enter the kingdom of Heaven was used to justify imprisonment, and the need to separate the good and the bad on the day of judgment served as a justification to strip opponents of their civil rights."[96] In *The Violent Bear It Away*, O'Connor explores ways in which benevolent missionaries might direct violence both outward and inward as they pursue the kingdom, and the power, in the name of benevolence.

So central is missionary work to *The Violent Bear It Away* that O'Connor places, midway in its pages, a chapter that stars a family of well-traveled evangelists. The night after fourteen-year-old Tarwater has appeared on Rayber's doorstep and been taken into his home, the hospitable uncle follows his nephew to a tabernacle, where they hear young Lucette Carmody proclaim the gospel. The preacher who introduces the Carmodys, a family of missionaries, declares that Lucette "has travelled the world over telling people about Jesus. She's been to India and China. She's spoken to all the rulers of the world."[97] Originally from Texas, Mrs. Carmody explains that she and her Tennessee-born husband have accompanied their charismatic daughter since the daughter began her vocation at six: "We saw that she had a mission, that she had been called. We saw that we could not keep her to ourselves and so we have endured many hardships to give her to the world, to bring her to you tonight." Blurring the foreign mission into the home mission that supports it, Mrs. Carmody uses her family's preaching to potentates abroad as a way of appealing to the listeners right in front of her: "'To us,' she said, 'you are as important as the great rulers of the world!'"[98]

As the self-important Rayber watches this missionary spectacle of saving souls and raising funds, O'Connor uses his fluid consciousness to overlay past and present so that all of the novel's major characters are brought onto the spot-lit stage with Lucette. Rayber judges the child missionary to be "exploited."[99] He may just be right, for the sensationalism of Lucette's performance seems as calculated as Mrs. Carmody's reference to the generosity of her audience. Inspired by this judgment, Rayber remembers what he considers his own exploitation, when his uncle Mason kidnapped him as a seven-year-old and brought him to Powderhead to be baptized. Rayber finds similarly exploitative the control that Mason, though now dead, still exerts over Tarwater, who has been attracted to this sanctuary. Finally, Rayber recalls how his developmentally delayed son Bishop is "exploited by the very fact that he is alive."[100] The exploited Lucette, standing in a white light at the center of the novel, focuses the political concerns of *The Violent Bear It Away*. The crippled child preacher with a wisdom beyond her years embodies Patricia Yaeger's claim that the grotesque in southern literature provides "a set of unacknowledged political coordinates." Yaeger views the grotesque "as a prose technique for moving background information into the foreground of a novel or story."[101] She further illustrates her definition with a scene from *Uncle Tom's Cabin* in which a young slave, entertaining two white men with his distorted mimicry, becomes "a site for reading cultural depravity."[102] In *The Violent Bear It Away*, O'Connor also uses a deformed child performer who copies adult behavior to reveal corrupted forms of magnanimity. As Lucette retells salvation history, she comes to speak of Herod, who feared that his dominion might be threatened by the birth of the upstart Jesus. Under the pretext of benevolence, the great ruler inquired of the Magi about the newborn king so that he might have any infant rivals massacred in an act of state-sanctioned violence. Rayber longs to save Lucette and all such exploited children from the ongoing victimization of Herod-like adults. However, he overlooks his own generous role in exploiting children. Illuminated on a dark stage, Lucette highlights the relationship between power and benevolence that O'Connor's principal characters, missionaries all, must violently face in the novel.

The most obvious of these missionaries is eighty-four-year-old Mason, a prophet who runs a backcountry "school for sanctity." Set some four miles off a rugged dirt road that leads to a mile-long wagon track and foot path, Powderhead seems so remote from the city where Rayber lives that it might as well be in Cuernavaca. The old man's pupil in this foreign land is the orphan that he took into his home as a baby. Mason has shown his own form of hospitality to his great-nephew, Tarwater. The preacher has "schooled him in the evils that befall prophets" and made it the mission of his old age to "instruct Tarwater . . . in the hard facts of serving the Lord."[103] Although the great-uncle teaches the youth reading, writing, and arithmetic as well as sacred and secular history, he also offers a lifelong lesson in the violence that will herald the kingdom. Mason's pedagogy at Powderhead is as brash as that of the "powerhouse," Illich, at his school for missionaries.[104] Convinced that God's reign will burst upon a corrupt world in need of salvation, the old prophet roars, hollers, hisses, slams his fist, grabs his nephew's overalls, and delivers angry denunciations of the sinners before him. Years before, Mason had succeeded in kidnapping both Rayber and Tarwater to baptize them, but he fails as the most domestic of missionaries when he tried to enter Rayber's house to claim young Bishop for Christ. So, he entrusts the task to Tarwater as "the first mission the Lord sends you."[105]

Although Mason's harsh missionary discipline is, in truth, a result of solicitude for Tarwater, the teen feels his great-uncle's violence as directed outward—toward him, and the sinful world. Mason seems too much like the "ecclesiastic conquistador" that Illich reproaches for being obsessed with saving souls and with counting baptisms; yet Mason also does not seem violent enough to Tarwater.[106] Once, when the pair traveled to the city, Tarwater was filled with scorn for his great-uncle because the elderly missionary did not denounce its sinful denizens with prophetic fury. Mason replied: "I'm here on bidnis. . . . If you been called by the Lord, then be about your own mission."[107] After Mason's death, Tarwater returns to the city to become a disciple of the uncle who claims to have renounced both Mason's violence and his Christianity. When Tarwater arrives at Rayber's home, he feels as if he has been "set down in the place of his mission."[108] As the newcomer bangs the brass knocker and then kicks the door with his work shoe, he stands violently on the threshold of what Illich identified as the political. Tarwater is the stranger who seeks entry, and Rayber responds as if well-schooled in the politics of friendship. He invites the boy into his home, feeds him, and gives him a room in which to sleep. Compared to Mason, the humanistic Rayber is a kind of antimissionary. Whereas Lucette delivers a Johannine-themed sermon on the Logos of Love, Rayber preaches the gospel of the self-redeeming powers of human intelligence. It is appropriate that Rayber is a teacher, for Illich charges that the "school has become the established church of secular times."[109] The benevolence of this priestly aca-

demic is purely intellectual. The pedagogue is convinced that he must save
Tarwater from the kind of seduction of the mind that Mason once practiced
on him as a boy, when the old man lured the seven-year-old Rayber away to
be baptized. The would-be benefactor insists that he tried to help Tarwater in the past when he sought to rescue the child from Mason's care, even
though the attempt was unsuccessful. He offers now: "I can help you. All I
want to do is help you any way I can."[110] So, Rayber converts his hospitality into a school for "de-sanctification." Through a rigorous regime of field
trips into the secular city, Tarwater's uncle hopes to "un-teach" the gospel of
Mason and to educate his disciple in the virtues of the mind. Typical of Rayber's progressive curriculum are his trips with Tarwater to a different restaurant every night, "run by a different color of foreigner so that he would
learn, he said, how other nationalities ate."[111] Whereas Lucette preached
in India and China, Rayber turns the foreign into an urbanite's exercise in
cultural diversity.

In rejecting Mason's violent God, and his violent bearing, Rayber seems
to have followed O'Connor's interpretation of Matthew 11:12. As she wrote
to Barnes, the violence needed to establish the kingdom of heaven must be
"directed inward."[112] The kindly minded schoolteacher has sublimated all of
the rage that keeps threatening to erupt toward Mason and Tarwater. In its
place he has cultivated an equipoise that perfects stoic indifference, turning
it into chilling anesthesia. However, the result of such nonviolent violence
is a killing kindness, for Rayber is guilty of far worse exploitation than what
he denounces in Lucette's parents. The uncle seeks not simply to convert
his nephew to his benevolent ideas about reason and progress but to convert
the teen himself into no more than an idea in his head. Such abstraction
"thinks away" Tarwater's humanity and thus provides a deadly intellectual
counterpart to Rayber's attempt to take away Bishop's life. Because his son
does not live up to the teacher's definition of the human as the intelligent,
Rayber once tried to drown his child at the beach. He envisions a future
century without children like Bishop, for doctors will be able "to put them
to sleep when they're born."[113] Although Rayber could not complete his own
version of such euthanasia, he tells Tarwater about the attempt in order to
provide an example for the youth's merciful murder of Bishop.

Tarwater lives divided between the violent benevolence of Mason and
the benevolent violence of Rayber. His dilemma is focused on the simple-
minded and good-hearted Bishop, who, like the hobbled Lucette, is a po-

litically charged grotesque. To welcome Bishop is to take a stand in favor of all who are exploited. Tarwater is drawn to Bishop, yet he also avoids looking his cousin in the eye. He senses the threshold implied by a face-to-face encounter—the kind of encounter that Illich prized as the foundation of political life. As the invisible stranger who befriends Tarwater warns the aspiring missionary, accepting Bishop could undermine the entire social order: "You have to quit confusing a madness with a mission. . . . If you baptize once, you'll be doing it the rest of your life. If it's an idiot this time, the next time it's liable to be a nigger."[114] Rayber also senses the possibility of such dangerous destabilization. He cares for Bishop so that he does not have to love the rest of the world, as if the interpersonal limits, rather than leads to, the political. Well-schooled by Mason, Tarwater sneers at how Rayber intellectualizes his fatherhood. Yet the nephew also sneers at how his ambivalent uncle seems to imitate the generous Mason by giving his life to "nurse an idiot."[115]

Both Rayber and Tarwater charge that the other still lives under the lingering influence of old Mason, the veteran missionary they profess to despise. The result of their mutual animosity is that by the time they travel to the Cherokee Lodge, the pair ride in silence, "the boy sitting as usual on his side of the car like some foreign dignitary who would not admit speaking the language—the filthy hat, the stinking overalls, worn defiantly like a national costume."[116] The scornful image maps how far the undiplomatic Rayber has traveled from Illich's threshold of the political. Lucette had "spoken to all the rulers of the world," but Rayber cannot even communicate with this ambassador from another land whose arrogant ethnicity he disdains.[117] Rayber's home version of the foreign mission fails because, a jingoist in his heart, he feels only contempt for the embodied alterity of his nephew from afar. Tarwater's country dress scandalously insists that the native son is not just an idea in the schoolteacher's head; however, his uncle and would-be father, like the missionary who clings to his own culture as normative, cannot get beyond his own provincialism.[118] Rayber later becomes so incensed with Tarwater that he wants to shout, "Go to hell! Go baptize the whole world!" as if confounding yet confirming Jesus's charge in Matthew (28:19) to spread the news of salvation that is the scriptural foundation for missionary work.[119]

Tarwater follows this double-voiced but unspoken command by carrying out the imperatives of both Mason and Rayber. At the lake by the

Cherokee Lodge, he drowns Bishop as his uncle had intended yet baptizes Bishop as his great-uncle had instructed. The murder is a missionary outrage. Bishop is not simply the spiritual kin of the evangelical Lucette but the embodiment of her message about the Logos. The boy who repeatedly seeks and gives affection suffers the same fate as the divine word of love. After drowning Bishop, Tarwater soon finds his flesh subjected to the most malign form of governance. When the youth is picked up by the driver of a cream-and-lavender-colored car, Tarwater crosses yet another threshold: he meets a man on a consummate mission, last in a line of roadside benefactors that, like the multiple avatars of Melville's *The Confidence Man,* are simply out to serve themselves. After the stranger offers the fourteen-year-old strange-tasting cigarettes and whiskey, he carries out the kind of bodily assault that aggressors have regularly inflicted on the victims of imperialism.[120] The master rapes his subaltern. The predator, by performing a vicious act of domination and occupation and then by leaving the teen, naked and bound, in the woods, asserts the eroticism of power and the power of eroticism.

The conclusion of O'Connor's novel shows how Tarwater moves from being a politicized body to becoming a member of the body politic. Although Tarwater's setting fire to the scene of his molestation might seem like a violent response to violence, it actually begins his agonized rejection of such vassalage. In its place, Tarwater develops a greater awareness of "the corporate body of the human community moving through history" that John Desmond views as characteristic of O'Connor's later work.[121] When Tarwater returns to Powderhead, he begins to make a fist at Buford Munson, the African American friend of Mason who buried the dead prophet while Tarwater lay drunk. However, Tarwater changes the hostile gesture to a wave, and he looks forward to dining with his black benefactor. That fellowship of the table deepens into sacramental sharing when Tarwater beholds a vision of Mason as one of the multitude enjoying a paradisal repast of loaves and fishes. The youth accepts his own spiritual hunger, which he has long tried to stifle by consuming insubstantial food and drink, because this yearning connects him to a tradition of truth-seekers who longed for God. Such communion broadens into service to the community as Tarwater hears the words, "GO WARN THE CHILDREN OF GOD OF THE TERRIBLE SPEED OF MERCY."[122] At the end of the novel, the youth sets out "toward the dark city, where the children of God lay sleeping," yet his burned-out eyes "seemed already to envision the fate that awaited him."[123] If Lucette's sermon about the Word is prophetic, Tarwater's destiny is grim indeed. Referring to Tarwater, O'Connor wrote to John Hawkes that she kept "wondering about how the children of God will finish him off."[124] However, the novel leaves Tarwater on the threshold of his missionary vocation and never depicts such final violence.

Equally unresolved is the fate of Roslyn Barnes. Although O'Connor's correspondence with Barnes chronicles one of the writer's important friendships in the early 1960s, the PAVLA missionary eventually vanishes from the letters collected in *The Habit of Being*. The volume includes no further communication from O'Connor to Barnes after Barnes departed in the fall of 1962 to teach chemistry at a Jesuit university in Valparaiso. As Sally Fitzgerald explains in a footnote, Barnes entrusted to Father McCown the letters that she had received from O'Connor and "left for South America, where she disappeared in the course of her missionary work. All efforts to trace her or learn her fate have failed."[125] On April 19, 1963, O'Connor wrote to McCown that Barnes seemed disheartened and would probably enjoy hearing from him. The following January, O'Connor informed Thomas Stritch that she had received a note from the *Review of Politics* acknowledging its receipt of an essay by Barnes.[126]

The article was an unlikely submission for the *Review of Politics*, a Notre Dame journal of political thought. Entitled "Inscape and Interiority: Their Nature and Dynamics," it was based on the third chapter of Barnes's thesis on Hopkins and Teilhard. The essay was actually submitted by O'Connor. In the absence of her friend, O'Connor befriended Barnes's writing instead, bringing it to the attention of friends, and friends of friends. In an unpublished letter, dated December 12, 1963, and now in the University of Notre Dame archives, O'Connor asked M. A. Fitzsimons, the editor of the *Review of Politics*, to consider the piece by Barnes. She mentioned that Thomas Stritch, her friend and a professor of communications at Notre Dame, had suggested the quarterly. O'Connor also sent Barnes's work to Brainard Cheney, the novelist and veteran of Washington and Tennessee politics, who had been her friend since 1953. Cheney called the submission to the attention of Andrew Lytle, editor of the *Sewanee Review*, but he later returned the essay to O'Connor, on April 25, 1964, with a comment that it needed to be shortened and better organized.[127] Earlier that month, on April 13, Fitzsimons had also returned Barnes's article to O'Connor and

explained that despite his efforts with the other editors, they could not recommend it for the *Review of Politics.*

Although the *Review of Politics* did not publish the section from Barnes's
thesis, O'Connor's efforts on behalf of the essay testify to the friendship that
supported Barnes's PAVLA work from her initial application to her departure for South America. In late October 1962, before Barnes left for her assignment, she spent a week at O'Connor's farm rather than staying with her
family, which did not approve of her missionary vocation. The friend who
was about to leave her homeland might have found in O'Connor's home the
welcome that Illich identifies as "the starting point of politics": "a practice
of hospitality recovering the threshold, the door through which I can invite
you, the table around which you can sit, and, when you get tired, the bed
where you can sleep, and from there generating seedbeds for virtue and
friendship on the one hand, and on the other, radiating out for the possible
rebirth of community."[128]

Then, after the visit to Andalusia, Barnes was gone. There is no satis-
fyingly dramatic closure to the plot of her life. Barnes was not Celia Cople-
stone in T. S. Eliot's *The Cocktail Party,* who abandons London society,
joins a nursing order, and is martyred in Kinkanja; the PAVLA volunteer's
disappearance did not, it seems, signify her achievement of "the ever more
complete offering of self and world as a true oblation" that she identified
in her thesis on Hopkins and Teilhard.[129] At best, there is the recent recollection of Peter Geniesse, a PAVLA colleague, who served in Antofagasta,
Chile, from 1963 to 1965. He recalls meeting Barnes "a couple of times for
PAVLA retreats in the environs of Santiago. However, she was a quiet, stu-
dious type, a bit of a loner who didn't take part in group activities."[130] The
elusive Barnes already seemed to be receding when a January 1964 letter from O'Connor to Stritch provided an intriguing final glimpse: "She is
presently lost in the wilds of Chile, the last letter she was somewhere for
Christmas that was just like Nazareth, no water no lights no nothing but
holy Indians and mud houses and she was eating it up. I guess I'm just old.
What piety I got is totally dependent on water, plumbing and electricity."[131]
O'Connor seems to smile at Barnes's connoisseurship of biblical starkness
in Chile, even as she smiles upon her friend's entry into a realm that was
as desolate as it was fulfilling. Much as the fiction writer speculated about
Tarwater's destiny beyond the final pages of the novel, readers might wonder about the fate of the missionary who was O'Connor's friend. Did Barnes

travel beyond her Nazareth-like Christmas in Chile and, like Mrs. Flood in *Wise Blood,* wander backward toward glimpsing the dot of a star that marked the Incarnation? Did she succumb to the discouragement that eventually beset so many of her PAVLA colleagues? Did she get wracked by the deeper sorrow that afflicts O'Connor's do-gooders when their hospitality leads to disaster, or did she continue the political action that Illich traced to being welcomed through the door and to the table? The questions look toward a mystery that is fit for the ending of an O'Connor story about the politics of benevolence.

Notes

1. PAVLA officially ended in 1971 because of poor communication, lack of support for those in the field, and problems with missionary assignments. Some volunteers worked in churches, schools, and clinics, but many were frustrated by the lack of clear goals and suitable jobs (see Gerald M. Costello, *Mission to Latin America: The Successes and Failures of a Twentieth Century Crusade* [Maryknoll, N.Y.: Orbis, 1979], 90–97; and David Agren, "Papal Volunteers: Nearly 50 Years Later, a Mixed Legacy," *Tidings* July 24 2009, Web).

2. Agren, "Papal Volunteers."

3. Costello, *Mission to Latin America,* 89–91.

4. Flannery O'Connor, *The Habit of Being: Letters of Flannery O'Connor,* ed. Sally Fitzgerald (New York: Farrar, Straus and Giroux, 1979), 446.

5. Ibid., 479.

6. John L. Hammond, *The Politics of Benevolence: Revival Religion and American Voting Behavior* (Norwood, N.J.: Ablex, 1979), 3–4.

7. Mine Ener, *Managing Egypt's Poor and the Politics of Benevolence* (Princeton: Princeton University Press, 2003), 24.

8. Flannery O'Connor, *Mystery and Manners: Occasional Prose,* ed. Sally and Robert Fitzgerald (New York: Farrar, Straus and Giroux, 1969), 27.

9. Ivan Illich, *Celebration of Awareness: A Call for Institutional Revolution* (Berkeley: Heyday, 1970), 28.

10. R. Neil Scott and Valerie Nye, *Postmarked Milledgeville: A Guide to Flannery O'Connor's Correspondence in Libraries and Archives,* ed. Sarah Gordon and Irwin Streight (Milledgeville: Georgia College & State University, 2002), 9.

11. O'Connor, *Habit of Being,* 428.

12. Ibid., 446.

13. Ibid., 508.

14. Ibid., 443.

15. For O'Connor's debt to Hopkins, see Sarah Gordon, *Flannery O'Connor: The Obedient Imagination* (Athens: University of Georgia Press, 2000), 144–52.

16. O'Connor, *Habit of Being*, 479.

17. Ibid., 482.

18. Ibid., 494.

19. Ibid., 486.

20. Ibid., 488, 490.

21. Ibid., 98–99.

22. Ibid., 304.

23. Ibid., 489.

24. Ibid., 493.

25. Ibid., 497.

26. O'Connor, *Mystery and Manners*, 34.

27. O'Connor, *Habit of Being*, 479, 482.

28. Francine du Plessix Gray, *Divine Disobedience: Profiles in Catholic Radicalism* (New York: Knopf, 1970), 248.

29. O'Connor, *Habit of Being*, 494.

30. Although Illich was an early critic of the Church's work abroad, his reservations would later be echoed by many missionaries and scholars in the field (see Costello, *Mission to Latin America*, 49–51).

31. Ivan Illich, *The Church, Change and Development*, ed. Fred Eychaner (Chicago: Urban Training Center Press, 1970), 112.

32. Gray, *Divine Disobedience*, 241–42.

33. L. Glenn Smith and Joan K. Smith, *Lives in Education: A Narrative of People and Ideas*, 2nd ed. (New York: St. Martin's, 1994), 434.

34. Illich, *Church, Change and Development*, 85.

35. Gray, *Divine Disobedience*, 243–46; Joseph P. Fitzpatrick, "Ivan Illich as We Knew Him in the 1950s," in *The Challenges of Ivan Illich: A Collective Reflection*, ed. Lee Hoinacki and Carl Mitcham (Albany: State University of New York Press, 2002), 36.

36. Gray, *Divine Disobedience*, 246–48; "Fiesta," *Time*, July 2, 1956. After Illich was ordered to leave Puerto Rico, Fordham gave the priest a position in its political science department and space at the university to develop CIF, whose first president was Fr. Laurence McGinley, president of Fordham (see Gray, *Divine Disobedience*, 251, 253; Fitzpatrick, "Ivan Illich as We Knew Him," 41; and Costello, *Mission to Latin America*, 107).

37. Todd Hartch, "Ivan Illich and the American Catholic Missionary Initiative in Latin America," *International Bulletin of Missionary Research*, October 1, 2009; "Boot Camp for Urbanites," *Time*, October 27, 1961.

38. Illich, *Church, Change and Development*, 113.

39. O'Connor, *Habit of Being*, 482.

40. Ibid., 347.

41. Daniel H. Levine and Alexander W. Wilde, "The Catholic Church, 'Politics,' and Violence: The Colombian Case," *Review of Politics* 39.2 (1977): 221–24.

42. Illich, *Church, Change and Development*, 30.

43. Ibid., 23–25.

44. Ibid., 35–38.

45. Ibid., 41.

46. Qtd. in Gray, *Divine Disobedience*, 252.

47. Hartch, "Ivan Illich and the American Catholic Missionary Initiative."

48. Illich, *Church, Change and Development*, 120–25.

49. O'Connor, *Habit of Being*, 497.

50. Ivan Illich, *Celebration of Awareness: A Call for Institutional Revolution* (Berkeley: Heyday, 1970), 43.

51. Gray, *Divine Disobedience*, 283, 279; Hartch, "Ivan Illich and the American Catholic Missionary Initiative"; "Boot Camp for Urbanites."

52. O'Connor, *Habit of Being*, 492.

53. Qtd. in Gray, *Divine Disobedience*, 283. Illich's work at Cuernavaca, critique of the Church's missionary endeavors, and call for reform of the Latin American clergy eventually led to his being summoned to the Vatican by the Congregation for the Doctrine of the Faith. Although Illich appeared there in the fall of 1968, he declined to answer questions on his beliefs about the clergy, liturgy, church law, and church doctrines (ibid., 233). In January 1969 the Apostolic Delegate prohibited priests, nuns, and monks from attending classes at CIF (ibid., 307), and in March Illich resigned from all of his responsibilities as a priest (except for his commitment to pray the Divine Office and to remain celibate) because he believed that the controversy surrounding him was obstructing his work and his life as a Christian (ibid., 313–14). By June the Vatican agreed to relax the ban on CIF as long as the Center was placed under the review of the Conference of Latin American bishops (ibid., 321). During the next decade Illich shifted his focus from the flawed policies of the Church to the counterproductivity in such Western institutions as education (*Deschooling Society*, 1971), transportation (*Energy and Equity*, 1974), health care (*Medical Nemesis*, 1976), and social services (*Disabling Professions*, 1977).

54. O'Connor, *Habit of Being*, 497; Gray, *Divine Disobedience*, 244.

55. O'Connor demurred but suggested that if Caroline Gordon were not busy teaching at the University of California, "she'd hop down there and teach it for him herself" (*Habit of Being*, 492).

56. O'Connor, *Habit of Being*, 208–9, 215, 227.

57. Illich, *Church, Change and Development*, 112.

58. O'Connor, *Mystery and Manners*, 68.

59. Illich, *Church, Change and Development*, 103.

60. O'Connor, *Habit of Being*, 157.

61. O'Connor, *Mystery and Manners*, 77; Illich, *Celebration of Awareness*, 22.

62. Illich, *Celebration of Awareness*, 21, 25.

63. Illich, *Church, Change and Development*, 51.

64. Qtd. in Deborah N. Cohn, *History and Memory in the Two Souths: Recent Southern and Spanish American Fiction* (Nashville: Vanderbilt University Press, 1999), 44. Noting how "political similarities have resonated in aesthetic solutions," Guerrilla Girl Alma Thomas has observed resemblances between O'Connor's grotesques and the postcolonial magical realism of García Márquez and Salman Rushdie (see Guerrilla Girl Alma Thomas, "Flannery & Other Regions," in *Flannery O'Connor: In Celebration of Genius*, ed. Sarah Gordon [Athens: Hill Street Press, 2000], 77).

65. Cohn, *Two Souths*, 1–10.

66. Jon Smith and Deborah Cohn, "Introduction: Uncanny *Hybridities*" in *Look Away! The U.S. South in New World Studies*, ed. Smith and Cohn (Durham: Duke University Press, 2004), 9–10.

67. O'Connor, *Habit of Being*, 197, 265.

68. Flannery O'Connor, *Collected Works*, ed. Sally Fitzgerald (New York: Library of America, 1988), 272.

69. Father Weatherbee in *The Second Coming*, for example, who has preached in the Philippines, or Father John in *Lancelot*, who has ministered in Africa.

70. O' Connor, *Habit of Being*, 101.

71. O'Connor's Milledgeville contemporary, Elizabeth Horne, claimed that Georgia itself seemed a "mission territory" to the Church at large (qtd. in Jean W. Cash, *Flannery O'Connor: A Life* [Knoxville: University of Tennessee Press, 2002], 35).

72. Smith and Cohn, *Look Away!*, 9.

73. O'Connor, *Mystery and Manners*, 200.

74. O'Connor's distrust of benevolence cannot be written off as sectional crankiness. Reservations about acts of charity seem almost as American as the impulse toward such goodness in the Puritan virtue of Cotton Mather and the civic-mindedness of Ben Franklin. In "Self-Reliance," Ralph Waldo Emerson asserted that to be faithful to his own nature he had to resist the campaigns of charitable agencies and hypocritical philanthropists (Emerson, *Essays* (Norwalk, Ct.: Heritage, 1962], 21). In *Walden*, Henry David Thoreau claimed that if he "knew for a certainty that a man was coming to my house with the conscious design of doing me good, I should run for my life" (Thoreau, *Walden, or Life in the Woods* [Norwalk, Ct.: Heritage, 1981], 80). Thoreau found much philanthropy stingy, self-serving, impersonal, and counterproductive.

75. O'Connor, *Collected Works*, 642.

76. Ibid., 499.

77. Illich, *Church, Change and Development*, 29.

78. O'Connor, *Habit of Being*, 125.

79. Paulo Freire, *Pedagogy of the Oppressed*, rev. ed. (New York: Continuum, 1993).

80. Darren R. Walhof, "Friendship, Otherness, and Gadamer's Politics of Solidarity," *Political Theory* 34.5 (2006): 584.

81. Ivan Illich and Carl Mitcham, "The Politics of Friendship," in *Dialogues* ed. Jerry Brown (Berkeley: Berkeley Hills, 1998), 60.

82. Ibid., 59.

83. Ibid., 61.

84. Jon Lance Bacon, *Flannery O'Connor and Cold War Culture* (Cambridge: Cambridge University Press, 1993), 8–40.

85. Illich and Mitcham, "Politics," 62.

86. O'Connor, *Habit of Being*, 329.

87. O'Connor, *Collected Works*, 246.

88. Ibid., 575.

89. Ibid., 587.

90. Ibid. 575.

91. Ibid., 632.

92. Illich, *Church, Change and Development*, 46.

93. Richard Giannone, *Flannery O'Connor, Hermit Novelist* (Urbana: University of Illinois Press, 2000), 172–73.

94. O'Connor, *Habit of Being*, 486.

95. Ibid., 382.

96. Illich, *Church, Change and Development*, 94.

97. O'Connor, *Collected Works*, 408.

98. Ibid., 411.

99. Ibid., 408.

100. Ibid., 412.

101. Patricia Yaeger, *Dirt and Desire: Reconstructing Southern Women's Writing, 1930–1990* (Chicago: University of Chicago Press, 2000), 25.

102. Ibid., 26.

103. O'Connor, *Collected Works*, 332.

104. O'Connor, *Habit of Being*, 479.

105. O'Connor, *Collected Works*, 335.

106. Illich, *Church, Change and Development*, 100.

107. O'Connor, *Collected Works*, 347.

108. Ibid., 385.

109. See Illich, *Celebration of Awareness*, 127, 126–29, for Illich's extensive parallels between education and church. David A. Gabbard argues that Illich's work has been excluded from much recent discussion about education because he challenged the belief that schooling can provide secular salvation (Gabbard, *Silencing Ivan Illich: A Foucauldian Analysis of Intellectual Exclusion* [San Francisco: Austin and Winfield, 1993]).

110. O'Connor, *Collected Works*, 397.

111. Ibid., 430.

112. O'Connor, *Habit of Being*, 486.

113. O'Connor, *Collected Works*, 435.

114. Ibid., 433.

115. Ibid., 419.

116. Ibid., 423.

117. Ibid., 408.

118. Illich, *Church, Change and Development*, 118–19.

119. O'Connor, *Collected Works*, 448.

120. Cf. Illich, *Church, Change and Development*, 124.

121. John F. Desmond, *Risen Sons: Flannery O'Connor's Vision of History* (Athens: University of Georgia Press, 1987), 64.

122. O'Connor, *Collected Works*, 478.

123. Ibid., 479.

124. O'Connor, *Habit of Being*, 359.

125. Ibid., 490. O'Connor did not keep Barnes's letters. She tore them up in one of her bimonthly fits at the paper she had accumulated (see *Habit of Being*, 514).

126. O'Connor, *Habit of Being*, 514; *Collected Works*, 1198.

127. *The Correspondence of Flannery O'Connor and the Brainard Cheneys*, ed. C. Ralph Stevens (Jackson: University Press of Mississippi, 1986), 188.

128. Illich and Mitcham, "Politics," 61.

129. Roslyn Barnes, "Gerard Manley Hopkins and Pierre Teilhard de Chardin: A Formulation of Mysticism for a Scientific Age," master's thesis, State University of Iowa, 1962, 80.

130. Peter Geniesse, "RE: PAVLA Missionary—Roslyn Barnes," e-mail to the author, July 31, 2010.

131. O'Connor, *Collected Works*, 1198.

11

"He Thinks He's Jesus Christ!"

Flannery O'Connor, Russell Kirk, and the Problem of Misguided Humanitarianism

Henry T. Edmondson III

Sometimes humane impulses turn sinister, and the damage done by the "humanitarian" may be directly proportionate to the fervor with which such humanitarianism is undertaken. Flannery O'Connor suggests such a possibility in her famous introduction to the "A Memoir of Mary Anne," a short biography of a young girl who succumbed to cancer in the care of the Dominican Sisters of Hawthorne's Atlanta house. In perhaps the most remarkable line in that stirring essay, she suggests that benevolence is in need of transcendence; if not, benevolence may, ironically, be injurious. "When tenderness is detached from the source of tenderness," she writes, "its logical outcome is terror. It ends in forced labor camps and in the fumes of the gas chamber."[1]

O'Connor influenced novelist Walker Percy in this regard, an influence apparent in his novel *The Thanatos Syndrome,* which is a mystery novel of sorts about a scheme run by a cadre of psychiatrists who tamper with the water supply of a rural region of Louisiana. Ingredients are added to the water to produce a chemical reaction in the brain so that crime decreases and academic and athletic performance improves. As a side effect, however, the men and women become superficial and bland—sheep-like. They are less thoughtful, and their daily routine is trivial; their conversation is full of platitudes. Worse, the scientific elite's "compassion" deteriorates to sexual abuse of the women and children under their care. Nonetheless, one of the doctors who perpetuates the experiment explains: "For the first time we have actually achieved the full meaning of the Greek word *eu* in euthanasia. . . . I think good is better than bad, serenity better than suffering."[2]

Father Smith is an eccentric and somewhat daft Catholic priest who resides in a fire tower in a manner reminiscent of Simeon Stylites, the fifth-century Syrian ascetic who reportedly sat upon a nine-foot pillar for thirty-six years so that he could fast and pray in relative solitude. Smith issues a prophetic warning to Dr. Thomas More, the novel's protagonist, who eventually uncovers the social experiment and visits Father Smith in his cramped elevated quarters. Father Smith warns that "people of the loftiest sentiments, the highest scientific achievements, and the purest humanitarian ideals" may become the most dangerous. He suggests it may be precisely those who have taken "the oath of Hippocrates" who are guilty of the benevolent abuse of those under their care without "a single letter of protest in the august *New England Journal of Medicine*." Although Percy provides no attribution, his priest echoes O'Connor when he asks the doctor:

> "Do you know where tenderness always leads?"
> "No, where?" I ask, watching the stranger with curiosity.
> "To the gas chamber."
> "I see."
> "Tenderness is the first disguise of the murderer."[3]

Although Percy and O'Connor readers might easily note the O'Connor connection, few may be aware that O'Connor's famous passage, lifted so boldly by Percy, is likely derivative of Russell Kirk: In her copy of Kirk's *The Conservative Mind,* O'Connor has notated this line: "Abstract sentimentality ends in real brutality."[4]

As Kirk explains elsewhere through one of his fictional characters, "Moral power is a catalyst, and can work for good or evil."[5] Kirk thus suggests that the humanitarian impulse is a kind of Aristotelian passion, like love or ambition. It is, in itself, ethically neutral, and if it is not informed by reason and guided by prudence, it may go awry, injuring anyone who happens to be in the line of fire. For her part, O'Connor makes the startling claim, "In the future, anybody who writes anything about me is going to have to read everything that I have written in order to make legitimate criticism, even and particularly the Mary Ann piece."[6]

A Conscience Speaks to a Conscience

There are several points of intersection between O'Connor's and Kirk's thought that provide a cautionary picture of the challenge of providing humanitarian aid so that such assistance might be beneficial and not harmful. This picture consists of shared concerns over a superficial reliance on statistics at the expense of rigorous moral discourse; a zeal for social improvement that may relieve the reformer of the obligation for personal virtue; the prevalence of "ideology" at the expense of principled practical wisdom; and the deterioration of traditional theology into a new kind of humanitarian religion in which the reformer seeks to fill his own spiritual emptiness with a kind of "do-goodism," anointing himself priest over his self-fashioned spirituality. Following introductory considerations, this essay will address the composite features of this philosophical portrait, each in turn, and in doing so, will illuminate Kirk's particular style of conservatism and consider the extent to which O'Connor's own thought might embody dimensions of that conservative thought. In so doing, the influence each had on the other comes into view. As Sarah Gordon has suggested, "O'Connor's privately held conservatism was of a piece with that of Russell Kirk."[7]

Kirk was especially appreciative that O'Connor could address these concerns through her fiction. Although he is more noted for his nonfiction writing, Kirk also turned his hand to fiction, since "fiction permitted Kirk to indulge his imaginative bent" as an alternate means to express his own philosophical concerns."[8] Kirk's narratives, occupied as they usually are with the occult or supernatural, often turn violent, as do O'Connor's. Yet those features exist for a purpose, a similar reason Kirk discerned in the writings of Flannery O'Connor: to lay bare human nature and, despite the ugliness and evil, to find the "grotesque face of God."[9] Kirk even fancied that his short story "'Off the Sand Road' . . . might have come from Flannery's typewriter."[10] Another Kirk short story, "The Invasion of the Church of the Holy Ghost," has a whole host of O'Connor-like characters: "Sherm" Tilton, blind "Fork" Causland, and the "mad" "wild-eyed" street preacher who uses a lifelike "white boy" mannequin as a prop. It is also a tale of temptation and raw evil. O'Connor, however, vigorously resisted the label "gothic" to describe her work, preferring the word "grotesque." Kirk and others readily described his fiction as "gothic," filled as it is with the ghostly and the ghoulish.

Kirk's influence on American conservatism is hard to overstate. He is the author of some thirty-two books, hundreds of periodical essays, and many short stories. Both *Time* and *Newsweek* described him as one of America's leading thinkers, and the *New York Times* acknowledged the scale of his influence when in 1998 it wrote that Kirk's 1953 book *The Conservative Mind* "gave American conservatives an identity and a genealogy and catalyzed the postwar movement."[11] His most successful novel, *Old House of Fear* (2007), is an intrigue about Scottish Marxist thugs who occupy a castle in the Hebrides from which they hope to encourage a revolution.[12] Kirk, though, was not a systematic political philosopher. Rather, he was a man of letters, a public intellectual, and a social critic: he wrote more about "principles" than theory or theoretical systems—except to criticize what he often regarded as sham schemes of thought.

Russell Kirk passed away in 1994; Flannery O'Connor met her untimely death thirty years prior, in 1964. Though they met only once, that encounter is described in some detail by both because, for both, it was significant. The two met at the home of Brainard and Frances Cheney of Nashville, Tennessee, a couple who sometimes hosted literary intellectuals of the day, and whose home often served as a kind of crossroads for discourse.[13] O'Connor became acquainted with Brainard Cheney after he insightfully reviewed her first novel, *Wise Blood*, in the autumn 1952 issue of the literary journal *Shenandoah*.[14]

By his own admission, Kirk was shy upon meeting O'Connor. That is, Kirk, a towering and influential intellect by anyone's standards on the Right or on the Left, held O'Connor in some awe and related to her with diffidence. O'Connor for her part, was not one to put another at ease with easy conversation. As O'Connor later explained, "He is non-conversational and so am I, and the times we were left alone together our attempts to make talk were like the efforts of two midgets to cut down a California redwood."[15] Perhaps in reference to the awkwardness of the moment she later wrote: "I enjoyed meeting Russell. . . . I also wish I could smoke cigars."[16]

That chance meeting made a lasting impact on Kirk, an impression that was deepened as he subsequently read O'Connor's works. O'Connor for her part, had already begun to appreciate Kirk's thought. She owned at least two of his books, replete with her annotations, which are now located in her personal library in Milledgeville, Georgia. O'Connor anticipates her meeting with Kirk to Betty Hester when she writes: "I crutches and all, am going to Nashville this weekend where I hope to hear Russell Kirk lecture at Vanderbilt. He wrote a book called *The Conservative Mind* which I admire." Kirk also happily noted in his memoirs that O'Connor had said that his was "the voice of an intelligent and vigorous conservative thought respected in this country."[17] She subsequently wrote to Hester:

> I didn't hear Russell Kirk lecture as that turned out to be on Mon. instead of Sat. as I had thought; however, he and I were visiting the same people for the weekend so I saw plenty of him. He is about 37, looks like Humpty Dumpty (intact) with constant cigar and (outside) porkpie hat. . . . He is starting a bi-monthly magazine to be called "The Conservative Review" which will be out in two weeks. It should be very good.[18]

O'Connor grew impatient waiting for the appearance of the *Conservative Review*, or at least she enjoyed poking fun at its delay. She wrote Brainard Cheney: "I hear from a friend at Notre Dame that Russell Kirk was last seen there. At that time the *Conservative Review* was two weeks distant—which is where it always appears to be."[19] Upon its appearance, the long-awaited journal was called *Modern Age;* Kirk had intended to include a review of *Wise Blood*, but the plan never materialized.[20]

By the time Kirk wrote his memoir, *The Sword of the Imagination*, he had read the *Habit of Being*, O'Connor's collected correspondence, which contains her account of their meeting. Accordingly, the subtitle of the section about O'Connor is entitled, "Flannery O'Connor: Notes by Humpty Dumpty." Kirk writes his autobiography, like Henry Adams, in the third person, and offers his account of the meeting: "At the house then called Cold Chimneys, in Smyrna, Tennessee, where Brainard and Fanny Cheney lived, Flannery O'Connor and Kirk met—for the first time and the last, here below. This occurred in October 1955; in Kirk's fancy, the occasion does not seem so far distant in time. For a conscience spoke to a conscience then, and the soul of Flannery O'Connor endures." Kirk continues:

She happened to greet Kirk in the broad entrance hall of the handsome old house, which had been built by a Carpetbagger. Kirk had not known that she too would be staying there, and he had read nothing of hers. As she says in her published letters, *The Habit of Being*, she and Kirk were shy with each other. Probably she had not expected the portentous author of *The Conservative Mind* . . . to look like "Humpty Dumpty (intact) with (outside) porkpie hat" (Flannery's description of Kirk). For Kirk's part, noticing her crutch and a bandaged leg, and knowing nothing of the disease that had fixed upon her. He inquired whether she had broken that leg; she said no, but did not explain. . . . Flannery explains she and Kirk were better at talking in the company of the Cheneys and of fellow guests than when left alone in a parlor.[21]

Like O'Connor, Kirk was a uniquely independent thinker, and so his thought is not easily pigeonholed. His biography prompted one reviewer to note that Kirk was "the champion of a kind of conservatism currently in eclipse."[22] Biographer James E. Person quotes the late conservative icon William F. Buckley's description of Kirk as "a neglected prince of conservative thought."[23] For example, before "environmentalism" came into fashion, Kirk was a serious conservationist, a passion too seldom shared by conservatives. His treks through his ancestral Scotland are legendary, and he preferred to walk whenever possible, eschewing the automobile. He sometimes covered twenty or thirty miles a day, often with his wife, Annette, on horseback at his side. Aware of his Scottish rambles, O'Connor once lightheartedly complained to her correspondent Betty Hester, "When anybody wants to get hold of Russell he is always in Scotland."[24] Kirk explained in the *Conservative Mind* that true conservatism *conserves* and that those efforts must include the environment, writing: "The modern spectacle of vanished forests and eroded lands . . . [and] wasted petroleum and ruthless mining . . . is evidence of what an age without veneration does to itself and its successors."[25] In one of his ghost stories, Kirk writes, "The heart of the town had been urban-renewed nearly out of existence."[26]

Reading this, one might recall O'Connor's two disturbing descriptions of the bulldozer in her short story "A View of the Woods." This disquieting story concerns a grandfather who controls his family by selling off the rural property on which they all live, parcel by parcel, thus inflicting on his family a kind of slow death by a thousand urban cuts. By so doing, he incurs the ill-fated enmity of his granddaughter, Mary Fortune, whose thought, he presumed, always agreed with his own. A bulldozer was at work carving into pieces Mr. Fortune's forest acreage, and the descriptions of destruction are placed like bookmarks at the beginning and end of the story. As the story opens, the ironically named Mary Fortune watches "the big disembodied gullet gorge itself on the clay, then with the sound of a deep sustained nausea and a slow mechanical revulsion, turn and spit it out." At the story's conclusion, her dying grandfather's last view is of "a huge yellow monster which sat to the side, as stationary as he was, gorging itself on clay."[27]

Kirk's conservative iconoclasm, however, went much further than the environment. As Persons explains, "Kirk criticized his fellow conservatives' obsession with economic matters; he did not believe that 'government was the problem'; he questioned the wisdom of indiscriminate attempts to export democratic capitalism around the globe;[28] [and] he believed that the small farmer and businessman should be protected."[29] Russello notes, "Kirk was never a free-market absolutist, and he had harsh words for global capitalism and the destructive tendencies of the free market."[30] Kirk is known for his use of the phrase "permanent things" to characterize those timeless principles that ensure the moral continuity of civilization. In a letter to Betty Hester, O'Connor employed the phrase at Kirk's expense, noting again the delays involved with the appearance of *Modern Age:* "I say Russell's articles will have to have permanent value as they will all be at least three years old before they appear."[31] Kirk once described O'Connor as "conservative politically," but perhaps he would acknowledge that this blunt description requires at least as much nuance in describing O'Connor as in describing himself.[32] It was certainly simplistic for Kirk to say that O'Connor "stood with the Agrarians—adding a Catholic element." Though O'Connor admired some of the activity of the Agrarians, she also thought they were utopian in their pronouncements: she noted of their manifesto, *I'll Take My Stand,* "It's futile of course like 'woodman, spare that tree.'"[33]

Both writers seemed to have enjoyed keen insight into the life and writing of the other. O'Connor wrote her friend Betty Hester about an (unknown) article they had shared and in doing so anticipated Kirk's later conversion to the Catholic Church in 1964: "That article was very Russell-like." She characterized his intellectual and spiritual curiosity by observing: "He is too intelligent a man to rest long content etc. Russell seems to me to be stuck and to need converting."[34] Kirk seemed to have helped O'Connor articulate some of her ideas, and O'Connor influenced Kirk as well, perhaps more than most realize. Kirk writes in his memoir—again in the third person: "Although Kirk's junior in years, [O'Connor] was in advance of him: when Flannery died in 1964, Kirk—then forty-five years old—had begun to apprehend truths that Miss O'Connor had [already] discerned at the age of thirty."[35]

Hazardous Humanitarianism

O'Connor and Kirk, then, were kindred spirits of a sort, and building upon this intellectual affinity, several areas of shared interest between the two point to a common concern over the dangers of overzealous humanitarianism. To begin, O'Connor, like Kirk, thought the reliance on statistics to answer crucial moral and political questions a matter of concern. In the introduction to the *Portable Conservative Reader,* which he edited, Kirk expresses a distrust of "sophisters and calculators."[36] In one essay in Kirk's *Beyond the Dreams of Avarice,* a copy of which is in the Georgia College O'Connor collection, Kirk, noting the modern tendency to slavishly follow opinion polls and indiscriminately consume statistics, argues: "It is time some of us pointed out that poll-takers, however diligent, are not prophets. . . . They want any god but God; and Statistics now serves."[37] Moreover, Kirk cleverly addresses a misplaced faith in numbers in his ghost story "Behind the Stumps." His epigraph for the story is the Old Testament passage from 1 Chronicles 21:1 in which the Lord condemns David for his stubborn insistence on "numbering" the Hebrew nation: "And Satan stood up against Israel / and provoked David to number Israel."[38] In Kirk's story, a blinkered census-taker named Cribben is warned by locals not to try to penetrate the treacherous backcountry of Pottawatomie County. Some people are better left alone, the locals explain. Cribben, though, is "devoid of imagination." Kirk writes, "he had not an ounce of fancy in him." He is reckless and unyielding in his counting—nothing will withstand his enumeration. Indeed, "truth," for Cribben, is "only an attribute of precision," and so he proceeds headlong into the mysterious backwoods of Barren Hill and attempts to do what no man has done before: count the strange Gholson clan. He is, Kirk writes, a "newfangled man": for him there is no mystery that does not yield to numerical analysis; consequently, he ventures where fools fear to tread and meets his grisly demise.[39]

Some of O'Connor's most memorable prose passages echo Kirk's cautions about an indiscriminate reliance on numeration; indeed, Kirk's comments seem to be in the not-so-distant background. At a lecture at Georgetown University, she confessed: "For someone like myself who is not a teacher, and not even a literary person in the accepted sense of the phrase, it's always difficult to throw off the habits of the story-teller and to come up with some abstract statement instead. I'd much prefer to be reading you one of my stories tonight, but these are times when stories are considered not quite as satisfying as statements and statements are considered not quite as satisfying as statistics."[40]

O'Connor elsewhere notes: "The novelist is asked to begin with an examination of statistics rather than with an examination of conscience. Or if he must examine his conscience, he is asked to do so in the light of statistics."[41] This is a rather ominous observation, for if statistics have come to challenge prudence and principle as a means of settling important moral and political questions, then the idea of individual human dignity is at risk: it all depends on utilitarian analysis. In *The Violent Bear It Away,* the schoolteacher Rayber is never able to grant his handicapped son the dignity of a human being. Early in the novel the older Tarwater notes the teacher's propensity to assess others as "parts and numbers" so that each discrete individual is "indistinguishable from the herd."[42] O'Connor further laments that writers are "invited to represent the country according to survey," which is to ask the writer "to separate mystery from manners and judgment from vision, in order to produce something a little more palatable to the modern temper. We are asked to form our consciences in the light of statistics, which is to establish the relative as absolute."[43] Both Kirk and O'Connor seem to have anticipated the character of contemporary discourse in which, to a disappointing degree, meaningful exchange about important religious, political, and moral matters is too often supplanted by reference to public opinion polls, in which conclusions are drawn by means of a statistical *argumentum ad populum.* Under such conditions, right and wrong are calculated by statistical advantage.

Both O'Connor and Kirk were insistent that, though continual social improvement is necessary and desirable, those so engaged should not neglect their own moral growth; to do so would be the worst sort of hypocrisy. O'Connor's personal library contains, among other Kirk volumes, *The Dreams of Avarice.* O'Connor often reviewed books on theology and philosophy for the Atlanta diocesan periodical the *Bulletin,* and in 1956, O'Connor wrote Hester: "I am reviewing Russell's latest for *The Bulletin.* . . . It's a collection of his essays called *Beyond the Dreams of Avarice.*"[44] Conspicuous is Kirk's insistence that personal improvement precede social reform: "[The conservative] . . . believes that the only sure reform which a man can effect is the improvement of one human unit, himself; and he thinks that the really important change required for the betterment of society is a change in heart."[45]

In O'Connor's "Everything That Rises Must Converge" a mean-spirited young man, Julian, callously mocks his mother's inbred social prejudice. When his mother is knocked to the ground by an indignant black mother for patronizing the woman's child with a "shiny, new penny," Julian mocks her misfortune—just before her weak heart gives way. Julian appears the real culprit, and the sorrow that descends upon him comes as redemptive punishment for his cruel behavior. O'Connor writes that suddenly "he was looking into a face he had never seen before" as a "tide of darkness seemed to be sweeping her from him." Julian's pretensions vanish as he employs cloying terms of endearment, pleading with his mother not to die: "'Mother!' he cried. 'Darling, sweetheart, wait!'" She collapses, however, on the pavement, and though he tries to run for help, "his feet moved numbly as if they carried him nowhere. The tide of darkness seems to sweep him back to her, postponing from moment to moment his entry into the world of guilt and sorrow."[46] To expect, then, that an individual will improve himself *before,* or at least *as,* he attempts to reform those around him, is not just the proper order of things, it is also a safeguard. It introduces a measure of humility and self-doubt in the reformer's psyche, which cannot help but blunt the dangerously sharp edge of zeal, while hopefully not enervating the reformer's moral energy.

If statistics can supplant conscience, as Kirk and O'Connor suggest, thereby facilitating a kind of bumbling if not dangerous "humanitarianism," then "ideology" becomes the turbo charged engine that drives misguided efforts to disaster. Kirk reports in his memoir: "Long after Flannery's death, Kirk would be shown her library books, desk, chair, and all plenishings—preserved in the library of Georgia College at her town of Milledgeville; and there he would find her copy of *The Conservative Mind,* with her marginalia."[47] *The Conservative Mind* provides the clearest and most comprehensive elaboration of Kirk's central conservative principle, namely, his warning against "ideology": "The Conservative simply does not possess an ideology in the strict sense of the word; and he does not desire one."[48] The ideologue, Kirk warns, takes ideas and makes a religion out of them: for the ideologue, ideas need only the commitment of faith, and they will come to pass; ideology is "inverted religion."[49] True conservatism, however, should be precisely the absence of faith in anything but God. This is the reason for Kirk's disagreement with some of the so-called neoconservatives of his day: he argued that they were insufficiently cautious in trying to export capitalism and democracy, lacking the prudential considerations of time, place, and manner by which such principles must be implemented.

This stance was evident in the inaugural issue of *Modern Age* in which, by way of introduction, Kirk asserts, "We are not ideologists: we do not believe we have all the remedies for all the ills to which flesh is heir." With reference to Edmund Burke, who wrote against the philosophical and bloody excesses of the French Revolution, Kirk announces, "We take our stand against abstract doctrine and theoretic dogma," continuing, "We confess a prejudice against doctrinaire radical alteration, and to a preference for the wisdom of our ancestors. Beyond this, we have no party line. Our purpose is to stimulate discussion of the great moral and social and political and economic and literary questions of the hour, and to search for means by which the legacy of our civilization may be kept safe." He further explains that "by 'conservative,' we mean a journal dedicated to conserving the best elements in our civilization; and those best elements are in peril nowadays. . . . Beyond this, we have no party line."[50]

In the next issue, Kirk was pleased to reprint several reviews of *Modern Age*. The *Sunday Oregonian* wrote, "This is an encouraging prospectus, considering that many who think of themselves as conservatives have tended to exhibit an intellectual octane too rich for easy assimilation and their impact is nil or near it."[51] The *Richmond News Leader* wrote of Kirk: "He is no right-wing fanatic, yelling shrilly on topical themes. He is a scholar, a philosopher, a thinker, gifted with an easy style of writing and an insatiable eagerness for intelligent debate."[52] The *London Times Literary Supplement* explained that *Modern Age* wants to take its stand "against abstract doctrine and theoretic dogma" and for "principle," even, in a sense, for healthy "prejudice."[53] Russello explains that, according to Kirk, "ideology is religious dogmatism in a political context," and such a posture is "inconsistent with a conservative outlook. Ideology eliminates the nuances and shades of gray that exist in actual political or social life."⁵⁴ Elsewhere, Kirk warns against the "drug of ideology."⁵⁵

Although she does not use the term "ideology," O'Connor addresses the danger of abstract theory when she writes, "The isolated imagination is easily corrupted by theory."⁵⁶ This is a consistent theme, even if she does not pursue it as systematically as Kirk does. This seems to be the concern behind her rueful observation after a lecture and question-and-answer period at an upscale private academy when she complained, "These young women live in a world that God never created." O'Connor once acknowledged that her first novel, *Wise Blood,* "was written by an author congenitally innocent of theory." She argues that "the beginning of human knowledge is through the senses." Accordingly, this is how she tries to communicate with her reader. To do so is more difficult than "to state an abstract idea." "Reformers" who try to change the world by theory "are conscious of problems, not of people, of questions and issues, not of the texture of existence, of case histories and of everything that has a sociological smack, instead of with all those concrete details of life that make actual the mystery of our positions on earth."⁵⁷ This is not an abstract debate for O'Connor; rather, it has real-world implications for reform and behavior. She once admonished Betty Hester: "Your views on morality are for never-never land. We don't live in it."⁵⁸ The earthy, unsettling resonance of O'Connor's fiction serves to force the reader to acknowledge the grit, spit, and dirt of human struggle: "Fiction is about everything human and we are made out of dust, and if you scorn getting yourself dusty, then you shouldn't try to write fiction. It's not a grand enough job for you."⁵⁹

Principles, Prudence, and the "Source of Tenderness"

In *The Politics of Prudence,* Kirk again addresses the danger of "political ideologies," on the left or the right. He offers "principles" guided by "prudence" as an antidote to injudicious ideology. Politics should be the art of the possible, Kirk argues, not the dream of the fanciful. The ideologue, on the other hand, thinks of politics as a revolutionary instrument for remaking society and transforming human nature. In his march toward Utopia, moreover, the ideologue may be merciless. In *The Politics of Prudence,* Kirk bars no holds—his prose is vigorous and insistent, a new urgency evident in his rhetoric. Ideology, he argues, is too often a substitute for religion. "Ideology provides sham religion and sham philosophy, comforting in its way to those who have lost or never have known genuine religious faith, and to those not sufficiently intelligent to apprehend real philosophy."[60]

In a startling passage, Kirk further warns, "The conservative 'movement' seems to have reared up a new generation of rigid ideologists. It distresses me to find them as numerous and in so many institutions." By contrast, to be "prudent," Kirk explains, means to be "judicious, cautious, sagacious. . . . A prudent statesman is one who looks before he leaps; who takes long views; who knows that politics is the art of the possible."[61] As one reviewer notes about *The Politics of Prudence*, "The picture of the true conservative that emerges from these essays is of someone who is humble about the prospects for positive change in society, humble about the value of new insights, especially his own, and realistic about the hidden hazards of change and the inevitability of further crises."[62]

Kirk's admiration for T. S. Eliot follows his perception that Eliot was a force against ideology in the tradition of Edmund Burke: "Since Eliot's death, we have slipped farther still into the antagonist world of armed doctrine and consuming appetite." Kirk notes the consequences of ideology on governance: he observes that a "party bound by political dogmas—an ideological party, that is, although Eliot does not use the term—discovers when in power that theory and circumstance often collide." Kirk complains that in the place of serious study in government, students are given "official propaganda about the holiness of the American Way or of the Free World Way or of the Democratic Capitalist Way." He continues, "Conservatism is not a fixed and immutable body of dogma, and conservatives inherit from Burke a talent for re-expressing their convictions to fit the time."[63]

Kirk's insistence on prudence finds an echo when O'Connor writes to Betty Hester: "I was reading that St. Thomas said Prudence was the highest of the virtues . . . because it articulated all the others. Anyway, the older I get the more respect I have for Old Prudence." In O'Connor's view, prudence does not negate principle; it simply guides—and at times restrains—its application. Prudence implies flexibility in the application of principle. O'Connor may have read Thomas Aquinas's prominent discussion on prudence in her one-volume compendium of the *Summa theologica*, also in her personal library. If not, she was obviously aware of his teaching. This helps us to understand her surprising remark about Aquinas when she wrote to Hester, "The more I read St. Thomas the more flexible he appears to me."[64]

O'Connor made the comment about "Old Prudence" at about the time she was finishing up one of her best short stories, "The Enduring Chill," which she reports completing in the fall of 1958. Walker Percy called it "witty . . . almost a masterpiece."[65] The protagonist of the story, a young man named Asbury, angrily and recklessly undertakes a reform of the social relationships of the family dairy farm. His crowning moment comes when, contrary to the farm rules, he defiantly takes a drink of unpasteurized milk in the presence of the black hired help. A year later he discovers he has unwittingly contracted "undulant fever"—also called "brucellosis" after the offending bacteria in the untreated milk. This disease would afflict him for the remainder of his life, with rising and falling (or undulating) fevers and chills, headaches, and general malaise. As Asbury demonstrates, the problem with the ideologue is that he knows what he knows, and no one can tell him anything different: Asbury's mother observes, "When people think they are smart—even when they are smart—there is nothing anybody else can do to make them see things straight."[66] Kirk warns that among others, university students are especially vulnerable to ideology;[67] Asbury's mother notes that although she managed to get Asbury and his sister through college, "the more education they got, the less they could do."[68]

Kirk admits that his position might be taken as a distrust of human reason. By his own admission, he is guilty as charged: "Human reason set up a cross on Calvary, human reason set up the cup of hemlock, human reason was canonized in Notre Dame."[69] It is not so much that tradition is unimpeachable; the problem, rather, is man's dangerous impulsiveness: "Tradition and sound prejudice provide checks upon man's anarchic impulse."[70] When Asbury suggests that the family physician Dr. Block is too ignorant to cure him of his malady, Block easily admits his limitations: "'Most things are beyond me,' Block said. 'I ain't found anything yet that I thoroughly understood,' and he sighed and got up. His eyes seemed to glitter at Asbury as if from a great distance."[71]

To be sure, neither O'Connor's nor Kirk's prudence is unprincipled cleverness, nor is it synonymous with utilitarianism; to the contrary, prudential positions can be highly impractical. O'Connor complained to Hester about Catholic clergy who tried to soft-pedal one of the Church's more difficult teachings:

The Church's stand on birth control is the most absolutely spiritual of all her stands and with all of us being materialists at heart, there is little wonder that it causes unease. I wish various fathers would quit trying to defend it by saying that the world can support 40 billion. I will rejoice in the day when they say: This is right, whether we all rot on top of each other or not, dear children, as we certainly may. Either practice restraint or be prepared for crowding.[72]

Prudence is a means of grappling with challenges that require an intellect informed by the Providential, or at least open to the transcendent. As Kirk explains: "Political Problems, at bottom, are religious and moral problems. . . . Providence is the proper instrument for change, and the test of a statesman is his cognizance of the real tendency of Providential social forces."[73] Elsewhere, he asks: "What ails modern civilization? Fundamentally, our society's affliction is the decay of religious belief."[74] O'Connor, in introducing herself to Betty Hester wrote darkly, "I think that the Church is the only thing that is going to make the terrible world endurable."[75] Neither Kirk nor O'Connor, however, ever advocated public religious practice as requisite for social and political action. For Kirk, such practice would contradict his opposition to ideological indoctrination; O'Connor was not absorbed with public policy; she was primarily interested in the action of grace in the individual. It is fair to say, though, that the two believed a society devoid of individual religious belief, and one that ignores or aggressively opposes religious inspiration, is destined for trouble.

Exactly how parochial this source of inspiration must be, or could be, is not entirely clear. What might be the "source of tenderness," to which O'Connor refers in her famous *Memoir*? Must it be Catholic, or Christian— or even religious? Kirk seemed to strive to be as broad-minded as possible in this regard. Person explains in respect to a passage in *The Conservative Mind,* "In later editions . . . he changed the words 'a divine intent' to 'a transcendent order, or body of natural law,' recognizing that the truths of the Tao remain true regardless of whether the people of a particular culture are theistic." In the preface to *The Conservative Reader,* which Kirk edited, he speaks of "a transcendent moral order, to which we ought to try to conform the ways of society."[76]

O'Connor, however, might be less inclined to characterize the "source of tenderness" so broadly. She explains time and again that her stories are about the operation of divine and natural grace, and though her principal concern may be with individual improvement, she does not draw sharp lines that would exclude broader moral and social concerns; such problems are, all too often, the collective effect of individual human weakness. Accordingly, grace is necessary because man is tainted by sin and stands in need of redemption. O'Connor explains: "I am no disbeliever in spiritual purpose and no vague believer. . . . This means that for me the meaning of life is centered in our Redemption by Christ and what I see in the world I see in its relation to that." O'Connor admits that this is not an easy or popular belief to hold: "I don't think that this is a position that can be taken halfway or one that is particularly easy in these times to make transparent in fiction." Her logic is important: redemption, she argues, is "meaningless" unless we can overcome the secular misconception that men and women, by virtue of some natural or acquired goodness, have no need of it; yet, O'Connor continues, man has an instinctive knowledge that he is indeed in need of such redemption. For that reason, she argues, "There is something in us, as storytellers and as listeners to stories, that demands the redemptive act, that demands that what falls at least be offered the chance to be restored."[77]

Kirk approvingly notes that in O'Connor's review of Kirk's *The Dreams of Avarice,* she writes, "It is . . . a rethinking in the obedience to divine truth which must be the mainspring of any enlightened social thought . . . whether it tends to be liberal or conservative."[78] The conservative, Kirk explains, stands against "the perfectibility of man and the illimitable progress of society: meliorism. Radicals believe that education, positive legislation and alteration of the environment can produce men like gods; they deny that humanity has a natural proclivity toward violence and sin." O'Connor, for her part, commended to Sally Fitzgerald her first collection of short stories, *A Good Man Is Hard to Find,* as "nine stories about original sin, with my compliments."[79] She further remarked that the advantage of writing in the South is that the South "still believes that man has fallen and that he is only perfectible by God's grace, not by his own unaided efforts." In contrast, "the Liberal approach is that man has never fallen, never incurred guilt, and is ultimately perfectible by his own efforts. Therefore, evil in this light is a problem of better housing, sanitation, health, etc. and all mysteries will eventually be cleared up."[80]

Tragic Naïveté

Ignorance of the theological dimension of social challenges may be accompanied by naiveté. Though O'Connor's story "The Partridge Festival" was not included in either of her short story collections, it is nonetheless an engaging, if overdone, portrayal of characters who suffer the consequences of their gullibility.[81] A young man named Calhoun visits the rural home of his grandmother, not for the annual festival but because a deranged denizen named Singleton has just been jailed for killing several of his fellow citizens at the previous year's celebration of the festival. Calhoun works successfully as a salesman a few months out of each year to support his self-styled avocation as a would-be novelist. He rejects the evidence that the killer was merely insane; instead, he interviews various townspeople to develop his thesis that Singleton had been misunderstood and alienated by the townspeople and thereby driven to his crime. Calhoun finds an unexpected kindred spirit in a mysterious local girl who seems to be more advanced than he in pseudo-intellectualism: strangely resolute in her views, Mary Elizabeth calls Singleton a "Christ-figure." She challenges Calhoun to join her in visiting Singleton in the state institution so as to sympathize with the killer's role of town "scapegoat" and to seek "an existential encounter with his personality."[82] The visit, though, is an ugly debacle as the disturbed killer behaves like the lunatic he is. When he crudely exposes himself, they flee the obscene spectacle in a panic.[83]

Such naiveté aggravates the hazard of risky charity, and the more naïve the humanitarian, the greater the danger. Here we also better understand O'Connor's and Kirk's warning that a thoroughly secular humanitarianism may be all the more dangerous because if the humility and caution born of traditional religious sentiments, or at least transcendent considerations, are alien to humanitarian efforts, then such activity may become a substitute religion. Such is the startling psychological insight O'Connor offers in her short story "The Lame Shall Enter First." Sheppard, a humanitarian social worker driven by his need to fill his own spiritual emptiness, perilously succumbs to spiritual pretensions. O'Connor notes, "The story is about a man who thought he was good and thought he was doing good when he wasn't."[84] O'Connor explained elsewhere that Sheppard represents the man who "fills up his emptiness with good works."[85]

"The Lame Shall Enter First" is arguably the most catastrophic of all of O'Connor's stories. It appears to end in irredeemable disaster with little hint of grace or redemption—unlike most of O'Connor's stories. Interestingly, O'Connor knew there was something different about this particular story, and it worried her. She admitted to fellow author Cecil Dawkins, "I don't know, don't sympathize, don't like Mr. Sheppard in the way that I know and like most of my other characters."[86] At times O'Connor doubted that the story was a successful one and noted to Betty Hester, "I am thinking of changing the title to "The Lame Shall Carry Off The Prey." She also admitted after it was published that she was reluctant to read it, because, again, she might be confronted with her failure. Most, however, find this an artful if disarming short story, dark though it may be.

The protagonist Sheppard is the recreational director for the unidentified city in which he lives, but the story is concerned but his self-styled avocation: Sheppard volunteers as a counselor at the reformatory where he discovers Rufus Johnson, a delinquent whose father died before he was born, whose mother is in the penitentiary, and whose grandfather beat him. Sheppard is an emphatic and self-professed atheist, whose "do-goodism" is thoroughly secular. Indeed, O'Connor suggests that Sheppard, having rejected the possibility of a deity, can only look to himself as a replacement. He is introduced early in the story as "a young man whose hair . . . stood up like a narrow brush *halo* over his pink sensitive face."[87] In the story's closing lines, as the revelation of his inadequacy crushes him, O'Connor explains: "Slowly his face drained of color. It became almost grey beneath the white *halo* of his hair" (italics mine). On another occasion, the shrewd delinquent Johnson complains to Norton about his father's presumptive, clumsy intrusiveness. His is a perceptive analysis of Sheppard's flawed humanitarianism: "'God, kid,' Johnson said in a cracked voice, 'how do you stand it?' His face was stiff with outrage. 'He thinks he's Jesus Christ!'"[88]

Sheppard's faithless benevolence, however, is sure to fail: he attempts to fill his own need, the void left in his soul by his rejection of the spiritual. O'Connor explained to a friend, "If Sheppard represents anything here, it is, as he realizes at the end of the story, the empty man who fills up his emptiness with good works."[89] As O'Connor writes, Sheppard "had stuffed his own emptiness with good works like a glutton. He had ignored his own child to feed his vision of himself."[90] Accordingly, his behavior is more selfish than benevolent. When Sheppard is trying to convince Johnson to stay despite Norton's objections, Sheppard's anxiety is palpable. He begs the juvenile delinquent to remain in his home. His motive, though, is not so much to rehabilitate the reprobate as it is to fill his own spiritual emptiness by pursuing Johnson's "salvation." He implores Rufus to stay with "desperation" in his voice.

Later, as Sheppard's aspirations begin to unravel, his judgment is still crippled by his own spiritual deprivation. Considering the possibility that Johnson may have to leave, Sheppard is distraught: "Oh my God, he thought. He could not bring it to that."[91] Even in the final scene of the drama when he is stung by ugly if superficial self-revelation, Sheppard merely switches the focus of his own deliverance from Rufus to his son, Norton. His reawakening to the possibilities of life with his own son "rush over him like a transfusion of life. The little boy's face appeared to him transformed; the image of his salvation."[92]

Conclusion: Charity and Anagogical Literature

Is O'Connor's edgy attitude toward misguided humanitarianism excessively harsh, leaving too little room for the compassion that leads to good deeds? Kirk was occasionally so accused, though he generally refuted such notions by his quiet example. Over the decades he and his wife, Annette, took into their home scores of needy souls: European refugees, unwed expectant mothers, the homeless, and itinerant hobos, including one recurrent drifter who, while tending the fireplace, started a fire that consumed the family estate, Piety Hill.[93] For her part, O'Connor thought "compassion" too often to be no more than sentimentalism, a shallow substitute for genuine, concrete acts of charity. She freely admitted to Betty Hester that she lacked vague feelings for "humanity"; instead she advocated charitable deeds. "I share your lack of love for the race of man," she wrote, but added, with reference to St. Thomas Aquinas, that such love is only a sentiment. She elaborates that after St. Catherine of Genoa's four years of penance, the saint then spent the remaining twenty-one years practicing "simple works of charity."[94] Elsewhere she explains that "there is nothing harder or less sentimental than Christian realism."[95] She once wrote William Sessions about the poet Gerard Manley Hopkins, who was asked by his friend Robert Bridges "how he could possibly learn to believe, expecting, I suppose, a metaphysical answer. Hopkins only said, 'Give alms.'"[96]

One reason O'Connor so disliked the conflation of charity and emotion is that sentiment becomes a substitute for compassionate action. If, in the face of need, one can emote sufficiently, one need not act at all. O'Connor admitted that the confusion between charity and sentimentality "is one reason I am chary of using the word, love, loosely. I prefer to use it in its practical forms, such as prayer, almsgiving, visiting the sick and burying the dead and so forth." O'Connor noted that, according to theologian Romano Guardini, "human love has been stifled, resting content with sympathy."[97] She also wrote: "To expect too much is to have a sentimental view of life and this is a softness that ends in bitterness. Charity is hard and endures."[98]

This disdain for sentimentality is evident in O'Connor's view of spirituality. O'Connor admitted: "I must say that the thought of everyone lolling about in an emotionally satisfying faith is repugnant to me. I believe that we are ultimately directed Godward but that this journey is often impeded by emotion."[99] In respect to the grace associated with the sacraments, she explains, "We don't believe that grace is something you have to feel." She continues, "The Catholic always distrusts his emotional reaction to the sacraments."[100] She once noted to a friend: "You are right that *enjoy* is not exactly the right word for our talking about religion. As far as I know, it hurts like nothing else."[101] O'Connor's interest in Edith Stein was encouraged because, as she explained, "If she is ever canonized, she will be one saint that I don't think they can sweeten up on holy cards and write a lot of 'pious pap' about."[102] O'Connor also found Guardini's disavowal of sentimentality attractive in her review of his *Prayer in Practice.* For example, she writes, "He speaks of having a 'sense of honor' in prayer, a sense which will be offended by the mawkish, sentimental and exaggerated."

One of O'Connor's most elegantly written stories is "The Displaced Person." This somber tale involves a Polish émigré who is accepted as a laborer at a rural southern family farm. He is soon rejected by an unlikely alliance of the black and white farm help, in part because he proves a far more diligent and grateful worker than they and in part because of his effort to help his white cousin escape the Holocaust by marrying one of the black laborers. In the mid-twentieth-century American South, such an interracial arrangement would have been taboo. The "D.P.," as the locals call him, is crushed in a tractor accident. The circumstances surrounding the tragedy are so artfully drawn that the reader is left suspecting that the D.P.'s coworkers—and even the farm owner—are passively if not actively complicit. The story is a disquieting commentary on both human nature and also, given the clever identification of the Pole with the redemptive work of Christ, man's need for a redeemer: "Christ was just another D.P.," says Mrs. McIntyre, without realizing the significance of her passing comment.

In an offhand remark, O'Connor seems to tie this story to Kirk's thought. She writes to Brainard Cheney, "I have been reading the *Conservative Mind* and just yesterday read your review of it and was so proud to see you did him justice. . . . I have been doing him some justice myself but in the short story form, having written another story about displaced persons."[103]

What exactly does O'Connor mean here? Although we may never know exactly, several inferences might be drawn. First, it suggests Kirk's keen appreciation for O'Connor's insistence that men and women are in need of redemption. In an essay entitled "Criminal Character and Mercy," Kirk gives another account of his meeting with O'Connor: "Georgia's most talented writer of this century, the late Flannery O'Connor, once read aloud to me the most famous of her short stories, 'A Good Man is Hard to Find.' . . . Flannery was no sentimentalist . . . she . . . perceived the whole depravity of our fallen nature."[104]

In "Adam's fall, we sinned all," Kirk recalls from the *New England Primer.* O'Connor, he concludes, though "a woman of humane letters, was no humanitarian—certainly not in the sense that man makes his own salvation."[105] When O'Connor ties her short stories to Kirk's philosophical project, she finds a common purpose for both fiction and political philosophy. She seems to think that through her art, she might pursue the same concerns that Kirk addressed in his essays on politics, culture, and social criticism: even though O'Connor was first an artist, philosophical ideas lurk in the shadowy background of her fiction.

Kirk believed literature to be at least as important a medium for individual and social well-being as other media. For example, he devotes two-thirds of his feisty book *Enemies of the Permanent Things* to a discussion of the importance of good literature in human flourishing. He announces his purpose on the first page with a simple assertion: "Good literature and bad literature exert powerful influences upon private character and upon the polity of the commonwealth." He continues: "If ethical understanding, then, is ignored in modern letters and politics, we are left at the mercy of consuming private appetite and oppressive political power. We end in darkness."[106]

Perhaps a key distinction between Kirk's exceptional essays and intriguing fiction and O'Connor's genius has to do with the level at which each respective author engages the reader. O'Connor explains that fiction operates on several levels, and she takes her cue from the medieval approach to interpreting scripture. She distinguishes the allegorical dimension, the moral dimension and the anagogical dimension: "[The] allegorical, in which one thing stands for another; the moral, which has to do with what should be done; and the anagogical, which has to do with the Divine life and our participation in it, the level of grace."[107]

At the same time, she admitted, "I certainly have no idea how I have written about some of the things I have, as they are things I am not conscious of having thought about one way or the other." She also acknowledges that "the hardest thing for the writer to indicate is the presence of the anagogical which to my mind is the only thing that can cause the personality to change.[108] The anagogical, then, is undeniably a dimension of O'Connor's fiction that renders it unique, presented as it is in her inimitable style. Reading O'Connor allows one to participate in the grace that issues from the "Divine life," and the opportunity for spiritual growth exists for the reader, just as it does for O'Connor's odd characters. By contrast, Kirk's cautionary tales seem to operate in the "moral" dimension but not in the wondrous anagogical manner that O'Connor's work consistently displays.

In 1979, fourteen years after O'Connor's death, *The Flannery O'Connor Bulletin* printed "A Memoir by Humpty Dumpty" by Russell Kirk, which, as noted, was later incorporated into his memoir. In that short piece Kirk reports that after their meeting in Nashville, "the impression that she made upon me by her presence was as strong as that created by her stories, which I began to read on my way back from Tennessee to Michigan." He concludes by offering O'Connor high praise indeed: "A day or two with Flannery O'Connor made such an enduring impression as might have required a decade of acquaintance with someone else."[109] Many readers might agree.

Notes

1. Flannery O'Connor, "The Catholic Novelist in the South," in *Collected Works* (New York: Literary Classics of the United States, 1988), 831–32.

2. Walker Percy, *The Thanatos Syndrome* (Princeton, N.J.: Farrar, Straus and Giroux, 1987), 351.

3. Ibid., 127–29.

4. Russell Kirk, *The Conservative Mind: From Burke to Santayana* (Chicago: Regnery, 1953), 141.

5. Russell Kirk, *Ancestral Shadows: An Anthology of Ghostly Tales* (Grand Rapids, Mich.: Eerdmans, 2004), 82.

6. Flannery O'Connor, *The Habit of Being* (New York: Farrar, Straus and Giroux, 1988), 442.

7. Sarah Gordon, "Mary Flannery O'Connor," in *Georgia Women: Their Lives and Times*, vol. 2, ed. Kathleen Ann Clark and Ann Chirhart (Athens: University of Georgia Press, 2014), 337.

8. Gerald J. Russello, *The Post Modern Imagination of Russell Kirk* (Columbia: University of Missouri Press, 2007), 32.

9. Quoted ibid., 57, from Russell Kirk, "Flannery O'Connor and the Grotesque Face of God," *The World and I*, January 1987.

10. Russell Kirk, *The Sword of the Imagination: Memoirs of a Half-Century of Literary Conflict* (Grand Rapids, Mich.: Eerdmans, 1995), 183; Russell Kirk, "The Invasion of the Church of the Holy Ghost," in *Ancestral Shadows: An Anthology of Ghostly Tales* (Grand Rapids, Mich.: Eerdmans, 2004), 353–94.

11. Qtd. at www.kirkcenter.org/index.php/about-kirk/.

12. Russell Kirk, *Old House of Fear* (Grand Rapids, Mich.: Eerdmans, 1960).

13. As Brad Gooch writes, the Cheney home "was a refuge for many of the leading figures in the "Southern Renaissance," dating from Brainard Cheney's Fugitive days at Vanderbilt. Among "the petit cercle" of visitors, as Caroline Gordon called them, were Robert Penn Warren, Randall Jarrell, Cleanth Brooks, Andrew Lytle, Eudora Welty, Allen Tate, Katherine Anne Porter, Jean Stafford, Peter Taylor, Eleanor Ross, Malcolm Cowley, Russell Kirk, Robert Lowell, and Walker Percy" (Gooch, *Flannery: A Life of Flannery O'Connor*, Kindle ed. [Hachette Book Group], Kindle locs. 3320–3323).

14. Brainard Cheney, *Shenandoah* (Autumn 1952): 55–60.

15. O'Connor, *Habit*, 112.

16. Milledgeville, October 18, 1955, p. 26, Georgia College archives. Used by permission.

17. Kirk, *Sword*, 183.

18. O'Connor, *Habit*, 110, 112. The "Conservative Review" was later renamed *Modern Age*.

19. C. Ralph Stephens, ed., *The Correspondence of Flannery O'Connor and the Brainard Cheneys* (Jackson: University Press of Mississippi, 1986), 34.

20. Kirk, *Sword*, 182.

21. Ibid., 181.

22. Jeremy Beer, review of *Russell Kirk: A Critical Biography of a Conservative Mind*, in *First Things*, May 2000, www.firstthings.com/print/article/2007/01/russell-kirk-a-critical-biography-of-a-conservative-mind-3?keepThis=true&TB_iframe=true&height=500&width=700.

23. James E. Person, *Russell Kirk: A Critical Biography of a Conservative Mind* (Lanham, Md.: Rowman and Littlefield, 2015).

24. O'Connor, *Habit*, 235.

25. Kirk, *Conservative*, 39.

26. Kirk, *Ancestral*, 398–99.

27. Flannery O'Connor, *Collected Works* (New York: Library of America, 1988), 525, 546.

28. Person, *Russell Kirk*, 56. As early as the inaugural issue of *Modern Age*, articles appeared warning against imperial pretensions. See, for example, Felix Morely, "American Republic or American Empire," 1, no. 1 (Summer 1957).

29. Person, *Russell Kirk*, 4, 209.

30. Russello, *Postmodern*, 8.

31. O'Connor, *Habit*, 1039. In his memoir, Kirk rues that under his editorship of the *Modern Age*, no article appeared on O'Connor (though one was planned), nor did he ever have the "occasion to write anything about Flannery but two or three syndicated newspaper columns, an unsatisfactory mode for discussing so complex and subtle a writer" (Kirk, *Sword*, 182).

32. Review of "Flannery O'Connor and the Grotesque Face of God," in Harold Fickett and Douglas R. Gilbert, *Flannery O'Connor: Images of Grace* (Grand Rapids, Mich.: Eerdmans, 1986), www.worldandischool.com/public/1987/january/school-resource12300.asp.

33. O'Connor, *Habit*, 56. Furthermore, as John Sykes explains in an essay in this collection, O'Connor did not so much "add" a "Catholic element" as she set herself apart from the Agrarians on the basis of her Catholicism.

34. Milledgeville, October 5, 1957 (Emory Collection). Used with permission.

35. Kirk, *Sword*, 182.

36. Kirk, *The Portable Conservative Reader*; qtd. in Person, *Russell Kirk*, 44.

37. Russell Kirk, *Beyond the Dreams of Avarice: Essays of A Social Critic*, rev. ed. (Chicago: Open Court, 2000), 78.

38. Kirk, *Ancestral*, 8.

39. Ibid.

40. O'Connor, *Collected*, 853.

41. Flannery O'Connor, *Mystery and Manners: Occasional Prose* (New York: Farrar, Straus and Giroux, 1969), 192.

42. Flannery O'Connor, *The Violent Bear It Away: A Novel* (New York: Farrar, Straus and Giroux), 17, 18.

43. O'Connor, *Mystery and Manners: Occasional Prose* (New York: Farrar, Straus and Giroux, 1957), 285.

44. O'Connor, *Habit*, 61. Kirk quotes O'Connor's review of his book, with evident pleasure, in his memoirs (Kirk, *Sword*, 183).

45. Kirk, *Beyond*, 56.

46. O'Connor, *Collected*, 500.

47. Kirk, *Sword*, 181. O'Connor personalized the volume to which Kirk refers with her brief inscription, "Flannery O'Connor, 1954."

48. Kirk, Russell, "American Conservative Action," *Chicago Review* 9, no. 3 (fall 1955): 65–75.

49. Russell Kirk, "The Drug of Ideology," in *The Essential Russell Kirk: Selected Essays* (Wilmington, Del.: ISI, 2007), 367.

50. *Modern Age* 1, no. 1, 2 (Summer 1957).

51. "Editorial Comments," *Sunday Oregonian* (Portland), 1, no. 2 (fall 1957): 215.

52. Editorial Comments, *Richmond (Va.) New Leader* 1, no. 2 (fall 1957): 216, "*The Progress of Modern Age*," www.mmisi.org/MA/01_02/letter3.pdf.

53. *Modern Age* (Winter 1957/1958): 105, www.mmisi.org/MA/02_01/london .pdf.

54. Russello, *Postmodern*, 61.

55. Kirk, *Essential*, 348.

56. O'Connor, *Mystery*, 53–54.

57. Ibid., 67–68.

58. O'Connor, *Habit*, 526.

59. O'Connor, *Mystery*, 68.

60. Kirk, *The Politics of Prudence* (Wilmington, Del.: Intercollegiate Studies Institute, 1993), 54.

61. Kirk, *Politics*, 63.

62. John Paul Wauck, review of *The Politics of Prudence*, in *National Review*, November 29, 1993.

63. Russell Kirk, *Eliot and His Age: T. S. Eliot's Moral Imagination in the Twentieth Century* (Wilmington, Del.: ISI, 2008), 7, 327, 70, 71.

64. O'Connor, *Habit*, 247, 97.

65. Walker Percy, *Conversations with Walker Percy*, ed. Lewis A. Lawson and Victor A. Kramer (Jackson: University Press of Mississippi, 1985), 232.

66. O'Connor, *Collected Works*, 551.

67. See, for example, Russell Kirk, *Enemies of the Permanent Things: Observations of Abnormality in Literature and Politics* (La Salle, Ill.: Sherwood, Sugden, 1984), 197–210.

68. O'Connor, *Works*, 551.

69. Kirk is quoting here from the English academic and author Keith Feiling.

70. Kirk, *Conservative*, 8.

71. O'Connor, *Collected*, 557.

72. O'Connor, *Habit*, 338.

73. Kirk, *Conservative*, 8.

74. Kirk, *Essential*, 114.

75. O'Connor, *Habit*, 90.

76. Person, *Kirk*, 37, 40.

77. O'Connor, *Mystery*, 32–33.

78. Kirk, *Sword*, 183.

79. Kirk, *Conservative*, 9; O'Connor, *Habit*, 74. The anthology is dedicated to the Fitzgeralds.

80. O'Connor, *Habit*, 302–3.

81. The events depicted in "The Partridge Festival" were inspired by actual events in Milledgeville, Georgia, O'Connor's home in 1953 during the city's sesquicentennial celebrations (see, for example, "The Genesis of O'Connor's 'The Partridge Festival' Carter Martin," *Flannery O'Connor Bulletin* 10 [1981]: 46–53; and "Marion Stembridge Rashomon in Milledgeville: Flannery O'Connor and Pete Dexter on the Stembridge Murders," *Flannery O'Connor Review* 9 [2011]: 69–82).

82. O'Connor, *Collected*, 796.

83. Ibid.

84. O'Connor, *Habit*, 490.

85. Ibid., 1174.

86. Ibid.

87. O'Connor, *Collected*, 1988, 595, 632, emphasis added.

88. Ibid., 609.

89. Ibid., 1174.

90. Ibid., 632.

91. Ibid., 614.

92. Ibid., 632. A school of thought in political science has arisen in recent decades detailing the destructive consequences of humanitarian activity, however benign the intentions of such activity might be. See, for example, Christopher J. Coyne, *Doing Bad by Doing Good: Why Humanitarian Action Fails* (Redwood City: Stanford Economics and Finance, 2013).

93. See Person, *Russell Kirk*, 175–76.

94. O'Connor, *Habit*, 335.

95. Ibid., 308, 90, 142.

96. Ibid., 161.

97. Romano Guardini, *The End of the Modern World* (Wilmington, Del.: ISI, 1998), 99.

98. O'Connor, *Habit*, 308.

99. Ibid., 100; O'Connor, *Collected*, 102, 952.

100. O'Connor, *Habit*, 346.

101. Ibid., 341.

102. Ibid., 173.

103. Ibid., 110.

104. Russell Kirk, *The Essential Russell Kirk: Selected Essays* (Wilmington, Del.: ISI, 2007), 341, 342.

105. Ibid.

106. Kirk, *Enemies*, 15.

107. O'Connor, *Habit*, 469.

108. Ibid., 179–80, 503.

109. Kirk, *Sword*, 182.

12

Flannery O'Connor and Political Community in "The Displaced Person"

John Roos

In such stories as "View of the Woods," "The River," and "The Artificial Nigger," Flannery O'Connor focuses on relations within the small community of the family. In "The Displaced Person," O'Connor moves from the question of how one treats one's children or parents to the question of how one treats the stranger—the other. Published in 1954, a time when American xenophobia was being fanned by Senator McCarthy's anti-Communist crusade, the story explores the terrible consequences of communities built on exclusionary principles.[1]

The events of the story occur shortly after the end of World War II and center on a farm owner, Mrs. McIntyre, and her chief hired hand, Mrs. Shortley. The quiet pattern of order in Mrs. McIntyre's farm community is disrupted when a local priest brings Mr. Guizac, a displaced person from a European refugee camp, to work on Mrs. McIntyre's farm. When Guizac's industry and efficiency threaten her place in the farm hierarchy, an enraged Mrs. Shortley and her family leave the community—but she dies of a heart attack in the process. Guizac further threatens the order of Mrs. McIntyre's farm community when he attempts to arrange a marriage between his cousin, still in the European refugee camp, and one of the black field hands. He is finally killed, at least through omission, by Mrs. McIntyre and her allies when they allow a tractor to roll over him. As the story ends, Mrs. McIntyre has a debilitating stroke, and a priest begins to visit her weekly and instruct her in the doctrines of the Catholic Church.

Although much of the critical literature has concentrated on explicitly religious themes in "The Displaced Person," such as the peacock as a symbol of transcendence and interpretations of Mr. Guizac as a "Christ figure," one can also read the story in a directly political way. A political reading looks upon Mrs. McIntyre's farm as a political community governed by a particular regime.[2]

Aristotle wanted to determine the best political community, and for him the central question was the character of its regime, the way in which a political community decides who shall hold power and for what purposes.[3] For Aristotle, regimes can be the rule of one person, the few, or the many, and in each case the regime can be directed to the exclusively private good or in the interest of the common good. The rule of one for the common good would be kingship, whereas the rule of one for private good would be tyranny. John Locke sets his sights lower: he wanted to avoid reliance upon religion, moral virtue, or the Divine Right of Kings to ground political authority and instead posited individual rational self-interest to account for entry into civil society. For Locke all contracts are based upon the self-interest of each individual, and this includes not only politics but economics, marriage, and family. According to Locke, we each aim to protect our life, liberty, and property rather than the common good.[4]

In "The Displaced Person," the question is who rules and toward what ends. The answer is clear—Mrs. McIntyre rules with the support of the loyal Mrs. Shortley, and the end is wealth, based upon profitably exploiting property. Mrs. McIntyre rules because she owns the land, but there are various classes of other persons involved in the community, all united under the rubric of social contract. People stay on Mrs. McIntyre's farm because it is to their advantage to do so. On Mrs. McIntyre's farm the motivation is not Aristotle's common good but rather the private good of Locke. Under the rule of Mrs. McIntyre we find a thoroughly Lockean regime where the self-interest of the individual is the only motivation for entry into political community. It is this orderly regime of self-interest that is challenged by the arrival of Mr. Guizac.[5]

We find in the story many elements of classical liberal and Lockean individualism. Unlike the contemporary usage of "liberal," which denotes state intervention to achieve social goals, classical liberal individualism rejects the primacy of the state and argues instead that everything must derive from the consent of individuals. Following Locke, one of its preeminent founders, it rejects divine right and any communitarian basis of state action. Classical liberalism and Locke argue that all associations—economics, parenthood, marriage, citizenship—arise only from the consent of individuals pursuing their own narrow self-interest.

Mrs. McIntyre is first and foremost concerned with profit, constantly lamenting that others will take advantage of her and diminish her property. "I've barely been making ends meet and they all take something when they leave," she says. "The niggers don't leave—they stay and steal. A nigger thinks anybody is rich he can steal from and that white trash thinks anybody is rich who can afford to hire people as sorry as they are. And all I've got is the dirt under my feet."[6]

All of Mrs. McIntyre's relations, including her marriages, are based upon individualistic contract. The Judge, her first husband, was the owner of the farm, and her marriage contract with him was primarily a calculation to exchange conjugal rights with an eye toward inheritance of his estate.[7] Mrs. McIntyre has had two other conjugal contracts, neither of which issued in children. One husband ended up in an insane asylum; the other, as an alcoholic. Since there was no need to care for children, the contracts were, in a thoroughly Lockean fashion, able to be terminated when they no longer served Mrs. McIntyre's purposes. In Locke, the marriage contract is wholly to share conjugal rights, with nothing else to indicate any residual obligation or concern for the welfare of the partner. Mrs. McIntyre has no sense of obligation or care for her ex-contract partners.[8]

For John Locke, the individual desires "life, liberty and estate" (property).[9] Mrs. McIntyre realizes this is precisely what holds her regime together. For Locke, until we make a decision to enter civil society, we are in a state of nature, bowing to no one. However, necessity and the prospect of mutual benefit eventually drive individuals out of the state of nature and into civil society. Mrs. McIntyre sees that neediness is the only thing that will drive people out of the state of nature onto her farm to work. Since she already has property, the more necessity on the part of others the better. As in Locke, nature is described as stingy.[10] The more poverty-stricken nature is, the greater the incentive to leave the state of nature. We see what nature provides outside Mrs. McIntyre's regime: as the Shortleys leave the farm, "the fields stretched away stiff and weedy, on either side."[11] After Mrs. Shortley's death, Mr. Shortley and his children are driven back into civil society. They return to renew their contract.

Mrs. McIntyre repeatedly relies upon material neediness to drive people into a contract or to induce them to work harder. She threatens, "Places are not easy to get now a days, for white or black."[12] About Guizac she says approvingly, "I have somebody now who has to work!"[13] She believes that "people ought to have to struggle," and if a person has property, then others' neediness can work to that person's advantage.[14] Mrs. McIntyre often repeats part of a saying of her husband the Judge: "One fellow's misery is the other fellow's gain."[15]

Mrs. McIntyre acts in a way that is consistent with Locke's addition to the fundamental law of nature in which one's self-preservation comes first: "When his own Preservation comes not in competition, ought he, as much as he can, to preserve the rest of Mankind."[16] She realizes that an obligation to charity binds only if there is something deemed not relevant to the preservation of one's own life, liberty, or estate. This means she would be obliged to give up something only when it became useless to her. In helping provision the Guizacs' quarters, "everything had to be scraped together out of things that Mrs. McIntyre couldn't use any more herself."[17] She denies any further obligations to the refugees from Europe by explaining that "she had not been responsible for any of this."[18] Later, she says to Guizac, "I am not responsible for the world's misery."[19] She has left untouched the room that was the inner sanctum of the Judge with a safe "set like a tabernacle in the center of it."[20] Property, then, is the civil religion of the McIntyre regime.

The African Americans in the story, Astor and Sulk, are on the lowest rung of this economy of need. They, like Locke's citizens who have only given tacit consent, have the option to leave their commonwealth and return to the state of nature or join another commonwealth rather than stay in this one.[21] Their choice will depend upon the calculation of self-preservation: Is it better to stay here as a day laborer or return to the state of nature? Mr. Shortley challenges Sulk one day, asking, "Why don't you go back to Africa?" Sulk replies, "I ain't going there. They might eat me up."[22]

Even Mr. Shortley acts as if he understands Locke's theory of property. John Locke says that one can claim property if it is not being used by anyone. Shortley has a second job making moonshine on the back of Mrs.

McIntyre's property, and he offers a perfectly Lockean claim to it because it was "on land that was not doing anybody any good."[23] This regime does not depend upon religion to support it, as we see in Mrs. Shortley's initial appraisal of religion as "essentially for those people who didn't have the brains to avoid evil without it."[24]

The virtues of the regime are instrumental ones. No one is ever praised for justice, temperance, fortitude, or prudence, much less faith, hope, or charity. Mrs. McIntyre praises Guizac because "he could work milking machines and he was scrupulously clean," and Mrs. Shortley notices that Guizac's motions are "quick and accurate."[25] Guizac is someone that Locke might call "rational and industrious."[26]

In the hierarchy within the regime, Sulk and Astor are at the bottom; above them are the "white trash" such as the Ringfields and the Collinses. Higher yet are people like the Shortleys, and, finally, the landowner Mrs. McIntyre sits at the apex.[27] It is a regime based on self-preservation and materiality, in which calculation and self-interest exhaust human reason—yet the regime across time is stable. Though the middle classes come and go, McIntyre and the field hands have enough mutual dependence to provide stability.[28]

The regime seems to have a basis in natural right, one that claims to be founded on natural principles and consent. Toward the end of the story, in trying to rally popular sentiment against Mr. Guizac, Mr. Shortley justifies his claims by retreating to the first principle of that regime, borrowing from America's Declaration of Independence. He proclaims, "all men was created free and equal."[29] It is clear, however, that the regime does not live up to its first principle.

The ability of the mutual benefit contract to function depends upon the principle of "free and equal," and in many ways the regime operates in that way, but with racial discrimination an obvious and glaring flaw.[30] In Mrs. McIntyre's regime African Americans are treated with a maternalistic tolerance while being denied the status of free and equal moral persons.[31] Time and time again Astor and Sulk are literally marginalized from the public arena. In the opening scene, "over by the tool shed, about fifteen feet away, the two Negroes, Astor and Sulk, had stopped work to watch. They were hidden by a mulberry tree but Mrs. Shortley knew they were there."[32] They are allowed to observe and to hold private discussions about the affairs of the regime, but they are never allowed a public voice.

Similarly, Mrs. Shortley treats the Guizacs as foreign and inferior rather than as free and equal. Both in Locke and in the American Declaration of Independence, the phrase "free and equal" is based upon the common rational nature of all humans. Mrs. Shortley ignores the principle by looking only at the Guizacs' material appearance; she immediately starts comparing their offspring with her own but only on a physical basis. Her assumption is that the Guizacs are not fully human because they do not share her external appearance. Shortley wonders whether they will ever know what color is since they speak a different language.[33] She immediately wants to know "what they are capable of" but does not assume or look for evidence of a rational soul as determining that capability.[34] Similarly she assumes that Astor and Sulk are incapable of rationality because of their external physical appearance. The injustice of her judgments is evident when she engages in a dialogue with Astor. When Astor asks who the Guizacs are, she replies "displaced persons." Asked for a definition, she replies, "It means they ain't where they were born at and there's nowhere for them to go." But that cannot be true, because they did find some place to go, America. Both on a literal level and on the claimed natural basis of the regime, Astor rationally comprehends this. "'It seems like they here though,' the old man said in a reflective voice. 'If they here, they somewhere.'"[35] On a literal level Astor claims they are not displaced if they have found a home; on a deeper level he suggests that by nature if they are rational human beings then they can become part of this regime. Mrs. Shortley dismisses this as "illogic" and proceeds to claim they belong somewhere else, simply on the basis of accident of birth, just as African Americans belong outside full citizenship simply on the basis of the color of their skin.

When Mr. Guizac finds Sulk stealing one of Mrs. McIntyre's turkeys, he reports him because Sulk has done wrong: he has violated the contract and should be held accountable for it. Guizac sees Sulk as a free and equal rational creature and, hence, as liable for upholding the social contract. Guizac is shocked and puzzled when Mrs. McIntyre refuses to punish Sulk. Since Mrs. McIntyre does not believe that all humans are free and equal, she believes that simply because of their skin colors "all negroes would steal."[36] Later Mrs. Shortley concurs, recalling that "when Gobblehook first came here you recollect how he shook their hands, like he don't know the difference, like he might have been as black as them, but when it comes to finding out Sulk was taking turkeys, he gone on and told her."[37] McIntyre and Shortley, in their absolution of Sulk's theft, do injustice to their own founding principles. They do injustice also to Sulk and Astor because they deny them that which they most deserve by nature, to be treated as fellow humans with rational souls.

The most serious challenge on the level of natural equality comes when it is discovered that Guizac wants Sulk to marry his cousin so that she can escape the refugee camp. Guizac reasons and believes that in a regime that proclaims all men are created free and equal, the color of one's skin cannot possibly be the basis for forbidding a contract of mutual benefit that will save the life of one of the parties. When he hears their responses, Guizac is now the one who suspects a lack of a common nature, that they may be doomed to separate and unintelligible languages. Mrs. McIntyre calls him a monster for trying to marry his cousin to a "half witted thieving black stinking nigger." Guizac, for the first time, truly cannot understand: "His face showed no comprehension. He seemed to be piecing all these words together in his mind to make a thought." Finally Guizac, perhaps like Huck Finn, can do nothing more than utter a prephilosophic claim of what is right by nature. All the laws of society, state, and religion proclaim that Jim is a slave, but Huck knows in his own heart that there is another standard by which Jim ought to be free. He cannot articulate or defend it, but he knows that to let Jim escape is the right thing to do. In what is one of the most moving lines of O'Connor's writings, Guizac can only utter: "She no care black. . . . She in camp three year."[38]

Guizac exposes the hypocrisy of the regime's claim to be just. The depth of his claim resonates with Lockean liberal premises but at the same time deepens them. In the terms of classical liberalism, Guizac should limit his claim to that of "harm" to a member of the social contract, but his claim goes beyond that since his cousin is not part of the contract. He points to some deeper horror. Guizac suggests some elemental recognition of the other as human, and this makes claims on us over and above those of positive contract. He believes that it is by nature wrong to deny relief to his cousin on the basis of race.

Guizac's first threat, then, is to claim that the regime is hypocritical. Though claiming to treat all as free and equal, the regime denies equality on the basis of color. A second and more formidable threat comes when his presence questions the stability of a political community maintained on the basis of rationality directed only toward utility. Self-interest can initially bind one to a political community if there is mutual utility, but what if the pursuit of material prosperity, while collectively beneficial, renders some individuals useless, without worth? Thomas Aquinas, like Aristotle, argues that material wealth is bounded by the common good, in which the parts find their completion in the whole, and conversely, in which the whole is for the benefit of all the parts.[39] In a regime in which the only definition of the good is the maximization of individual utility, some individuals may not be beneficial partners to anyone. To be truly "displaced," one has to be useless to everyone. Astor realized that Guizac ceased being displaced when Mrs. McIntyre accepted him into her regime. But what if the long-term dynamics of that regime are such that some become truly displaced, useless, worthless, to no one's benefit and hence to no one else's advantage as a contract partner? If they cannot emigrate to another regime, Locke would say that they could revert back to the state of nature, and perhaps to the state of war.[40]

Guizac is an ideal contract partner—efficient, hardworking, precise— and he is intelligent enough to manipulate machinery. Guizac is the ideal laborer increasing productivity in an industrializing economy. In doing so, he successively threatens all the classes of the regime. First Astor and Sulk replaced mules, making mules worthless. Now machines, guided by industrious and willing (needy) workers like Guizac, threaten not only Astor and Sulk but the Shortleys as well: "The tractor, the cutter, the wagon passed, rattling and rumbling and grinding before them. 'Think how long that would have taken with men and mules to do it.'"[41]

Mules became worthless, then humans become worthless. This is no local regime problem; it is worldwide. Emigration is no option if a person is not wanted anywhere. Guizac is both victim and threat. Having been forced from his own county, he now threatens the position of some in his new country. Time and again, characters raise the question of a surplus of humans making some useless. Mrs. McIntyre says: "Do you know what's happening to this world? It's swelling up. It's getting so full of people that only the smart energetic ones are going to survive." Later, "'people are selfish,' she said. 'They have too many children. There's no sense in it any more.'"[42] Humans become interchangeable, substitutable, and ultimately expendable. Shortley proclaims, "She says it's ten million more like them, Displaced Persons, she says that there priest can get her all she wants."[43] Later she ominously refers to Guizac as "extra."[44]

Here the reason for the recurring images of death camps becomes clear. The inhabitants of Mrs. McIntyre's regime all want to understand the death camps as foreign, alien, inapplicable to themselves: "Every time Mr. Guizac smiled, Europe stretched out in Mrs. Shortley's imagination, mysterious and evil, the devil's experiment station."[45] She and the others believe they are exempt because they, unlike Europeans, are "advanced." But perhaps, Mrs. Shortley thinks, Guizac could be carrying the germ of "murderous ways" like "rats with typhoid fleas."[46] Perhaps the seeds of these murderous ways are present in the regime itself, but Guizac does nothing except hold the regime accountable to its own standards. He demands that it treat all humans as free and equal, but he also shows that the only answer being given to the question of what rationality says about humans is that they are to be treated as either useful or useless. O'Connor suggests in powerful ways that a regime that has no deeper bond of political community may thinly cover a terrible abyss.[47] Faced with her own possible uselessness, Mrs. Shortley responds apocalyptically. In the reaction of Mrs. Shortley, O'Connor portrays a soul experiencing that abyss. O'Connor shows that there is a kind of madness that results when a soul is starved of its real needs above and beyond mere self-preservation.[48]

Mrs. Shortley has no resources to help her weather this threat to her identity; she has only the gospel of material progress. She has neither education in the moral life within a well-ordered polis, nor the experience of the contemplative life, nor the life of grace. So when Mrs. Shortley, seeing her regime challenged at the core, faces the prospect of becoming useless, she has to search her soul for other resources, with no aid from her community to guide her. Mrs. Shortley does turn to the Bible, specifically to Revelation and Ezekiel. As a result she has the first of two visions (the second occurs as she dies at the end of part 1 of the story). It is easy to misread this section, perhaps assuming that O'Connor was simply an apocalyptic writer whose characters plunge into the realm of grace in an unquestioned and unquestionable fashion. Such a reading is found in Frank Kessler's *Flannery O'Connor and the Language of Apocalypse.*[49] Kessler thinks O'Connor has no interest in the question of the stability of the good regime. He equates O'Connor with romantics like Blake and says that in "The Displaced Person" the connection between the parts of the story "cannot be discovered by analyzing social relations."[50] In analyzing Mrs. Shortley's visions, Kessler is unable to distinguish between their extraordinarily different political implications. He sees the first vision as consistent with, and preparing for, the second: "The vision from Ezekiel replaces her outer world so that when her eyes are later directed toward an exterior place 'all vision in them might have been turned around, looking inside her.' Consequently at her death, she approaches a transcendent vision, although from a worldly viewpoint she only 'seems to contemplate for the first time the tremendous frontiers of her true country.'"[51]

A more careful reading suggests a quite different interpretation. Before Mrs. Shortley's first "vision," she has begun to lapse into a kind of Manichean xenophobia. The only way she can redefine the political community is by defining it as the exclusive holder of a truth comprised primarily of a division of the world into clean and unclean. Rather than finding a true basis for a reformed regime, she leaps into the mad tyranny of unlimited assertion of self against other. She imagines the weakening of the regime until only she and Mrs. McIntyre are left with Guizac and an additional Polish family. She imagines a battle of uncomprehending words warring with one another: "She saw the Polish words, dirty and all-knowing and unreformed, flinging mud on the clean English words until everything was equally dirty."[52] Rather than moving, as Aquinas does, through nature to grace, Shortley has arrogated to herself the power of remaking and redefining the world. In this redefinition there is no possibility of limit or measure or understanding. Unlike Job in the Old Testament, there is no talking with God. There is only the violent assertion of one's own claim to knowledge and to power. O'Connor shows the totalitarian impulses that may accompany the disordered soul's attempt to remake the world within time.[53] Mrs. Shortley asserts her own privileged place in that remaking when she says that "she saw that the Lord God Almighty had created the strong people to do what had to be done and she felt that she would be ready when she was called."[54]

In this tyrannical mood Mrs. Shortley has her first "vision," the wheels of Ezekiel's chariot. A voice tells her to "prophesy," and in terrible words she does: "'The children of wicked nations will be butchered' she said in a loud voice. 'Legs where arms should be, foot to face, ear in the palm of hand. Who will remain whole? Who will remain whole? Who?'" Returning to the farmhouse, she sees the priest's car, which reminds her of Guizac, "unreformed religion," and the threat to her and her regime. She labels her enemy the anti-Christ: "'Here again,' she muttered. 'Come to destroy.'"[55]

Absent any real experience of either reason or grace revealing the grounds of genuine community, Mrs. Shortley has taken her rage and pride and fashioned her own religion of retribution. In effect, "vengeance is mine" says Mrs. Shortley, placing herself in a line of false prophets, both secular and religious, who having experienced fragility, contingency, and despair at the emptiness of their lives are willing to resort to terror, justifying any and all slaughter to remake the world.

If one reads Ezekiel and Revelation, as O'Connor intends the careful reader to do, one finds several things. First, Mrs. Shortley's prophesies occur nowhere in these books. Mrs. Shortley has made them up. Second, they falsify the essential character of Ezekiel's message. Ezekiel is a minister to those who have, like Mrs. Shortley, seen their material city crumble with the fall of Jerusalem and the exile of the Jews to Babylon. Ezekiel prophesies to a displaced people. God does promise judgment, but it is God's judgment, not Ezekiel's or Israel's. God says, "I myself will judge between the fat sheep and the lean sheep."[56]

Third, the fundamental thrust of Ezekiel's prophecy is to repent. God will distinguish between a people or nation and the individuals within it. Talking in the context of both Jew and non-Jew, God says to Ezekiel: "Again, though I say to the wicked, 'you shall surely die,' yet if he turns from his sin and does what is lawful and right, if the wicked restores the pledge, gives back what he has taken by robbery, and walks in the statutes of life, committing no iniquity; he shall surely live, he shall not die."[57]

Fourth, the culmination of God's judgment occurs at the end of time. Whatever ambiguities rest in Revelation, at least this was clear to O'Connor: the God of the Last Judgment is transcendent, not immanent. To act in God's name within history to bring about the Last Judgment is to sin against God and God's word.

Finally, O'Connor contrasts the false prophecy with a true vision that Mrs. Shortley has as she is dying, while she is leaving the McIntyre farm. This vision occurs precisely at the center of the story: "Then all at once her fierce expression faded into a look of astonishment and her grip on what she had loosened. Her eyes like blue-painted glass seemed to contemplate for the first time the tremendous frontier of her true country."[58] Shortley is "astonished" because the Lord's judgment is nothing like the one she has proclaimed. Revelation is about the gathering of those who are saved, where God and only God decides finally who are the fat and lean sheep. Mrs. Shortley certainly prefigures Ruby Turpin in the story "Revelation."[59]

In that story we find O'Connor's only fully articulated attempt by to portray a grace-ful vision—it is an unmistakable vision of mercy. O'Connor leads us to reflect upon the natural basis of our regime and its flaws. She also leads us to reflect about the terrible dangers involved when people are displaced and a regime crumbles without some tangible better alternative.[60] In Mrs. Shortley we find a warning against the kind of irrationalism that has plagued so much of political action in the twentieth century.

The question arises as to whether there is any vision of a well-ordered regime in the story. In one sense the answer is no. Caricatures of the flawed and negative critiques are much more prevalent in O'Connor than any direct presentation of the good. Here, though, she adopts the mode of her mentor, Aquinas, by using the via negative: the good is presented indirectly by pointing to what is absent. In "The Displaced Person" we do find hints of what a well-ordered regime might look like, but only in focusing on small instances where the author points out what is missing or ignored.

At the very beginning of the story Mrs. Shortley is at the height of her power, unaware of the shifting sands upon which she stood "on two tremendous legs, with the grand self-confidence of a mountain, and rose, up narrowing bulges of granite, to two icy blue points of light that pierced forward, surveying everything." O'Connor contrasts her apparent solidity with the "tangle of limbs" she will become at her death, but she also alerts the reader to something missing. The peacock, most associated in the story with the Church and the old priest who compares it to the Transfiguration of Jesus, prefigures the transformation of all creation at the end of time. At the Last Judgment Mrs. Shortley will discover her "true country," but at the beginning of the story, she is unaware of this. At that point, as O'Connor states, the peacock's neck "was drawn back as if his attention were fixed in the distance on something no one else could see."[61]

That "as if" clause has been widely noted as a marker for the narrator's move to the realm of mystery, which in turn is almost always interpreted as the realm of universal grace.[62] Interestingly, though, this is the second proximate use of the "as if" clause. Immediately preceding this, Mrs. Shortley "ignored the white afternoon sun which was creeping behind a ragged wall of cloud as if it pretended to be an intruder and cast her gaze down the red clay road that turned off from the highway."[63] With many other writers one would simply conclude that the author is repeating herself and that the failure to see what the peacock sees is simply identical with the failure to look toward the sun rather than downward to the world of mere appearances. In this construction one would conclude that the only alternative is supernatural grace and that the region of mystery is limited to supernatural grace alone. But another way of reading the double "as if" clauses suggests that O'Connor saw a plurality of connected alternatives. Consider the possibility that in "The Displaced Person," both grace *and* nature are either absent or ignored—and that O'Connor, following Aquinas, took both utterly seriously.[64]

Although O'Connor has been linked both with the concept of grace and with the teaching of Aquinas, one finds virtually no analysis of his treatment of grace in the critical literature. For Aquinas, grace, like virtue, is a quality of the soul, and hence, in the diction of Aristotle's categories—which Aquinas follows—it is an accident rather than part of our substantial identity. A being has a power, such as reason. Reason is part of our substance, and hence as humans we always have the capacity for reason. Humans are essentially rational animals. But the perfection of that power, that is for that power to be virtuously exercised, is accidental. To be beautiful or ugly, wise or foolish, brave or cowardly, to be filled with grace or not—these are "accidental" qualities.

Aquinas sees the soul as having several powers, such as reason, will, desires, and sense. He finds, however, that grace is not in any single power, and certainly not in the will alone. Grace is in the soul as a whole, and hence grace is a precondition for excellent function of each of the individual powers, and hence grace is prior to virtue. Further, grace is a special gift of the rational human soul.[65] God governs other creatures but not in the special way that humans participate in God's Eternal Law. For Aquinas, rather than stressing our irrational dimension, grace flows from our unique status as intellectual creatures. To choose anything without apprehending and in some way understanding it would be an inhuman act. Reflexive obedience without knowing the reason for obedience or the good involved in obedience would be subhuman, moving toward the good as other animals do.

In his first article on grace, Aquinas treats the crucial question of whether there can be any knowledge without grace. One stream of religious thought claims no and hence rejects nature and reason as guides to human action, saying that only God's supernatural grace can save us. Aquinas rejects this answer by giving a different perspective on grace: while agreeing that all knowing depends on grace, he proceeds to show that grace has two dimensions, one natural and the other supernatural.[66]

Aquinas argues that there are two kinds of things that can be known: those things that are within the grasp of our natures, and those things that are above our natures. The former are known through a natural intellectual light; the latter, through "a stronger light, viz., the light of faith or prophecy that is called the light of grace, inasmuch as it is added to nature."[67] Further he says that the Holy Ghost, the symbol of the supernatural in so much Christian tradition, is the source of both the natural light and the light of grace.[68]

At this juncture Aquinas introduces a metaphor for the way in which we experience God, through the Holy Ghost, as the ultimate source of natural knowing: "The material sun sheds its light outside us; but the intelligible sun, Who is God, shines within us. Hence the natural light bestowed upon the soul is God's enlightenment, whereby we are enlightened to see what pertains to natural knowledge; and for this there is required no further knowledge, but only for such things as surpass natural knowledge."[69]

The movement from ignorance to knowledge was for O'Connor always a mystery. But the content of this mystery has two distinguishable dimensions: that which she saw as within the grasp of our natures and that which she saw as beyond our nature. In terms of the broad theme of "rising and converging," which she adopted from Teilhard de Chardin, both are "risings." Ultimately they converge because of a common source.[70] But one must distinguish between the rising that is a rising to grasp natural truth and that which is a rising to supernatural truth.[71] For O'Connor, the turning around in Plato's cave, whereby one begins painfully to ascend from the shadows, is a mystery, but not the mystery of supernatural grace, that "stronger light" whereby we know that which is above our natures. Only in the closing passage of one story, "Revelation," do we grasp some glimpse of what the content of that illumination might be.

In "The Displaced Person," Mrs. Shortley ignores two things as she vainly presides over her countryside. The first is the realm of natural intelligibility represented in this story by the sun; the second, represented by a peacock, is that which can only be fully known outside of time, at the Last Judgment. The realm of nature, and its relationship to the political, can be seen most clearly in Astor, and in the brooding references to the Judge. The explicit realm of grace can be seen, but only slightly, by the peacock, which points us in the direction of the Creator.[72]

Frequently in O'Connor's fiction, the marginalized who are not fully

part of the liberal acquisitive society are the most able to rise to a knowledge of nature as revealed by the intelligible sun. In "View of the Woods,"
for example, Mary Fortune discerns an intimation of something not infinitely malleable and infinitely substitutable. In "The Displaced Person," it
is Guizac and Astor. Guizac is able to disregard the accident of color in trying to find a way out of the camps for his cousin. Astor is able to reflect that
since Guizac was there, he was somewhere.

Astor is also able to recognize that Guizac makes a claim that is outside the realm of ordinary contractual obligations. Astor is the character
most associated with sunlight per se; the priest is most associated with the
peacock. At one point Astor is described as "half in the sunlight and half
out." At another place, "bars of sunlight fell from the cracked ceiling across
his back and cut him in three distinct parts."[73] Astor is also associated with
speech. He talks to Sulk, to Mrs. McIntyre, and to Guizac. Sometimes he
even has conversations with himself, imitating a dialogue: "a careful roundabout discussion, question and answer and then refrain."[74]

Through this habit of speech and reflection, Astor is able to come to
more reasonable insights than other characters in the story. In addition to
his realization of Guizac's human claim, Astor apprehends some bond between himself and Mrs. McIntyre beyond the perpetual transactions and
transitory alliances of commerce. Mrs. McIntyre says, "We've seen them
come and seen them go." Astor, realizing that there is some "we" amid the
endless shifting of individuals, says, "And me and you is still here."[75]

Mrs. McIntyre resents Astor's claim that they are capable of a relationship that transcends commerce and utility, and she reminds Astor of her
power: "'I've spent half of my life fooling with worthless people,' she said in
a severe voice, 'But now I am through.'" Astor enigmatically replies, "Black
and White is the same."[76] The line can be read in two different but compatible ways. On one level is Astor's claim that by nature, each human is worthy because of his or her equal status as rational beings; but simultaneously,
there is also the suggestion that black and white are the same because of
the neediness and vulnerability of each. Whether black or white, each can
be treated as worthless, and each can be excluded from human friendship.

As the conversation continues, the Judge is remembered. Mrs. Mc-
Intyre is fond of recalling the Judge's platitudes that reinforce her self-
satisfied status as owner: "One man's gain is another man's misery; you can't
have your pie and eat it too." But Astor remembers a saying that unsettles

Mrs. McIntyre because of its double-edged character: "'Judge say he long for the day when he be too poor to pay a nigger to work,' he said. 'Say when that day come, the world be back on its feet.'"[77] On the one hand, the line could be interpreted as Mrs. McIntyre desires. If she becomes poor, she will still have power, the power to fire the hired help, so she uses her power as a threat to Astor. But Astor seems to suggest something else: perhaps the Judge really meant it; perhaps to be poor would be to renounce the endless quest for acquisition and the striving for advantage entailed in it. In that construction, leaving aside wealth and acquisition would be the precondition for leaving aside utility and wealth as the sole measure of human relationships. Only then could friendship emerge.

Astor restates the latter interpretation to Sulk, who fears that like the mule, he too will become worthless—as prophesied by Mrs. Shortley: "'Never mind' the old man said, 'your place too low for anybody to dispute with you for it.'"[78] Poorness of status, like poorness of ambition for gain, can exempt one from the brutal competition of exchange in which utility is the only measure.

Astor is the rational counterpoint to the grasping Mr. Shortley, who uses self-contradictory arguments to condemn Guizac. Shortley proclaims that all men are free and equal and proudly trumpets his service in World War I where he fought to defend the truth of that proposition—and yet Shortley immediately turns around and radically relativizes the human. Like his now-deceased wife, who saw the battle of clean English words with dirty Polish words, Shortley sees language as historical and conventional, trapping persons in their own idiosyncratic cultures. Rather than genuinely affirming that all men are free and equal as the basis of some human characteristic underlying history, Shortley prefers China or Africa since "you go to either of them two places and you can tell right away what the difference is between you and them." Rather than any openness to the other, to the "foreign," to the different—on the basis of some commonality underlying surface difference—Shortley, talking to Sulk, sees difference as a justification for abolition: "For a moment he only looked at him while a great deal of meaning gathered in his wet eyes. Then he said softly, 'revenge is mine saith the Lord.'"[79] Of course Shortley thinks he is the one who should mete out the revenge. For Shortley, as for Locke, there is no natural basis for a human community of friendship. The distinction between political society and the state of nature is ultimately fragile. The state of war can erupt at any time and with it, the right of the individual to punish, including both reparation and deterrence.

Astor, on the other hand, acknowledges his natural desire to live with others in some community bound together by ties greater than utility. At the end of the story we find a small hint of that: Astor was not implicated in the death of Guizac; only he and the priest escaped. All the others begin to live out the consequences of that complicity. For example, Mrs. McIntyre begins her long process of trying to heal her soul; she forgoes her desire for unlimited acquisition (where the two ends never meet since one end, the desire for more, is unlimited) and decides to "live on what she had."[80] The priest visits her, trying to explain the doctrines of the Church. Sulk and Shortley flee with no real explanation, but the reader assumes that they somehow cannot live with the constant reminder of their guilt.

Astor leaves too, but in his case the reason is given: "The old man could not work without company."[81] O'Connor could have written "help" rather than "company." Help would indicate a physical incapacity on Astor's part. But she chose "company" instead. Astor cannot work without conversation, others with whom to converse, others with whom, however imperfectly, he can experience something of his desire for a polity of friendship. Work for the others was simply a way of gratifying ultimately private preferences. For Astor, being together with others in speech was an end in itself. Control over physical nature is instrumentally necessary but ultimately not the genuine end of distinctly human activity. For Astor, as for Aquinas and Aristotle, politics may originate in the desire for mere life but continues for the sake of the good life whose highest expression is friendly speech.

There is another hint at an alternative contract, and that hint centers on the ambiguous character of the Judge. Though often interpreted for us by Mrs. McIntyre as the ultimate commercial individual, we have seen his ambiguous claim, perhaps more accurately reported by Astor, that to be poor and hence free of the desire to acquire and master the world is better than a life driven by acquisition. So, even for Mrs. McIntyre, there is some scandal, some anomaly in the Judge. Mrs. McIntyre's surface account of her marriage to the Judge is perfectly Lockean, since the marriage is aimed at her advantage. She calculates rightly that the contract will be short given the Judge's advanced age, and in fact he dies within three years. She calculates wrongly that she will inherit great wealth from him, since he leaves little behind. But even Mrs. McIntyre is forced to acknowledge some other relationship to the Judge: "She had married him when he was an old man and because of his money but there had been another reason that she would not admit then, even to herself: she had liked him."[82] McIntyre could not admit "she liked him" because such acknowledgment would undermine her view of the world as one of autonomy, freedom, and calculation. To admit love would be to admit neediness and responsibility rather than unfettered freedom and stark equality. Such an admission would make her liable to concern over a common good between her and the Judge, rather than the solitary pursuit of her own private good. It would make the relationships between her and the Judge "free, equal, and friendly."

Two other details about the Judge reinforce this view. The Judge, though constantly complaining that he was the poorest man alive, was the one who had bought the peacocks. Mrs. McIntyre is letting them die off because they are not useful, but the Judge bought them precisely because they were not for use but rather because they were beautiful. In Locke's state of nature there are no peacocks, only real and potential violators of the laws of nature, willing to plunge all into a state of war. Those who violate the laws of nature are like lions and tigers, savage beasts that one has a right to destroy.[83] In Locke's thought, nature is stingy and mean, giving almost nothing to humankind. Locke says that nature provides at best only one out of a thousand parts of the value of a thing. Only transformative human labor can compensate for this poverty-stricken state. But for O'Connor and for the Judge, there are peacocks, whose beauty is bounteous, beyond expectation. The Judge said that he was the poorest man alive, and yet "he had liked to see then walking around the place for he said they made him feel rich."[84] For all its incompleteness, nature sometimes offers a taste of limitless bounty, an overflowing that cannot be exhausted.

The other action of the Judge that hints at an alternative is his buying the granite cherub to place over his gravesite. The cherub has been vandalized by former tenants, the Herrins, who chopped the angel from its base with an axe when they left. Because Mr. Herrins aimed poorly, the cherub broke off, leaving the toes. The vandalized cherub, then, is an illustration of O'Connor's use of the absent: she describes a granite base, out of which arise granite toes, which abruptly end in a jagged line. The cherub is absent, and yet the presence of the broken toes indicates that they were, or are—or could be—not solitary and independent, but part of some larger whole.

So too, the original whole cherub invokes this same idea. The Judge bought it for two reasons: one, because it reinforces the presence of the peacocks in that it represents something beyond utility, a value beyond price— "he had wanted a genuine work of art over his grave."[85] The other reason is that "its face reminded him of his wife."[86] O'Connor, then, in a series of analogies, presents an ascent to the reader that ultimately links the realm of nature and grace. The Judge experiences the love of a particular woman, whose beauty attracts him. He then connects that concrete love of the beautiful to the love of a higher beauty, the artwork represented by the angel. The granite angel in turn suggests that it might only be an instance, an imitation of an actual beautiful angel, which further suggests someone who is the source of the angel's beauty. This ascent is made possible by the natural light of intelligibility that allows us to encounter glimpses of truth, goodness, beauty, and unity.

O'Connor, moreover, indicates that the love engendered by these glimpses cries out for fulfillment and that it is in the fulfillment or culmination of this love that grace works its healing power. Mrs. McIntyre remains at the lower end of the ascent; O'Connor explains that she had "never noticed the resemblance to herself." Because she remains trapped in her habit of acquisition, she has no resources to devote to the higher and more beautiful; after the cherub is vandalized, "Mrs. McIntyre had never been able to afford to have it replaced."[87]

"The Displaced Person" raises themes that recur in later stories such as "Revelation." O'Connor shows an opposition between a liberal individualistic vision and the vision of Aquinas. In what liberals would simply lump together as the private sphere, that is outside the realm of politics and what is public, O'Connor finds two dimensions, one natural, the other supernatural. Further, O'Connor finds some clear demarcation between politics and the Divine. Mrs. Shortley's first vision is a false one and is to be rejected; final judgment is not ours, and neither is the sword of that judgment. As we hear in snatches from the Judge and from Astor, the genuine basis of a good regime seems to be not in coercion but in the spoken word.

Notes

1. Flannery O'Connor, "The Displaced Person," in *The Complete Stories* (New York: Noonday, 1993), 194–235. This article is partially based on my previous treatment of "The Displaced Person." See John Roos, "Flannery O'Connor and

Natural Law: A Reading of 'The Displaced Person,'" paper presented at Northeast Political Science Association, November 13, 1992.

2. See, for example, Carter W. Martin, *The True Country: Themes in the Fiction of Flannery O'Connor* (Nashville: Vanderbilt University Press, 1968), 94. See also Miles Orvell, *Invisible Parade: The Fiction of Flannery O'Connor* (Philadelphia: Temple University Press, 1972), 150.

3. Aristotle, *Politics,* ed. and trans. Carnes Lord (Chicago: University of Chicago Press, 1984), 1278b 9–10. All references to *Politics* are to this edition.

4. John Locke, *Second Treatise of Government,* ed. Peter Lasslett (Cambridge: Cambridge University Press, 1988). On rejection of Divine Right, see ibid., chap. 1, par. 1–2. On joining political society see ibid., chap. 9, par. 89; on economics and property, see ibid., chap. 5, esp. par. 51; on marriage, see ibid., chap. 7, esp. 78–83; on family, see ibid., esp. par. 58–73; on aiming at life, liberty and property, see ibid., chap. 9, esp. par. 123–24.

5. Ibid, chap. 8, par. 95.

6. O'Connor, *Complete Stories,* 203.

7. Ibid., 218.

8. Mrs. Shortley's marriage also shows Lockean elements. When Mr. Shortley courted her, there were no tokens of affection or freely given love (206). Instead there is only the sensual appeal of his trick with the burning cigarette, suggesting a devil-like sensuality.

9. Locke, *Second Treatise,* chap. 9, par. 123.

10. Ibid., chap. 5, par. 38.

11. O'Connor, *Complete Stories,* 213.

12. Ibid., 199.

13. Ibid., 215.

14. Ibid., 219.

15. Ibid., 203.

16. Locke, *Second Treatise,* chap. 1, par. 6.

17. O'Connor, *Complete Stories,* 196.

18. Ibid., 219.

19. Ibid., 225.

20. Ibid., 221.

21. Locke, *Second Treatise,* chap. 8, par. 121. Locke says most persons are part of the commonwealth only because of tacit consent rather than a formal declaration. Those with tacit consent have the right to emigrate, that is, leave. But, they must leave all their property and they have to be able to find some place that is more conducive to their life, liberty, and estate. Astor and Sulk may resent Mrs. McIntyre's commonwealth, but they do not think they can find anyplace better.

22. O'Connor, *Complete Stories,* 232.

23. Ibid., 204.

24. Ibid., 203.

25. Ibid., 201.

26. Locke, *Second Treatise,* chap. 5, par. 34.

27. The enigmatic figure of the Judge suggests that he might be above Mrs. McIntyre. As we shall see later, he may in some ways transcend the regime itself.

28. Astor tells Sulk that he need not worry about being fired because "your place too low for anybody to dispute with you for it," and Mrs. McIntyre says to Astor: "We can get along without them. We've seen them come and seen them go—black and white" (O'Connor, *Complete Stories,* 231).

29. Ibid., 232. The shift from "are" to "was" seems not only colloquial. It is ironic, because Shortley does not want to include Guizac under the umbrella of the principle.

30. In one ironic twist, Mrs. McIntyre's regime operates more radically than the American regime of the time with respect to gender. In the story a woman is in charge, with a woman lieutenant. In the Shortley family, Mr. Shortley rightly concludes that Mrs. Shortley is by nature more capable, effective, and shrewd than he, and hence should have the ruling power in their family—"Mr. Shortley had never in his life doubted her omniscience" (ibid., 211).

31. Unlike some of her regional literary antecedents among the Agrarians, who condoned paternalistic racism, O'Connor shows in this story the moral bankruptcy of such a position. See, for example, *I'll Take My Stand: The South and the Agrarian Tradition by Twelve Southerners* (New York: Harper Torchbooks, 1962).

32. O'Connor, *Complete Stories,* 194.

33. This passage has numerous ironies. It turns out that of course they can know color, but they can know it rightly, that is, as relevant to some things and not relevant to others. By truly knowing color one knows that the color of a person's skin is irrelevant to their human nature. It is Shortley and McIntyre who do not "know what color is."

34. O'Connor, *Complete Stories,* 196.

35. Ibid., 199.

36. Ibid., 202.

37. Ibid., 207.

38. Ibid., 222.

39. *Summa theologica* (Westminster, Md.: Christian Classics 1981), II–II, Q. 66, Art. 7, in which Aquinas talks about the natural basis of property in service to the common good.

40. In this case, unlike that of racial equality, O'Connor agreed with the Agrarian analysis (see esp. Lyle Lanier, "A Critique of the Philosophy of Progress," in *I'll Take My Stand,* 122–54).

41. O'Connor, *Complete Stories*, 205.

42. Ibid., 216.

43. Ibid., 201.

44. Ibid., 231.

45. Ibid., 205.

46. Ibid., 196.

47. Ibid., 212. Mr. Shortley is perhaps an exception to this. He has been willing to fight for his country and risk his life. His is not a thin attachment to the community, but this willingness to sacrifice seems in no way coherently derived from the regime. He simply asserts that he was willing to die to defend that proposition of freedom and equality, but in the same context he wants to discriminate against Guizac on the simple ground of self and other. In this sense he is the exception that proves the rule. For the criticism of Locke concerning self-sacrifice, see Robert Goldwin, "John Locke" in *History of Political Philosophy*, ed. Leo Strauss and Joseph Cropsy (Chicago: University of Chicago Press, 1987).

48. In this respect O'Connor's artistic explorations parallel so much of European and American thought in the immediate postwar period. The late 1940s and early 1950s were a period of profound explorations of alternatives to liberal individualism and the narrow view of instrumental rationality it engendered. The cumulative experience of what followed the giddiness of pre–World War I Vienna had crushed for many the optimistic view of the unchecked progress in the enterprise of mastering nature and transforming it into our own image. The relentless slaughter of a generation of youth in the trenches of the Marne was followed by the unprecedented horrors of Hitler's Holocaust. The gas ovens and the boxcars became the most pervasive image reflecting what "civilized" life had become. Leo Strauss's attempt to recapture an original Greek horizon of nature, Eric Voegelin's attempt to reconcile history with order, Hannah Arendt's attempt to recapture a nontechnological and nondeterministic space for human action, and Jacques Maritain's attempt to reinvigorate a natural basis for morality are all bound together as attempts to find a firmer barrier to totalitarian terror than the flimsiness of liberal individualism.

49. Edward Kessler, *Flannery O'Connor and the Language of Apocalypse* (Princeton, N.J.: Princeton University Press, 1986).

50. Ibid., 39.

51. Ibid., 38.

52. O'Connor, *Complete Stories*, 209.

53. In this she may be following the analysis of Eric Voegelin, a political philosopher whose writings could be found in O'Connor's library. For an interpretation that stresses the Voegelinian influence, see Marion Montgomery, *Why Flannery O'Connor Stayed Home* (Athens: University of Georgia Press, 1968).

54. O'Connor, *Complete Stories*, 209.

55. Ibid., 210.

56. Ezekiel 34:20 (p. 1045). All references to the Bible are to *The Oxford Annotated Bible with the Apocrypha*, ed. Herbert G. May and Bruce M. Metzger (New York: Oxford University Press, 1965).

57. Ibid., 33:14–15 (p. 1043).

58. O'Connor, *Complete Stories*, 214.

59. Flannery O'Connor, "Revelation," in *Complete Stories*, 488–509.

60. Here, too, O'Connor follows Aquinas, who urges that natural law be the basis of human law but warns against changing human law whenever something better occurs. Aquinas says with striking sobriety: "Consequently, when a law is changed, the binding power of law is diminished, in so far as custom is abolished. Therefore human law should *never* be changed, unless, in some way or other, the common welfare be compensated according to the extent of the harm done in this respect" (see Thomas Aquinas, *Summa theologica*, I–II, 97, Art. 3, I ans. that.).

61. O'Connor, *Complete Stories*, 194.

62. Kessler, *O'Connor and the Language of Apocalypse*, 8. See also Ruthann Johansen, *The Narrative Secret of Flannery O'Connor* (Tuscaloosa: University of Alabama Press, 1994), 23–28.

63. O'Connor, *Complete Stories*, 194.

64. One of the problems encountered in both Aquinas and O'Connor is the complexity of the terms and experiences they attempt to represent. Thomas often calls our attention to the need to make an analytic distinction in regard to something that actually cannot be divided. So, for example, he makes a distinction between the intellect per se and the rational appetite designated as the will. Taken too far, this may at times lead to the reification of the will as a separate autonomous faculty, ready for Nietzsche to choose as the source of our identity. Closer examination, though, reveals that the objects of the analytically divided powers are in fact not really separate. The intellect aims at truth, the will at the good, but for Aquinas they are not finally or fundamentally different. One cannot really separate the good from the true. Or to put it another way, the encounter with truth simultaneously involves the encounter with the good. In a similar vein, Aquinas develops accounts of nature and grace, which need to be analytically distinguished but may not always be really separate. For example, Thomas claims that part of the Divine Law, given by God in special revelation and known with the aid of grace, is also accessible to the unaided natural human reason. If known through natural reason, it is then also part of the natural law.

65. Aquinas, *Summa theologica*, I–II, 4, reply obj. 3.

66. In the body of the article Thomas proceeds to explain the way in which all knowledge, corporeal and spiritual, depends upon God. Aquinas, citing both Paul

and Aristotle as his authorities, says that this dependence on God has two dimensions: God as creator of our rational form, and the creator of that which moves this form to act. In simple terms, Aquinas says we do not cause or create ourselves, and we do not move ourselves. Both our form and existence as rational creatures and that upon which this intellectual form acts is from God as simple first mover. In even simpler terms, for me to do or know anything, there has to be a me, and there has to be something other than myself to know. I do not cause either of these by myself. For both I am dependent upon the whole of which I am a part. For Aristotle, this phenomenon is covered by a teaching of nature and the first cause of nature. For Aquinas, who generally accepted Aristotle's account as far as it went, there is a need to add that which is the cause of things simply and that which preserves them in being. This leads to the great divide between Aristotle and Aquinas on whether nature is eternal or created. About this they agreed on one fundamental proposition: no rational proof existed to determine the matter either way.

67. Aquinas, *Summa theologica*, I–II, 109, 1, I ans. that.

68. Ibid., reply obj. 1.

69. Ibid., reply obj. 2.

70. For O'Connor, as for Aquinas, this origin from and convergence toward a common source has the clear consequence that there can be no contradiction between the two. What has been demonstrated in nature cannot be contradicted by revelation. There can be no doctrine of "two truths."

71. As one would expect in a 1,500-page book like the *Summa*, things get complicated. Sometimes that which is knowable by nature can be repeated by revelation because we humans forget things or fail to learn them in the first place. Hence the very intent of the moral precepts of the Decalogue, though knowable by nature, are repeated by Divine revelation. But given the two truths, Thomas would say that Revelation and Reason cannot disagree, properly understood, about what that common content is. In some, and only some, cases two persons could arrive at the same truth by different avenues. One could arrive at the natural truth by unaided reason, i.e., nature. The other could arrive at the same truth by the grace of particular revelation.

72. O'Connor, *Complete Stories*, 508. Note that this is one of the few places in O'Connor's work where she shows the content of the particular revelation.

73. Ibid., 214.

74. Ibid., 217.

75. Ibid., 214.

76. Ibid., 215.

77. Ibid.

78. Ibid., 206.

79. Ibid., 233.

80. Ibid., 235.

81. Ibid.

82. Ibid.

83. Locke, *Second Treatise*, chap. 2, par. 11

84. O'Connor, *Complete Stories*, 218.

85. Ibid., 221. O'Connor of course cannot drop her sense of the ridiculous. One doesn't wonder very long whether the granite cherub was "a genuine work of art." But the point seems to be the Judge had an impulse toward something genuine, something of beauty.

86. Ibid.

87. Ibid.

13

Future Flannery, or, How a Hillbilly Thomist Can Help Us Navigate the Politics of Personhood in the Twenty-First Century

Christina Bieber Lake

A self-described "hillbilly Thomist," Flannery O'Connor was a national anomaly. Equal parts Georgia hillbilly and devoted Catholic writer, she wrote stories about common southerners for no other reason than that they were her people, as blessed by God as anybody. If she wrote about intellectuals, politicians, or pseudo-celebrities, it was only to make fun of them, to take them down a notch or two. The people she wrote about because she loved them were the "folk": people like Obadiah Elihue Parker, as "ordinary as a loaf of bread." Her stories were all about how ordinary things are capable of extraordinary transformations.

It turns out that this is exactly the Flannery O'Connor we may need now more than ever before. Her love for the "folk"—in her case, love for people of all mental capacities simply because they are family—has become an increasingly radical position to take. Were she alive today, O'Connor would likely agree with Martha Nussbaum in her assessment that utilitarian ethics, with its way of aggregating statistics instead of considering individuals, dominates ethical discourse today, significantly impacting decision makers.[1] In *Poetic Justice: The Literary Imagination and Public Life,* Nussbaum argues that it is in the very nature of narrative fiction to resist this kind of aggregation, for it operates at cross purposes with cost-benefit analyses that tend to reduce the complexities of individual lives to tabular form. The more politics resembles a technocracy in which leaders make decisions by leaning over actuarial tables in big-city offices, the more important literature—with its concern for the moral imagination—becomes.

Martha Nussbaum, Wayne Booth, and many others have thus urged policymakers to give literature a greater role in their decisions. Literature is increasingly indispensable in these arenas, argues Nussbaum, because it "expresses, in its structures and its ways of speaking, a sense of life that is incompatible with the vision of the world embodied in the texts of political economy; and engagement with it forms the imagination and the desires in a manner that subverts that science's norm of rationality."[2] In other words, literature does not let us get away with converting people into numbers in order to decide which decisions yield the greatest happiness for the largest number.

The widespread acceptance of a utilitarian norm of rationality—the norm that Nussbaum claims fiction subverts—is especially evident in the recent history of the word "person." In his illuminating book *Persons: The Difference between "Someone" and "Something,"* Robert Spaemann explains that since its early modern development, the word "person" has been used to establish equality and basic human rights for all individuals. Today, however, the word is used to differentiate between members of the human species. In other words, "person" does not apply to every human being equally but is used to delineate who has rights and who does not:

> Only human beings can have human rights, and human beings can have them only as persons. The argument then runs: but not all human beings are persons; and those that are, are not persons in every stage of life or in every state of consciousness. They are not persons if from the first moment of their lives they are refused admission to the community of recognition, for that is what makes human beings persons. And they are not persons if, as individuals, they lack the features that ground our talk of human beings as persons in general, i.e. if they never acquire or lose, temporarily or permanently, the relevant capacities.

Small children are not persons, for example; neither are the severely handicapped and the senile.[3]

This position—usually called "personism"—is held most recognizably by Peter Singer, the famous Princeton utilitarian ethicist. Singer argues that parents should have the right to commit infanticide when they give birth to a severely disabled child. Singer can make this argument because widespread practice already supports the reasoning behind it. The existence of prenatal testing for Down syndrome, for instance, presumes the moral acceptability of aborting a fetus for no other reason than that it has been diagnosed with this disability. Abortion statistics confirm the prevalence of this belief in the right to discriminate between which persons should be born and which should not be. For example, one hospital-based study published in 1998 revealed that 86 percent of couples who obtained a prenatal diagnosis of Down syndrome chose to terminate their pregnancies.[4] At the very least, these statistics reveal a practical affirmation of the belief that it is acceptable to think of a fetus with Down syndrome as replaceable.

Singer simply extends the reasoning behind this common practice. Since an infant prior to age two is equally not capable of "regarding itself as a distinct entity with a life of its own to lead," he or she does not meet the standard definition of "person."[5] And as such, to kill an infant because he is severely disabled is not categorically different from aborting a fetus for the same reason. Since neither the fetus nor the young infant are persons, a different ethical standard applies to them. Parents who abort a fetus with Down syndrome, just as those who might choose to end the life of a disabled infant, are simply hoping to replace that child with a "normal" one. Singer writes, "I cannot see how one could defend the view that fetuses may be 'replaced' before birth, but newborn infants may not be."[6] When made into a legislative standard, personism allows individuals to make decisions for others on the basis of the existence or nonexistence of definable personal traits. With this standard in place, there is no need to consider any subjectivities beyond those of the parents or caregivers.

Although most would consider infanticide to be morally abhorrent, Singer's argumentation reveals how the eugenic and utilitarian ideas behind personism have steadily become an invisible cultural norm in the United States. For example, the advent and increasing use of preimplantation genetic diagnosis (PGD) not only assumes that it is acceptable to discard unselected fertilized embryos, but it also assumes that it is acceptable to discriminate between desirable and undesirable embryos based on future traits that the children will evince, presumably for their benefit. As Eric Cohen explains, this represents a clear move toward a eugenic attitude regarding the vulnerable:

> By making reproduction into a process of division by class, we transform the welcoming attitude of unconditional love into a eugenic attitude of conditional acceptance. Of course, we would do this in the name of compassion, or mercy, or equality. We seek to give our children healthy genetic equipment, and to spare those who would suffer by "nipping them in the bud." But the pursuit of genetic equality requires a radical program of genetic discrimination. Whatever we might think about the moral status of the early embryos tested in PGD, they are certainly not nothing.[7]

This changing view of persons affects more than American reproductive practices. In his book *The Future of Human Nature,* Jürgen Habermas explains how significantly (in the West) the ethical self-understanding of the human species has changed. Specifically, the increasing availability and acceptance of technologies like PGD have reinforced an instrumental view of persons, the definitive characteristic of which is to treat life more as made than as given. Habermas believes that an instrumental view of persons, inherent in utilitarian reasoning, is more threatening than we recognize. An instrumental view of persons threatens the "great achievement of modernity," the idea of egalitarian universalism. For although egalitarian universalism is a moral norm that nobody wants to challenge directly, it could be toppled. Not overnight or dramatically, he argues, but "by the silent consequences of practices we will become numbly accustomed to."[8]

It is precisely this "numbing" that concerns a prophetic writer like Flannery O'Connor. Like Walker Percy, who proclaimed that a "twentieth-century novelist should be a nag, an advertiser, a collector, a proclaimer of banal atrocities," O'Connor was aware of subtly shifting attitudes toward those persons who society values least.[9] Though she likely never heard the term "posthuman," anticipated the normalization of abortion, or conceived of the idea of pre-implantation genetic diagnosis, she identified the instrumental view of persons that lies underneath such changes, and she warned against its increasing prominence. Like Martha Nussbaum, she believed that stories, by their nature, work against utilitarian ethical reasoning. By centering her stories around misfits, the mentally or physically disabled, ignorant backwoods prophets, and ordinary rural folk, O'Connor argues for the equal dignity of all persons. By telling stories that hinge on the recognition and acceptance of the "least of these," O'Connor refuses to say that a person is a person based on his or her attributes. In her vision, a person is a person simply by being born into the human family. The important thing is to be able to recognize and take responsibility for that fact.

It is stunning to note how many of O'Connor's stories have this theme of recognition as their ethical core. In the oft-anthologized "A Good Man Is Hard to Find," a self-righteous grandmother must learn to see a criminal as someone who might have been her own son. In "The Life You Save May Be Your Own," a drifter, himself unloved, is unable to learn to love others and continues the cycle of his own abandonment, leaving a mentally disabled girl in a restaurant. In "Revelation," Ruby Turpin has to learn to see her own foibles before she can recognize how she has lived a life of judgment on, and rejection of, other people. In the novella *The Violent Bear It Away*— the focus of this essay—the protagonist's redemption centers around the question of whether or not he will baptize a child with Down syndrome, a child whose own father does not consider him worthy of the water spilled over him. In this novella, O'Connor violently turns the table on ethicists who assert the power to grant or deny personhood to others. *The Violent Bear It Away* links Francis Marion Tarwater's redemption—and his freedom—to his recognition of the claim that others have on him. For Flannery O'Connor, it is that recognition of the other that is constitutive of true freedom.

The Violent Bear It Away is something of a retelling of *Wise Blood*, Flannery O'Connor's first novel. In *Wise Blood*, Hazel Motes was the reluctant prophet who has to learn that he does, in fact, believe that Jesus has redeemed him and called him to himself. In *The Violent Bear It Away*, Francis Tarwater is a reluctant prophet who must learn the same thing. Whereas Haze's redemption depends on his rejection of his own adopted atheism (achieved through rejecting the "new jesus," a mummified body that stands for the "body of death" that atheism leads to), Tarwater's redemption depends on his acceptance of responsibility for others. Specifically, he must accept the mission to preach salvation to the children of God who "lay sleeping in the city." That acceptance pivots around the question of whether or not he will submit to what his great-uncle said would be his first mission: to baptize his "dim-witted" cousin, Bishop.

The novel begins when the death of Tarwater's great-uncle (old man Tarwater) leaves young Tarwater completely on his own for the first time. It then traces the story of Tarwater's violent struggle for and against this call to be a prophet (depicted in his resistance to his uncle, Rayber); his angry fulfillment of the role (in which he murders the child as he unintentionally baptizes him), and his eventual repentance and full acceptance of the calling. The full acceptance comes only after Tarwater himself is violently sodomized by someone who shows as little regard for his personal dignity as he had shown for Bishop's.

This is not a story for the faint of heart. The first thing to notice about it is that O'Connor refuses to sentimentalize the issue of Tarwater's call to love Bishop and to preach the gospel to others. The story is instead a kind of exposition of Jesus's words in Matthew 11, quoted in the epigraph of this novella: "The kingdom of heaven suffereth violence, and the violent bear it away." Many writers have tried to make sense of this difficult teaching of Jesus. As Erasmo Leiva-Merikakis points out, it needs to be taken in context of the gospel of Matthew. That gospel includes the following: Jesus's teaching that he came not to bring peace but a sword; his teaching that if anyone loves their own family more than Jesus they are not worthy to follow him; and his teaching that whoever loves him must take up their cross and follow him. Leiva-Merikakis writes: "All of these are particular aspects of the salutary interior violence a person must do to himself in order to be 'worthy of Jesus,' an heir of the Kingdom, and a child of the Father of the Word." So the particular verse "appears to mean that the 'violence' or 'forcefulness' that God himself is using so as to tear down the barriers that the human heart has erected against the approach of grace must be matched by the decision on the part of individuals to respond *just as violently and forcefully* in embracing that grace."[10] The violent bear away the kingdom of God because it is they who recognize the reality that to love God and others unconditionally will be a struggle in an age of cheap grace.

Flannery O'Connor's interest in this passage reveals her conviction that it is not *feelings* of love for other people that matter but proper *recognition:* first of Jesus: as who he claims he was, and then of others as who they are: beings worthy of self-sacrificial love. As this segment of the gospel of Matthew is centered on John the Baptist's recognition of Jesus as the coming Messiah, so is *The Violent Bear It Away* centered on the question of recognition. As John the Baptist recognizes that the one who comes after him is greater than he, so Tarwater must recognize that Bishop, contrary to societal teaching, is also a child of God. Bishop is so loved by God that God sent his son to die for him.[11] This kind of love involves a violent struggle against evil. And in *The Violent Bear It Away,* evil is located accordingly: Evil stems directly from the failure of the modern world to recognize that we are all children of God, worthy of dignity, worthy of sacrifice.

The *Violent Bear It Away* illustrates this failure beginning early in the novel. It opens with the death of old man Mason Tarwater, who is Francis Tarwater's great-uncle and guardian. While young Tarwater had promised the old man he would bury him in a deep grave, Tarwater's first act of rebellion is to break this promise. He declares, "Now I can do anything I want to."[12] He receives encouragement to break this promise from the voice of the "stranger" who is representative both of the demonic and of the dark and self-centered half of his conscience. The stranger tells him that he doesn't have to bother with respecting the old man's wishes or his body. Besides, the stranger tells him, he's been raised by a crazy person, and "in the rest of the world they do things different than what you have been taught" (*CW* 345). Tarwater wants to believe that the stranger is right. He wants to believe that he does not owe his uncle anything, that there is no final resurrection, and no Day of Judgment (*CW* 468). So he takes off, leaving his great-uncle's body unaccounted for.

As much as young Tarwater wants to join this modern rebellion against his great-uncle's teaching about the resurrection of the body, Tarwater still believes it to be true. He has what O'Connor would describe as wise blood. He also still believes everything else the old man taught him, and the narration moves back and forth in time in order to show how much of young Tarwater's upbringing has remained with him. What Tarwater has retained from his great-uncle is the idea of taking responsibility for others. Most notably, two or three years before his death, his great-uncle had taken Tarwater into the city. While there, the young Tarwater is drawn to the mass of humanity that he encounters:

> Before coming he had read facts in the almanac and he knew that there were 75,000 people here who were seeing him for the first time.

He had wanted to stop and shake hands with each of them and say his name was F. M. Tarwater and that he was here only for the day to accompany his uncle on business at a lawyer's. His head jerked backwards after each passing figure until they began to pass too thickly and he observed that their eyes didn't grab at you like the eyes of country people. Several people bumped into him and this contact that should have made an acquaintance for life, made nothing because the hulks shoved on with ducked heads and muttered apologies that he would have accepted if they had waited. (*CW* 346)

O'Connor's description of Tarwater's memory is not an attack on city life in favor of an idealized version of country living; instead, she draws on images of the anonymity of the city as a symbol of the modern failure to recognize the central fact of the humanity of all others that we encounter. When he has this experience of people in the city, young Tarwater "realized, almost without warning, that this place was evil—the ducked heads, the muttered words, the hastening away. He saw in a burst of light that the people were hastening away from the Lord God Almighty" (*CW* 346). Tarwater believes that to hasten away from others is also to hasten away from God, to give evil an opening. So when Tarwater is tempted now, upon his uncle's death, to do his own thing, it means that he wants the anonymity of autonomy. He does not want to take responsibility for preaching to these others who are walking away from God and from each other. This is the central struggle of the plot. Tarwater feels encouraged to rebel against his great-uncle by the voice of the demonic "stranger," who lays it out for him: "It ain't Jesus or the devil. It's Jesus or *you*" (*CW* 354). Tarwater must choose between unfettered freedom or responsibility to others. He knows they cannot coexist.

Tarwater's strongest effort to escape that responsibility is his rejection of his call to baptize Bishop, a child with Down syndrome. Bishop is Tarwater's cousin, the son of his uncle Rayber. The old man Mason Tarwater believed that either he or young Tarwater was sent by God to baptize Bishop. Old man Tarwater had told him that "that boy cries out for his baptism . . . Precious in the sight of the Lord even an idiot!" (*CW* 350). But Rayber had not permitted the old man to get anywhere near Bishop. Because Rayber, a schoolteacher, wants to be the paragon of the modern enlightened man, he is trying to convince himself (and now, young Tarwater, whom he is trying to parent) that his uncle is crazy. Rayber deliberately contradicts the Christian understanding of the dignity of every human person by insisting that Bishop was a mistake of nature, that he is useless, and that baptism would be a useless rite. "'You'll never lay a hand on him,' the schoolteacher said. 'You could slosh water on him for the rest of his life and he'd still be an idiot. Five years old for all eternity, useless forever. Listen,' he said, and the boy heard his taut voice turn low with a kind of subdued intensity, a passion equal and opposite to the old man's, 'he'll never be baptized—just as a matter of principle, nothing else. As a gesture of human dignity, he'll never be baptized'" (*CW* 351).

When the old man dies, Tarwater knows that the task of baptizing Bishop has fallen to him. As soon as Tarwater sees Bishop again, he knows "with a certainty sunk in despair" that the old man was right and that "he was called to be a prophet and that the ways of his prophecy would not be remarkable" (*CW* 388). When he was a small boy, Tarwater had wanted a dramatic calling. Now he knows that his task is first to recognize the value of a "useless" child and then to turn those same eyes toward the city, where the children of God lay sleeping.

Because Tarwater is trying to rebel against his prophetic calling and live for himself, he resists that calling. So when Rayber takes Tarwater to live with him and his son Bishop, he avoids looking at Bishop. Tarwater's refusal to look at Bishop is not just a refusal to accept his life as a prophet; it is a refusal to see Bishop as a person. This is why he keeps trying to convince himself that there's no difference between Bishop and a hog (*CW* 403). Rayber, the child's father, has also been trying to avoid looking at Bishop for the same reason. It turns out that Rayber has the same struggle as Tarwater; he, too, feels the influence of old man Tarwater's views. Although Rayber tries to think of the child abstractly, as "an x signifying the general hideousness of fate," he cannot (*CW* 401). Every time he looks at him he feels overwhelmed and horrified by a love he cannot explain. He thinks of his love as horrifying precisely because it is irrational, "it was love without reason, love for something futureless, love that appeared to exist only to be itself, imperious and all demanding, the kind that would cause him to make a fool of himself in an instant. And it only began with Bishop. It began with Bishop and then like an avalanche covered everything his reason hated" (*CW* 401).

This passage reveals the strong link between O'Connor's conception of the person and that of many prominent Catholic thinkers of her day, including neo-Thomist philosophers, and theologians associated with *la nouvelle théologie.*[13] O'Connor's library contained many works by Christian personalists, such as those by Gabriel Marcel, Baron von Hügel, Emmanuel Mounier, and Claude Tresmontant.[14] O'Connor underlined passages and made marginal comments in her copies of these books; in Mounier's *Personalism,* she wrote the words "the violent bear it away."[15] In *Personalism,* Mounier argues that it is Christianity that gave us the decisive original notion of the person, because all persons were created by God through love and for love: "The supreme Being which through love brings them into existence no longer makes the world a unity through the abstraction of the idea, but by an infinite capacity for the indefinite multiplication of these separate acts of love."[16] The superabundance of creation is not the impersonal result of Darwinian evolution but the loving act of a creator. Similarly, Claude Tresmontant, in *A Study of Hebrew Thought,* argues that Christianity follows the Hebrew way of thinking about creation and the person, in defiance to the Greek way. "Hebrew thought runs in a direction opposite to the current of Greek thought," since Greek thought deems "all tangible stuff to be born from a *decline,* a degradation, while the Hebrew considers it the result of an *ascent,* the result of a truly positive act: creation."[17] God's love for persons is indicated by how significant names and naming are in the Bible: "Each one's name, each one's essence is unique and irreplaceable."[18] Finally, and most decisively for Christian personalists, the Incarnation of Christ represents and effects God's decisive positive valuation of particular persons.[19]

The Violent Bear It Away is a veritable hymn to Christian personalism. Bishop triggers Rayber's intuitive valuation of and love for particular persons—and indeed, for all of creation. The kind of love Rayber feels for Bishop moves beyond that which comes from the fact he is his father. It touches on and mimics God's love for all of creation, even and especially for the "least of these." Try as he might, Rayber simply cannot see him as an abstract "x," for he is Bishop, a named particular person. Tarwater feels that same love too, and also fights it.

As with all of O'Connor's reluctant prophets, Tarwater's wise blood does not let him get away. At this point in the story, Rayber is trying to normalize Tarwater and make him believe that the old man was just a crazy hoot. The demonic stranger, who has now become Tarwater's "friend," is trying to convince him of the same thing. But when Tarwater sees Bishop jump in the fountain, he makes a move, in spite of Rayber and the friend, to baptize him. When Tarwater looks at Bishop in the water, he sees a spot of light that "rested like a hand on the child's white head" (*CW* 432). The biblical resonances with John the Baptist's baptism of Jesus are unmistakable in this scene.[20] Unlike John, Tarwater resists the attraction and listens to the voice of the friend who is telling him to take the opportunity to drown Bishop. Because if he baptizes Bishop now, the friend tells him, he'll be doing it for the rest of his life: "If it's an idiot this time, the next time it's liable to be a nigger. Save yourself while the hour of salvation is at hand" (*CW* 433).

Tarwater's "friend" defines salvation as freedom from the responsibility to love *all* of humanity, especially the ones that it is inconvenient to love. So eventually Tarwater takes the friend's advice and rids himself of the problem of Bishop by drowning him. The scene is O'Connor's most stunning move: Tarwater does drown Bishop, but when he does so, he *accidentally* baptizes him. Many critics have written about this scene, about its violence, its apparent heartlessness. One thing is clear: it is a scene that cannot be read sentimentally. Readers are not permitted to pity Bishop, because O'Connor knew that having feelings of pity for the vulnerable is not enough. Pity does not necessarily lead to recognition of the child's humanity; one can feel pity for animals. Without a theological motive, pity can be downright dangerous. After all, it is chiefly pity that enables eugenic thinking. This poor child—wouldn't it be better if he were not born at all? In one of her essays, O'Connor explained that by this kind of pity, "we mark our gain in sensibility and our loss in vision." She then aptly describes pity as the tenderness that leads to the gas chamber (*CW* 830–31).

By taking sympathy and any sentiment out of the picture, O'Connor turns the pivotal scene of Tarwater's recognition of the dignity of others on a decision of his will: the decision to accept or reject Bishop's value to God. O'Connor would likely agree with Spaemann on what lies at the core of this decision. To recognize the dignity of the other is not simply to put ourselves into the other's shoes, to feel sympathy or even empathy because we recognize elements of our own plight. It is instead to recognize the "same incomparable uniqueness" of the other. Human beings as human beings, explains Spaemann, "may be more or less similar; but as persons they are not similar, but equal—equal in their distinctive uniqueness and incommensurable dignity."[21] That Tarwater has little natural empathy for Bishop only makes the point more richly: Tarwater must come out of himself and see this other child, who is in many ways very different from him, as loved by God. It is a step into a "wholly new form of relation" that moves beyond seeing our well-being as wrapped up in theirs. That is why this definition of the person is best illustrated in those cases, argues Spaemann, where there is no motive of sympathy or empathy to make it easier, "so that personal relations assume the elementary form of justice."[22]

Tarwater's redemption requires that he do justice: he must learn to love Bishop for no other reason than that God does. Earlier, when Bishop had been saved from drowning by a bystander at the lodge, Rayber had said, "It wouldn't have been no great loss if he had drowned. . . . [I]n a hundred years people may have learned enough to put them to sleep when they're born" (*CW* 435). O'Connor devotes a single-sentence paragraph to Tarwater's response: "Something appeared to be working on the boy's face, struggling there, some war between agreement and outrage" (*CW* 435). Because Bishop either is or is not a member of the human family by birth, agreement or outrage are the only possible responses to Rayber's comment. During the fatal scene when he is alone in the boat with Bishop, the decision that Tarwater must make is equally simple. To baptize Bishop is to recognize him in love; to kill him is to refuse to recognize him as a person. Since Tarwater is still trapped in ambivalence, he does both at once. The moment thereby underscores the violence of the dilemma inside of Tarwater, a dilemma whose poles had been correctly outlined by his "friend": "It's Jesus or you."

As is frequently the case with O'Connor, it is not just about an individual person's actions, as if what someone does or does not do can ultimately save or condemn her. Tarwater's decision both to kill Bishop and to baptize him activates a greater mystery, a mystery that is fundamentally outside of his doing. The Apostle Paul describes this mystery as "being buried with Christ in baptism." Baptism, for Catholics, is not merely symbolic. According to the Catechism of the Catholic Church: "The Church does not know of any means other than Baptism that assures entry into eternal beatitude; this is why she takes care not to neglect the mission she has received from the Lord to see that all who can be baptized are 'reborn of water and the Spirit.' God has bound salvation to the sacrament of Baptism, but he himself is not bound by his sacraments."[23] By baptizing Bishop, Tarwater also names him as a member of the Church, a fact O'Connor signifies by naming the child after a high priest, a bishop.[24] Specifically, according to the catechism: "The baptized have become 'living stones' to be 'built into a spiritual house, to be a holy priesthood.' By Baptism they share in the priesthood of Christ, in his prophetic and royal mission. They are 'a chosen race, a royal priest-hood, a holy nation, God's own people, that [they] may declare the wonder-ful deeds of him who called [them] out of darkness into his marvelous light.' *Baptism gives a share in the common priesthood of all believers.*"[25]

The mystery of baptism is external to both Tarwater and Bishop's thoughts and intentions. Though Tarwater's selfishness distorts the scene, the baptism still also symbolizes his recognition of Bishop as a member of God's family. Although he is discussing baptism in a different context, John Ford explains that baptism is "the archetypical Christian sign of personal identity," because it nonidentically repeats Jesus's baptism (along with his death and resurrection) as well as the baptism of every other Christian.[26]

That this baptism is a symbolic, efficacious, and nonidentical repetition of Jesus's baptism is essential to understanding the significance of the scene for Tarwater's development. Tarwater cannot escape the significance of his actions, though he tries to get away from the scene and forget about it. After the murder he hitches a ride with a truck driver, and in spite of himself, Tarwater plays the scene over and over in his mind. He remembers it in a way reminiscent of the first chapter of the gospel of John: "They were sitting facing each other in a boat suspended on a soft bottomless darkness only a little heavier than the black air around them, but the darkness was no hin-drance to his sight. He saw through it as if it were day. He looked through the blackness and saw perfectly the light silent eyes of the child across from him. They had lost their diffuseness and were trained on him, fish-colored and fixed" (*CW* 461).

In John, Jesus is described as the life that was the light of men, a light that is not overcome by darkness. And the light reveals that Jesus gives peo-ple the "power to be made the sons of God, to them that believe in his name. Who are born, not of blood, nor of the will of the flesh, nor of the will of man, but of God" (Douay-Rheims version). Bishop is not Jesus, or even necessarily a Christ figure in this passage. Instead, O'Connor's evocation of the gospel of John reveals that the issue is Tarwater's *recognition* of Bishop as made by God, a child of God, a being worthy of the loving recognition and rebirth that is baptism. Bishop's eyes are fish-colored, just like old man Tarwater's. Francis Marion Tarwater has been called to be a fisher of men, and here he is in a boat with one of them. The call overtakes Tarwater enough for him to let the words of baptism "spill out" over Bishop. Since he also drowns the child, it is clear that the battle for Tarwater's soul is not over.

Although Tarwater does baptize Bishop in spite of himself, the participation in this mystery, and Tarwater's memory of it, is not yet enough to win
him over to his calling. At this point he still does not fully comprehend the
idea that people must be loved, not used. He has yet to repent for his failure
to bury his great-uncle's body and his murder of a helpless child. Though
the trucker offers him some food, he finds that he cannot eat or drink, so
strong is his hunger for the "bread of life." Tarwater gets out of the truck
and decides to walk back home, convinced he can shut down these thoughts
and live "with all of the old man's fancies burnt out of him, with all the old
man's madness smothered for good" (464). But try as he might, he cannot
get the memory of the drowning and baptism out of his head. He gets more
and more hungry and thirsty. The hound of heaven is after him, for when he
stops for a "purple drink," he gets angelic judgment in the form of an imposing female clerk instead: "She did not speak but only looked at him and he
was obliged to direct a glance upward at her eyes. They were fixed on him
with a black penetration. There was all knowledge in her stony face and the
fold of her arms indicated a judgment fixed from the foundations of time.
Huge wings might have been folded behind her without seeming strange."

"The niggers told me how you done," she said. "It shames the dead"
(*CW* 468).

This judgment sinks into Tarwater, but he still resists. He tells her that
it doesn't matter that he disregarded his great-uncle's wishes, because the
"dead are dead and stay that way" (*CW* 468). Tarwater's refusal to bury his
great-uncle to prepare him for resurrection is roughly equivalent to his refusal to bury Bishop with Christ in baptism. In both cases, he puts his own
freedom ahead of a loving responsibility for those who are the most vulnerable. This woman calls him to account for it, but he is not yet ready to hear.

It is on the question of Tarwater's freedom that O'Connor's story is the
most radically countercultural, and where it attacks the utilitarian values
undergirding much of contemporary political life. O'Connor correctly pre-
dicted that her audience would identify with and root for Rayber in his effort to get Tarwater to forget about his calling.[27] O'Connor recognized that
modernity's obsession with individual autonomy leads to a particular view
of persons that looks a lot like "live and let live"—unless or until one's own
autonomy is threatened by the other. O'Connor rejects this account of autonomy by illustrating that its attainment is illusory: autonomy proffers a
false sense of freedom, not true freedom.

Tarwater will be a slave to himself, or he will be a slave to Jesus and his calling; there is no other alternative. In his struggle with the old man over who would bring up young Tarwater, Rayber—the proponent of the modern ideal of individual autonomy—makes it plain that he believed the old man had ruined his life, and he wasn't going to let him ruin his nephew's: "This one is going to be brought up to live in the real world. He's going to be brought up to expect exactly what he can do for himself. He's going to be his own saviour. He's going to be free!" (*CW* 375). What readers soon begin to recognize is that Rayber himself is not free, and not, as he assumes, because of the indoctrination of his pernicious upbringing. He is not free because of Bishop: Bishop is his stumbling block; Bishop starts the fount of "irrational" love. Rayber confesses that he had tried to kill Bishop once but lost his nerve. Tarwater pins it down: "You didn't have the guts. . . . [Old man Tarwater] always told me you couldn't do nothing, couldn't act" (*CW* 435). So when Tarwater kills Bishop, he succeeds in doing what Rayber had wanted to do. He takes his uncle's beliefs to their proper conclusion; he becomes truly "free." But since this freedom can come only at a brutal price to the other, O'Connor gives the lie to modern definitions of freedom. Moderns only see freedom as freedom *from* something, not freedom *to* something. Tarwater correctly surmises that his action to kill Bishop did attain to a greater freedom than his uncle's inability to act, but he does not initially recognize that it failed to free him from himself. His actions make him more of a slave to himself than before. His misery is its own prison.

This is where Spaemann's definition of persons illuminates both O'Connor's story and our current ethical landscape. Spaemann insists that true freedom is not autonomy. True freedom is freedom from ourselves that can be attained only in the act of recognizing other persons, and their claims upon our freedom:

> Only the affirmation of other centres of being, through recognition, justice, and love, allows us the distance on ourselves and the appropriation of ourselves that is constitutive for persons—in sum, "freedom from self." This we experience as a gift. It is simply the emotional and practical side of that opening up, that light in which persons see themselves placed and in which they see whatever encounters them as what it is in itself, not merely as an element in their world serving their organism and their interests. The human capacity for truth is the op-

posite of autonomy. It is a step into the open, a step towards freedom, where the existent reveals itself as itself.[28]

When Tarwater baptizes Bishop, he takes a step into the open, toward the kind of freedom Spaemann describes. But when he murders Bishop, he takes a step in the opposite direction. Clearly, Tarwater is mired in a dilemma. How can such a dilemma ever be resolved?

For O'Connor, that resolution must come through Tarwater being brought to understand that his failure to recognize the other (in Bishop) is not trivial but is the very starting point of evil. As has been noted by Henry Edmondson, O'Connor's definition of evil follows the classic description of evil as the absence of good, the deprivation of being. Noting how O'Connor once insisted that "if you live today, you breathe in nihilism," Edmondson explains how this pervasive attitude includes, among other things, "an impertinent disrespect for the mystery inherent in human existence."[29] Spaemann argues that when a person recognizes another person and acts accordingly, it is the beginning of love, but when a person refuses that recognition, it is the beginning of evil. Although all human beings have a "natural egocentrism" that is innocent and morally neutral, when it is brought to a decision point, the will takes over and we become morally culpable. The will to be "merely natural" is thus a decision to act against the community, and is evil.[30] Cold-blooded murder is taking this decision to a logical end.

It is in this light that we can understand why it is not until Tarwater is himself so disregarded that he accepts his calling. After he receives the judgment from the clerk, he walks again toward Powderhead and is thirsty to the "point where it could not get worse." He makes up his mind to get into the next car that passes by because he wants to justify his actions to someone (468). But the next car happens to contain a man dressed in lavender, clearly meant to be an incarnation of his demonic "friend." The man gives Tarwater drugged whiskey, rapes him, and abandons him. It is not just the violence of the attack that makes it significant. The man in lavender epitomizes a demonic culture that uses other human beings for its own pleasure and then throws them away. The man rejected the reality of Tarwater as an other with equal dignity and due the utmost respect, and it is in this unequivocally evil action that Tarwater sees the truth of his own behavior toward Bishop and others. Disgusted and angry, Tarwater immediately sets fire to the spot where his body had lain. He has a vision, and then his eyes are scorched; they "looked as if, touched with a coal like the lips of the prophet, they would never be used for ordinary sights again" (*CW* 473). As Isaiah's lips had to be burned to speak truth, Tarwater's eyes must be burned to see all of humanity as loved by God. He smears his forehead with a handful of dirt from old man Tarwater's grave and sets his face "toward the dark city, where the children of God lay sleeping" (*CW* 479). Tarwater has now fully accepted his calling, which is to preach to people who live in the city, to tell them about the "terrible speed of mercy" that was unleashed through the death and resurrection of Jesus Christ. Because his calling is defined by the gospel message—that Christ died to redeem all of humanity—it makes sense that Tarwater's only gateway to that calling was the recognition of the "least of these."

Telling Tarwater's story in *The Violent Bear It Away* gave O'Connor the opportunity to hit the nail squarely on the head. Instead of giving Tarwater vices he must reject, she gives him a vulnerable child he must learn to accept. So, too, does O'Connor's story reveal that it is always real people, not abstractions, who stand at the crossroads of political decisions. Bishop is a child who can make no argument for his own membership in the human community. He is completely at the mercy of the recognition or nonrecognition of others. While neither O'Connor nor Spaemann would argue that God deliberately caused Bishop to miss a chromosome and become disabled, both would see the child as a kind of acid test for the character of the people who have the power to decide his fate.[31] Spaemann argues that it is precisely because of their dependence on others that the disabled actually "give more than they get": the larger community is humanized by learning how to care for the vulnerable. Because disabled persons lack the properties we associate with "normal" humanity, they force the issue. Will we respect the other who is different from us? The disabled thus "evoke the best in human beings; they evoke the true ground of human self-respect. So what they give to humanity in this way by the demands they make upon it is more than what they receive."[32]

O'Connor was not sentimental about human nature. She knew that if the vulnerable among us are capable of evoking the best in human beings as we learn to recognize, accept, and care for them in loving responsibility, they are equally capable of evoking the worst in human beings who reject them in the name of freedom. By telling a story that reveals what is at stake in that choice, she uncovers the rot that lies below the surface in a culture increasingly unable to see what we are choosing between. And that is as Tarwater's friend had said: "It's Jesus or you."

Notes

1. Martha Craven Nussbaum, *Poetic Justice: The Literary Imagination and Public Life* (Boston: Beacon, 1995).

2. Ibid., 1.

3. Robert Spaemann, *Persons: The Difference between 'Someone' and 'Something'* (Oxford: Oxford University Press, 2006), 2.

4. T. M. Caruso, M. N. Westgate, and L. B. Holmes. "Impact of Prenatal Screening on the Birth Status of Fetuses with Down Syndrome at an Urban Hospital, 1972–1994, *Genetics in Medicine: Official Journal of the American College of Medical Genetics* 1, no. 1 (1998): 22–28.

5. Peter Singer, *Writings on an Ethical Life* (New York: Ecco, 2000), 191.

6. Ibid.

7. Eric Cohen, *In the Shadow of Progress: Being Human in the Age of Technology* (New York: Encounter, 2008), 93.

8. Jürgen Habermas, *The Future of Human Nature* (Cambridge, U.K.: Polity; distributed in the USA by Blackwell, 2003), 95.

9. Walker Percy and Patrick H. Samway, *Signposts in a Strange Land* (New York: Farrar, Straus and Giroux, 1991), 340.

10. Erasmo Leiva-Merikakis, *Fire of Mercy, Heart of the Word: Meditations on the Gospel According to Saint Matthew* (San Francisco: Ignatius, 1996), 660.

11. Philippians 2:3–8: "Do nothing out of selfish ambition or vain conceit. Rather, in humility value others above yourselves, not looking to your own interests but each of you to the interests of the others. In your relationships with one another, have the same attitude of mind Christ Jesus had: Who, being in very nature God, did not consider equality with God something to be used to his own advantage; rather, he made himself nothing by taking the very nature of a servant, being made in human likeness. And being found in appearance as a human being, he humbled himself by becoming obedient to death—even death on a cross!" (Today's New International Version).

12. Flannery O'Connor, *Collected Works,* vol. 39 (New York: Library of America, 1988), 345. Hereafter cited parenthetically as *CW.*

13. See, for example, Peter M. Candler Jr., "The Anagogical Imagination of Flannery O'Connor," *Christianity and Literature* 60, no. 1 (autumn 2010): 11–33.

14. "Personalism," as I am using the term here, refers to a specific school of thought developed by Christian philosophers around the 1940s and 1950s, largely

in response to Marxism and atheistic existentialism. It should not be confused with "personism," the utilitarian concept developed later.

15. For an account of the marginalia, see Arthur F. Kinney and Flannery O'Connor, *Flannery O'Connor's Library: Resources of Being* (Athens: University of Georgia Press, 1985).

16. Emmanuel Mounier, *Personalism* (1952; Notre Dame: University of Notre Dame Press, 1970), xx. Spaemann, continuing in the twenty-first century in the same vein as Tresmontant and Mounier, explains that Greek thought was nowhere near this understanding of persons: "Plato never once conceived the thought that we have when we use the term" (Spaemann, *Persons: The Difference between "Someone" and "Something,"* 18).

17. Claude Tresmontant, *A Study of Hebrew Thought* (New York: Desclee, 1960), 4.

18. Ibid., 98. Flannery O'Connor had underlined the entire paragraph in which this sentence occurs (Kinney and O'Connor, *Flannery O'Connor's Library: Resources of Being*, 22).

19. I develop this argument elsewhere; see Christina Bieber Lake, *The Incarnational Art of Flannery O'Connor* (Macon, Ga.: Mercer University Press, 2005).

20. See especially Richard Giannone, *Flannery O'Connor and the Mystery of Love* (1989; New York: Fordham University Press, 1999).

21. Spaemann, *Persons: The Difference between "Someone" and "Something,"* 185.

22. Ibid., 186.

23. Catholic Church, "Second Catechism of the Catholic Church," www .scborromeo.org/ccc/p2s2c1a1.htm#1234.

24. The fact that the character is named Bishop seems also to signify that O'Connor would weigh in on the Catholic debate over universal vs local church on the side of universal. Bishops are connected to the pope and receive authority from that connection (Fr. Daniel Callam CSB, "What Happens at Baptism? the Ratzinger-Kasper Debate," http://catholicinsight.com/online/theology/article_299 .shtml). In any case, the child's membership in the Church marks and seals him as a child of God.

25. Catholic Church, "Second Catechism of the Catholic Church," www .scborromeo.org/ccc/p2s2c1a1.htm#1234.

26. Richard Ford, *Self and Salvation: Being Transformed* (Cambridge: Cambridge University Press, 1999), 162.

27. Martha Stephens both describes and represents this trend (see Stephens, *The Question of Flannery O'Connor* [Baton Rouge: Louisiana State University Press, 1973], 101–2).

28. Spaemann, *Persons: The Difference between "Someone" and "Something,"* 217.

322 *Christina Bieber Lake*

29. Henry T. Edmondson, *Return to Good and Evil: Flannery O'Connor's Response to Nihilism* (Lanham, Md.: Lexington, 2002), 3.

30. Spaemann, *Persons: The Difference between "Someone" and "Something,"* 217.

31. For a thorough treatment of this issue, see Timothy J. Basselin, *Flannery O'Connor: Writing a Theology of Disabled Humanity* (Waco, Tex.: Baylor University Press, 2013).

32. Spaemann, *Persons: The Difference between "Someone" and "Something,"* 244.

Bibliography

Basselin, Timothy J. *Flannery O'Connor: Writing a Theology of Disabled Humanity.* Waco, Tex.: Baylor University Press, 2013.

Callam CSB, Daniel. "What Happens at Baptism? The Ratzinger-Kasper Debate." http://catholicinsight.com/online/theology/article_299.shtml.

Candler, Peter M., Jr. "The Anagogical Imagination of Flannery O'Connor." *Christianity and Literature* 60, no. 1 (Autumn 2010): 11–33.

Catholic Church. "Second Catechism of the Catholic Church." www.scborromeo.org/ccc/p2s2c1a1.htm#1234.

Cohen, Eric. *In the Shadow of Progress: Being Human in the Age of Technology.* New York: Encounter, 2008.

Edmondson, Henry T. *Return to Good and Evil: Flannery O'Connor's Response to Nihilism.* Lanham, Md.: Lexington, 2002.

Ford, Richard. *Self and Salvation: Being Transformed.* Cambridge Studies in Christian Doctrine. Cambridge: Cambridge University Press, 1999.

Giannone, Richard. *Flannery O'Connor and the Mystery of Love.* New York: Fordham University Press, 1989.

Habermas, Jürgen. *The Future of Human Nature* [Zukunft der menschlichen Natur]. Cambridge, U.K., and Malden, Mass.: Polity, 2003.

Kinney, Arthur F., and Flannery O'Connor. *Flannery O'Connor's Library: Resources of Being.* Athens: University of Georgia Press, 1985.

Lake, Christina Bieber. *The Incarnational Art of Flannery O'Connor.* Macon, Ga.: Mercer University Press, 2005.

Leiva-Merikakis, Erasmo. *Fire of Mercy, Heart of the Word: Meditations on the Gospel According to Saint Matthew.* San Francisco: Ignatius, 1996.

Mounier, Emmanuel. *Personalism.* 1952. Notre Dame: University of Notre Dame Press, 1970.

Nussbaum, Martha Craven. *Poetic Justice: The Literary Imagination and Public Life*. Boston: Beacon, 1995.

O'Connor, Flannery. *Collected Works*. Library of America. Vol. 39. New York: Library of America, 1988. Cited parenthetically as *CW*.

Percy, Walker, and Patrick H. Samway. *Signposts in a Strange Land*. New York: Farrar, Straus and Giroux, 1991.

Singer, Peter. *Writings on an Ethical Life*. New York: Ecco, 2000.

Spaemann, Robert. *Persons: The Difference between "Someone" and "Something."* Oxford Studies in Theological Ethics. Oxford: Oxford University Press, 2006.

Stephens, Martha. *The Question of Flannery O'Connor*. Southern Literary Studies. Baton Rouge: Louisiana State University Press, 1973.

Tresmontant, Claude. *A Study of Hebrew Thought*. New York: Desclee, 1960.

IV

Beyond Politics

In Defense of Being

Flannery O'Connor and the Politics of Art

John F. Desmond

Flannery O'Connor is not usually considered to be a political writer. She would not be included in the ranks of George Orwell, Fyodor Dostoevsky, Graham Greene, or even Joseph Conrad, one of her favorite writers, in this regard. Obviously she was interested in the major historical and cultural events of her day—the effects of the Holocaust, the atom bomb, the politics of changing southern society, and racial strife across the United States, to name a few—but to measure her significance as a political writer, a much broader and deeper perspective is needed, one that includes not only contemporary events but also the philosophical and theological foundations of political order, especially the vision of history and order inherent in her Catholic faith. This is the perspective that informed her fiction and shaped the political dimension of her art. In addition to their artistic brilliance, her stories reveal her profound insights into, and deep concern for, the *good* of the sociopolitical order—in the South, in America, and in Western culture as a whole.

The notion of "politics" in O'Connor's writings must be understood in the classical sense; that is, as having to do generally with the idea of order (and disorder) in the communal life of man in society, and with the individual's relationship to the sociopolitical order. Justification for this approach to O'Connor's politics of art is found in Plato's belief that the transcendent divinity, not man, is the measure of reality; that "a polis is man written large"; and that disorder in society is a reflection of disorder in the human psyche.[1] Her anthropological, ethical, and theological views presuppose her political vision. Anthropologically, her view of humanity is that man *by nature* participates in the divine-human order. As Aristotle maintained, the human mind is "itself divine or the most divine thing in us."[2] Similarly, Plato affirmed that as humans we live in the *metaxy*, "in between the divine and the human, the One and the Many."[3] Moreover, political philosopher Eric Voegelin, a writer whose work O'Connor studied carefully and reviewed for the *Georgia Bulletin*, argued that given the fact that man by nature participates in the divine-human order, "the life of reason is thus firmly rooted in a revelation."[4] In a passage O'Connor marked in her study of *Plato and Aristotle*, volume 3 of Voegelin's *Order and History*, Voegelin states that "the paradigm of a good polis is revealed by an inquiry into man's existence in a community that lies not only beyond the polis, but beyond any political order in history."[5]

To say that man by nature lives in the *metaxy* is to say that we live in mystery, both the mystery of our being and of our existential situation in history. At the same time, for O'Connor, the Catholic believer, the human mystery of being and of history has been superseded by the mystery of Christ's Incarnation, the entrance into and transformation of history by the God-man Jesus. For her, the Incarnation and our redemption by Christ is the center of existence: "I see from the standpoint of Christian orthodoxy. This means that for me the meaning of life is centered in our Redemption by Christ and what I see in the world I see in its relation to that. I don't think that this is a position that can be taken halfway or one that is particularly easy in these times to make transparent in fiction."[6] The Christian vision is, for O'Connor, the foundation of the spiritual order of the world, and thus of the sociopolitical order and of man's relation to the community. It commands a social ethic based on charity and love, and a recognition and acceptance of one's participation in the communal process of redemption. O'Connor's view echoes that of the monk Fr. Zossima in *The Brothers Karamazov*, who says that "all men are guilty and everyone is responsible for everyone else."[7] Ultimately, her vision of community is a vision of the mystical body of Christ, inclusive of both the living and the dead. A refusal to participate in this divine-human community—whether by rejection, isolation, rebellion, betrayal, or closure to the spiritual truth of reality—must therefore promote sociopolitical disorder and chaos. Without faith in Christ, the social order, and so mankind itself, is threatened.

O'Connor stated her general view of contemporary culture in midcentury America in a letter to her friend Betty Hester: "If you live today you breathe in nihilism. In or out of the Church, it's the air you breathe," which indicates the general toxicity she saw pervading modern culture.[8] We inhabit what Ellis Sandoz has called the "Age of Nihilism."[9] The term "nihilism" includes all those ideologies that emerged from the Enlightenment and began to flower in the nineteenth century—rationalism, positivism, materialism, scientism, secularism—and whose fundamental metaphysical assumption is the atheistic one that man, not God, is the measure of all reality. Belief in a transcendent spiritual order is either categorically rejected or "immanentized" so that man comes to be seen as the sole architect of his destiny, and as capable of self-redemption, in the context of secular history. In her review of Voegelin, O'Connor noted how he traced the etiology of the disease of modern nihilism back to classical roots: "Plato's enemies were the Sophists and Socrates' arguments against them are still today the classical arguments against the sophistic philosophy of existence which characterizes positivism and the age of enlightenment. These are also Voegelin's enemies; he makes it plain in this volume that the murder of Socrates parallels the political murders of our time."[10]

Under the metaphysical assumptions of the age of nihilism and its anthropological view of man as an autonomous, self-redeeming individual, the godly ideal of community, one based on charity and love, is displaced in favor of a privatized ethic. At best, secular humanism; at worst, naked self-interest. Moral responsibility based on transcendent spiritual principles and Christian revelation, and aimed at the *good* of the whole sociopolitical order, is rejected. Spiritually and ethically, man suffers a consequent diminishment. Writing to a friend about her audience, O'Connor said: "It is easy to see that the moral sense has been bred out of certain sections of the population, like the wings have been bred off certain chickens to produce more white meat. This is a generation of wingless chickens, which is what I suppose Nietzsche meant when he said God was dead."[11] Simply stated, O'Connor's strategy as a writer, like that of Dostoevsky, was to vigorously oppose the sociopolitical disorder she saw manifested in the various forms of nihilism that dominated the age. For her, the Church—by which she meant belief in the mystical body of Christ—was "the only thing that is going to make the terrible world we are coming to endurable."[12] More specifically, her strategy was to expose and oppose the disease in the psyche, or disorder in the soul, of most of her characters, whom she made to mirror the general nihilism of the age.

Like Dostoevsky, O'Connor understood that the real thrust of modern nihilism—in the guise of progressive movements toward social justice and intellectual freedom—was to attack God. For both writers, the nihilistic roots of such movements, and their destructive consequences, had to be exposed. Politically, then, O'Connor's stories aim both to record the effects of nihilism and to point prophetically to visible and invisible sources of true order open to her audience.

How does O'Connor represent the ethos of nihilism in modern culture, and what Eric Voegelin calls "the closure of mind" to the transcendent order?[13] In chapter 3 of *Wise Blood*, the narrator describes the cosmic backdrop to Hazel Motes's entrance into the city of Taulkinham: "The black sky was underpinned with long silver streaks that looked like scaffolding and depth on depth behind it were thousands of stars that all seemed to be moving very slowly as if they were about some vast construction work that involved the whole universe and would take all time to complete. No one was paying attention to the sky."[14] Citizens of Taulkinham, symbolic city of modern Western culture, are completely oblivious to the transcendent order and to the unfolding process of human/divine history. Likewise, they are indifferent, or hostile, to Haze and his obsession with Jesus. They worship mechanical gods, gathering around the altar of a huckster selling potato peelers. As for religion, even cynically false preachers like Asa Hawks and Onnie Jay Holy (who preaches a humanistic gospel of rational, sentimental self-redemption) cannot hold their attention for long. A violent, lost people, they are mesmerized by such diversions as movies, bestiality, and lurid sex, as personified by Enoch Emery and Sabbath Lily Hawks. Self-interest, sentimentality and cynicism govern the social order, subverting any ethic of charity and love. Taulkinham is O'Connor's version of Voegelin's "closed world," with modern Western humanity slouching toward spiritual suicide and self-destruction.

O'Connor's ironic beacon of hope in this wasteland culture is Haze Motes, a "Christian malgre lui" whose defiant quest to escape his knowledge of sin and redemption, and so to escape Jesus, is thwarted at every turn by his conscience, and by his counterquest after truth.[15] Living during the age of nihilism has stifled neither the truth at the heart of his spiritual condition nor his existential freedom. Throughout Haze's quest, the "wild ragged figure" of Jesus relentlessly stalks him "from tree to tree in the back of his mind."[16] Unlike the other city dwellers—O'Connor's "wingless chickens"—Haze intuits what is ultimately at stake. He invests his hope of escaping Jesus in a mechanical god, his rat-colored Essex, proclaiming that "nobody with a good car needs to be justified."[17] When his god/car fails, the haunting presence of Jesus draws him back to confront both his sin and the meaning of his existence. But in the "terrible world" in which Haze finds himself, there is nothing beyond the self, nothing within the decadent sociopolitical order, to sustain either belief or a defiant disbelief. In this modern city, egotism and ego-satisfaction hold sway. The best Haze can do is to cling to his integrity and accept the hard consequences of his failed attempt to escape the knowledge of sin and the need "to pay" for it. In his final suffering and death, Haze becomes O'Connor's ironic sign and "stumbling block," her mysterious witness shining as a small beacon of light in the chasm.

Nowhere in O'Connor's fiction is the stark opposition between the terrifying consequences of the age's nihilism and the ethical demands of charity and love based on the recognition that "all are guilty and all are responsible for all" dramatized more clearly than in her signature story "A Good Man Is Hard to Find." The grandmother is a familiar type: the nominal "Christianity" divorced from its sacred roots and reduced to a decadent social form. Jesus the God-man has been reduced in her mind to a "good" man, as defined by the profane norms of class, manners, and material success. O'Connor's antagonist, the Misfit is, like Haze Motes, a guilt-ridden, Jesus-haunted rebel who nevertheless understands what is ultimately at stake in modern society: the salvation or damnation of the soul. Through him, O'Connor poses for her audience the central question Jesus asked his followers: "Who do you say that I am?" (Luke 9:20). But like his rationalist forefather Ivan Karamazov, the Misfit rejects faith in Jesus as an answer to the mystery of evil and suffering. Faced with the incomprehensible awareness of his own evil, the Misfit, like Ivan, demands rational justice. "I call myself 'The Misfit,'" he says, "because I can't make what all I done wrong fit what I gone through in punishment." Jesus, he says, "thown everything off balance. If He did what he said, then it's nothing for you to do but thow away everything and follow Him, and if He didn't, it's nothing for you to do than enjoy the few minutes you got left the best way you can—by killing somebody or burning down his house or doing some other meanness to him. No pleasure but meanness."[18] As Ivan Karamazov observed, without God or Christ "everything is permitted."[19] The radical opposition between faith and nihilism could not be more clearly stated.

The Misfit scoffs at the blandishments offered by modern secular culture—respectability and the comforts of home—saying "nobody had nothing I wanted."[20] He is aware of Christianity's eschatological framework, and his radical nihilism foreshadows apocalyptic destruction, or what O'Connor called "the terrible age we are coming to." Without faith in Jesus, and finding nothing in the social order to justify belief, the Misfit chooses random violence. He murders the grandmother and her entire family—although even meanness brings him "no pleasure." However, since he also takes the Christian message of redemption with utmost seriousness, his mind is not entirely closed to the transcendent. He still lives in the *metaxy*, still wrestles with the mystery of evil and suffering. Though he is a pathological killer, he may yet, as O'Connor suggested, one day become "the prophet he was meant to be."[21]

As suggested, the hypocritical grandmother personifies another manifestation of disorder in the sociopolitical order: Christianity reduced to social convention. In her conversation with the Misfit, she initially tries to equate "goodness" with social class, that is, with morality reduced to good breeding, good manners, and social status. Only in desperation does she mention the name of Jesus, muttering that He will help the Misfit if the Misfit prays. The Misfit dismisses her coy maneuvers and, implicitly, her caricaturized version of the hard challenge of commitment to Jesus. Yet O'Connor reminds us that the grandmother has "a conscience," however distorted; when faced with death, her "head clears" momentarily as her heart is mysteriously touched by the anguish of the Misfit. She sees a fellow sufferer and intuitively grasps the truth that "all are guilty and all are responsible for all"—the ethical answer to the Misfit's isolation from God and humanity. The grandmother's intuition moves her to a gesture of real compassion when, just before he shoots her, she touches the Misfit's shoulder and proclaims: "Why you're one of my babies. You're one of my own children!"[22] For O'Connor, the mysterious light of divine grace can, through suffering and the humiliation of pride, penetrate even nihilism and decadence. Recognition of communal responsibility, of humanity bonded in guilt and charity, is faith in action, and a testament to the true meaning of the sociopolitical order.

The grandmother's version of Christianity derives from a broad segment of American society for whom the genuine message of faith, when not ignored altogether, had been reduced to a moribund cultural form—a spiritual disorder that O'Connor exposed and attacked throughout her fiction. Many of her characters try to create, or to maintain, their own kingdoms, in which materialism and self-interest—variant forms of nihilism—rule in opposition to the transcendent order. O'Connor's fictional assaults on such self-created kingdoms are meant to reawaken a true sense of reality in her protagonists. The suffering inflicted may seem gratuitous on one level, but on a deeper level, it removes several of her heroines from the prideful, God-like roles they have assumed and initiates them into the community of human frailty and need. Paradoxically, their "fortunate" downfall is often a consequence of their own calculated acts of charity—"calculated" because they use these gestures as further attempts to exercise control over their own domains. For them, man (or woman), not God, is the measure.

In "A Circle in the Fire," Mrs. Cope treats the delinquents who invade her farm with polite deference, offering them Coca-Colas and crackers. But then she is forced to watch helplessly as the delinquents ransack the farm and set the woods—her protective wall against the evils of the world outside—ablaze. As the woods burn, Mrs. Cope's young daughter sees her mother's initiation into the world of evil and suffering etched on her face: "It was the face of the new misery she felt, but on her mother it looked old and it looked as if it might have belonged to anybody, a Negro or a European or to Powell himself."[23] Mrs. Cope's isolation is shattered as she becomes a participant in the real order of human misery, loss, and grief, for which there is no rational answer, only the redemptive mystery of divine love.

In "The Displaced Person," O'Connor presents two defenders of an order deformed by racism and exclusivity—the farm owner Mrs. McIntyre and her farmhand Mrs. Shortley. As Mrs. Shortley succumbs to a stroke, she is displaced from her self-appointed role as prophet and protector of the status quo, and united, both symbolically and "bodily," with the Holocaust victims she has earlier denounced as part of Europe's evil—an evil that includes the Catholic Church, as represented by the Guizac family, who are therefore a threat to "pure" America. In death, Mrs. Shortley is left "to contemplate for the first time the tremendous frontiers of her true country."[24] For her boss, Mrs. McIntyre, the collapse of the material kingdom comes after Mr. Guizac, the Polish handyman, is killed. Mrs. McIntyre is complicit in Mr. Guizac's death. She is then left alone and in failing health to listen to her only visitor, the priest, who comes regularly to instruct her in the doctrines of the Church, the earthly manifestation of the eternal kingdom of Christ.[25]

In "Greenleaf," Mrs. May's material order is disrupted by an errant bull that finally gores her to death. Mrs. May's "religious" views are summed up pithily when she confronts Mrs. Greenleaf during the latter's prayer healing, just as Mrs. Greenleaf cries out, "Jesus, Jesus." With scathing irony, O'Connor's narrator reports that Mrs. May "thought the word, Jesus, should be kept inside the church building like other words inside the bedroom. She was a good Christian woman with a large respect for religion, though she did not, of course, believe any of it was true." When Mrs. Greenleaf continues to grovel on the ground, Mrs. May scolds her: "Jesus would be *ashamed* of you. He would tell you to get up from there this instant and go wash your children's clothes!"[26] Mrs. May's Jesus would be a clean, respectable "gentleman." Only when she is stabbed in the heart by the bull's horn—an echo of Mrs. Greenleaf's prayer plea, "Jesus, stab me in the heart!"—is Mrs. May granted the vision of a true order of being, centered in Christ: "One of his horns sank until it pierced her heart and the other curved around her side and held her in an unbreakable grip. She continued to stare straight ahead but the entire scene in front of her had changed—the tree line was a dark wound in a world that was nothing but sky—and she had the look of a person whose sight has been suddenly restored but who finds the light unbearable."[27] All three of these stories reveal O'Connor's clear sense that the old sociopolitical order of the South, based on class distinction and race, was crumbling.

Nihilism takes many forms in O'Connor's fiction, one of the most insidious being the spirit of gnosticism. Eric Voegelin, whose monumental work *Order and History* O'Connor reviewed for the *Bulletin,* saw gnosticism as *the* prevailing disorder in modern Western society.[28] For Voegelin, gnosticism represented, first of all, a "deformation of consciousness" characterized by a "closure of mind" to the transcendent; by abstraction from the true incarnate mystery of the divine/human person; and by isolation from the corporate body of society. All of these characteristics of gnosticism find expression in modern ideologies that, for him, constitute an abandonment of true reason.[29] Second, gnosticism meant a deformation of the sociopolitical order, in which belief in transcendent reality was rejected in favor of the "deification" of man and society. Gnosticism and its particular manifestations in the ideologies of secular humanism, progressivism, and scientism all purport to bring about a spiritualized salvation of mankind in secular history. Gnostic man becomes his own self-appointed savior, his mind and heart closed to the transcendent order of reality under God.[30] Under the Gnostic impulse, Christ is displaced as the center of all reality in favor of secular human reason.

Several of O'Connor's characters are infected with the spirit of gnosticism, in various forms. In *Wise Blood*, Onnie Jay Holy preaches a gospel of self-salvation based on secular reason and positivism. "You don't have to believe nothing you don't understand or approve of," he proclaims. "If you don't understand it, it ain't true, and that's all there is to it."[31] A sociopolitical order based on such a premise would lead to a totally privatized ethic and, ultimately, barbarism and chaos. In "The Life You Save May Be Your Own," itinerant handyman Mr. Shiftlet's Gnostic spirit takes the form of Manichean dualism—a separation of body and spirit: "The body, lady [Mrs. Crater], is like a house: it don't go anywhere; but the spirit, lady, is like a automobile: always on the move, always."[32] A more sophisticated form of gnosticism afflicts Hulga Hopewell in "Good Country People." A proud intellectual and self-proclaimed nihilist—"I am one of those who see *through* to nothing"— her philosophy proves to be a delusion, blinding her to her belief in "simple" innocence and to the reality of evil.[33] It takes an encounter with the satanic salesman Manley Pointer to shatter her Gnostic self-deception and force her to see both the limits and the deformation of her own mind.

For Julian in "Everything That Rises Must Converge," gnosticism takes the form of an abstract, liberal political philosophy that posits the gospel of social progress and racial equality, an ideology that blinds him to his own elitism. An heir to the "Godhigh" family, Julian longs for a return to the paternalistic southern aristocratic order now feebly represented by his ailing mother. But that decadent order has passed, as O'Connor shows us; and with his mother's collapse and death—she is slugged by an irate Negro woman—Julian is forced to confront the truth of his deep, reactionary dependence on his mother, and the hollowness of his pose as a progressive liberal. In "The Enduring Chill," Asbury Fox, living in New York City, listens as friends discuss what he thinks is his "approaching death" and the impossibility of "self-fulfillment" or "salvation" for himself as a writer. Gnosticism devolves into nihilism as Fox's friend Goetz, echoing Hulga Hopewell, proclaims that "salvation is the destruction of a simple prejudice and no one is saved." When Asbury asks a Jesuit priest to comment, the priest says: "There is a real possibility of the New Man, assisted, of course, by the Third Person of the Trinity."[34] The priest's doctrine of "self-fulfillment" is not Gnostic but Pauline—spiritual transformation made possible *only* by faith in Christ as redeemer and by the gift of the Holy Spirit. After he returns home to the South "to die," Asbury learns that his illness is "undulant fever," a persistent but not fatal malady. Faced with the bitter truth that he will not die immediately, Asbury receives the gift of the Holy Spirit, the Paraclete descending, ironically, in the form of an icy water-stain. With his self-pity and pride lacerated, Asbury is left to face life as an enduring chill.

O'Connor's most explicit attack on gnosticism—as manifested in proposed social programs based on progressive ideology—came in her second novel, *The Violent Bear It Away,* and in the companion story, "The Lame Shall Enter First." Both George Rayber, the antagonist in the novel, and Sheppard in "The Lame Shall Enter First" try to govern life according to secular Gnostic-humanism. Rayber intends to make a "new man" of his nephew Francis Tarwater along humanistic lines, by stripping him of any vestiges of Christian belief or identity. Sheppard has a similar plan for the delinquent Rufus Johnson. That both men hold respectable positions as "counselors" within the modern sociopolitical order is O'Connor's trenchant comment on the state of the culture at large. Propelled by their deformed theories of man, their faulty anthropologies, both men wreak destruction and death on vulnerable children—Rayber's son Bishop and Sheppard's son Norton. In both men, Gnostic dream has trumped human reality so that, as under Nazism and Stalinism, individual persons—those "sacred in the eyes of the Lord," as O'Connor believed—become expendable. In both these cases, O'Connor shatters Gnostic delusion, opening her characters to a bitterly chastening self-knowledge, and to the mystery of reality beyond the enclosed self. Sheppard must face the truth of his own complicity in the death of his son Norton, who hangs himself in the hope of reaching his deceased mother in heaven. Likewise, Rayber must face the truth of his own responsibility when his son Bishop is drowned by Tarwater; in addition, he must face his utter failure to make Tarwater into the "new man" of atheistic humanism. Rayber "feels nothing" after hearing his son Bishop's death cry, which is O'Connor's chilling comment on how the schoolteacher's rationalistic theory has dried up the well of human love and charity within him. Rayber is one of those who would attempt to transform history through an atheistic ideology.

For his part, young Tarwater tries to escape history and his call to be a prophet, only to be chastened and corrected by undergoing a brutal rape. Nevertheless, the chastened Tarwater is, in the end, granted a vision of the true, eternal community beyond human history as he stares for the last time over the field at Powderhead:

> The boy remained standing there, his still eyes reflecting the field the Negro had crossed. It seemed to him no longer empty but peopled with a multitude. Everywhere, he saw dim figures seated on the slope and as he gazed he saw that from a single basket the throng was being fed. His eyes searched the crowd for a long time as if he could not find the one he was looking for. Then he saw him. The old man was lowering himself to the ground. When he was down and his bulk had settled, he leaned forward, his face turned toward the basket, impatiently following its course toward him. The boy too leaned forward, aware at last of the object of his hunger, aware that it was the same as the old man's and that nothing on earth would fill him. His hunger was so great that he could have eaten all the loaves and fishes after they were multiplied.[35]

O'Connor's diagnosis of, and attack on, the nihilism of the age is not simplistic. She recognized that vital pockets of belief exist in the sociopolitical order. She believed, like Eric Voegelin, that while "the closure of the soul in modern gnosticism can repress the truth of the soul, it cannot remove the soul and its transcendence from the structure of reality." Consequently, even today in deformed society, "the classic and Christian tradition of Western society is rather alive."[36] O'Connor reveals this truth through the many characters in her fiction that, as a group, can be said to constitute a remnant of believers struggling against the nihilistic forces of the age. The most conspicuous character in this regard is old Mason Tarwater in *The Violent Bear It Away*, a prophet figure who battles heroically to save his kinsmen—Francis Tarwater, Bishop, and even George Rayber—from the solipsism of modern disbelief by baptizing them into the life of Christian

faith. The novel itself dramatizes young Tarwater's struggle with the opposing influences of his great-uncle Mason, the believer, and his uncle Rayber,
the rationalizing agnostic, a struggle that climaxes when young Tarwater
accepts his vocation as prophet and returns to the "dark city" to warn the
sleeping "children of God" of the "terrible speed" of God's mercy.

Even given the generally nihilistic ethos of the age, O'Connor, like
Voegelin, affirmed the truth of divine "irruptions" in history, intrusions of
grace that she represented microcosmically in her stories. Stated more precisely, she aimed to dramatize the "in-break" of the Holy Spirit into the
deformed, mostly Gnostic consciousness of her characters, thus opening
them to the mystery of reality beyond the immanent. These "irruptions"
are registered through the shock of violence—a roadside execution, an artificial leg stolen, a rape, a drowning, an act of self-blinding. But the surface
acts of violence are incidental to the deeper shock registered in the characters' souls and minds. As she insisted, "the (true) violence is internal."[37]
Her violence shatters her characters' self-sufficient egotism, leaving them
scourged and humiliated but more open, at least potentially, to deeper and
truer knowledge of themselves and of the mystery of their existential situation in history. In this regard, O'Connor is principally concerned with the
ultimate consequences of the shock of grace received, and what her characters as free beings choose to do with gift of grace offered. She emphasized,
for example, the situation of Hulga Hopewell after her artificial leg is stolen,
of Julian after his mother dies, of Asbury Fox after the descent of the Paraclete, and of Ruby Turpin after she is assaulted by Mary Grace and receives
a final revelation. Ultimately, the truth of fiction, as O'Connor knew, lies beyond fiction itself. It is dependent, just as political order itself is dependent,
upon the larger truth of transcendent order under God.

O'Connor's focus on the "irruptions" of the divine in human experience, and on the mystery of existence, reveals that the politics of her art
must be understood in relation to her prophetic stance as a writer. Her prophetic stance is fundamental to her political strategy of opposing nihilism
in all its modern manifestations. Prophetic witness is what gives her fiction
its powerful authority and truth. Her prophetic stance was based on a belief
in, and insistence upon, the truth of an objective order of reality beyond the
self, and on a view of history shaped not exclusively by the flow of immanent
events but by divine revelation. In her copy of Eric Voegelin's *Israel and
Revelation*, O'Connor underscored the author's affirmation of the objec-

tive order: "Now historical form, understood as the experience of the present under God, will appear as subjective only, if faith is misinterpreted as a 'subjective' experience. If, however, it is understood as the leap in being, as the entering of the soul into divine reality through the entering of divine reality into the soul, the historical form, far from being a subjective point of view, is an ontologically real event in history."[38] In her essay "Novelist and Believer," O'Connor stated her own belief in the objective order of reality, as well as her criticism of the subjective viewpoint in fiction writing:

> The artist penetrates the concrete world in order to find at its depth the image of its source, the image of ultimate reality.
> For the last few centuries we have lived in a world which has been increasingly convinced that the reaches of reality end very close to the surface, that there is no ultimate divine source, that the things of the world do not pour forth from God in a double way, or at all. . . . In twentieth-century fiction it increasingly happens that a meaningless, absurd world impinges upon the sacred consciousness of author or character; author and character seldom now go out to explore and penetrate a world in which the sacred is reflected.[39]

Belief in the objective order of reality and in "irruptions" of the divine in human affairs called her, as a writer, to the prophetic vocation. Again, in her reading of Voegelin, she underscored the significance of this vocation: "The leap in being entails the obligations to communicate and to listen. Revelation and response are not a man's private affair; for the revelation comes to one man for all men, and in his response he is the representative of mankind. And since the response is representative it endows the recipient of revelation, in relation to his fellow man, with the authority of the prophet."[40] Put simply, O'Connor always insisted on the prophetic role of the writer and understood her own talent to be a "gift" from God, an obligation to be fulfilled by sharing her vision, especially her analysis of the modern spiritual disorder, with her audience: "The fiction writer should be characterized by his kind of vision. His kind of vision is prophetic vision. Prophecy, which is dependent on the imaginative and not the moral faculty, need not be a matter of predicting the future. The prophet is a realist of distances, and it is this kind of realism that goes into great novels."[41] As one whose vision is "a matter of seeing near things with their extensions of meaning and thus seeing far things close up," her role as a prophetic artist was to measure the distance between the disorder of modern culture and the ultimate source of reality from which it has strayed.[42] The "ultimate source" of reality, as we have seen and as Voegelin affirmed, is the transcendent world beyond the world of the polis, a transcendence in which man by nature participates. Given this, political order is finally to be understood and judged in terms of how it conforms, or fails to conform, to its transcendent source, under God. Thus, for O'Connor, prophetic witness and the politics of her art were inextricably intertwined.

Some critics have argued that O'Connor's embrace of the prophetic role is an escape from the tension of history, an arbitrary transcending of the immanent order. This criticism was stated most forcefully by Lewis P. Simpson, who argued that because O'Connor saw herself as a participant in "the transcendent mystery of the history behind history," she "embraced the mode of revelation."[43] Having embraced "the vocation of prophesy," she abandoned the tension between history and memory that, according to Simpson, has been the defining mode of great modern southern writers such as William Faulkner, Eudora Welty, and Robert Penn Warren. For Simpson, these writers dramatize the self's struggle to survive the catastrophes of history, especially the "historicism of consciousness" in which all external reality—the past, tradition, religious belief, man, and God—is subsumed in the mind: "Ultimately, through its will to analytic interpretation, the human mind would transfer God and man, nature and society, and even mind itself, into mind." The effect of this process would be to alienate man from the world and from himself: "The radical subjectivity of this process—which implies that from the end of the Middle Ages on history in its most fundamental aspect is the movement of existence into mind—makes it impossible for the human mind to deal with itself save on its own terms of self-interpretation."[44] One obvious implication of this view is that man alone is now the measure of reality; God is either dead or reduced to a datum of human consciousness. The human mind is effectively "closed" to objective, transcendent reality. The great writer is, for Simpson, a "survivor" of history, one who invests himself, like Joyce's Stephen Dedalus, as sole authority over creation. Novelist Walker Percy, a Catholic, agreed with Simpson, saying that "most contemporary novelists have moved on into a world of rootless and isolated consciousnesses for whom not even the memory and the nostalgia [for the Christian tradition] exists."[45]

It must be noted, however, that the condition Simpson describes—the human mind's absorption of all reality—is a description of modern gnosticism that is completely antithetical to the Incarnation vision of Judeo-Christianity. For O'Connor, as well as for Voegelin and others, history begins in a divine revelation to the Hebrews and reaches its axial point of meaning in the Incarnation of Jesus, the effects of which continue as a vital force in human history through the Holy Spirit.[46] The Gnostic view rules out the possibility of divine grace acting in the world; it separates secular history and the human political order from the transcendent order of reality. In this regard, we recall again Voegelin's insight that "historical form, understood as the experience of the present under God, will appear as subjective only, if faith is misinterpreted as a 'subjective' experience. If, however, it is understood as the leap in being, as the entering of the soul into divine reality through the entering of divine reality into the soul, the historical form, far from being a subjective point of view, is an ontologically real event in history."[47]

Simpson focused his criticism of O'Connor's prophetic stance on the ending of her late story "Revelation," in which Ruby Turpin challenges God for allowing the Wellesley student Mary Grace to assault her and call her a "wart hog" from hell. Simpson finds an "incongruity" between "Ruby's profound question and questioner," one that "makes the whole situation in 'Revelation' unconvincing" because "it moves into depths of a self that Ruby, as a member of her historical society, does not possess." Simpson's conclusion about O'Connor's artistic strategy is worth quoting in full because it signifies a larger school of criticism of her authorial stance: "The movement is interpreted as the working of God's grace, which surely can yield a vision beyond one's level of theological sophistication. But even in the domain of southern Protestantism visions come to those in some way prepared for them. We are not convinced that time, place and eternity find a location in Ruby's story because it is not *her* story. It is the author's, and it is Miss O'Connor—as poet prophet, as participant in the mystery of the history behind history—who assigns the location." As a consequence, Simpson believes that in the story "the great metaphysical juncture is located in the self (in older terms, the soul) of the writer." Simpson then extrapolates from this assertion to a general criticism of O'Connor's prophetic stance as a writer:

Flannery O'Connor suppresses the motive of the Southern literary imagination known to Faulkner, Eudora Welty, and Warren: a tension

between memory and history. Ascribing to the southern writer a transcendent religiosity of consciousness, she parodies the quest to resist
the historicist compulsion. . . . [S]he fails to realize that her conception
of a simultaneous descent into the self and into the South is a way of
avoiding the historicism of consciousness; that the problem of locating
the transcendent juncture of time, place, and eternity is ironically involved with the modern self's tendency to enclose history in the self.
(Thus) she oversimplifies the modern situation of the self; her stories
employ a series of characters who lack the sophistication to grapple
inwardly with the subtleties of the self as a creature of modern secular history. . . . Her vision is directed toward timeless order and the
ultimate beatitude of the soul. Prophesying the irresistibility of God's
grace in the life of the individual, her stories follow a compelling aesthetic of revelation. The result is that, in spite of their detailed portrayal of the manners of her region, they divest it of a tension toward
historical order.[48]

Though Simpson's criticism is to be taken seriously, it is difficult to credit
either his reading of the ending of "Revelation" or his view of the fate of the
theological and anthropological beliefs that underpin O'Connor's aesthetic.
For one, although Ruby Turpin's Christian belief is woefully distorted by
pride, her thoughts and her conversation in the doctor's office reveal that
she does indeed know her scripture. Consequently, she is not ignorant of
history and the biblical tradition. She is as "prepared" for her final vision, an
"irruption" of the grace of insight, as St. Paul was on the road to Damascus,
or the ordinary fishermen working the Sea of Galilee when Jesus called
them to follow Him. Grace, for O'Connor, is not dependent on human
knowledge or intellectual "sophistication" or subtlety of mind. In fact, in
her stories the opposite is usually the case. So-called intellectual sophistication—most often seen in the agnostic minds of characters like Hulga
Hopewell, Julian, Asbury Fox, and George Rayber—is a stumbling block
to grace. Simpson's view seems to arbitrarily restrict or even rule out the
possibility of the divine Spirit as a direct agent in history—for example in
the experience and heart of a Francis Tarwater, Ruby Turpin, or Asbury
Fox—except as "created" by the author.

More importantly, as previously noted, Simpson's view presumes that
independent objective reality and the transcendent order have been en-

tirely subsumed by the mind of the self-conscious self. If true, if "the historicism of consciousness" is an overpowering fact, then the self, including O'Connor's self, is trapped in subjectivity. But O'Connor, schooled in the aesthetics of St. Thomas Aquinas and Jacques Maritain, believed the opposite. From them she learned that belief in a "pristine independent subjectivity" is a fiction. As Rowan Williams points out, for Maritain "there is never a confrontation between those two mythological entities of modern epistemology—the innocent receptacle of the disinterested mind and the uninterpreted data of external reality. The mind itself is already an agency with a 'shape,' a tendency to respond thus and not otherwise; it makes patterns of what it confronts according to the patterning it has received in its primordial contact with God's agency. The artist's knowledge is a kind of self-knowledge."[49]

In short, Simpson's notion of the mind of the writer as engaged in "detached observation and suspension of judgment" is itself a fiction because any writer's mind and art is already shaped by presuppositions rooted in a primordial intuition of being, and not merely by historical circumstance. Human consciousness is itself a mystery, part of the larger mystery of the human/divine reality, the dynamic world of life lived in the *metaxy*. Simpson's view assumes that human "memory" is the only resource available to the writer to resist "the compulsion to historicism." The possibility of an "irruption" of grace in the act of writing itself, as well as the possibility of representing it in fiction, is excluded.

Finally, when one considers characters like the Misfit, Mr. Fortune, Hulga Hopewell, and George Rayber, Simpson's claim that O'Connor prophesied the "*irresistibility* of grace" in her stories is clearly oversimplified (my emphasis). When the opportunity for acceptance of grace arises in their stories, these characters firmly resist it. O'Connor leaves them "in freedom," denying the immediate "irruption" but open to the future.

Simpson also charges that O'Connor "oversimplifies the modern situation of the self; her stories employ a series of characters who lack the sophistication to grapple inwardly with the subtleties of the self as a creature of modern secular history."[50] In effect, he claims that her characters are too primitive to adequately represent the modern self. As noted earlier, O'Connor stated that she was not interested in exploring her characters' subjectivity. Her reasons were deeply theological and philosophical. She believed that we exist in a divine/human matrix—the *metaxy*—and in an objective order of reality. For her, this meant that every aspect of the story must be rendered in objective, dramatic fashion. As she indicated in "Novelist and Believer," she did not believe an approach to fiction writing through her characters' subjectivity could adequately represent the religious experience, the encounter with God. The "ordering" of experience and the past through "memory," in the manner of Faulkner, Welty, and Warren, could produce great naturalistic fiction, but it could not dramatize the mystery of grace in the encounter with God.[51] O'Connor's characters are not "subtle" or highly self-conscious, self-doubting individuals. Indeed, she said to her friend Betty Hester: "I am not one of those subtle, sensitive writers like Eudora Welty. I see only what is outside and what sticks out a mile, such things as the sun that nobody has to uncover or be bright to see."[52] Before catastrophe strikes them, most of her characters are self-righteously convinced of what they know and believe, whether in a religious or a secular sense. But that is precisely a mark of their pride, egotism, and assumed "self-sufficiency"—the pride of the secular modern age that O'Connor, as a prophetic artist, felt called upon to shatter by awakening these characters, and hopefully her audience, to an awareness of their radical dependency within a larger order of reality. Once again, her strategy was political, aimed at revealing the truth of this larger order in her characters' lives; her art is not just aimed at "artistic" effects for their own sake. As she said, "to the hard of hearing you shout, and for the almost-blind you need to draw large and startling pictures."[53]

Simpson's error is to locate the juncture of "time, place and eternity" exclusively within the mind, particularly the self-conscious mind. Thus, his critical perspective endorses the kind of subjectivity of viewpoint recognized in many modern writers but rejected by O'Connor as inadequate to represent the deepest, transfiguring experiences of God in His relation to humanity. Simpson takes the "sophisticated, highly self-conscious" self to be representative of all modern selves and thus oversimplifies the fullest range and complexity of modern characters. In contrast, the powerful reality of O'Connor's characters, the truth of their personalities, seems clear evidence of her repeated success in fictionalizing the mystery of the human-divine encounter.

O'Connor defended her practice in a letter to Betty Hester: "You have to be able to dominate the existence you characterize. This is why I write about people who are more or less primitive."[54] In what sense are we to understand O'Connor's description of her characters as "primitive"? First, it reveals that she recognized her limitations as a writer, that she wrote best through the lens of irony and satire that required a certain exaggeration and "flattening" of characters to make her point. She did not intend simply to create three-dimensional, naturalistic types.[55] As she said in a letter to Cecil Dawkins: "I am a pretty insensitive soul for subtleties and so forth but then one never writes for a subtle reader. Or if you do, you shouldn't."[56] But more importantly, the primitivism of her characters reflects what she saw as the prideful "innocence" of those children of the age of nihilism who are blind to the reality of their own evil and sin. Caught up in their willfulness, they have inured themselves to this dark knowledge and so have closed themselves into what Richard Giannone has called "archaic modes of thought."[57] Given this moral blindness, O'Connor's task, as she understood it, was to shatter closed minds and hearts. Her "authority" is not the self-generated perspective of the modern secular writer who explores human subjectivity; her authority as a writer is modeled on divine Revelation. Her goal was to return her characters, and her audience, to a true sense of their "place" in the order of being and in the true human community, because they are not just self-conscious, Gnostic "minds" but hypostatic creatures living under God. Her aim of returning her characters and her audience to a true sense of being—the goal of *metanoia*—was the implicit political goal of her art.

O'Connor understood that her politics of art, her attack on the pervasive nihilism of the culture, her fictional voice of prophetic authority, was a bracing counterpoint to the literary zeitgeist of the age. She had no illusions about her religious views gaining a wide acceptance. Given the age's intellectual deformations and the lack of a unified, coherent ontology, general acceptance of her prophetic vision was not to be expected. As she said: "I don't believe that we shall have great religious fiction until we have again that happy combination of believing artist and believing society. Until that time, the novelist will have to do the best he can in travail with the world he has. He may find in the end that instead of reflecting the image at the heart of things, he has only reflected our broken condition and, through it, the face of the devil we are possessed by. This is a modest achievement, but perhaps a necessary one."[58] At the same time, O'Connor also said that "people without hope don't write books," and her hope in writing was that, even in a broken sociopolitical order, the light of the transcendent order, of grace, even the grace of the *via negative*, would shine through to her audience.[59]

Notes

1. Eric Voegelin, *The New Science of Politics: An Introduction* (1952; Chicago: University of Chicago Press, 1957), 61, 67–70. Voegelin also cites Plato's formula "God is the measure," from *Laws* 716c.

2. See Gerhart Niemeyer, "Eric Voegelin's Philosophy and the Drama of Mankind," *Modern Age* 20, no. 4 (1976): 33. See also Aristotle, *Nic. Ethics:* 1177a15.

3. Neimeyer says: "It was Plato, however, who achieved the most important development of Anaximander's insight, in *Philebus* 16c–17a, noting that all things have their being 'from the One and the Many, and conjoin in themselves Limited (*peras*) and Unlimited (*apeirian*),' so that the domain of human knowledge is 'in-between' the One and the Unlimited. The Greek word for 'in-between' is *Metaxy*, which in Voegelin's vocabulary becomes a noun, the Metaxy, working something like a space but also serving as something like a synonym for both the *condicio humana* and 'human nature'" ("Eric Voegelin's Philosophy," 33).

4. Eric Voegelin, *The Ecumenic Age,* vol. 4 of *Order and History* (Baton Rouge: Louisiana State University Press, 1974). This is cited by Niemeyer, "Eric Voegelin's Philosophy," 33. O'Connor reviewed three volumes of Voegelin's *Order and History* for the diocesan newspaper, the *Bulletin:* vol. 1, *Israel and Revelation* (*Bulletin*, 11/15/58); vol. 2, *The World of the Polis* (*Bulletin*, 1/24/59); vol. 3, *Plato and Aristotle* (*Bulletin*, 5/2/59). See *The Presence of Grace and Other Book Reviews by Flannery O'Connor,* comp. Leo J. Zuber (Athens: University of Georgia Press, 1983), 60–61, 67–68, 70–71.

5. Voegelin, *Plato and Aristotle,* vol. 3 of *Order and History* (Baton Rouge: Louisiana State University Press, 1957), 92.

6. Flannery O'Connor, *Mystery and Manners: Occasional Prose,* ed. Sally Fitzgerald and Robert Fitzgerald (New York: Farrar, Straus and Giroux, 1961), 32.

7. Fyodor Dostoevsky, *The Brothers Karamazov,* trans. Richard Pevear and Larissa Volokhonsky (New York: Farrar, Straus and Giroux, 1990), 320.

8. Flannery O'Connor, *The Habit of Being: Letters,* ed. Sally Fitzgerald (New York: Farrar, Straus and Giroux, 1979), 97.

9. Ellis Santoz, *Political Apocalypse: A Study of Dostoevsky's Grand Inquisitor* (Wilmington, Del.: Intercollegiate Studies Institute, 2000), xix.

10. Flannery O'Connor, *The Presence of Grace and Other Book Reviews,* ed. Carter W. Martin (Athens: University of Georgia Press, 1983), 71.

11. O'Connor, *Habit of Being*, 90.

12. Ibid., 97.

13. The best discussion of this process of "closure" or "deformation" of the modern mind can be found in Voegelin's chapter "Gnosticism: The Nature of Modernity" in *The New Science of Politics: An Introduction*, 107–33.

14. Flannery O'Connor, *Collected Works*, ed. Sally Fitzgerald (New York: Library of America, 1988), 19.

15. O'Connor, *Mystery and Manners*, 114.

16. O'Connor, *Collected Works*, 11.

17. Ibid., 64.

18. Ibid., 151–52.

19. Dostoevsky, *Brothers Karamazov*, 263.

20. O'Connor, *Collected Works*, 150.

21. O'Connor, *Mystery and Manners*, 113.

22. O'Connor, *Collected Works*, 152.

23. Ibid., 250–51.

24. Ibid., 305.

25. Ibid., 327.

26. Ibid., 506–7.

27. Ibid., 523.

28. *Bulletin* (see note 4 above for full citation).

29. Niemeyer, "Eric Voegelin's Philosophy," 30.

30. Voegelin, *New Science*, 117–32.

31. O'Connor, *Collected Works*, 86.

32. Ibid., 179.

33. Ibid., 280.

34. Ibid., 550.

35. Ibid., 477–78.

36. Voegelin, *New Science*, 165.

37. O'Connor, *Habit of Being*, 36.

38. Eric Voegelin, *Order and History*, vol. 1, *Israel and Revelation*, ed. Maurice P. Hogan (Columbia: University of Missouri Press, 2001), 130. For reference to O'Connor's underscoring, see Arthur F. Kinney, *Flannery O'Connor's Library: Resources of Being* (Athens: University of Georgia Press, 1985), 139.

39. O'Connor, *Mystery and Manners*, 157–58.

40. Eric Voegelin, *Order and History*, vol. 2, *The World of the Polis*, ed. Athanasios Moulakis (Columbia: University of Missouri Press, 2000), 6; Kinney, *Flannery O'Connor's Library*, 141.

41. O'Connor, *Mystery and Manners*, 179.

42. Ibid., 44.

43. Lewis P. Simpson, *The Brazen Face of History: Studies in the Literary Consciousness of America* (Baton Rouge: Louisiana State University Press, 1980), 245–46.

44. Lewis P. Simpson, *Imagining Our Time: Recollections and Reflections on America Writing* (Baton Rouge: Louisiana State University Press, 2007), 30, my emphasis.

45. Walker Percy, *Signposts in a Strange Land*, ed. Patrick Samway (New York: Farrar, Straus and Giroux, 1991), 209.

46. O'Connor, *The Presence of Grace*, 60–61.

47. Voegelin, *Israel and Revelation*, 130; Kinney, *Flannery O'Connor's Library*, 139.

48. Simpson, *Brazen Face of History*, 247–48.

49. Rowan Williams, *Grace and Necessity: Reflections on Art and Love* (London: Bloomsbury Academic, 2006), 24–25.

50. Simpson, *Brazen Face of History*, 247–48.

51. O'Connor, *Mystery and Manners*, 160.

52. O'Connor, *Habit of Being*, 141.

53. O'Connor, *Mystery and Manners*, 34.

54. O'Connor, *Habit of Being*, 106.

55. Flannery O'Connor was well aware that she needed to make her characters more "human" in order to overcome the limitations of caricature and farce. She worked hard to achieve this, especially in creating George Rayber. At the same time, however, she aimed to create characters who were "unnatural" in the sense that they strained to transcendent the natural order in their quest for God, which often led to them being characterized as "freaks" by mundane standards of human behavior.

56. O'Connor, *Habit of Being*, 296.

57. In his introduction to *Flannery O'Connor: Spiritual Writings*, ed. Robert Ellsberg (Maryknoll, N.Y.: Orbis, 2003), 31–48.

58. O'Connor, *Mystery and Manners*, 168.

59. Ibid., 77.

15

Flannery O'Connor, Eric Voegelin, and the Question That Lies between Them

Marion Montgomery

Flannery O'Connor was much taken with Erie Voegelin's great undertaking, *Order and History*. She reviewed the first three volumes for the *Bulletin*, her diocesan weekly, and the volumes in her library are heavily marked, showing how closely she read them. But we may well consider a possible limit to her interest, particularly in relation to a central question raised by the most recent volume of that work, *The Ecumenic Age*, a question implicit from the beginning and one of which she must have been aware. It is a question Voegelin himself raises in this fourth volume of his projected five, as if he has reached an impasse in his great attempt. The acute awareness of the difficulty, which he expresses in his "Preface" and in the course of the volume itself, yields finally a strengthening of our respect for the man, as his work has commanded an increasingly general respect for the mind in that work. Our approach to this question must of necessity be a delicate one, guarded by fear and trembling before such a remarkable mind. For the question itself, at the last, shifts us from the more limited intellectual dimension of Voegelin's pursuit into the spiritual realm. It is in the region of faith and belief that we at last find ourselves, which is not to say that the ground is any safer if one respects the proper relation to and importance of reason to faith. It is to say that we come to a country of the mind in which the drama of man's journey toward order reveals a range of uneasy kinships reflected in the words of our journeying. In that drama itself, as in Mrs. Turpin's vision of that bridge toward Heaven, strange and curious relationships emerge among struggling souls. It is in that dramatic region, then, that one may with cautious propriety speak of a relationship between Haze Motes and Saint Paul, between Haze and the highly sophisticated Mr. T. S. Eliot, or between Eric Voegelin and Eliot and Saint Paul.

In her review for the diocesan *Bulletin* of the first volume of Voegelin's study, *Israel and Revelation,* Flannery O'Connor remarks it a study which is an "advance over Toynbee in that it satisfactorily answers the comparativism which sees all spiritual movements as fundamentally the same and of equal importance." It is a remark of some prophetic irony, in the light of Voegelin's latest volume, published in 1975. In that volume, Voegelin seems to take a radical departure from the apparent linear, chronological pursuit of man's struggle toward leaps of being, his earlier "chronological" approach to Western thought. But Miss O'Connor from the beginning has praised him particularly for his sense of the irregularity of intensity in visions occurring at different points along the scale of time from the ancient East into the modern world. From her position, she detects in Voegelin an intellectual pursuit of those leaps of being which to her mind must at last require the complementary explanation of the gifts of grace to man. Voegelin looks at man's struggle toward transcendence from man's intellectual side, a limitation appropriate to the scholar, for whom the addition of a faith in grace must prove an additional handicap to persuasiveness, given an age in which the popular spirit is largely controlled by Enlightenment limitations upon reason. What Miss O'Connor detects in Voegelin is that he is content neither with that frozen conception of history as an endless process of repetition, an entrapment in a determinist conception of history such as one finds in Vico, or in Toynbee, as she suggests, nor with a progressivist conception of history, in which one sees mankind moving inexorably toward some divine far-off consummation. In this latter respect, one may remark that the linear study in Voegelin's first three volumes does not correspond to that large visionary poem by Teilhard de Chardin, *The Phenomenon of Man,* which sees in its cosmic sweep a growing intensity and concentration of being in an orderly, progressive, and inevitable scale such as leads Teilhard to his visionary postulate of Point Omega.

Voegelin declares, in *The Ecumenic Age,* in what has appeared to some reviewers a sharp break with the linear movement of his first three volumes of the study, that "History is not a stream of human beings and their actions in time, but the process of man's participation in a flux of divine presence that has eschatological direction." So far, the parallel to Teilhard holds reasonably well, with a comparable direction in their sense of order in time. But Voegelin goes on to say that "The process of history, and such order as can be discerned in it, is not a story to be told from the beginning to its happy, or unhappy end; it is a mystery in process of revelation." What one begins to notice is Voegelin's shift from an attention to the sweep of the vision he articulates to a concern for the articulator of that vision, as if he is returning to his own mind again with a new understanding of that mind in its complexity—a complexity beyond its rational faculties. It is, we may say, a return to the grounds of individual being, a constant ground of tensions in which—in its dramatic perspective—we find ourselves in that country where (as Miss O'Connor says) one finds "a peculiar crossroads where time and place and eternity somehow meet." We are in that country of the "In-Between," which Voegelin describes in an unpublished manuscript (quoted by John H. Hallowell in his preface to *From Enlightenment to Revolution,* viii). It is a description of that crossroads which defines the ground on which we meet Eliot and Voegelin and Haze Motes and Saint Paul: on the road to Damascus, it is a crossroads which sets them quite apart from Oedipus toward Thebes. Voegelin says:

> If anything is constant in the history of mankind it is the language of tension between life and death, immortality and mortality, perfection and imperfection, time and timelessness, between order and disorder, truth and untruth, sense and senselessness of existence; between *amor Dei* and *amor sui, Fame ouverte* and *Fame close;* between the virtues of openness toward the ground of being such as faith, hope and love and the vices of infolding closure such as hybris and revolt; between the moods of joy and despair; and between alienation in its double meaning of alienation from the world and alienation from God.

That passage is worth our reflective pause, since it applies so particularly to those abiding agonies of the mind which we have so insistently considered peculiarly modern. Voegelin's point is that for the particular mind—whether it be Plato's or Paul's, Prufrock's or Hazel Mote's, Poe's or Hawthorne's,

Heidegger's or Sartre's—the ground is the same. We meet in that ground those tensions which reason alone cannot dissolve or resolve. In a very real way, I suggest, Voegelin is returning to the place from which he set out and seeing that place with new eyes. The intellectual point from which we set out in reflecting here on Voegelin is that the returning is implicit from the beginning of his study. That he should come to this country at last is not surprising, and Miss O'Connor would certainly not be surprised. For above all she has from the beginning an awareness of those grounds of tension, the grounds within which the individual "person," as she is fond of saying (or "personality") attempts through risk to discover his being, only to discover that his being is dependent upon the gift of grace. If Heidegger and Sartre focus our attention most particularly upon the "modern" problem of the grounds of being, Voegelin asserts them ancient ground, the one constant in our history. If those are the grounds a poet like Eliot dramatizes as a projection of his own wrestling with the angel in the wilderness, it is also the ancient ground of older pilgrims, reflected in the most homely of ways— in story or song. Whitehead, entering upon this ground himself, cites the tension in an old hymn:

> Abide with me
> Fast falls the eventide
> The darkness deepens
> Lord with me abide.

In *Process and Reality,* Whitehead cites the hymn as expressing that tension between the sense of flux and the desire for permanence: "Here . . . we find formulated the complete problem of metaphysics." And in that confrontation one comes to see, if he is an Eliot,

> That the past experience revised in the meaning
> Is not the experience of one life only But of many generations. . . .

It is the profound human dilemma, the tension between memory and desire, between hope and despair, which Miss O'Connor dramatizes in a comic way, herself using folk expressions of that dilemma. Her "children," in "The Temple of the Holy Ghost," counterpoint each other; the big dumb Church of God ox with his guitar sings:

I've found a friend in Jesus,
He's everything to me,
He's the lily of the valley,
He's the One who's set me free!

In response to "The Old Rugged Cross," the silly convent girls sing:

Tanturn ergo Sacramentum
Veneremur Cernui:
Et antiquuam documentum
Novo cedat ritui:
Praestet fides supplementum
Sensuum defectui.

The harmony of a common station within the grounds of being is obscured by the stirrings in these adolescents as they turn toward their own centers; as they preen the feathers of the ego in sexual flirtations through their complementing hymnings. But Miss O'Connor's central character in the story, the child who watches such a display with disgust, is very much in the turmoil of those tensions by which Voegelin and Eliot and Whitehead—among a legion of great minds—are caught. One may find it stated with less artistry than in Eliot's careful measurings of those tensions in the *Four Quartets*, or in Whitehead's citation of that widely known hymn—which one may still hear regularly sung (if he will) with little art, much heart, and quite often accompanied by twangy guitars. Such a combination of a high matter in a discordant art suggests a strategy of Miss O'Connor's comic seriousness. To miss that suggestion leads one to undervalue, for instance, the serious burden carried in those constant clichés she develops like musical phrases. It is to miss the profound core in her comic and comical agents. She turns to the simplest and sometimes most irritating—irritating to the aesthetic sensibilities—level of that tension in the grounds of being, as if to demonstrate the common in mankind when seen with the light of grace's rescue. The theme itself, as Whitehead knows, occurs and recurs in folk literature of a range of artistic merit. An instance is on my local station as I write:

This world is not my home
I'm just a-passing through;

If Heaven's not my home,
Oh Lord, what will I do
The Angels beckon me
To Heaven's open door,
And I can't feel at home
In this world anymore.

Voegelin's "mystery in the process of revelation" draws a disparate mankind, the multiple creatura of men, into a common ground.

When one perceives that truth about our individual existence, it must follow that revelation must be uneven in its intensity and clarity, for revelation is accessible to particular and so disparate persons in that ground, and at various times and in strange and common places. But what lies in that mystery so disparately perceived is full and complete in itself. If its revelation varies in the flux of time and place, as revealed in the old battle of the ancients and moderns, initiated with new intensity by the Enlightenment, we require a cautious review. The sense of progress toward a universal promised land, whether in the secularized view of history out of the Enlightenment or in Teilhard's attempt to reconcile that view to Christian eschatology, reveals a deterministic pattern such as Voegelin in his early volumes examines and, as Miss O'Connor notes, finds unsuited even at that early stage of his study.

Since the mystery of being reveals itself in varying intensities to man's intellectual faculties, as Voegelin's reconsideration of the historical problem suggests, and in varying times and places, it follows that it may be revealed fully and completely in any time and place, hut with a fullness of comprehension of that revelation restricted by the limits of man's faculties. That, Miss O'Connor would be quick to affirm, is precisely the meaning of the Incarnation. There too lies the source of the continuous presence of grace, through which an illumination occurs to individual minds. In regard to this point, Professor Gerhart Niemeyer raises a crucial question about the position reflected in *The Ecumenic Age*. For it is apparent that Voegelin shies away from a direct address to that intrusion upon history by the God Man, Christ. Instead, he addresses himself to the mind of Saint Paul, being drawn by Paul's insight that (in Voegelin's words) "transfiguration is in process in untransfigured history." Here Voegelin is held by that insistence in Paul that man must be born again in Christ, an insistence that the old man must he put off and the new put on. The question about Voegelin's position, as Professor Niemeyer puts it, is why he does not address himself directly to the question of the Incarnation.

I think the answer lies partly in Voegelin's being in one sense a continuation of nineteenth-century thought, but I think as well that we see him working free of an entrapment by that thought. Professor Niemeyer at one point comments on a shift "from the paradox of reality to the abolition of paradox, *i.e.,* toward the vision of a reality in which both disorder and mortality are vanquished by God." To neutralize paradox requires a balance under the control of reason; the poles between which one achieves that balance are the terms of the paradox, separated by rational thought—the God and the Man in our present instance. It is such a separation as reason seems to demand, and in this careful weighing in Voegelin one perhaps hears an echo out of Heidegger. Heidegger sets "emptiness" in relation to "presence" for instance, and "being" in relation to "Being-itself," and in each instance keeps at bay the object toward which mystery draws one, being hesitant to articulate the God as Being. It is an attempt to use reason to its fullest possibility, that mind may gain a respect as authority in a skeptical age. The paradox involved in Heidegger's balanced terms is accepted and, as it were, consumed by Saint Paul's faith. A most particular instance, since Miss O'Connor herself is drawn to use it in the story we last mentioned, is Saint Paul's reading of man as the temple of the Holy Ghost. The philosopher, committed to reason, divides paradox so that by reason he may walk that careful line which holds the poles in separate suspension by mind, not fully accepted by the act of faith. That is the state of the philosopher's mind which Marcel describes metaphorically when he says, "My thought . . . is above all a travelling along a ridge above an abyss." For philosophy, as philosophy, abhors paradox as Newton a vacuum, though it be always driven toward paradox.

Voegelin's concern for man's participation in history is a point that again makes one aware of echo out of Heidegger's divisions and balances, though one can't help noticing that Heidegger's "Being-itself" sounds suspiciously like the Holy Ghost as it might be presented by the theologian. The impulse to neologism, which Heidegger asserts a necessity because of the complexity of his thought, appears rather an effect of our alienation from scholastic thought; but it may also be the beginning of our progress toward its recovery, in which respect Voegelin's strictness of terms is a healthy beginning, though a torturous experience to the modern mind. Voegelin's own call for a new Thomas, rather than for neo-Thomism, I think, is a further sign of his origins in late nineteenth-century continental thought, though his evaluation of the opaqueness of our inherited images and forms is surely an important contribution in his thought.[1] The question central here is whether the opaqueness is in the eye or in the image, and for an Eliot or an O'Connor the conclusion is that the difficulty lies in the eye of the beholder of the world as he looks through images and forms. (One might pursue this point at length in Eliot's poetry as it concerns itself with the image and the blinded eye, to the opening of the eye in vision; it is a progress which gives a narrative continuity to the body of his poetry.) We must concern ourselves more fully with Heidegger's neologisms when we turn to Poe in our second volume, since that concern sheds particular light upon the poet's problem with form and image in relation to reality, a problem which reaches its crucial limit in the nineteenth-century poet.

Up to *The Ecumenic Age,* Voegelin has devoted himself to the strict discipline of reason in pursuit of the grounds of being, made objective by his examining that pursuit as revealed in other minds in history. This means, in Professor Niemeyer's words, that for Voegelin, philosophy is inseparable from history, "both the historical past as the genesis of crucial insights and the historical process as the drama of existence; it is also inseparable from experience of reality intelligible only through its divine ground; it is inseparable finally from the experience of human participation in the divine through revelation." But if this is the position Voegelin holds (and I believe Professor Niemeyer's is an accurate reading of that position), the problem remains to come to terms with grace as the medium or agency of human participation in the divine ground. Voegelin, examining his own findings with a skeptical eye turned increasingly upon his own mind, asks a number of questions of his findings which tend toward this very problem of grace: "Why must the epochal truth go through the historical torment of imperfect articulation, evasion, skepticism, disbelief, rejection, deformation, and of renaissance, renovations, rediscoveries, rearticulations?" For Voegelin— that is, for the public Voegelin, the Voegelin of the studies—revelation must be made to yield to the rational; to the contrary, a Saint Thomas or a Maritain, a Niemeyer or Flannery O'Connor, would put the matter rather that man is required to pursue revelation with the reason as a price of Original Sin, reason necessarily giving way to faith. For Thomas, necessary reasons cannot demonstrate the tenets of faith, only show them not contrary to reason. On that position, Maritain builds: "Religious faith is above reason, but normally presupposes the rationed conviction of God's existence." In the long journey back from the loss of faith in the popular spirit, whether one see it in the poetry of Wordsworth or Hölderlin, or in the thought of Heidegger and Voegelin and Teilhard, the attempt is to discover the true path by means of one's sensibilities and reason—that is, the attempt is to work back to faith through man's powers and from the world itself. When Miss O'Connor remarks, on reading Teilhard, that Teilhard's way, that of spiritualizing matter with the aid of science's advances, "is actually a very old way," one obscured by a variety of heresies over the ages since the Incarnation, she is expressing an awareness of his attempt to work back to an old position, an attempt in which he may not himself be fully aware of his action of recovery, as Claude Tresmontant suggests in his tribute, *Pierre Teilhard de Chardin*.

Miss O'Connor's belief in Original Sin throws a certain light upon Voegelin's troubled question, a question which, in effect, laments the failure of man to progress in history. If her answer does not satisfy the reason in every point, it at least makes the question less poignant, less conducive to despair, when one comes to believe man indeed fallen and insufficient to his own rescue. History as a process and history as a drama: that is the Voegelinean message Miss O'Connor reads as a welcomed complement to those necessities she faces as a dramatist—as a narrative dramatist. Epic, we are told, begins *in medias res*. But in the larger focus of one's metaphysical concerns, so does drama. *Oedipus Rex* is a point very late in the narrative sequence, but the burden of the past is heavy upon it, as if past history were the thumbprint of fate. Miss O'Connor's drama, we may observe, is a linear one, however skillfully she foreshortens and condenses her narrative element to the crucial moment in the life of a protagonist. And so we may observe that the linear in history has an attraction to the fiction writer separate from its "truth." It suggests analogical dimensions to the history of the individual soul, the recognition of which Eliot comes to in discovering that a past experience, when one comes to understand it, is not the experience of one life but "of many generations." (Miss O'Connor would have it, the many generations of Adam.) The significant "progress" is that of the individual soul, whose relation to God at any moment through grace is decisive and not dependent upon a progressive development under the auspices of

reason. Thus she remarks that "Christ didn't redeem us by a direct intellectual act, but became incarnate in human form, and he speaks to us now
through the mediation of a visible Church. . . . [T]he main concern of the
fiction writer is with mystery as it is incarnated in human life." Voegelin's
recognition of this point in relation to history, a recognition that revelations
leading to leaps of being are uneven in their intensity and independent of
an absolute dictate of time and place, is an indication of a movement of his
mind toward Christianity.

If grace is the decisive element in history, it is not thereby continuously
intense in history, either in the history of a people or the history of a person.
There is no reason, consequently, to suppose that Miss O'Connor intends us
to conclude that Mrs. Turpin is rescued by her vision, that she is no longer
susceptible to "backsliding." For individual spiritual life is a continuous act
of dying to the old mem in us that we may be reborn. Death as sister to her
imagination, as Miss O'Connor says it is, is a larger death than the physical,
though the physical death is a fictionally suitable term for that larger reality
which her art attempts to reflect. It is so, whether one deal with Oedipus or
Lord Jim or Prufrock or Hazel Motes. But the sense of order, proportion,
duration which fiction requires be satisfied in us is the aesthetic sense. The
shards of an urn or a part of a bust of Apollo lead us to imaginative comple-
tions; we find ourselves compelled to similar acts of completion within our
responses to the figures of man projected dramatically. That is why "slices
of life" as art do not fully satisfy the aesthetic hunger in us, though they
often whet the aesthetic appetite. For, as Miss O'Connor says, "There is
something in us, as story-tellers and as listeners to stories, that demands the
redemptive act, that demands that what falls at least be offered the chance
to be restored." A reader who looks for this motion is right she says, though
he has largely forgotten the cost of restoration. The sacrifice necessary can
be imitated in art, but it is error to suppose art the medium itself of restoration, a confusion which leads a reader to expect in fiction, for instance, to be
"transported, instantly, either to a mock damnation or a mock innocence."
What she is saying, in effect, is that the modern reader requires of art a sentimental use of art's catharsis, in which the sense of evil "is diluted or lacking altogether." In that sentimental approach to the desire for rescue, one
has a parallel in the protestant emphasis in Miss O'Connor's fictional agents
of the necessity of being born again—beyond whatever initial baptism one
may have undergone. It is a point in time to which one refers in testimony, at

which he was "saved." This "born-again" doctrine is counterpointed by Miss O'Connor in the continuing agony of her protagonists, who must struggle continuously with becoming the new man. A most striking instance is her portrait of old Tarwater, as we see in the language he speaks, in his eyes attempting to burst their blood-lined net of the body.

We may say, then, that literal death as it occurs in Miss O'Connor's fiction is not the *deus ex machina* it may be taken to be. It brings to rest, to a completion, the movement of a story or novel with a suggestion of abiding duration in the art object itself. In its relation to the spiritual content of drama, Haze's death or the grandmother's in "A Good Man Is Hard to Find," does not mean to suggest that the reality of individual salvation requires the literal death of the particular person in a literal time and place. Art gives a range of the possible or probable (and Miss O'Connor emphasizes the *possible* in her remarks that echo Aristotle) in particular moments of a life, in an ordered relationship to the distant, the absolute. Neither art nor life permits for Miss O'Connor one's ignoring that distant reality, of course. As she says, "Those who have no absolute values cannot let the relative remain merely relative; they are always raising it to the level of the absolute." But the dramatizing of a particular moment of grace does not obscure to us Miss O'Connor's constant belief that the very fact of our existence at any moment—not simply at our high moments—is evidence of a continuing grace. That it is also a contingent moment as well, a relative moment, in our rescue or loss is in a balance beyond art's resolution. That is to say, in the reality of the world we continue in those grounds of tension of which Voegelin speaks, most particularly suspended by *amor Dei* and *amor sui*. As we speak of continuous creation in the new astronomy, we may speak of each creature's continuous creation, or in Miss O'Connor's words of a "good under construction." In the realization of this participation in the grounds of being lies that exhilarating terror, joy, and awe of being, through which Being is at last recognized, the dramatic consummation Miss O'Connor attempts to imitate in her fiction.

O'Connor's "linear" drama casts her protagonist toward revelation, toward the intrusion of grace as a turning point in her agent. In this respect, both Voegelin and Teilhard are encouraging analogues to the vision she would make incarnate in fiction. But it does not mean that she takes that progress as a necessary version of reality, of a progress toward complete revelation at Point Omega as in Teilhard. In reality, any moment is that mo-

ment at the crossroad where time and place and eternity coincide. In the
moment of revelation, time and place are consumed by eternity, in grace's
revelation.[2] That is an action, however, within the individual, a transformation such as St. Paul experienced on the road to Damascus. Voegelin as philosopher of history looks at moments of "differentiating consciousness" to
discover leaps in being. But, as Professor Niemeyer asks, "From where will
he look at them?" He quotes Voegelin's own awareness of this problem: "To
accept the process of differentiation as the exclusive source of knowledge
means, negatively, to renounce all pretense to an observer's position outside
the process. Positively, it means to enter the process and to participate both
in its formal structure and the concrete tasks imposed on the thinker by his
situation in it."

It would be presumptuous in the extreme, in the light of this dilemma, to attempt to enter into that "differentiation" we call Jesus of Nazareth, and Voegelin's turning to Paul instead of attempting the more obvious
temptation is a sign of a piety in Voegelin. Yet, more than piety is involved.
The hesitation between renouncing the pretension of the detached observer and entering into the process is not so much an intellectual difficulty
as a spiritual one, as Voegelin of all our philosopher-historians of the moment seems most aware. If there is a movement of thought in nineteenth-
century continental philosophers such as Husserl's and twentieth-century
minds such as Heidegger's (both of whom were Voegelin's teachers), one
may say that Voegelin has moved that thought to the point where it must
yield either to madness or to a consent to enter at last upon vision itself. He
has brought us to that point which Michael Polanyi talks about in *Personal
Knowledge*:

> This then is our liberation from objectivism: to realize that we can
> voice our ultimate convictions only from within the whole system of
> acceptances that are logically prior to any particular assertion of our
> own, prior to the holding of any particular piece of knowledge. . . . I
> believe that the function of philosophical reflection consists in bring-
> ing to light, and affirming as my own, the beliefs implied in such of
> my thoughts and practices as I believe to be valid; that I must aim at
> discovering what I truly believe in and at formulating the convictions
> which I find myself holding; that I must conquer my self-doubt, so as to
> retain a firm hold on this programme of self-identification.

In the tradition of that disciplined mind which characterizes the best (and, in weaker minds, the worst) of nineteenth-century thought, Voegelin follows the reason, strictly controlled, in the course of which journey seemingly unanswerable questions present themselves. It is in history, and in particular minds out of history that he examines his own particular mind, attempting to establish a place from which to look at differentiating consciousness, just as in a parallel instance Heidegger attempts to stand in his own mind and summon being to presence. In other words the attempt is to work with the givens of consciousness, and work through them to the Giver, rather than assume the Giver as premise, as once seemed possible and necessary to the philosopher, as in the thought of Saint Thomas. It is, once more, an attempt which assumes a power in the pilgrim reasoner, a power which Zarathustra shouts: "I will." But Voegelin has, in that searching journey, reached the position Polanyi speaks of, at which it is necessary to bring to light and affirm as belief the implied principles of that particular consciousness named Eric Voegelin. In venturing upon such hazardous grounds, one ought to remark once more that we are considering the mind as revealed in the public work. It is possible, and perhaps even probable, that in Voegelin one has that ancient pleasure to the philosopher, a heritage from Plato, of a dramatic enactment of the quest and that the man Voegelin is himself far in advance of our questions, having rather imitated the progress of the modern mind back toward a faith he already holds as a particular being in the troubled grounds of being. Such a possibility is suggested in his remarks on modern man's pathetic state: "The man who once could demonstrate not only himself but even the existence of God, has become the man who is condemned to be free and urgently wants to be arrested for editing a Maoist journal."

In either event, we may observe that when one comes to the position Voegelin occupies in *The Ecumenic Age*, in the process of which journey he has become the most encyclopedic mind of our day, it is a spiritually shocking dilemma to find one's position as observer so sharply in question. To enter into and participate in the "formal structure and the concrete tasks imposed on the thinker by his situation," it may be discovered, requires a surrender such as Eliot speaks of in *The Waste Land* and more fully in *Little Gidding*. It is to come to that point of consciousness requiring an "awful daring of a moment's surrender / Which an age of prudence can never retract." The age of prudence, since the Enlightenment, is our age, which is reduced from Saint Thomas's conception of prudence as the virtue leading toward one's proper end in God; for prudence as virtue when secularized becomes a devotion to *amor sui*. Eliot comes to a surrender to that Calling which costs "no less than everything," that is, no less than everything to the popular spirit of an age whose energy is out of *amor sui*. That energy, consolidated in power out of the gnostic triumph over being, still holds one fiercely in the "old man." On the point, Polanyi remarks, again in *Personal Knowledge*, that in his rising eminence in nature, man stands at least

> at the confluence of biology and philosophical self-accreditating, . . . rooted in his calling under a firmament of truth and greatness. Its teachings are the idiom of his thought: the voice by which he commands himself to satisfy his intellectual standards. . . . He is strong, noble and wonderful so long as he fears the voices of this firmament; but he dissolves their power over himself and his own powers gained through denying them, if he turns back and examines what he rejects in a detached manner. Then law is no more than what the courts will decide, art but an emollient of nerves, morality but a convention, tradition but an inertia, God but a psychological necessity. The man dominates a world in which he himself does not exist. For with his obligations [lost] he has lost his voice and his hope, and been left behind meaningless to himself.

What Polanyi describes here as failure is the ultimate triumph of gnosticism, that movement which has so troubled Voegelin and which he so brilliantly reduces to its fundamental absurdity as thought. And having done so, he is brought at last to the sound of his own voice, and to the significance of the words he has been saying. The illusion of having a place to stand, untrammeled by assumptions such as lead out of the self and its own powers: that is what Miss O'Connor herself presents rather tellingly, as in Haze Motes's frenzied confidence in his Essex: "Since I've had it," Haze says, "I've had a place to be that I can get away in." A student of Miss O'Connor remarked in my presence that "Nobody in his right mind identifies himself with Flannery O'Connor's protagonists." But our very point is that the mind working itself back to right-mindedness works itself through the agonies she dramatizes in her protagonists. Since she sees the causes of the mind's difficulties in intellectual failures since the Enlightenment, and in the degree to which her reading of that failure is valid, one finds her protagonists mythical figures of those failures, so that it is highly revealing to speak of Haze Motes in relation to such thinkers as we have associated him with.

If her comic presentation of the Western intellectual obscures to that intellect his own kinship to a Haze, that (as we have said) is part of the mischief in her. It is a mischief through which she remarks a confusion between intellectual and spiritual dimensions of man's being. In C. Vann Woodward's *The Burden of Southern History* and in his chapter on "The Populist Heritage and the Intellectual," she has marked a sentence that speaks to this mischief. Woodward, commenting on "liberal intellectuals" who "have in the past constructed a flattering image of Populism," out of their "sympathy with oppressed groups," says that the intellectuals "attributed to [the Populists] . . . values, tastes, principles, and morals which the Populists did not actually share. It was understandably distasteful to dwell upon the irrational or retrograde traits of a people who deserved one's sympathy and shared some of one's views." In marking that sentence, Miss O'Connor recognizes in it the sentimental romanticizing of the "southerner," the down-trodden southerner, through which he is denied his being. That is, the southern "populist" is a man, too, with all the weaknesses as well as those strengths which the "liberal intellectual" would separate and conserve at the expense of denying the complexity of man's being. There is, of course, a species of idolatry involved in such a distortion, in which one man is made over in the image of another, by that generous imagination which denies reality, whether that limited imagination is displayed in moonlight-magnolia romances of the southerner or the liberal portrait of the populist. The intellectual's image of man as intellectual is incomplete, and Miss O'Connor's irony is the product in part of her yoking Haze Motes to Nietzschean thought. This is her historical dimension, then; it brings to focus the sentimental drift of reason since the Enlightenment as it comes to dominate the popular spirit of the age. That drift Eric Voegelin has exposed by his reasonable assessment of the unreasonable drift. And it has brought him to the present moment, the "confluence of biological and philosophical self-accrediting," about which he raises questions which turn toward his own mind. He moves from the intellectual sphere toward the spiritual, in which movement the question of faith becomes paramount, a question "costing no less than everything."

In the surrender which faith requires, we are told by Eliot, one comes to see that the pursuit of history is not an act whereby we "ring the bell backward," as had seemed the consequence of that pursuit at the time of *The Waste Land.* At that earlier point in the journey, the reward of history had seemed only echoes out of dry cisterns in the desert. By the time of *Little Gidding,* the necessary surrender has shown a different effect. The self comes to discover that

> while the light fails
> On a winter's afternoon, in a secluded chapel
> History is now and England.

For time is seen at last enfolded by the Rose of Time, which reveals itself in history as the Incarnation. Such a long journey back to Bethlehem, involving the constant terror of surrender, brings one to an end of the journey, a surprising end, since we "arrive where we started / And know the place for the first time." It is dangerously presumptuous to assume the role of prophet in such matters, especially when one fears himself insufficiently supported by the grace of vision, but one's reason suggests nevertheless that in the promised final volume of Eric Voegelin's *Order and History* we shall find just such a surrender and a return to the lost garden. The alternative would seem to be only a continuation of those questions he asks of himself in *The Ecumenic Age.*[3] One sees him in this volume, not at an intellectual, but at a spiritual crossroads. Or better perhaps: one sees him in a state of spiritual awareness very like that old one on the road to Damascus at which the particular intersection of history by grace differentiated Saul of Tarsus from Saint Paul. If this is more strongly probability than merely possibility, I think we shall see in the body of Voegelin's work, as it reflects such an awe-inspiring mind, a sojourn which in its spiritual significance (which is deeper than the spectacle of its history) a parallel to the modern journey of the Western mind out of the illusion foisted upon it that all creation is a meaningless desert, the illusion that being has been exiled from our awareness by gnostic power. It is the journey Miss O'Connor dramatizes for us as that from Eastrod to Taulkinham, but a journey that goes beyond that city of man to Bethlehem. The kinship of Miss O'Connor's protagonist to such a great mind as Eric Voegelin's will not be so disparate as the spectacle of her fiction makes the comparison at first appear.

For the comparison speaks to a brotherhood of the creatures called man, established by gift in the grounds of man's being at a level more fundamental and essential than the disparity of our gifts of intellect. Haze Motes comes at last to a point where he woos silence, in spite of Mrs. Flood's troublesome intrusions. He is at last on that road which Josef Pieper speaks of in *The Silence of St. Thomas*. Pieper's words are perhaps applicable to Voegelin, but hopefully to us all: "The fullness of truth can never be grasped by a neutral and indifferent mind, but only by a mind seeking the answer to a serious and urgent existential problem." Nevertheless, "man, in his philosophical inquiry, is faced again and again with the experience that reality is unfathomable and Being is mystery—an experience . . . which urges him not so much to communication as to silence. But it would not be the silence of resignation and still less of despair. It would be the silence of reverence."

Notes

Originally published as "Flannery O'Connor, Eric Voegelin and the Question That Lies between Them," *Modern Age*, spring 1978, 133–43. Reprinted with permission by the Intercollegiate Studies Institute.

1. "When not only the substance is lost, but when also the active center of intellectual life has shifted to the plane of our knowledge of the external world, the symbols expressive of Christian spiritual life acquire . . . opaqueness. . . . The symbols will either be abandoned entirely because they have become irrelevant or, when the sentiments of tradition are still strong, they will be submitted to rational simplification, psychological interpretation and utilitarian justification. . . . [T]he combination of opaqueness of the symbols with traditional reverence for them, is the position of Newton and Voltaire" (*From Enlightenment to Revolution*, 25).

2. She wrote Maryat Lee (October 8, 1957): "The only thing that irked me about your last letter was your use of the word eternity in the plural, with airless in front of it. I don't mind you being a pathetic quaver, but eternity means the beatific vision to me and my quaver, or anybody elses, has nothing to do with it" (*Flannery O'Connor Bulletin* 5 [Fall 1976]: 58).

3. Some light is thrown on my speculation by Voegelin's essay "The Gospel and Culture," his contribution to the *Pittsburgh Theological Seminary 175th Anniversary Festival of the Gospels*, vol. 2, ed. Donald G. Miller and Dikran Y. Hadidian (1971), 59–101.

Acknowledgments

In a project that has stretched over as long a period of time as this one has, two problems arise: there are too many people to thank, and I can't remember half of them. That said, let me first thank the contributors to this volume for both their contribution and their patience. My wife, Dorothy Marie, has displayed the patience of Job once again, as she does with all of my endeavors. Special Collections at Georgia College, O'Connor's alma mater, has been supportive as usual, especially Nancy Davis Bray. Finally, but very importantly, Jude Marr, who began to assist me in the last year of this project and who made all the difference.

Hank Edmondson
Milledgeville, Georgia
Pentecost, 2016

Selected Bibliography

Works by Flannery O'Connor

The Complete Stories. New York: Farrar, Straus and Giroux, 1971.

Conversations with Flannery O'Connor. Edited by Rosemary M. Magee. Jackson: University Press of Mississippi, 1987.

The Correspondence of Flannery O'Connor and the Brainard Cheneys. Edited by C. Ralph Stevens. Jackson: University Press of Mississippi, 1986.

Everything That Rises Must Converge. New York: Farrar, Straus and Giroux, 1965.

Flannery O'Connor: Collected Works. New York: Library of America, 1988.

Flannery O'Connor's Library: Resources of Being. Edited by Arthur F. Kinney. Athens: University of Georgia Press, 1985.

A Good Man Is Hard to Find and Other Short Stories. New York: Harcourt Brace Jovanovich, 1977.

The Habit of Being: Letters of Flannery O'Connor. Edited by Sally Fitzgerald. New York: Farrar, Straus and Giroux, 1979.

Mystery and Manners: Occasional Prose. Edited by Sally Fitzgerald. New York: Farrar, Straus and Giroux, 1969.

A Prayer Journal. Edited by W. A. Sessions. New York: Farrar, Straus and Giroux, 2013.

The Presence of Grace and Other Book Reviews. Compiled by Leo J. Zuber. Edited by Carter W. Martin. Athens: University of Georgia Press, 1983.

The Violent Bear It Away. Farrar, Straus and Giroux, 2007.

Wise Blood. Reprint, New York: Farrar, Straus and Giroux, 2007.

Biographies

Cash, Jean. *Flannery O'Connor: A Life.* Knoxville: University of Tennessee Press, 2002.

Gooch, Brad. *Flannery: A Life of Flannery O'Connor.* Boston: Little, Brown, 2009.

Rogers, Jonathan. *The Terrible Speed of Mercy: A Spiritual Biography.* Nashville, Tenn.: Thomas Nelson, 2012.

Interpretive Works

Amason, Craig, and Sarah Gordon. *A Literary Guide to Flannery O'Connor's Georgia.* Athens: University of Georgia Press, 2008.

Asals, Frederick. *Flannery O'Connor: The Imagination of Extremity.* Athens: University of Georgia Press, 1982.

Bacon, Jon Lance. *Flannery O'Connor and Cold War Culture.* Cambridge: Cambridge University Press, 1993.

Basselin, Timothy J. *Flannery O'Connor: Writing a Theology of Disabled Humanity.* Waco, Tex.: Baylor University Press, 2013.

Baumgaertner, Jill P. *Flannery O'Connor: A Proper Scaring.* Wheaton, Ill.: Harold Shaw, 1988.

Bosco, Mark, S.J. *Revelation and Convergence: Flannery O'Connor and the Catholic Intellectual Tradition.* Washington, D.C.: Catholic University of America Press, 2017.

Brinkmeyer, Robert. *The Art and Vision of Flannery O'Connor.* Baton Rouge: Louisiana State University Press, 1989.

Ciuba, Gary M. *Desire, Violence and Divinity in Modern Southern Fiction: Katherine Anne Porter, Flannery O'Connor, Cormac McCarthy, Walker Percy.* Baton Rouge: Louisiana State University Press, 2007.

Desmond, John F. *Risen Sons: Flannery O'Connor's Vision of History.* Athens: University of Georgia Press, 1987.

Edmondson, Henry T. *Return to Good and Evil: Flannery O'Connor's Response to Nihilism.* Lanham, Md.: Lexington, 2002.

Elie, Paul. *The Life You Save.* New York: Farrar, Straus and Giroux, 2003.

Ellsberg, Robert, ed. *Flannery O'Connor: Spiritual Writings.* Maryknoll, N.Y.: Orbis, 2003.

Feeley, Kathleen. *Flannery O'Connor: Voice of the Peacock.* New York: Fordham University Press, 1972.

Gentry, Bruce, and Craig Amason, eds. *At Home with Flannery O'Connor: An Oral History.* Milledgeville, Ga.: Flannery O'Connor Andalusia Foundation, 2012.

Giannone, Richard. *Flannery O'Connor and the Mystery of Love.* New York: Fordham University Press, 1989.

———. *Flannery O'Connor, Hermit Novelist.* Urbana: University of Illinois Press, 2000.

Gretlund, Jan Nordby, and Karl-Heinz Westarp, eds. *Flannery O'Connor's Radical Reality.* Columbia: University of South Carolina Press, 2006.

Gordon, Sarah. *Flannery O'Connor: In Celebration of Genius.* Athens, Ga.: Hill Street Press, 2000.

———. *Flannery O'Connor: The Obedient Imagination*. Athens: University of Georgia Press, 2000.

Hewitt, Avis, and Robert Donahoo. *Flannery O'Connor in the Age of Terrorism*. Knoxville: University of Tennessee Press, 2011.

Johansen, Ruthann. *The Narrative Secret of Flannery O'Connor*. Tuscaloosa: University of Alabama Press, 1994.

Kessler, Edward. *Flannery O'Connor and the Language of Apocalypse*. Princeton: Princeton University Press, 1986.

Kilcourse, George. *Flannery O'Connor's Religious Imagination: A World with Everything Off Balance*. New York: Paulist Press, 2001.

Lake, Christina Bieber. *The Incarnational Art of Flannery O'Connor*. Macon, Ga.: Mercer University Press, 2005.

———. *Prophets of the Posthuman: American Fiction, Biotechnology, and the Ethics of Personhood*. Notre Dame, Ind.: University of Notre Dame Press, 2013.

Magee, Rosemary M. *Conversations with Flannery O'Connor*. Jackson: University Press of Mississippi, 1987.

Marshall, Bruce Gentry. *Flannery O'Connor's Religion of the Grotesque*. Jackson: University Press of Mississippi, 1986.

Martin, Regis. *Unmasking the Devil: Dramas of Sin and Grace in the World of Flannery O'Connor*. Washington, D.C.: Catholic University Press, 2002.

May, John R. *The Pruning Word: The Parables of Flannery O'Connor*. Notre Dame, Ind.: University of Notre Dame Press, 1976.

McKenzie, Barbara. *Flannery O'Connor's Georgia*. Athens: University of Georgia Press, 2013.

McMullen, Joanne, and Jon Parrish Peede, eds. *Inside the Church of Flannery O'Connor*. Macon, Ga.: Mercer University Press, 2007.

Michaels, Ramsey J. *Passing by the Dragon: The Biblical Tales of Flannery O'Connor*. Eugene, Ore.: Cascade, 2013.

Montgomery, Marion. *Hillbilly Thomist: Flannery O'Connor, St. Thomas and the Limits of Art*. 2 vols. Jefferson, N.C.: McFarland, 2006.

———. *Why Flannery O'Connor Stayed Home*. The Prophetic Poet and the Spirit of the Age series. Peru, Ill.: Sherwood Sugden, 1981.

Murray, Lorraine V. *The Abbess of Andalusia. Flannery O'Connor's Spiritual Journey*. Charlotte, N.C.: Saint Benedict, 2009.

O'Gorman, Farrell. *Catholicism and American Borders in the Gothic Literary Imagination*. Notre Dame: University of Notre Dame Press, 2017.

———. *Peculiar Crossroads: Flannery O'Connor, Walker Percy, and Catholic Vision in Postwar Southern Fiction*. Baton Rouge: Louisiana State University Press, 2004.

Ragen, Brian Abel. *A Wreck on the Road to Damascus. Innocence, Guilt and Conversion in Flannery O'Connor*. Chicago: Loyola University Press, 1989.

Scott, R. Neil, and Valerie Nye, eds. *Postmarked Milledgeville: A Guide to Flannery O'Connor's Correspondence in Libraries and Archives.* Milledgeville, Ga.: Flannery O'Connor Review, 2002.

Scott, R. Neil, and Irwin H. Streight, eds. *Flannery O'Connor: The Contemporary Reviews.* Cambridge: Cambridge University Press, 2009.

Spivey, Ted Ray. *Flannery O'Connor: The Woman, the Thinker, the Visionary.* Macon, Ga.: Mercer University Press, 1995.

Srigley, Susan. *Dark Faith: New Essays on Flannery O'Connor's "The Violent Bear It Away."* Notre Dame: University of Notre Dame Press, 2012.

———. *Flannery O'Connor's Sacramental Art.* Notre Dame, Ind.: University of Notre Dame Press, 2004.

Stephens, Martha. *The Question of Flannery O'Connor.* Baton Rouge: Louisiana State University Press, 1973.

Sykes, John D., Jr. *Flannery O'Connor, Walker Percy, and the Aesthetic of Revelation.* Columbia: University of Missouri Press, 2007.

Whitt, Margaret Earley. *Understanding Flannery O'Connor.* Columbia: University of South Carolina Press, 1995.

Wood, Ralph C. *The Comedy of Redemption: Christian Faith & Comic Vision in Four American Novelists.* Notre Dame: University of Notre Dame Press, 1991.

Wood, Ralph C. *Flannery O'Connor and the Christ-Haunted South.* Grand Rapids, Mich.: Eerdmans, 2004.

Contributors

Benjamin B. Alexander is professor of English and humanities at Franciscan University of Steubenville. He also has taught at George Mason University, the Catholic University of America, Hampden-Sydney College, Marymount University, Washington College, and Hillsdale. In addition to his academic posts, he was a speech writer and consultant at USIA and the U.S. Department of Education from 1990 to 1992.

Mark Bosco, S.J., is associate professor at Loyola University Chicago, holding a joint position in the Departments of English and Theology. He also directs Loyola's Joan and Bill Hank Center for the Catholic Intellectual Heritage, a research center on Catholic thought and culture. His scholarship focuses on the intersection of religion and art, especially on the twentieth-century Catholic literary revival in Britain and North America. He is the author of, among other works, *Graham Greene's Catholic Imagination* (2005) and, most recently, a new collection of essays, *Revelation and Convergence: Flannery O'Connor and the Catholic Intellectual Tradition* (2017).

Gary M. Ciuba is professor of English at Kent State University. He is the author of *Walker Percy: Books of* Revelations (1991) and *Desire, Violence, and Divinity in Modern Southern Fiction* (2007), which received the C. Hugh Holman Award for 2007 from the Society for the Study of Southern Literature.

John F. Desmond is professor of English emeritus at Whitman College. He is the author of *Risen Sons: Flannery O'Connor's Vision of History* (1987); *At the Crossroads: Ethical and Religious Themes in the Writings of Walker Percy* (1997); *Walker Percy's Search for Community* (2005); and *Gravity and Grace: Seamus Heaney and the Force of Light* (2009). He has published dozens of essays on Flannery O'Connor and has been a board member of the Flannery O'Connor Society. He has also published numerous essays on Walker Percy, William Faulkner, Eudora Welty, Seamus Heaney, Bernard Malamud, Mark Twain, and Don DeLillo.

Henry T. Edmondson III is professor of government at Georgia College and State University, Flannery O'Connor's alma mater. He is the author of numerous essays on politics and literature; educational philosophy and reform; and leadership and literature. He is the editor of *The Moral of the Story: Literature and Public Ethics* (2000) and the author of *Return to Good and Evil: Flannery O'Connor's Response to Nihilism* (2005). He was codirector of "Reason, Fiction & Faith: An International Flannery O'Connor Conference," April 20–22, 2009, in Rome, Italy, and codirector of "Flannery O'Connor and the Mystery of Place: An International Conference on the 50th Anniversary of Her Death," July 24–26, 2014, in Dublin, Ireland.

Sarah Gordon is professor emerita at Georgia College and State University, served as editor of the *Flannery O'Connor Bulletin,* and is founding editor of the *Flannery O'Connor Review.* She is the author of *Flannery O'Connor: The Obedient Imagination* (2000) and *A Literary Guide to Flannery O'Connor's Georgia* (2008); and the editor of *Flannery O'Connor: In Celebration of Genius* (2000, 2010). Gordon is a widely published poet, with recent poems appearing or forthcoming in the *Georgia Review, Shenandoah, Confrontation, Arts & Letters,* and the *Sewanee Review.*

Christina Bieber Lake is the Clyde S. Kilby Professor of English at Wheaton College, where she teaches classes in contemporary American literature and literary theory. Lake has authored several essays on Flannery O'Connor as well as a monograph entitled *The Incarnational Art of Flannery O'Connor* (2005). Her most recent book is *Prophets of the Posthuman: American Fiction, Biotechnology, and the Ethics of Personhood* (2013), which was awarded Indiana Wesleyan University's 2014 Aldersgate Prize for integrative scholarship.

The late **Marion Montgomery** was a native and resident of Georgia. For thirty-three years he taught composition, literature, and creative writing at the University of Georgia. While teaching, he wrote hundreds of poems, twenty-seven short stories, three novels, and one novella. He received numerous awards for his fiction and verse in the 1960s and early 1970s. In 2001, he received the Stanley W. Lindberg Award for outstanding contributions to Georgia's literary heritage. Montgomery also published seventeen books of literary-cultural criticism. Montgomery's antagonist is modernity, an intellectual attitude that divorces man from both tradition and transcendence. Montgomery was a close friend of Flannery O'Connor's and is considered by many to have been the "dean" of O'Connor studies. Montgomery passed away in 2002.

Farrell O'Gorman is professor of English at Belmont Abbey College and author of *Peculiar Crossroads: Flannery O'Connor, Walker Percy, and Catholic Vision in Postwar Southern Fiction* (2004). His book *Catholicism and American Borders in the Gothic Literary Imagination* is forthcoming in 2017.

George Piggford, C.S.C., is associate professor of English at Stonehill College in Easton, Massachusetts, where he has also served as director of the Moreau Honors Program and Martin Fellow in Catholic Studies. He has published on British and American literature in *Christianity & Literature, Cultural Critique, English Studies in Canada, Flannery O'Connor Review, Modern Drama,* and *Mosaic,* as well as in volumes such as *American Gothic: New Interventions in a National Narrative* and *Through a Glass Darkly: Suffering, Sacred, and the Sublime.* In 2014 he was an NEH Summer Scholar at the Revisiting Flannery O'Connor Institute at Georgia College, and in November of that year he reflected on "Flannery O'Connor's Faith" at the induction of O'Connor into the American Poets Corner at the Cathedral of St. John the Divine in New York. His essay is dedicated, with great fondness and gratitude, to William A. Sessions.

John Roos is professor emeritus in the Department of Political Science at University of Notre Dame. His work has focused on American institutions and political theory with a special emphasis on Thomas Aquinas, Flannery O'Connor, and religion and politics.

Michael L. Schroeder is professor of English and chair of the Department of English, Languages, and Cultures at Savannah State University, and serves on the board of the Flannery O'Connor Childhood Home Foundation in Savannah. In addition to O'Connor, his research interests include writers of the Harlem Renaissance and connections between literature and the visual arts.

John D. Sykes Jr. is Mary and Harry Brown Professor of English and Religion at Wingate University. He has published two books on the literature of the American South, *The Romance of Innocence of the Myth of History: Faulkner's Religious Critique of Southern Culture* (1989) and *Flannery O'Connor, Walker Percy, and the Aesthetic of Revelation* (2007). His academic articles have appeared in such periodicals as *Mississippi Quarterly, Renascence, Modern Theology, Flannery O'Connor Review, Religion & Literature, Tennessee Williams Annual Review, Literature and Theology, and Zygon.*

Margaret Earley Whitt is professor emerita of English at the University of Denver, where she taught American literature and civil rights history and literature courses for twenty-seven years. In the fall of 2015, she led her third tour through Alabama's now historic and iconic civil rights places.

Ralph C. Wood is University Professor of Theology and Literature at Baylor University, where he teaches in the Great Texts program, the Department of English, and the Department of Religion. He serves as an editor-at-large for the *Christian Century* and as a member of the editorial board of the *Flannery O'Connor Review.* He is the author of *The Comedy of Redemption: Christian Faith and Comic Vision in Four American Novelists* (1988); *The Gospel According to Tolkien: Visions of the Kingdom in Middle-earth* (2004); *Flannery O'Connor and the Christ-Haunted South* (2004); *Literature and Theology* (2008); and *Chesterton: The Nightmare Goodness of God* (2011).

Index

CPSIA information can be obtained
at www.ICGtesting.com
Printed in the USA
BVOW04*2232020617
485391BV00003B/6/P